Budgeting: Key to
Planning and Control

Budgeting: Key to Planning and Control

Practical Guidelines for Managers

Revised Edition

REGINALD L. JONES AND H. GEORGE TRENTIN

American Management Association, Inc.

International standard book number: 0–8144–5253–1
Library of Congress catalog card number: 74–141679

First Printing, Revised Edition

Foreword

IMPROVEMENTS IN THE ART of designing management systems in the few years since the first edition of this book was published have compelled this revision. Rather than detracting from the importance of sound budgeting systems, these new developments have emphasized the essentiality of good budgeting as a prerequisite to the more advanced techniques inherent in financial models, risk analysis, and management information systems development.

Financial models are claiming an increasing share of management's attention, and many companies have begun to experiment with this new technique. As we gain more experience with modeling, we are impressed with the interaction between modeling systems and budgeting systems. Budgeting is intimately associated with planning, and computerized models make it possible quickly to test various alternatives as a basis for management's final plan of action. Also, the relationships between various aspects of the business (such as costs and revenues, return on investment, and variability of expenses at different levels of operation) that are essential ingredients in building a financial model can be derived with ease from the kind of complete budgeting system outlined in this book. Accordingly, we have included in this revised edition an entire new chapter to explain this important interaction.

The original chapter on the capital expenditure budget has been expanded to incorporate two important new ideas. First, in computing return on investment of alternate proposals, a reliable figure for cost of capital must be used. Since most capital investments are financed from some combination of debt and equity, suggestions are made for valid conclusions relating to a company's true cost of capital. Second, we have illustrated the usefulness of risk analysis in capital investment decisions. Return on investment computations are based on estimates of revenue, costs, and life of equipment, which have varying degrees of probability of error. We have explained how using a range of probabilities, instead of single values, gives management a more reliable basis for making capital investment decisions.

The concluding chapter has been substantially expanded to describe and illustrate the essential role a budgeting system plays in an integrated management information system. Both systems must deal with each functional area of the business, such as marketing, manufacturing, and purchasing. The management information subsystems developed for each functional area provide the decision rules, operational plans, and results whose financial consequences must be reflected in the appropriate functional segments of the budget system. Understanding the complementary nature of these systems will permit both the businessman and the designer of systems to do a better job.

In addition to these major enhancements, we have put to good use several more years of experience in budgeting, as well as the critiques of readers, to improve our explanations and illustrations in areas such as sales forecasting, production reporting, maintenance budgeting, cash management, and profit improvement. We have adhered to the original style and purpose of addressing the business manager, rather than the budget technician, in businessman's language to help him increase profits and improve management performance.

The material has been drawn largely from our experience in various management-oriented assignments with business firms. Some of it has been taken from the budgeting course developed in conjunction with, and for use by, the American Management Association. We have received valuable assistance in this work from our associates in the firm. Among others, Kurt H. Schaffir helped on inventory budgeting and sales forecasting; Granville R. Gargiulo, program budgets and retail merchandising; John J. Stephens, budget variance analysis and management action; John W. Konvalinka, general and administrative budgets; Stephen B. Zimmerman, capital expenditure budgeting; and Henry Johansson, financial modeling.

We owe a special debt of gratitude to Mrs. Evelyn Nethercott for the hours she and her department devoted to the preparation of graphic exhibits, and to Mrs. Shirley D. White and other secretaries, who cheerfully assumed the role of typing the manuscript and taking care of a multitude of details.

REGINALD L. JONES
H. GEORGE TRENTIN

Contents

Tables

Evaluations

Forms

Index

1

The Role of Budgeting in Management

THE MERITS OF AN EFFECTIVE BUDGETING SYSTEM—one that is directed at helping managers perform their major management functions—can be fully appreciated by all executives who have been frustrated by improperly conceived budgeting procedures. The significance of that statement is all too evident to those readers who have been subjected to such experiences as the following:

- Although a department is asked to perform far more work than anticipated, budget allowances are left unchanged.
- Despite constructive efforts at efficient management, a manager is ordered to effect a 5 or 10 percent across-the-board cut in budgeted expenses.
- In spite of a straightforward request for clarification of cost variations from budget, the resultant financial reports pinpoint neither the causes of the variations nor the persons responsible for controlling the variances.
- Although sales are increased by hard work, substantial increases in allocated "home office" expenses wipe out any prospect of profit gains.
- Although an executive asks for information relative to the financial impact of alternative planning assumptions, his staff merely reshuffles myriads of historical cost averages and takes weeks doing it.

While these are isolated examples, they are representative and, more importantly, rooted in a common cause: the lack of a systematic budgeting process based on sound concepts of planning and control.

The role that good budgeting plays in the management of a business is best understood when related to the fundamentals of management. The many existing definitions of business management can be expressed in terms of three major functions: planning, execution, and control. Those are the key elements of the management process. Business management must plan its activities in advance, carry out the plan, and institute appropriate techniques of observation and reporting to insure that the deviations from plan are properly analyzed and handled.

A budget can be regarded as primarily a plan or goal or objective, and we know of no better definition of budgeting than to say it is primarily a *planning* and *control system*. Each word in that definition is important for a full understanding of budgeting's proper role. The planning and control aspects relate to the fundamentals of the management process mentioned previously. To regard budgeting as a system is most important, because this implies a continuing process throughout the year—the key to good budgeting in any business operation.

Contrary to some views, budgeting is not a financial function performed by budget departments, bookkeepers, or accountants. They merely record and report plans and comparisons of operating results with those plans; they help management analyze, interpret, and react. Budgeting also is not forecasting as such, if by that we mean predicting the outcome of events rather than planning for a result and controlling to maximize the chances of achieving that result. Many companies complain about the lack of effectiveness of budgets. But their "budgets" are little more than forecasts, all too often prepared by the finance department and not by the operating people; the result is a superficial set of figures rather than a grass-roots budget.

This forecasting approach to budgeting can be illustrated by a very common occurrence in business. During the month of October, the president calls the controller and asks whether it isn't time to begin to think about the budget for the next year. The controller generally agrees but bemoans the fact that he has many other pressing problems. Eventually he gets around to thinking about and working on the budget for next year. One day he finds himself in the president's office with summary financial statements showing what the results for the current year will be in relation to the budget adopted about a year ago and with some ideas as to how this trend will continue into the next year. The president usually has some definite ideas about the state of the economy and, in particular, how his business is doing. In addition to having an opinion about sales volume, he and others in the business have an idea of the trend in costs as a result of major union negotiations, price level changes, and so on. This meeting generally concludes with some percentages which are used to adjust the current year's figures. Out of this process evolves a forecast of the results of next year's operations.

This is forecasting, not budgeting, because planning and budgeting have to be a grass-roots operation in which all levels of management participate. It is true that budgeting does involve some forecasting, primarily in the area of sales budgets, but the process is basically one of detailed analysis and planning—not one of predicting future results. Too many businesses are using the inefficient forecasting approach rather than the planning and control type of budget system. It is the latter type which is the subject matter of this book.

All this is not to say that the controllership function in the budget process is unimportant. Indeed, the financial people play a very important role. Basically, the controller receives the operating plans of the line managers and other department heads and translates those plans into a comprehensive projection of financial condition and operating results. It is obvious that a final judgment should not be made until this is done and until the effect of the plans can be estimated by the president in terms of their impact on company resources and profits.

The code of accounts is the principal means by which the translation of operating plans into dollars is made. This code might be described simply as a standardized classification of expenditures and other transactions made by a business, generally in terms of the nature of the expenditure. For instance, we are all familiar with accounting classifications for such expenditures as salaries, fringe benefits, rents, and taxes. When businesses were relatively small and simple, accountants found this one-dimensional description of expenditures adequate.

As businesses became more complex, a concept known as "responsibility accounting" or "responsibility reporting" was developed to add a second important dimension to that of the classification of expenditures. This second dimension can be regarded primarily as a control device. The addition of this element was required as a result of the need for budgeting in terms which could be related to managers responsible for the expenditures. This dimension, then, largely reflects the organizational structure of a company.

Reporting transactions in two dimensions—first by the nature of the expenditure and second by the organizational unit responsible for the action—permits management to pinpoint responsibilities for the dollar consequences of planning, execution, and control. Dollar budgets and actual performance against those budgets can be reflected in separate statements for each block on the organization chart, thus permitting businessmen to make budgeting an integral part of the management function.

During the period when this second dimension was being added to that of account codes, the controller was also busy developing a parallel improvement in the financial techniques for budgeting. Starting in the early days with what is now called a fixed budget, he subsequently developed the variable budget concept—an integral part of any sound budget program.

The concept of the fixed budget is easy to understand. When business was relatively simple and stable, it was possible to develop plans a year in advance which were fairly representative of what actually would take place. Assume that a company is in a relatively stable position, with sales volume showing a moderate increase from year to year and a reasonably well-established seasonal pattern. It is possible in a situation like this to prepare a monthly budget of expected sales, projected manufacturing costs, general and selling expenses, and net profit month by month for the next year. Accordingly, say in the month of October, this business would prepare a budget statement showing these figures for each of the months in the next calendar year.

Jump ahead to next June. It would be a rare coincidence indeed if the sales experienced in that month were the same as those projected the previous October. However, under the fixed budget concept, the budgeted expense estimates made in October for the following June are compared with the actual figures for June. Obviously, if environmental conditions preclude reasonably accurate predictions of sales volume, budget comparisons of this nature are rather meaningless and useless for controlling operations.

The variable budget concept was developed to overcome this deficiency; and it must be used in any effective budget program, since most businesses have become complex and since the volume of business activity generally fluctuates in an unpredictable way. The first step in this approach is the same as that for the fixed budget, and the result is a financial projection of what resources and profits will materialize if the projected volume prevails throughout the budget period. However, as already noted, expense budgets computed on a fixed basis are not useful to the line manager for controlling operations when volumes differ from those included in the original budget. For example, if projections made in October indicate projected sales of $100,000 for next June but sales turn out to be only $75,000, the budgeted expense allowances for June should be adjusted downward from the amounts originally calculated on the basis of $100,000 of sales. The bases for these volume-induced budget adjustments are (1) ratios developed from an analysis of historical data relating to the way expenditures vary with volume and (2) standards adopted by management. If the actual monthly volume throughout the year happens to be the same as the planned operating volume, the variable and fixed budgeting techniques give the same answer; but this rarely happens in real life.

Because of the growing complexity of business and business problems and because of the movement toward decentralization in large enterprises, increased attention is being given to better planning and control techniques; accordingly, the use of sound budgeting techniques is becoming more prevalent in industry. Also, personal experience and survey results indicate a trend toward placing the responsibility for budgeting at higher levels in the organization. Whereas in earlier days it was customary to find the budget function buried deeply in the accounting operation, today it is not uncommon to have the budget function report to levels of management above the controller. Although it is still usual for the budget director to report to the controller, the trend toward reporting at a higher level is a recognition of the need to have the budget function broadly based in all of the operating areas of the business.

To accomplish this purpose better, many companies are turning to the use of budget committees, in spite of the criticisms one hears about the ineffectiveness of committee operations. If properly administered, the budget committee can perform the very useful role of encompassing and reconciling the many diverse interests which make up a modern business.

Before turning to the specifics of budgeting in a business, we might consider certain features of budgeting which are intangible but nevertheless have a vital bearing on the success or failure of the effort. Many studies have been made in this area, and the results carry important lessons for the businessman interested in making the most of his budget system.

One study discusses the effects of manufacturing budgets upon the front-line supervisor. The conclusion is that the budgets studied were used as pressure devices for constantly increasing efficiency, but, because of the effects on people, the budgets tended to generate a long-run result of decreased efficiency. Interestingly enough, this is attributed to the lack of participation in the budget-preparation phase by those being budgeted and to the lack of sales ability on the part of accounting personnel. Another study concludes that budgeting is more concerned with concepts of human relationships than with rules of accounting and that if good principles of human relationships are applied, successful budget practices will be inevitable. Still another appraisal of current business budgeting indicates that important weaknesses in practice are the result of superficial appreciation of budget concepts by management, inadequate techniques, and absence of a disciplined environment in many organizations.

Upon reflection, it becomes apparent that the requirements for a successful budget operation are not restricted to accounting techniques but are more broadly based and that the successful managers are those who keep such considerations in mind while executing the more mechanical aspects of the budgeting process.

To put what has been said about the overall role of budgeting into more concrete terms, consider how *A* Manufacturing Company controls operations through its budgeting and responsibility-reporting system. It is a growing multiproduct company in the metal-converting field. Annual sales are approximately $12 million. The company employs about 800 people and has a fairly typical organization. Top executives are able to control every area of the organization through a system of budgetary planning and control reporting by responsibility area. Yardsticks of performance are provided for all productive and service areas, and results of operations are accumulated and reported in terms of these yardsticks at all supervisory levels.

Sales and profit contribution are compared with previous plans; thus lower- or higher-than-planned results are readily determined. Selling expenses are controlled by budgeting, accounting, and reporting in terms of personnel responsible for those expenses. These measurements of sales and of selling expenses result in effective control of *income*.

Production costs are measured by appropriate controls over materials costs, labor costs, and manufacturing overhead expenses. Costs incurred for materials are controlled through standards; price variations are segregated; and materials utilization is measured by charging excess issues of productive materials to the departments responsible for spoilage and comparing these charges with variable budget allowances. Productive labor costs are measured against standards, and variances are reported in terms of the departmental foreman responsible for such variances. Manufacturing overhead expenses are controlled by reporting actual expenditures compared with variable or fixed-amount budgets in terms of the individual who has participated in planning these budgets and who has responsibility for the expenditures made. Control over services of *auxiliary departments*—that is, over general overhead expenses—is effected through comparing such costs (in terms of departments and of individuals incurring the costs) with expenditures previously planned and approved for levels of required service or for programs adopted.

Responsibility in budget preparation and in cost control is a major feature in the company's control system. It pinpoints responsibility for all controllable costs by individuals and integrates standard cost reporting with the company's budgetary

EXHIBIT 1

Organization Chart: *A* Manufacturing Company

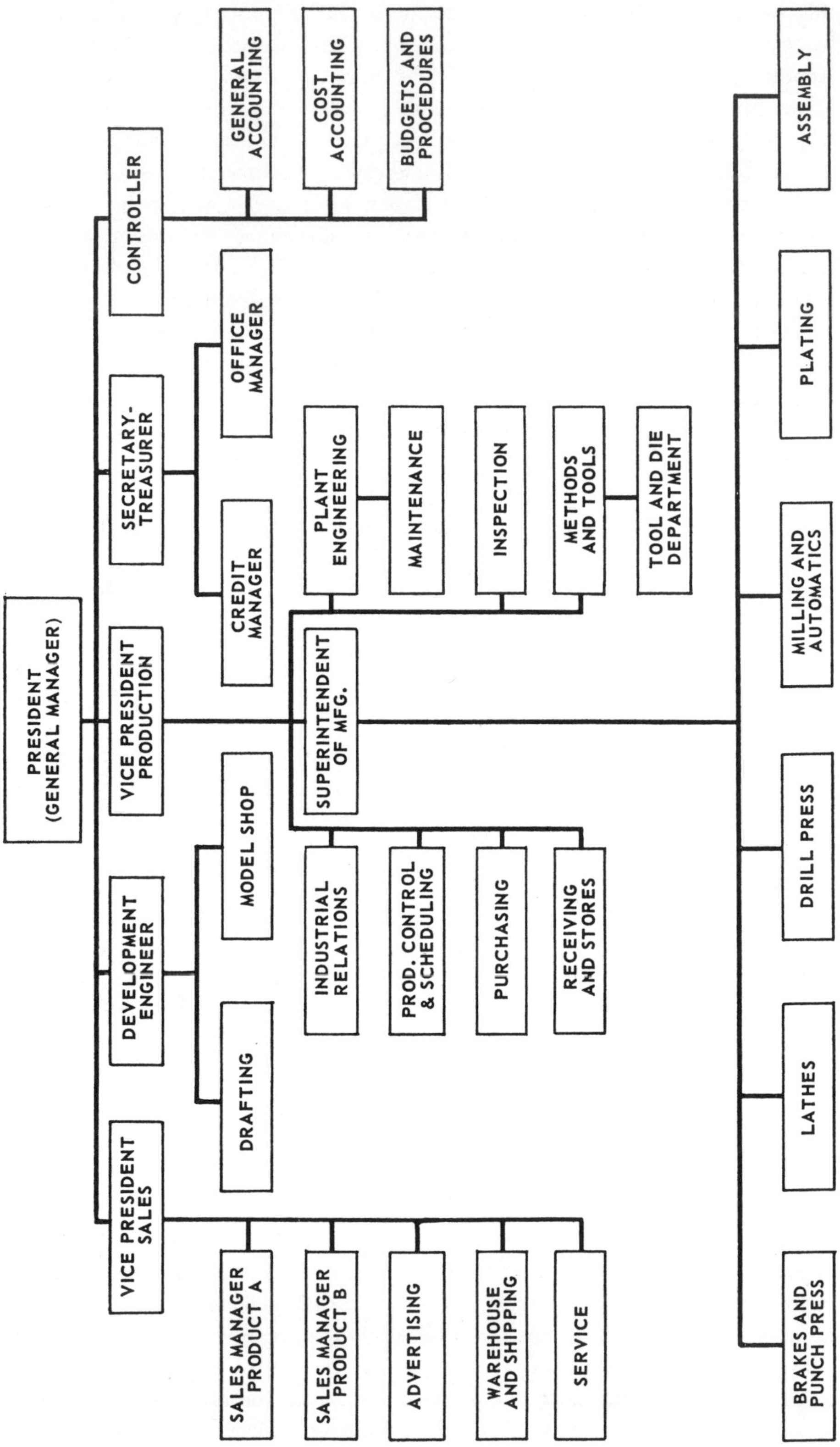

EXHIBIT 2

LEVELS OF RESPONSIBILITY REPORTING

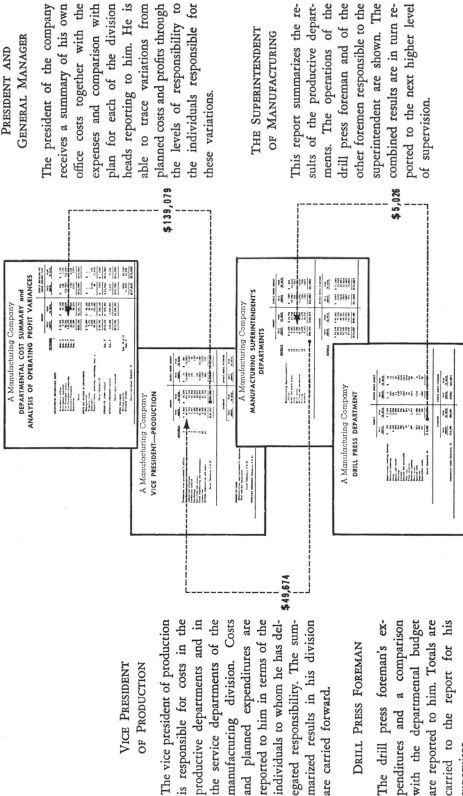

PRESIDENT AND GENERAL MANAGER

The president of the company receives a summary of his own office costs together with the expenses and comparison with plan for each of the division heads reporting to him. He is able to trace variations from planned costs and profits through the levels of responsibility to the individuals responsible for these variations.

THE SUPERINTENDENT OF MANUFACTURING

This report summarizes the results of the productive departments. The operations of the drill press foreman and of the other foremen responsible to the superintendent are shown. The combined results are in turn reported to the next higher level of supervision.

VICE PRESIDENT OF PRODUCTION

The vice president of production is responsible for costs in the productive departments and in the service departments of the manufacturing division. Costs and planned expenditures are reported to him in terms of the individuals to whom he has delegated responsibility. The summarized results in his division are carried forward.

DRILL PRESS FOREMAN

The drill press foreman's expenditures and a comparison with the departmental budget are reported to him. Totals are carried to the report for his supervisor.

7

EXHIBIT 3 STATEMENT OF INCOME—*A* MANUFACTURING COMPANY

		Amount		(Over) Under Budget	
	From Exhibit:	This Month	Year to Date	This Month	Year to Date
Net Sales	12 & 13	$1,069,281	$3,977,542	$ (18,006)	$ (24,092)
Cost of Sales	4	760,328	2,824,324	(25,086)	(23,370)
Gross profit on sales		$ 308,953	$1,153,218	$ 7,080	$ (722)
Expenses					
Development engineering	5	$ 11,546	$ 45,265	$ 138	$ 1,470
Selling and shipping	6	93,162	347,357	(10,701)	(18,039)
General and administrative	7	50,213	197,213	31	3,528
Total		$ 154,921	$ 589,835	$ (10,532)	$ (13,041)
Profit from operations		$ 154,032	$ 563,383	$ 17,612	$ 12,319
Other (Income) Expense					
Interest expense		$ 2,708	$ 10,882	$ (8)	$ (82)
Other (net)		(3,420)	(18,640)	580	(2,640)
		$ (712)	$ (7,758)	$ 588	$ (2,558)
Net profit before income taxes		$ 154,744	$ 571,141	$ 18,200	$ 9,761
Provision for Income Taxes		84,000	309,000	10,000	5,000
Net profit		$ 70,744	$ 262,141	$ 8,200	$ 4,761

controls. Reports are prepared for all levels of management—from the operating foremen and service department supervisors to the president of the company. The reporting system is designed as a tool for all levels of supervision in controlling their operations and their costs. It emphasizes information which is useful to the individual supervisor and de-emphasizes the bookkeeping aspects of reporting.

The company's reports are tailored to the company and to the executives who use them. This tailoring is carried down to the individual report rendered to each supervisor. The supervisor of each department determines, within a general framework, the extent of the detailed information he requires to control operations for which he is held accountable. Following the organizational lines indicated by Exhibit 1, the cost totals of one level of responsibility are carried forward to the report prepared for the next higher level of responsibility (Exhibit 2). Accounting allocations over which the individual has no control are not included in these reports. (The company's management recognizes that control of wage and salary costs correspondingly influences payroll-connected fringe benefit costs. Similarly, control of appropriations for fixed plant additions and of the inventory level largely determines the costs of depreciation, property taxes, and insurance.)

Largely supported by departmental cost control schedules (not shown), income and cost control summaries (Exhibits 3–13) in two ways group costs over which individuals have control. First, such costs are reported by type of expense—cost of sales, development engineering, and so on (Exhibits 4–7)—which support a conventional income statement (Exhibit 3). Second, such costs are grouped by executive responsibility (Exhibits 5, 6, 9–11), and these divisional costs are in turn summarized in

Exhibit 8, which shows total cost incurred. The transitional link between the responsibility reports and conventional cost-of-sales and expense statements is the simple set of predetermined cost transfers shown on conventional statements but not needed on the responsibility reports. Exhibit 8 also summarizes by responsibility areas all factors accounting for the operating-profit variation indicated in the statement of income, Exhibit 3.

Cost control aspects of accounting are stressed in these exhibits. Variations from planned profits, costs by conventional classifications, and costs by any level of management responsibility can be traced directly to the individual responsible. Product costs required for sales pricing and inventory purposes are not included in the exhibits. Such costs are obtained through normal supplementary analysis.

While the *A* Manufacturing Company utilizes standard costs, this system of responsibility reporting, with suitable modification, can be applied to manufacturers using job cost or process cost systems on an actual-cost basis.

(*text continued on page 14*)

EXHIBIT 4

COST OF SALES—*A* MANUFACTURING COMPANY

	From Exhibit	Amount This Month	Amount Year to Date	(Over) Under Budget This Month	(Over) Under Budget Year to Date
Production Costs Incurred at Standard					
Manufacturing overhead					
Controllable factory costs	9	$139,079	$ 549,645	$ (4,466)	$ (5,963)
Costs not charged to departments	8	60,701	245,140	(51)	(540)
Transfers to other departments (net)		(8,735)	(34,705)	—	—
Variances (see below)		(5,754)	4,830	5,754	(4,830)
Total standard manufacturing overhead		$185,291	$ 764,910	$ 1,237	$(11,333)
Productive labor	9	110,365	457,922	2,335	(7,122)
Materials	9	419,837	1,817,091	19,513	(59,691)
Total standard costs incurred		$715,493	$3,039,923	$ 23,085	$(78,146)
Costs Expensed or Capitalized		(6,019)	(13,945)	3,263	2,561
Inventory (Increase) or Decrease		44,366	(192,189)	(44,946)	42,750
Standard cost of sales		$753,840	$2,833,789	$(18,598)	$(32,835)
Cost Variances					
Manufacturing overhead					
Controllable factory costs	9	$ 4,466	$ 5,963	$ (4,466)	$ (5,963)
Costs not charged to departments	8	51	540	(51)	(540)
Volume variances		1,237	(11,333)	(1,237)	11,333
Total		$ 5,754	$ (4,830)	$ (5,754)	$ 4,830
Productive labor	9	1,951	14,583	(1,951)	(14,583)
Materials	9	(1,217)	(19,218)	1,217	19,218
Total cost variances		$ 6,488	$ (9,465)	$ (6,488)	$ 9,465
Actual cost of sales (to Exhibit 3)		$760,328	$2,824,324	$(25,086)	$(23,370)

9

EXHIBIT 5 DEVELOPMENT ENGINEERING EXPENSES—*A* MANUFACTURING COMPANY

(Development Engineer)

	From Schedule:	Amount This Month	Amount Year to Date	(Over) Under Budget This Month	(Over) Under Budget Year to Date
Controllable Costs					
Chief product engineer's office	20	$ 3,665	$14,680	$(75)	$ (320)
Drafting department	21	3,679	13,645	238	2,023
Model shop	22	1,885	7,673	(25)	(233)
Total (Exhibit 8)		$ 9,229	$35,998	$138	$1,470
Transfers from other departments, net		2,317	9,267	—	—
Total (to Exhibit 3)		$11,546	$45,265	$138	$1,470

EXHIBIT 6 SELLING AND SHIPPING EXPENSES—*A* MANUFACTURING COMPANY

(Vice President of Sales)

	From Schedule:	Amount This Month	Amount Year to Date	(Over) Under Budget This Month	(Over) Under Budget Year to Date
Controllable Costs					
Sales vice president's office	23	$ 5,224	$ 21,152	$ (4)	$ (272)
Sales manager, Product *A*	24	17,320	62,204	(1,647)	(1,012)
Sales manager, Product *B*	25	14,475	56,220	(662)	32
Advertising department	26	30,489	106,227	(7,554)	(14,487)
Warehouse and shipping	27	12,224	51,463	35	(2,427)
Sales service department	28	7,219	25,273	(869)	127
Total (to Exhibit 8)		$86,951	$322,539	$(10,701)	$(18,039)
Transfers from other departments, net		6,211	24,818	—	—
Total (to Exhibit 3)		$93,162	$347,357	$(10,701)	$(18,039)

EXHIBIT 7 GENERAL AND ADMINISTRATIVE EXPENSES

(A Manufacturing Company)

	From:	Amount This Month	Amount Year to Date	(Over) Under Budget This Month	(Over) Under Budget Year to Date
Controllable Costs					
President's office	Sch. 1	$15,511	$ 62,125	$ 314	$1,175
Secretary-treasurer's departments	Exh. 10	12,895	48,652	(72)	2,610
Controller's departments	Exh. 11	21,600	85,816	(211)	(257)
Total		$50,006	$196,593	$ 31	$3,528
Transfers from other departments, net		207	620	—	—
Total (to Exhibit 3)		$50,213	$197,213	$ 31	$3,528

DEPARTMENTAL COST SUMMARY AND ANALYSIS OF OPERATING PROFIT VARIANCES   **EXHIBIT 8**

(A *Manufacturing Company*)

		Amount		Profit Contribution Above (Below) Plan	
	From:	This Mo.	YTD	This Mo.	YTD
Departmental Controllable Costs					
President's office	Sch. 1	$ 15,511	$ 62,125	$ 314	$ 1,175
Development engineer	Exh. 5	9,229	35,998	138	1,470
Vice president—sales	Exh. 6	86,951	322,539	(10,701)	(18,039)
Vice president—production	Exh. 9	139,079	549,645	(4,466)	(5,963)
Secretary-treasurer	Exh. 10	12,895	48,652	(72)	2,610
Controller	Exh. 11	21,600	85,816	(211)	(257)
Total		$285,265	$1,104,775	$(14,998)	$(19,004)
Costs Not Charged to Departments					
Depreciation		$ 15,890	$ 64,438	$ —	$ —
Property taxes		9,371	36,910	—	—
Insurance		4,855	21,140	(111)	475
Payroll taxes, pensions, vacations, etc.		30,585	122,652	60	(1,015)
Total (to Exhibit 4)		$ 60,701	$ 245,140	$ (51)	$ (540)
Productive Labor—Actual	Exh. 9	$112,316	$ 472,505	$ (1,951)	$(14,583)
Materials Purchased—Actual	Exh. 9	418,620	1,797,873	1,217	19,218
Total costs incurred		$876,902	$3,620,293	$(15,783)	$(14,909)
Other Variances					
Selling profit	Exh. 12 & 13			(592)	(8,743)
Overhead volume	Exh. 4			(1,237)	11,333
Total variances (to Exhibit 3)				$(17,612)	$(12,319)

EXHIBIT 9

VICE PRESIDENT—PRODUCTION

(A *Manufacturing Company*)

		Amount		(Over) Under Budget	
	From:	This Mo.	YTD	This Mo.	YTD
Production vice president's office	Sch. 2	$ 9,044	$ 35,859	$ 71	$ 601
Manufacturing superintendent's departments	Sch. 3	49,674	193,673	(3,803)	(4,962)
Industrial relations	Sch. 4	4,724	19,794	197	(110)
Production control	Sch. 5	7,921	32,066	107	46
Purchasing	Sch. 6	2,650	10,643	—	(43)
Receiving and stores	Sch. 7	6,528	26,832	184	16
Plant engineering and maintenance	Sch. 8	31,981	122,099	(2,004)	(2,188)
Inspection	Sch. 10	6,936	27,569	(102)	(233)
Methods engineering and tools	Sch. 11	19,621	81,110	884	910
Total (to Exhibits 4 & 8)		$139,079	$ 549,645	$(4,466)	$ (5,963)
		Standard		(Over) Under Standard	
Productive Labor					
Manufacturing superintendent's departments	Sch. 3	$110,047	$ 457,220	$(1,849)	$(14,367)
Tool and die department	Sch. 12	318	702	(102)	(216)
Total (to Exhibits 4 & 8)		$110,365	$ 457,922	$(1,951)	$(14,583)
Materials Purchased (to Exhibits 4 & 8)	Sch. 6	$419,837	$1,817,091	$ 1,217	$ 19,218

11

EXHIBIT 10   SECRETARY-TREASURER'S DEPARTMENTS
(A *Manufacturing Company*)

		Amount		(Over) Under Budget	
	From Schedule:	This Month	Year to Date	This Month	Year to Date
Secretary-treasurer's office	29	$ 3,376	$11,802	$ 87	$1,990
Credit manager	30	4,520	18,066	(6)	(10)
Office manager	31	4,999	18,784	(153)	630
Total (to Exhibits 7 & 8)		$12,895	$48,652	$(72)	$2,610

EXHIBIT 11   CONTROLLER'S DEPARTMENTS
(A *Manufacturing Company*)

		Amount		(Over) Under Budget	
	From Schedule:	This Month	Year to Date	This Month	Year to Date
Controller's office	32	$ 3,731	$16,635	$ 350	$(309)
General accounting	33	3,751	14,916	(16)	24
Cost accounting	34	8,465	34,072	—	(212)
Budgets and procedures	35	5,653	20,193	(545)	240
Total (to Exhibits 7 & 8)		$21,600	$85,816	$(211)	$(257)

EXHIBIT 12   SALES, PRODUCT MIX, AND ADJUSTMENTS—THIS MONTH
(A *Manufacturing Company*)

	Sales			Selling Profit	
	Amount	(Over) Under Budget	Standard Gross Profit Percentage	Amount	(Over) Under Budget
Product Line *A*					
Item No. 1	$ 63,032	$ 12,437	54.6%	$ 34,401	$ 6,447
Item No. 2	71,643	790	30.8	22,076	437
Item No. 3	42,131	1,018	38.1	16,046	388
Item No. 4	93,332	(16,173)	19.2	17,930	(3,105)
Item No. 5	100,313	(542)	28.0	28,084	(152)
Item No. 6	54,432	(1,701)	29.6	16,108	(503)
Item No. 7	22,516	412	24.5	5,522	101
Total	$ 447,399	$ (3,759)	31.3%	$140,167	$ 3,613

	Sales			Selling Profit		
	Amount	*(Over) Under Budget*	*Standard Gross Profit Percentage*	*Amount*	*(Over) Under Budget*	**EXHIBIT 12** *(concluded)*
Product Line *B*						
Item No. 100	$ 300,857	$ 5,223	26.3%	$ 79,230	$ 1,374	
Item No. 200	213,761	(10,061)	34.2	73,037	(3,441)	
Item No. 300	55,266	(7,781)	17.9	9,876	(1,393)	
Total	$ 569,884	$(12,619)	28.5%	$162,143	$(3,460)	
Service Parts	$ 82,520	$ (2,520)	52.9%	$ 43,653	$ (453)	
Totals	$1,099,803	$(18,898)	31.5%	$345,963	$ (300)	
Sales Adjustments						
Cash discounts allowed	(10,209)	409		(10,209)	409	
Outbound freight	(20,313)	483		(20,313)	483	
Totals (to Exhibits 3 & 8)	$1,069,281	$(18,006)	29.5%	$315,441	$ 592	

SALES, PRODUCT MIX, AND ADJUSTMENTS—YEAR TO DATE   **EXHIBIT 13**
(A *Manufacturing Company*)

	Sales			Selling Profit		
	Amount	*(Over) Under Budget*	*Standard Gross Profit Percentage*	*Amount*	*(Over) Under Budget*	
Product Line *A*						
Item No. 1	$ 207,659	$ 14,895	54.6%	$ 113,382	$ 8,133	
Item No. 2	297,708	1,101	30.8	91,694	339	
Item No. 3	140,098	2,406	38.1	53,377	917	
Item No. 4	420,294	(17,540)	19.2	80,696	(3,368)	
Item No. 5	350,245	75	28.0	98,069	21	
Item No. 6	210,147	(4,158)	29.6	62,204	(1,231)	
Item No. 7	105,073	(1,971)	24.5	25,743	(483)	
Total	$1,731,224	$ (5,192)	30.3%	$ 525,165	$ 4,328	
Product Line *B*						
Item No. 100	$ 945,158	$ 4,103	26.3%	$ 248,577	$ 1,079	
Item No. 200	883,516	(8,288)	34.2	302,162	(2,834)	
Item No. 300	226,018	(1,889)	17.9	40,457	(338)	
Total	$2,054,692	$ (6,074)	28.8%	$ 591,196	$(2,093)	
Service Parts	$ 329,304	$(14,304)	50.1%	$ 165,070	$ 5,030	
Totals	$4,115,220	$(25,570)	31.1%	$1,281,431	$ 7,265	
Sales Adjustments						
Cash discounts allowed	(42,949)	699		(42,949)	699	
Outbound freight	(94,729)	779		(94,729)	779	
Totals (to Exhibits 3 & 8)	$3,977,542	$(24,092)	28.8%	$1,143,753	$ 8,743	

Among the financial summaries and analyses not illustrated but which are called for by the accompanying exhibits and which might be included as part of a complete monthly financial report for *A* Manufacturing Company are the following:

- Comparative statement of income.
- Statement of financial position.
- Statement of net income and rate of return by product line.
- Statement of changes in cash position—financial ratios, and so on.
- Statement of inventories, commitments, and order backlog.
- Statement of accounts receivable.
- Statement of plant and equipment and plant appropriations.
- Payroll analysis and employment data.

The content of such statements will be covered in subsequent chapters dealing with inventories, cash flow, capital investments, and other balance sheet transactions.

2

The President
and the Budget Plan

As STRANGE AS THIS MAY SOUND TO SOME, the president is a key participant in the budget process, and, ordinarily, the success or failure of the budget plan depends on the degree of his involvement. Too many people believe that a competent budget director is the only requirement for success. However, every chief executive has plans for the operation of his business, and the budget system is the means by which he can formalize and publish such plans and observe the performance of his line managers in carrying them out.

There are some businessmen who say that they run their business quite successfully without a budget. In most of those cases, particularly if the business is truly successful, the essential ingredients of good budgeting *are* present but have not been formalized into a system. Such informal systems can work satisfactorily, particularly in smaller companies and in those dominated by strong top executives. However, informal approaches are becoming less adequate as businesses grow and as the need for good communications increases.

The ingredients essential to the operation of even the informal budget system consist of *criteria* or *control* standards. These may not be obvious; but upon probing deeply enough, one finds that every successful management has developed such guidelines and has formally or informally, consciously or unconsciously, used them to run the business. Two illustrations will help clarify this important point.

A large manufacturer and wholesale distributor handled a rather standardized industrial product line. The line consisted of perhaps 100 different products, and each product was made in several grades. Distributed nationwide through about 150 warehouses, the products were used primarily in industrial and home construction and decoration. At the end of each month, the president of this company took considerable delight in calling the controller into his office and asking him how the company's profits fared for that month. The controller, having been subjected to this treatment before, was quick to tell the president that the books had not yet been

15

closed, that an estimate of earnings would not be available until about the fifteenth of the following month, and that an absolutely reliable figure would not be ready until about the end of that month. In other words, what he told the president represents the reply most controllers would give; that is, net profits are not finally determined in most businesses until two to four weeks after the close of the month in question.

The president asked whether the controller had the sales figures for the month; usually these were available on the second or third day of the following month. When the sales figures were supplied, the president (with a knowing smile on his face) predicted that profits for the month in question were $100,000, for example. Some time around the fifteenth, the controller told the president that it looked like the net profit for the previous month was $95,000—or some other figure reasonably close to the president's estimate. Two weeks later he laid the formal statement of profit and loss on the president's desk and pointed to the net profit figure of $96,000.

On many occasions the controller marveled at the ability of the president to forecast profit, once having been given the total sales for the month. But deeper analysis indicated the logic of the president's method. He was very close to the business and participated in determining standard markup ratios, manning tables for the various warehouses, personnel additions or reductions at the headquarters offices, and many other policy matters which influenced final profits. This is not to say that his business always operated in accordance with policy and never deviated from standard markups and so forth. Quite the opposite was true, since his business was quite competitive and he often had to authorize price cuts or other concessions to remain competitive.

This was a business in which standard gross profit margins were clustered about a general average of approximately 25 percent on sales. Selling and distribution expenses had been managed to fall within an overall control limit of approximately 15 percent of sales, consisting of 10 to 12 percent for selling and distribution and 3 to 5 percent for general and administrative expenses (including interest). This was designed to leave approximately 10 percent before taxes. With such a standard operating and financial plan, the president—who kept in day-to-day touch with major developments of the business—was able to make quick mental calculations of the effect of any material departures from the plan and to make a fairly reliable estimate of net profits after he knew sales for the month.

Another illustration of the importance of basic standards is apparent in the following approach used by a defense products manufacturer. Not surprisingly, defense industries are subject to rather sudden and drastic changes in volume as a result of changes in Government procurement programs. Accordingly, most knowledgeable businessmen in this field recognize that profitability depends on the ability to react quickly to changes in volume.

The way most businesses are constituted, a drop in sales volume evokes a fairly quick reaction of reducing such direct expenditures as production labor and materials. This is easy to understand: If Government orders for a product are cut to $5,000 a month for 10 months, from $10,000 a month for 12 months, it does not take a very imaginative management to realize that it needs less people on the production lines and less material to make the product. Where most defense businesses run into trouble is in their failure to react quickly to changes in sales volume by reducing the *indirect* elements of expense.

Upon analysis, it is obvious that if there are fewer people on the production line, there is less need for supervisory and support personnel. This affects the number of foremen, timekeepers, payroll department personnel, and so on. It is also obvious that if less material is used, fewer purchasing department personnel, storeroom clerks, material handlers, and so forth are required. With reductions in all of these service activities, there should also be a reduction in the more general support activities, such as production control, accounting, and general office activities.

Unfortunately, the business in question had several unhappy experiences in which substantial losses were realized as a result of canceled orders, because of delays in taking the necessary retrenchment steps. Out of hard experience, the president of this company developed rather effective techniques for monitoring this situation. This system principally involved charts, which were kept on a very current basis, showing the relationship between indirect personnel and direct personnel. As a matter of fact, the president prominently displayed these charts in his office because they played such an important role in the new control system. The charts were the principal means of focusing on current problems at the usual staff meetings; out of this approach evolved a quick-response system of adjusting indirect activities when direct activities contracted. One day the charted ratio of indirect to direct personnel exceeded the control limit, and the president issued orders to the controller to set the example by eliminating a specified number of people from his department and by publishing guidelines for similar reductions in the other overhead departments. Although such use of charts may appear as a somewhat arbitrary procedure, it was the heart of a planning and control system that brought the company from an unsuccessful to a successful basis of operation in the volatile defense products field.

As can be appreciated from these examples, what is needed for good budgeting are substantive planning and control standards. Although informal systems have sometimes been successful, the advantage rests with companies using good budgeting techniques. The most successful systems are those which achieve the right balance between technique and form, on the one hand, and substantive planning and control standards, on the other.

Standards must be related to a company's situation and objectives, but what other similarly situated businesses are able to do is an important supplement to conclusions reached by analyzing one's own past performance. More information on competitors' experience is available to the public than most people realize. Typical of such information is that shown in Exhibits 14 and 15, dealing with various financial ratios.

The following pages describe the correct budgeting process in its more formal aspects. Less formal approaches may be adopted if warranted in particular situations. The process involves three phases: preplanning, budget preparation, and control of operations.

The preplanning phase of budgeting consists of work that, generally, must be done in the last half of the year preceding the budget year in order to provide the framework for budget preparation. In this period an analysis is made of previous experience, the state of the economy, and company objectives—an analysis leading

Phase One:
The Job of
Preplanning

EXHIBIT 14
14 IMPORTANT RATIOS IN MANUFACTURING AND CONSTRUCTION LINES—1968

Line of Business (and number of concerns reporting)		Current assets to current debt (Times)	Net profits on net sales (Per cent)	Net profits on tangible net worth (Per cent)	Net profits on net working capital (Per cent)	Net sales to tangible net worth (Times)	Net sales to net working capital (Times)	Collection period (Days)	Net sales to inventory (Times)	Fixed assets to tangible net worth (Per cent)	Current debt to tangible net worth (Per cent)	Total debt to tangible net worth (Per cent)	Inventory to net working capital (Per cent)	Current debt to inventory (Per cent)	Funded debts to net working capital (Per cent)
2871-72-79 Agricultural Chemicals (42)	Upper Quartile	3.49	4.92	13.18	30.83	4.86	12.06	33	12.1	32.1	24.4	46.8	43.0	84.3	21.4
	MEDIAN	2.15	2.22	5.72	13.65	2.84	5.07	58	7.4	45.7	43.2	112.7	70.8	130.3	86.8
	Lower Quartile	1.36	0.67	2.92	3.23	1.59	3.16	109	5.2	73.4	81.6	190.3	127.4	296.2	160.6
3722-23-29 Airplane Parts & Accessories (57)		2.64	6.46	19.47	40.56	4.11	7.84	30	7.7	38.0	30.2	45.9	73.8	76.6	35.4
		1.94	4.14	13.78	23.40	3.24	4.87	48	5.4	60.8	57.1	85.3	95.0	100.0	50.1
		1.54	2.17	7.94	12.52	2.45	3.73	63	3.9	79.6	88.1	164.7	139.5	136.6	93.0
2051-52 Bakery Products (83)		2.58	4.81	18.13	70.67	5.26	20.48	15	40.1	61.4	18.1	33.1	28.4	150.2	31.4
		2.00	2.78	10.80	40.97	3.82	14.73	21	29.8	82.9	25.5	52.7	52.0	210.7	82.2
		1.46	1.07	5.46	17.15	2.77	8.73	26	24.4	107.2	39.2	99.2	81.3	301.6	163.0
3312-13-15-16-17 Blast Furnaces, Steel Wks. & Rolling Mills (63)		3.38	5.68	10.03	24.38	2.55	5.33	30	7.4	43.8	17.0	26.3	76.2	51.4	33.9
		2.58	3.74	7.22	16.57	1.93	4.10	35	4.8	61.1	23.5	49.3	86.1	65.8	68.3
		1.98	2.48	4.36	8.82	1.50	3.24	43	3.9	85.9	35.6	83.9	104.7	98.5	123.4
2331 Blouses & Waists, Women's & Misses' (69)		2.36	1.95	17.09	19.70	13.99	15.88	33	16.1	3.8	62.0	122.0	59.2	125.4	9.8
		1.57	1.21	10.31	11.08	9.96	10.90	43	12.9	8.6	150.0	235.9	94.2	156.4	14.5
		1.33	0.61	4.11	4.57	6.20	7.64	51	8.4	14.7	252.6	318.1	156.6	253.6	26.3
2731-32 Books; Publishing & Printing (39)		3.65	7.17	16.51	21.33	3.39	6.32	46	9.7	14.7	24.0	50.3	50.2	50.7	10.8
		2.38	3.45	8.78	14.70	2.18	3.78	59	4.2	40.8	48.0	72.6	83.9	92.5	38.8
		1.53	1.41	3.54	7.34	1.63	2.20	76	2.6	63.2	85.6	134.9	116.4	151.7	91.8
2211 Broad Woven Fabrics, Cotton (44)		4.77	4.70	9.27	20.21	2.12	5.11	38	5.9	38.9	15.1	27.0	62.2	46.1	22.1
		3.11	4.15	7.01	13.85	1.84	4.03	53	4.9	54.3	22.6	42.3	78.9	58.1	53.6
		2.24	2.26	4.53	9.93	1.43	2.78	62	3.8	67.0	31.7	88.3	104.4	79.8	76.0
2031-32-33-34-35-36-37 Canned & Pres. Fruits, Veg. & Sea Foods (68)		2.69	4.36	14.86	30.26	4.78	10.75	17	8.5	38.4	27.2	56.5	90.1	61.7	15.9
		1.65	2.83	9.35	16.19	3.11	6.66	25	4.9	53.1	58.1	118.2	149.8	88.1	52.1
		1.27	0.97	4.22	11.21	2.03	4.62	34	2.9	72.1	115.9	190.3	286.5	115.2	75.9
2751 Commercial Printing except Lithographic (72)		3.16	4.48	13.56	31.22	4.25	9.93	29	**	35.0	20.1	42.9	**	**	16.3
		2.34	2.63	7.07	16.45	2.64	6.43	41	**	53.6	33.3	74.2	**	**	54.1
		1.73	1.08	3.71	8.13	1.96	4.10	52	**	85.3	70.7	144.0	**	**	124.0
3661-62 Communication ... (66)		3.74	5.08	15.05	23.83	4.01	5.66	38	6.9	22.5	28.3	45.8	46.2	64.0	20.4
		2.58	4.15	11.82	14.12	2.71	3.44	51	4.9	41.4	39.1	68.5	84.8	92.5	41.5
		1.45		7.66	8.89	2.22		79	3.8		78.3	130.0	113.1	115.5	

Selected statistics from *Key Business Ratios in 125 Lines of business 1968*; published by Dun & Bradstreet, Inc.

EXHIBIT 15

14 IMPORTANT RATIOS IN RETAIL AND WHOLESALE LINES—1968

RETAIL LINES

Upper Quartile / MEDIAN / Lower Quartile

Line of Business (and number of concerns reporting)	Current assets to current debt (Times)	Net profits on net sales (Per cent)	Net profits on tangible net worth (Per cent)	Net profits on net working capital (Per cent)	Net sales to tangible net worth (Times)	Net sales to net working capital (Times)	Collection period (Days)	Net sales to inventory (Times)	Fixed assets to tangible net worth (Per cent)	Current debt to tangible net worth (Per cent)	Total debt to tangible net worth (Per cent)	Inventory to net working capital (Per cent)	Current debt to inventory (Per cent)	Funded debts to net working capital (Per cent)
Children's & Infants' Wear Stores (40)	5.80 / 2.82 / 2.09	3.54 / 1.70 / 0.04	15.77 / 5.98 / 0.18	17.29 / 7.39 / 0.20	5.65 / 4.17 / 2.60	6.96 / 4.36 / 2.97	* / * / *	6.3 / 4.4 / 3.1	6.0 / 14.3 / 24.6	18.9 / 39.6 / 88.2	99.5 / 118.4 / 152.8	81.4 / 105.2 / 131.0	25.8 / 44.9 / 80.7	10.0 / 28.0 / 58.5
Clothing & Furnishings, Men's & Boys' (213)	4.48 / 2.62 / 1.92	4.19 / 2.77 / 1.11	15.36 / 9.33 / 3.81	18.27 / 11.09 / 4.34	4.40 / 3.40 / 2.29	5.35 / 3.73 / 2.68	* / * / *	5.1 / 3.9 / 3.0	5.2 / 10.8 / 22.5	26.0 / 50.4 / 92.9	78.1 / 111.0 / 183.9	67.7 / 98.2 / 131.4	33.9 / 63.6 / 88.2	12.8 / 27.1 / 52.9
Department Stores (239)	4.25 / 2.85 / 2.00	2.88 / 1.93 / 1.06	10.32 / 6.16 / 2.88	14.31 / 7.68 / 3.77	4.57 / 3.14 / 2.44	6.09 / 4.13 / 3.12	* / * / *	6.9 / 5.4 / 4.4	12.0 / 24.4 / 46.3	24.1 / 38.8 / 66.0	44.1 / 70.7 / 119.6	58.6 / 81.0 / 106.5	46.8 / 69.7 / 100.7	12.3 / 31.9 / 57.6
Discount Stores (233)	2.26 / 1.83 / 1.46	3.25 / 2.00 / 1.03	20.57 / 13.97 / 8.01	29.55 / 17.08 / 8.67	9.73 / 6.71 / 4.84	13.19 / 8.26 / 5.65	* / * / *	7.1 / 5.2 / 4.0	12.9 / 24.1 / 48.0	62.7 / 95.7 / 144.6	92.6 / 142.2 / 199.4	110.5 / 159.3 / 229.0	58.8 / 75.2 / 100.0	15.7 / 39.6 / 74.9
Discount Stores, Leased Depts.	2.19 / 1.92	3.37	22.21 / 15.26	30.65 / 17.46	9.50	11.49 / 7.22	*	6.0	13.1 / 23.1	69.0 / 106.5	94.2 / 158.8	112.8 / 160.7	56.2 / 75.3	10.1 / 24.7

WHOLESALE LINES

5077 Air Condtg. & Refrigtn. Equipt. & Supplies (52)	3.29 / 2.16 / 1.60	3.28 / 1.82 / 1.04	16.61 / 9.32 / 6.25	18.65 / 13.41 / 7.69	7.85 / 5.20 / 3.28	11.22 / 5.83 / 4.23	34 / 49 / 65	9.8 / 6.5 / 4.9	6.6 / 12.4 / 32.4	33.6 / 75.5 / 149.4	48.5 / 89.3 / 186.8	59.0 / 85.5 / 141.2	62.7 / 109.0 / 155.6	15.5 / 30.6 / 61.8
5013 Automotive Equipment (185)	3.96 / 2.62 / 1.92	3.24 / 1.83 / 1.07	11.85 / 7.60 / 3.79	16.37 / 8.87 / 5.14	5.22 / 3.84 / 2.99	6.59 / 4.70 / 3.37	29 / 36 / 46	6.7 / 4.9 / 3.8	6.4 / 12.1 / 29.4	30.3 / 52.2 / 85.2	56.3 / 99.0 / 154.4	70.6 / 96.2 / 125.9	45.9 / 68.3 / 94.8	15.7 / 29.6 / 51.1
5095 Beer, Wine & Alcoholic Beverages (85)	3.29 / 2.19 / 1.54	1.99 / 1.07 / 0.54	13.10 / 7.52 / 4.14	16.95 / 10.32 / 5.44	9.69 / 6.79 / 4.92	13.21 / 9.26 / 6.60	11 / 25 / 40	13.3 / 9.2 / 6.3	5.4 / 18.3 / 42.0	28.8 / 65.9 / 143.9	68.6 / 156.1 / 234.9	69.9 / 94.6 / 141.6	58.9 / 91.6 / 128.6	8.7 / 27.9 / 49.2
5029 Chemicals & Allied Products (53)	2.63 / 1.83 / 1.44	3.56 / 1.89 / 0.46	12.75 / 8.72 / 3.67	27.30 / 13.26 / 6.76	7.77 / 5.37 / 2.34	15.00 / 7.45 / 4.27	32 / 43 / 53	17.1 / 11.3 / 7.6	10.9 / 22.2 / 49.9	30.3 / 69.3 / 135.8	58.7 / 149.8 / 199.0	46.9 / 77.2 / 113.5	113.4 / 144.7 / 218.2	14.7 / 33.8 / 83.8
5037 Clothing & Accessories	3.45 / 2.26 / 1.59	2.17 / 1.09	15.04 / 7.37 / 3.30	20.56 / 10.99 / 3.00	8.07 / 6.10 / 3.88	10.50 / 6.89 / 4.30	22 / 37 / 53	23.0 / 8.7 / 6.0	2.0 / 6.2 / 18.0	31.0 / 74.9 / 130.7	72.6 / 113.2 / 157.2	38.1 / 72.2 / 113.2	64.1 / 115.4 / 181.1	11.1 / 21.1

Selected statistics from *Key Business Ratios in 125 Lines of Business 1968*; published by Dun & Bradstreet, Inc.

to the development by the president of the ground rules for the preparation of the budget for the next fiscal year.

Businessmen constantly concern themselves with economic and industry trends; the financial pages of most publications contain forecasts of economists, polls of business opinions, and surveys of past performance which help set the mood for next year's budgeting.

This budget preplanning activity is akin to the long-range operational and financial planning activities which take place in an increasing number of companies these days. Most managements have found that it is not sufficient to face the problems of a business on a day-to-day basis or even on a year-to-year basis; accordingly, they try to plan at least five years in advance. Generally such planning involves a projection of the total market for the company's products and an assessment of what the company's share of that market should be, based on historical performance and management objectives.

Once a decision is made as to what the sales objectives should be for the next five years, management must decide how it will provide the resources to satisfy the projected volume. This usually involves capital budget projections for plant, manpower development programs, and the means by which funds will be obtained to finance the effort.

This process also deals with questions of policy and company objectives, such as:

1. The extent to which expansion will be financed from internally generated funds, equity funds, or debt.
2. The methods of distribution.
3. The development of sources of raw materials.
4. The decisions pertaining to the company's image in terms of price and quality of product.

Obviously the degree of accuracy of the projections and plans varies with the period covered. As a matter of fact, in view of the many uncertainties involved in projecting activities over a five-year period, the usual procedure is to prepare plans for the first year in considerable detail and then to resort to summary projections for the remaining four years. As each year's planning is done, refinements are made on the basis of recent experience and a new fifth year is added. Whether or not operational and financial planning is done over a five-year period, it is necessary to follow this preplanning procedure on at least a one-year basis in order to lay a sound foundation for running the business and preparing the budget for the next year.

Commencing with this preplanning activity, Exhibit 16 diagrams the flow of activity through all phases of the budget function. Although Exhibit 16 assumes the existence of a planning staff and a budget director, these positions may not be present in a given company. But the actual functions are performed, however informally, by some individual or group. In this example, detailed planning for next year starts with a general discussion between the president and his planning staff. This normally occurs about mid-year, and the planning staff has prepared economic evaluations of national, geographic, and industry trends in consumer demands. Keeping abreast of these types of data is the continuing function of the planning staff, which has access to a great abundance of statistics from governmental sources, trade associations, and market surveys by the company's own salesmen or market research organization. This is not to say that cold statistics of past activities contain the answer to the future development of a company. However, the future is sometimes quite clearly foretold by the past, and much planning lacks effectiveness because it does not make full use of all the material available for studying the past.

Paralleling the accumulation of these data relating to economic trends, the sales vice president will have been accumulating and analyzing the company's past performance in various areas and making an assessment of the company's competitive position and potential for the future based on the trends developed by the planning staff.

An additional piece of information is required in the preplanning phase before the president can successfully assess the company's position and establish objectives for the next year. This is information relating to the important area of how competitors are doing. Although detailed data are normally kept confidential by most companies, revealing trends and results may be derived from the large quantity of relevant published information. For example, *Fortune* annually ranks this nation's 500 largest industrial corporations by sales and lists assets, profits, and return on investment. Such data give the planning staff and the president some indication of how their company is faring competitively. In this process they must ask themselves, "Are we maintaining our share of the market?" Sometimes the growth of the economy may result in increasing sales for a particular company, but closer analysis may reveal that it is losing its share of the market to competitors—a trend that will be fatal in the long run if not arrested.

If the company appears to be holding its own in the marketplace, the next question is whether it is making a sufficient profit. Comparative percentages of profit return on sales and profit return on investment usually give quite conclusive indications as to whether the company is operating in an economical fashion.

Exhibit 17 presents a sampling of the many statistics available from the Government on relative profitability of different companies. Note how the detail varies as the series progresses, permitting the selection of the pertinent level of detail. Another example of Government-provided statistics is the set of input-output tables available from the U.S. Department of Commerce. The tables show the input-output relationships for 86 industries by indicating how each industry's sales and purchasing dollars are divided among the other industries. Designed to help forecasters calculate the impact of a major change in the demand for the products of any of the industries, the tables are made up of a grid of 86 rows and 85 columns so that each company falling in one of the 86 categories can see what dollar allotment of each of the other 85 industries' expenditures its industry receives.

Regardless of what competitors are doing, eventually the president must decide what his company's objectives and policies will be. At this point he has a wealth of information about his company's performance as related to the economy in general and to the experience of competitors. A good president does not accept statistical projections but sets his own goals based on what he thinks is possible regarding the introduction of new products, the development of new channels of distribution and

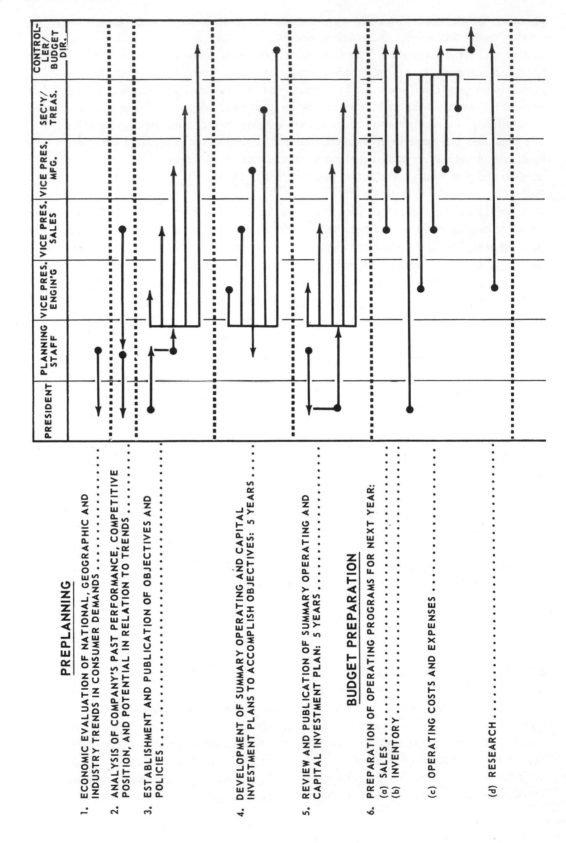

EXHIBIT 16   SIMPLIFIED DIAGRAM OF THE PLANNING AND BUDGETING PROCESS

PRESIDENT | PLANNING STAFF | VICE PRES. ENGIN'G | VICE PRES. SALES | VICE PRES. MFG. | SEC'Y/ TREAS. | CONTROL-LER/ BUDGET DIR.

PREPLANNING

1. ECONOMIC EVALUATION OF NATIONAL, GEOGRAPHIC AND INDUSTRY TRENDS IN CONSUMER DEMANDS . . . .

2. ANALYSIS OF COMPANY'S PAST PERFORMANCE, COMPETITIVE POSITION, AND POTENTIAL IN RELATION TO TRENDS . . . . . .

3. ESTABLISHMENT AND PUBLICATION OF OBJECTIVES AND POLICIES . . . .

4. DEVELOPMENT OF SUMMARY OPERATING AND CAPITAL INVESTMENT PLANS TO ACCOMPLISH OBJECTIVES: 5 YEARS . . . . .

5. REVIEW AND PUBLICATION OF SUMMARY OPERATING AND CAPITAL INVESTMENT PLAN: 5 YEARS . . . .

BUDGET PREPARATION

6. PREPARATION OF OPERATING PROGRAMS FOR NEXT YEAR:

(a) SALES . . . .
(b) INVENTORY . . . .

(c) OPERATING COSTS AND EXPENSES . . . .

(d) RESEARCH . . . .

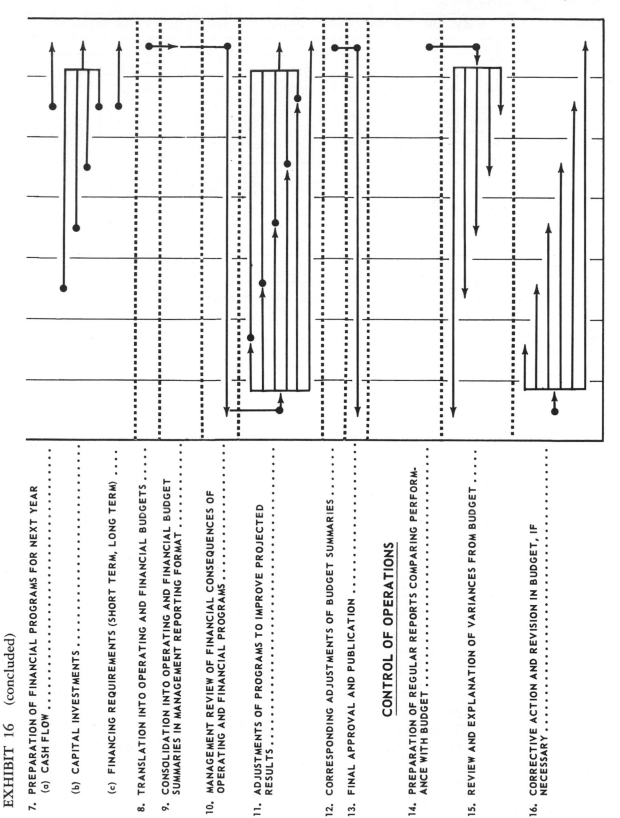

EXHIBIT 16 (concluded)

7. PREPARATION OF FINANCIAL PROGRAMS FOR NEXT YEAR
   (a) CASH FLOW . . . .

   (b) CAPITAL INVESTMENTS . . . .

   (c) FINANCING REQUIREMENTS (SHORT TERM, LONG TERM) . . . . .

8. TRANSLATION INTO OPERATING AND FINANCIAL BUDGETS . . . . .

9. CONSOLIDATION INTO OPERATING AND FINANCIAL BUDGET
   SUMMARIES IN MANAGEMENT REPORTING FORMAT . . . .

10. MANAGEMENT REVIEW OF FINANCIAL CONSEQUENCES OF
    OPERATING AND FINANCIAL PROGRAMS . . . .

11. ADJUSTMENTS OF PROGRAMS TO IMPROVE PROJECTED
    RESULTS . . . .

12. CORRESPONDING ADJUSTMENTS OF BUDGET SUMMARIES . . . . . .

13. FINAL APPROVAL AND PUBLICATION . . . .

CONTROL OF OPERATIONS

14. PREPARATION OF REGULAR REPORTS COMPARING PERFORM-
    ANCE WITH BUDGET . . . .

15. REVIEW AND EXPLANATION OF VARIANCES FROM BUDGET . . . . .

16. CORRECTIVE ACTION AND REVISION IN BUDGET, IF
    NECESSARY . . . .

EXHIBIT 17   RATES OF RETURN (AFTER TAXES) ON STOCKHOLDERS' INVESTMENT

Industry	Number of Corpora-tions	Rate of Return After Taxes (%)									
		1958	1959	1960	1961	1962	1963	1964	1965	1966	1967
Dairy Products	10	11.8	11.6	11.3	10.5	10.5	10.7	11.6	11.9	11.9	11.5
Bakery Products	11	10.4	10.6	10.4	8.9	9.3	10.2	10.7	11.4	12.6	14.1
Bread	8	10.6	10.1	8.4	5.7	4.9	5.5	6.0	6.7	8.8	11.6
Biscuits & Crackers	3 1/	10.2 1/	11.1 1/	12.4	12.0	13.6	14.9	15.2	15.7	15.9	16.3

Industry	Rates of Return After Taxes (%)									
	1958	1959	1960	1961	1962	1963	1964	1965	1966	1967
Dairy Products										
4 Largest Companies	12.2	12.0	11.6	10.9	10.8	10.9	11.9	12.4	12.5	12.1
6 Other Companies	8.5	8.4	9.2	8.0	8.2	9.3	9.8	8.9	8.1	7.4
Total 10 Companies	11.8	11.6	11.3	10.5	10.5	10.7	11.6	11.9	11.9	11.5

	Rate of Return (After Taxes) (%)									
	1958	1959	1960	1961	1962	1963	1964	1965	1966	1967
Dairy Products										
Borden Co., The	11.2	11.6	10.0	10.8	10.8	10.9	11.4	11.0	10.8	9.5
National Dairy Products Corp.	13.3	12.8	12.5	10.9	10.9	10.9	12.2	12.6	12.7	12.5
Carnation Co.	11.3	10.6	11.1	11.4	11.1	11.0	12.0	13.8	14.2	14.3
Beatrice Foods Co.	11.3	11.0	10.2	10.3	10.3	10.8	12.1	14.5	15.1	15.8

202-DAIRY PRODUCTS

	Total Assets		Rank		Stockholders' Average Investment		Net Income After Taxes		Rate of Return (%)	
	1966	1967	1966	1967	1966	1967	1966	1967	1966	1967
Companies Ranked 1 to 4	$2,461,111	$2,683,712			$1,524,535	$1,652,725	$190,902	$200,440	12.5	12.1
Companies Ranked 5 to 8	400,740	468,139			241,525	271,831	19,999	20,962	8.3	7.7
Companies Ranked 9 to 12 1/	50,549	57,915			28,094	29,333	2,145	2,110	7.6	7.2
Total 12 Companies	2,912,400	3,209,766			1,794,154	1,953,889	213,046	223,512	11.9	11.4
Registered Cos. Incl. Above:										
Beatrice Foods Co.	286,418	343,446	4	4	201,005	237,055	30,275	37,399	15.1	15.8
Borden Co., The	909,984	1,011,597	1	1	534,439	585,076	57,660	55,301	10.8	9.5
Carnation Co.	380,191	413,325	3	3	208,510	221,894	29,506	31,620	14.2	14.3
Dean Foods Co.	45,740	44,015	7	7	16,991	18,120	1,763	1,884	10.4	10.4
Deltown Foods, Inc.	16,290	15,715	A	A	8,983	9,051	25	376	0.3	4.2
Fairmont Foods Co.	77,395	96,170	6	6	52,342	57,018	3,941	5,048	7.5	8.9
Knudsen Creamery Co. of Calif.	29,995	33,795	8	8	21,624	23,192	3,013	3,642	13.9	15.7
National Dairy Products Corp.	884,518	915,344	2	2	580,581	608,700	73,461	76,120	12.7	12.5
Pet, Inc.	247,610	294,159	5	5	150,568	173,501	11,282	10,388	7.5	6.0

A – Ranks are not shown where they would disclose the approximate size of unregistered companies.
1/ Penn Dairies, Inc., with total assets of $11,105,000, a registered company, places among the companies ranked 9 to 12. One unregistered company whose total assets places it among the companies ranked 9 to 12 is included here instead of Penn Dairies, Inc., in order that a report may be made of companies of this size category without disclosing unpublished information on any individual company.

Selected statistics from *Report of the Federal Trade Commission on Rates of Return for Identical Companies in Selected Manufacturing Industries, 1958–1967.*

markets, and the application of good old-fashioned hard work and initiative, which he is very influential in motivating and achieving after he has called for this sort of effort.

The preplanning phase of the budget function culminates in a broad operating plan for the year, developed from two basic sources of data: environmental factors and company objectives. This plan is issued to the operating departments for the development of their individual plans and budgets to accomplish the objectives. An example of such a budget planning report is presented in the final section of this chapter.

The receipt of the budget planning report from the president by the various line managers initiates the budget preparation phase. Each of these managers prepares an operating plan for the next year and submits it to the budget director. (It may be helpful to refer again to Exhibit 16 for the sequence of events in this phase of budgeting.)

For example, the vice president of engineering prepares a recommended program of research and development, indicating priorities applicable to the projects recommended. This is important, since the decisions as to how much can be spent on research will have to await the financial budget review procedure. It is usually the case, and desirable, that the research budget be prepared on an overabundant basis. This will permit the president to make the selection which best meets the company's operating and profit objectives. Like all of the other line managers, the vice president of engineering must also prepare his program for operating the engineering and research and development departments—a program that will become the basis for his operating cost and expense budgets.

The sales vice president in his turn prepares the sales projections and the operating plans for the various sales activities and advertising campaigns. The manufacturing vice president prepares the inventory and manufacturing plans. The treasurer and controller also complete programs for the operation of their departments.

In addition to these operating plans of the various department heads, the budget director must be furnished with details of the financial programs for the year. The treasurer must prepare projections of cash requirements, preferably in the form of cash flow statements, and indicate sources of additional financing if required. The capital investment programs required by the various line managers to accomplish their operating programs must also be furnished to the budget director so that he may complete the capital expenditures budget.

With all of these basic data in hand, the budget director commences the task of assigning dollar values to the operating and financial programs submitted to him. Generally this is accomplished by translating the programs into dollars and by utilizing the format of responsibility reports, which are normally issued to each of the line managers. This involves two basic steps. First, the programs must be related to the chart of accounts so that the effect in each department and account can be determined. Second, the trend of costs and prices must be ascertained so that appropriate adjustments can be reflected in the budget. For example, if the workforce contemplated in the operating plans of the manufacturing vice president is to be the same as in the current year but a wage increase of 5 percent is contemplated in June of next year, the manufacturing cost budgets should reflect this. In a similar fashion, based on the planning assumptions of the planning staff and the president, the budget director must incorporate projected changes in other costs.

Having completed the preparation of the individual departmental budgets, the budget director consolidates them into operating and financial budget summaries in a form identical to that normally used when reporting operating and financial results to management. In other words when the budget department has completed its work, it has a product that looks exactly like the monthly operating and financial reports of the business, except that the figures contained therein represent projections for the next year instead of actual results for a completed period. These usually show operating results for each month of the budget year. Normally, cash flow statements are also presented for each month of the year, but other balance sheet items may be shown on only a quarterly or semiannual projected basis.

At this point the budget director submits the budget summaries to the president with comments and recommendations. As a result of the work involved in the preparation of these summaries, the budget director has had an opportunity to gain a real insight into the operating plans of the various managers and has determined the consequences in financial terms, which the president may now review in a comprehensive way. The effective budget director helps the president analyze the plan and develop possible alternatives if the projected results appear unsatisfactory. As pointed out previously, the budget director acts as an analyst and catalyst but does not make operating decisions or plans. However, at this point the good budget director is separated from the less effective budget director: The former has the ability to point up why the projected result is or is not satisfactory and what the president can do to change the situation if he so desires.

It is not unusual to find in this phase of the budget operation that the financial consequences of the initial plans are not satisfactory and that the president must ask his line managers and department heads to adjust their programs in specified ways to accomplish the desired profit and return-on-investment goals. In effect, he returns the operating and financial programs included in the budget requests to the originating line managers with specific suggestions for change. After the line managers have made the suggested changes, these programs are resubmitted to the budget director, who makes the corresponding financial adjustments and resubmits consolidated operating and financial budget summaries to the president for final approval and publication.

The procedure just described is not an unusual one. An actual example of the budget preparation phase, disguised to conceal confidential information, involves a large, well-known manufacturer of durable goods for the consumer market. This company is organized into a number of divisions on a product-line basis. Its preplanning cycle is a part of longer-range planning and covers a three-year forward period.

Each division manager annually submits a plan of operations for the ensuing three years, summarizing expected sales and operating levels, including costs and expenses. These plans are compared with the prior year's performance, and the approved budget and the significant deviations for the current year are evaluated and explained. The president's staff consolidates division plans and prepares a summary of profit and return on investment as well as sales and operating levels for the corporation as a whole. The president has one unyielding policy: The corporation and its divisions must show improvement from period to period. An improvement is specifically related to better profits and more efficient performance. When the budget officers reviewed these three-year plans with the president, he found the overall consolidated picture unsatisfactory. He said the forecast sales level for the first year of the three-year period looked all right; but for the second and third year, estimates were too optimistic. He told his budget officer to reduce the sales forecast for each of those two years by 100,000 units. The president said the profit shown for the first year was inadequate and asked for an improvement running into millions of dollars. The budget officer was directed to assign the requested overall profit improvement to the various divisions and to keep the president informed so the latter can identify how much of an improvement each division manager is required to produce.

After this initial meeting, the budget director made the requested profit-improvement breakdown in consultation with various staff groups and identified areas—such as manufacturing cost, general and administrative expense, and selling and promotional cost—where reduction in expenses could be made. In follow-up meetings with division general managers, the president and budget director reviewed improvement goals; as an outgrowth of this, the president subsequently placed a ceiling on the upcoming year's general and administrative expenses for each division. This ceiling was included in a letter to the managers.

In addition, each division was given an indication of how cost reductions could be made, such as by improving gross profit by one or two percentage points or by deferring certain routine maintenance projects. As a matter of policy, the president of this company does not permit the staff to tell the division managers specifically how these improvements should be achieved, because the corporate budget director is not running the business of the various operating divisions. As a result, some division managers chose courses of action other than those originally suggested.

To summarize, the president reviewed three-year plans on a consolidated basis; for each division where the projected profit was unsatisfactory, he asked his budget director and staff to recommend cost reductions or other improvements necessary to achieve the desired profit level. He accepted or rejected forecasts of sales and operating levels on the basis of their attainability. Once these changes were communicated to the divisions, they had to work them into revised budget plans and were then ready to go forward with the operating budget for the next year.

With the approval and publication of the budget for the new year and with the commencement of the year, the third or control-of-operations phase of the budgeting function begins. Basically, this involves the preparation of periodic reports comparing performance with the budget. Variances or departures of actual operations from the budget plan are highlighted in these reports, and the budget director analyzes these variances and determines and publishes the causes for the benefit of management.

Phase Three: Control of Operations

At this point the analyst's role terminates, and management must begin to perform its primary function of managing. Basically, one of three decisions can be made by the line managers, with the concurrence of the president:

1. The plan of operations can be changed to achieve the budgeted result. For example, if reduced activity in January is anticipated and a department projected a reduction in personnel for that month but failed to make the reduction, the variance report for January will show an unfavorable condition for that department. Releasing the excess personnel will bring actual operations into line with budget operations in future periods.

2. A departure from the plan can be authorized. Assume the situation in No. 1 above but that volume actually increased contrary to expectation, and, accordingly, the full complement of personnel was kept on. The budget report

for January will indicate the same excess costs, but under these circumstances management might, and probably will have to, authorize running in excess of the original personnel budgets because of the increase in volume.

3. A change in the budget plan can be authorized. As indicated later in this book, management should avoid changing its budget too frequently, since this has the effect of detracting from a long-range effort toward an established goal. However, there may be situations in which such drastic economic or other changes have taken place that continuing with the existing budget would be rather meaningless.

It is well to emphasize that management's response to budget variances must be very judicious and, in the last analysis, not in any sense automatic. In one instance the president of a firm which was engaged largely in research and development for space products said he was very fearful of a paperwork system that would interfere with true research objectives. For example, he pointed out that results quite often are not apparent or achieved until the very end of a planned research activity. He said that in his many years in this kind of work he saw too many projects on the verge of success almost abandoned, and a few which were actually abandoned, because of budget stringencies. Accordingly, he wanted to build into his budget system a signal, in addition to all of the regular reporting procedures, which would indicate to him when 90 percent of the expenditures had been made. At this point he would personally review each project and decide whether the results to date warranted exceeding the budget. The record of his accomplishment in the space field attests to the wisdom of exceeding budget under the proper circumstances.

Another interesting case involved a large motion picture producer and exhibitor that had fallen into financial difficulties with the advent of television and competition from other entertainment media. The company was sorely in need of management information and control systems, especially cost accounting and budgeting in the studio activity. However, there was a definite lack of appreciation of such planning and control techniques by studio personnel in Hollywood. The studio manager said that what the company needed was artistic excellence, and the fact that it hadn't won an Oscar in quite a few years was a reflection on how cost reduction programs and planned financial approaches had impaired the effectiveness of the Production Department. This notion was not rejected out of hand, although it was apparent that the studio was being run too loosely and that a budget plan somehow had to be implemented which would meet the needs of management.

However, an extensive review of the history of some of the big motion picture successes and failures did confirm the importance of what the studio manager had said. Generally budgets for motion picture productions ran anywhere from a few million dollars up to $30 million. No one has been able to determine in a very positive way what accounts for box office success, but a pattern of key ingredients has evolved, including individual stars, successful predecessor novels or plays, spectacular scenes, and so on. In certain cases, the payment of an additional few hundred thousand dollars for one of the more popular stars has resulted in millions of additional dollars at the box office. The same could be demonstrated for any of the other factors contributing to a successful motion picture.

This condition was so pertinent that it had to be incorporated into management strategy and consequent budget principles. To illustrate, if there is an opportunity to engage Star *B* for twice the price of Star *A*, the budget must be flexible enough to permit this added cost if management decides that such action will more than repay itself at the box office. Thus a cost control and budgeting plan was developed which met the needs of top management and yet was acceptable to studio management as being a reasonable plan that would not hamper artistic efforts.

In review, the three basic phases of budgeting are preplanning, budget preparation, and control of operations. It should be clear at this point that the president plays a vital role in the process and must work closely with the budget director and the various line managers to arrive at the right answer for his company. As a detailed example of the president's role in the preplanning phase, the following budget planning report is presented.

To All Vice Presidents:

Since our founding 30 years ago, we have grown with the industry in the manufacture and sale of plastic products. From our modest beginning, we have expanded our manufacturing and general offices to the modern facilities we enjoy today. We are also very proud of the addition, over the years, of the branch sales offices in New York, Atlanta, Chicago, New Orleans, and San Francisco.

Last year our annual sales volume grew to $22 million, and profits amounted to $820,-000. In spite of sales attaining a record high volume, the margin of profit declined from the previous year and the percentage of net to sales declined from the level of the past four years. This trend must be reversed, and the planned improvement should be reflected in your budgets to be prepared for the next year. Table 1 illustrates the unsatisfactory condition experienced last year.

INCOME STATEMENTS—PREVIOUS FIVE YEARS

(In Thousands of Dollars)

TABLE 1

	Last Year	2 Years Ago	3 Years Ago	4 Years Ago	5 Years Ago
Net sales	$22,384	$20,980	$19,830	$18,782	$17,436
Cost of sales	16,849	15,550	14,645	14,060	12,972
Gross profit	5,535	5,430	5,185	4,722	4,464
% of sales	24.7%	25.9%	26.1%	25.1%	25.6%
Selling expenses	2,627	2,540	2,416	2,124	1,977
General and administrative	1,237	1,203	1,160	1,108	1,087
Operating profit	1,671	1,687	1,609	1,490	1,400
% of sales	7.5%	8.0%	8.1%	7.9%	8.0%
Other income	103	16	41	36	29
Other expense	115	33	27	24	18
Net profit before income taxes	1,659	1,670	1,623	1,502	1,411
Provision for taxes	839	840	813	760	721
Net profit	$ 820	$ 830	$ 810	$ 742	$ 690
% of sales	3.7%	4.0%	4.1%	4.0%	4.0%

TABLE 2   PER-SHARE EARNINGS AND RETURN ON INVESTMENT

	Earnings Per Share		Return on Average Investment	
	Amount	Increase (Decrease)	Percent	Increase (Decrease)
5 years ago	$3.45	—	11.9%	—
4 years ago	3.71	8%	12.3%	3%
3 years ago	4.05	9%	12.7%	3%
2 years ago	4.15	2%	12.2%	(4%)
Last year	4.10	(1%)	11.3%	(7%)

There are certain underlying basic factors which must be considered by each department in the preparation of the budget. The planning staff, with the concurrence of the budget committee and with my approval, has set forth the following planning assumptions to be considered by you:

1. Growth. The industry is expected to continue its expansion at the rate of 5 to 6 percent because of population growth. Our products have continued to sell well and are expected to perform better than the industry average.
2. Business conditions. General business conditions are expected to maintain the present growth rate during the first half of the year, with a leveling off during the last half.
3. Capital. All anticipated expansion is to be financed from cash flow. The recent $1.2 million sale of ten-year debentures anticipated capital requirements; therefore, we do not expect to obtain any additional financing in the immediate future.

Investment and earnings. Our primary objective of strengthening the financial structure of the organization cannot be overemphasized. We must not only maintain profits for continued existence but also achieve profit growth at an optimum level and improve the return on our investment.

Our five-year record of per-share earnings and return on investment is noted in Table 2. These results and our recent growth rate are completely unsatisfactory. Our study of business and general industry trends indicates that we are capable of earning $5 per share this coming year. This would represent a net income of $1 million after taxes and a return on investment of 13.4 percent. Such increases of almost 22 percent in earnings and 19 percent in return on investment represent attainable improvements in our operating results. Accordingly, our primary objective this coming year is to earn $1 million after taxes, with the same level of capitalization as last year.

Supplementing this objective of improving the rate of return on investment, we must improve our capital investment program; this must include a creative search for, and analyses of, profitable opportunities. Alternatives offering improved return should be explored in depth for the best payout selection consistent with the company's objectives.

Volume and profit. To achieve our higher earnings objective, there must be an increase in gross profit. This can be brought about by any one of four actions:

1. Increase total sales.
2. Increase production of the more profitable products or introduce new product lines.
3. Increase sales prices.
4. Decrease costs.

A combination of these alternatives is required to achieve the optimum gross profit.

COMPARISON OF RESULTS   **TABLE 3**
(*000's Omitted*)

	Our Company	Industry Average
Sales	$22,384	$21,181
Cost of sales	16,849	14,381
Gross profit	$ 5,535	$ 6,800
Selling, general, and administrative	3,864	4,400
Operating profit	$ 1,671	$ 2,400
Federal income taxes, etc.	851	1,214
Net income	$ 820	$ 1,186

Therefore, we must plan to attain the proper level and mix of sales at prices producing the gross profit necessary for earnings of $1 million after taxes.

With this in mind, the decision has been made to add a new product, *XYZ*, to our product line starting next February 1. Forecast sales of one million units in the first year have been based upon extensive advertising in the first year to establish the product and, in subsequent years, upon advertising proportionate to that for our other products to maintain the sales level.

Productivity and penetration. Branch and district sales results indicate that the market potentials have not been fully exploited. Moreover, comparisons of selling expenses and order value per salesman indicate that not all branches are operating at acceptable effectiveness. This indicates the need for greater promotional effort and a revision in sales campaigns to capture a greater share of the market. You should analyze the causes for unfavorable market penetrations and plan corrective action to improve selling productivity.

Control of costs. The many "crash programs" to reduce costs have not had significant permanent results. However, a continuing effort must be made to eliminate nonproductive elements of expense. The prime responsibility for control of costs rests with the head of each department. In the coming year this responsibility can best be discharged by submitting requests for departmental expense budgets which have been pared of all nonproductive costs. Continuing control must be exerted to keep expenses within the budget, and we must be alert to additional opportunities for cost reduction throughout the year.

The budget committee will review all expense budgets and recommend reductions whenever it deems such action appropriate. Except for direct manufacturing and selling expenses associated with anticipated higher sales volume, all expense budgets equal to or higher than last year's budgets probably will be unacceptable.

Profit analysis. Last year's performance fell short of the performance of the industry as a whole. Our 11.3 percent return on average invested capital is seriously below that of the industry average, 15.2 percent. In Table 3 this unfavorable performance is illustrated through a comparison of our results with results experienced by a company of our size as computed from industry averages.

We spend considerably more on cost of sales than the industry average and somewhat less on selling, general, and administrative expense. Additionally our break-even point is higher than the industry because of our greater fixed costs. This, coupled with poor return on capital, indicates apparent unused plant capacity.

Products. An analysis of our three products (Table 4) shows considerable difference in gross profit contribution.

TABLE 4   PRODUCT PROFITABILITY DATA FOR LAST YEAR
(Per 100 Units)

	A	B	C
Sales Price	$120.00	$300.00	$450.00
Variable Costs and Expenses			
Manufacturing costs			
Standard			
Material	$ 36.91	$ 60.84	$ 92.58
Labor	23.71	46.12	78.82
Overhead	29.84	48.33	82.58
	$ 90.46	$155.29	$253.98
Variances	.91	3.20	3.32
Manufacturing marginal contribution	$ 28.63	$141.51	$192.70
% to sales	23.9%	47.2%	42.8%
Operating expenses			
Salesmen's commissions	$ 2.51	$ 6.28	$ 9.42
Advertising and sales promotion	3.22	9.80	14.71
Other variable selling expense	2.94	5.46	7.54
	$ 8.67	$ 21.54	$ 31.67
Net marginal contribution	$ 19.96	$119.97	$161.03
% to sales	16.6%	40.0%	35.8%
Fixed Costs and Expenses			
(including associated variances)	17.63	34.02	61.37
Net operating income	$ 2.33	$ 85.95	$ 99.66
% to sales	1.9%	28.7%	22.1%

Because of its relatively low profit contribution, product *A* should not be produced in preference to one of the more profitable products. Also, it would be unwise to run another shift merely to produce these items if the added costs cancel the contribution made by the product.

Sales campaigns should be employed to achieve the product mix producing the best overall contribution. A significant increase in marginal profit would more than offset a sizable decrease in volume. Additionally, a sizable decrease in product *A* volume would complement not only the introduction of *XYZ* but also the expanded production of products giving us more favorable profit contributions.

Branch sales analysis. Market penetration is considerably smaller in some branches than in others:

Market	% Penetration Last Year
Atlanta	21
San Francisco	20
New Orleans	16
Chicago	16
New York	12

SALES ANALYSIS—NEW ORLEANS **TABLE 5**
(*All Products*)

District	Total Sales in Dollars			% Market Penetration		
	Last Year	1 Year Ago	2 Years Ago	Last Year	1 Year Ago	2 Years Ago
1	$142,806	$ 210,728	$ 211,066	17%	18%	18%
2	159,021	174,286	190,211	14	18	20
3	186,186	205,817	212,309	13	16	22
4	214,686	287,809	291,512	12	19	20
5	296,514	220,711	205,184	26	21	18
All districts	$999,213	$1,099,351	$1,110,282	15.8%	18.3%	19.5%

Although our share of the New York and Chicago markets is smaller than the other markets, it accounted for over 70 percent of total sales. Since the New York and Chicago markets offer considerable long-range potential for expanding sales, we should begin to achieve increased market penetration. Also consideration must be given to increasing promotion in areas which have the greatest sales return per dollar of promotion expenditure:

Market	Sales Payback Per Promotional Dollar
San Francisco	$369
Chicago	302
New York	299
New Orleans	133
Atlanta	97
Average	$240

Total sales in New York have increased 10 percent in the last three years. However, on balance the sales of the least profitable product increased as much as the more profitable products. This further demonstrates the lack of selection in product promotion and sales improvement programing. The New Orleans branch has lost both sales and share of the market in the last three years, as shown in Table 5. District 5 is the only district which has a favorable trend. The reasons for the slippage in the other districts must be explored in depth and corrective action taken to improve our performance.

General. In requesting budget estimates from department heads, you should pass along guidelines which are consistent with those contained in this report. Our budget director will shortly issue a timetable for completion of the various phases of the budget.

THE PRESIDENT

The process of preplanning, preparation of the budget, and control of operations involves a very close relationship between planning and budgeting. Before moving on to the preparation of the various functional budgets, we should take note of an important new development which will assist in planning not only for the coming budget year but also for the more extended time spans (five years or more) covered by the long-range planning program of the company. Generally, manual methods of

Use of Models in the Budgeting and Planning Process

making the planning computations are time-consuming, with the result that only a few alternative plans of operation can be fully evaluated. Computerized financial models have been developed to assist in simulating what the results would be under many different assumptions as to volume, products, and plan of operation.

The full impact of this statement is not realized unless one has been closely associated with the preparation of all phases of a budget as illustrated in Exhibit 16. Most steps usually involve some alternative assumptions or decisions, and the final outcome of the budget process can vary greatly in terms of the profits and resources which will result from each assumption or decision. As a practical matter, the burden of making the planning and budgeting computations under even one set of assumptions is generally considered to be all that a company can expect its people to carry in addition to their other current operating responsibilities. Very often the work is such that deadlines are missed and budgets for the new year are not available on time.

The computerized financial model takes the drudgery out of the computations, once the computer programs are prepared, by applying the given relationships to different sets of assumptions and conditions. This process of simulating different methods of operation is a big help in exploring the alternatives available in the planning process. Chapter 14 discusses this process in detail, linking the relationships in models to those used in budgeting, and illustrates the principles by means of a case study.

3

The Sales Manager's Role

ALL TOO FREQUENTLY the optimistic characteristics of salesmen and sales managers lead them to view budgeting as a restrictive process and a necessary evil. Such a viewpoint is extremely unfortunate; good budgeting is quite the reverse. When a system of budgetary planning and control is properly conceived and implemented, it offers a prime creative opportunity to improve market penetration and sales effectiveness.

To be of any real use to management, budgeting must facilitate the basic management process, as mentioned in prior chapters. This process of planning, execution, and control involves four fundamental management requirements: anticipation, coordination, control, and payout evaluation. Generally the success of management can be measured by how well it handles those four requirements.

What is true for management in general is certainly true for sales and marketing in particular. Sales managers are constantly faced with the problem of anticipation—anticipating customer requirements, new-product needs, competitor strategies, and various changes in distribution methods or promotional techniques. No sales executive needs to be shown the value of beating competitors by anticipation. In a similar vein the value of good coordination is highly respected in marketing. A product "deal" promotion has to be coordinated with advertising, store display, and shelf-space arrangements. Or an order for parts to be furnished by a subcontractor must be delivered on schedule for a major contractor's assembly. Sales management is also acutely interested in control. No better evidence is necessary than the widely used quota system for field salesmen. Pressure is usually exerted regularly to assure quota attainment.

Finally, payout evaluation is of particular interest to sales management, as there is considerably more flexibility in the economics of sales activities than in other functional areas of business. This is simply saying that sales management generally has far more ability than other managers to make money by spending money. Production and administrative departments typically operate in a less flexible environment. Since sales management realizes that expenditures for new-product development, market research, more salesmen, broker or distributor agreements, increased advertising and promotion, and so forth could increase revenue and possibly profit, the evaluation of payout is a matter of frequent review.

What have been mentioned are typical day-to-day management problems in sales. Their relationship to budgeting is very direct. In fact the entire concept of budgeting is built around the four crucial requirements or problems of management just described. Particularly in the development of the sales budget do we see how a good budget system copes with the basic management problems of anticipation, coordination, control, and payout evaluation.

Chapter 2 presented an overview of the budgetary process to demonstrate how good budgeting systematically relates one function to another. This integration of planning has great pertinence to the sales officer, because the sales budget is the key budget in this process. It becomes the cornerstone of the overall corporate budget simply because it sets the basic level of activity for the entire business. This point can be illustrated by contrasting an integrated budget system to a routine or old-fashioned budgeting method still practiced by some companies today and widely used by government agencies. Under this routine method, budgeting consists of each department preparing an estimate or forecast of its expenses for the next year, usually by reference to what was spent last year. Apart from the obvious tendency to perpetuate inefficiencies, this method assumes the level of activity will be the same in the budget year as in the prior year. Stated another way and from the sales manager's point of view, such a budget routine has the effect of letting expense budgets establish the marketing plan. This may be too harsh an oversimplification, because top management frequently seeks a sales forecast as well as expense budgets; nevertheless, the principle of expense budgets based on last year's figures is not planning, and salesmen soon recognize this as budgeting backwards. Thus the feeling of restrictiveness results.

Effective coordination in budgeting requires the identification of a common activity level throughout the business, based on the sales budget. This is the real challenge to the sales executive, but there is no escaping it in an economy where customer choice is exercised at the point of sale. The sales order is the focal point of business reality. Either a sales budget is well conceived or else a company cannot hope to earn a good return and enjoy future growth. The sales executive is not a totally free agent, however. His budget must recognize the production, engineering, and transportation capabilities of the company. This is an internal link of only slightly less importance than the reality of the marketplace.

Bearing on this point is the following conversation among a company's top executives. The chief manufacturing officer outlined the company's profit-making problem as a simple one: All that is required is for sales personnel to sell exactly what the manufacturing department can best produce and in precisely the right order-size to effect maximum production efficiency. The proposal was seriously and sincerely offered but reflected an obvious commercial naïveté. Sales management countered that production should arrange and even replace facilities so that the orders available in the marketplace could be run efficiently and hence sell at a lower price. This approach was also rather impractical on any short-run basis. Top management frequently faces such a conflict, and quite frankly a good budgetary process highlights it in the search for an adequate solution. The solution lies in the key sales budget.

The sales budget is not a sales forecast. The distinction is important. A budget is a planning and control document which shows what management intends to accomplish. In this sense it is active rather than passive. A sales forecast, however, is a projection or estimate of the available customer demand. A forecast reflects the environmental and competitive situation facing the company, whereas the sales budget shows how management intends to *react* to this environmental and competitive situation. It is necessary to emphasize this, because good budgeting hinges on aggressive management control rather than on passive acceptance of what the market appears to offer. Many companies have failed to make that distinction; consequently, they have found the budget more of a figure exercise than a working tool. A good example of the distinction is reflected in the way budget revisions are handled. If the budget is revised casually and frequently because actual performance is not up to budget, then the budget is probably viewed as more of a forecast than a tool of management control.

Sales budget preparation can be viewed as involving the following four interrelated steps:

Sales Budget Preparation

1. The sales forecast.
2. The marketing plan.
3. The advertising and promotion budget.
4. The selling expense budget.

Before examining each of those four steps individually, it will be helpful to discuss briefly their interrelationship.

As the first step in preparing the sales budget, the sales forecast expresses demand potential and opens the way to intelligent marketing planning. To convert the forecast to a marketing plan, management must make certain policy decisions about such matters as pricing, share of market, size of sales force, level of promotional activity, and ability to and cost of manufacture. These decisions and management plans imprint management control on the passive sales forecast and thus add the vital element of creative sales planning. The marketing plan is based not only on the sales forecast but also on certain assumptions regarding the level of advertising and sales promotion expenses and regarding the level of selling expenses. Therefore, it is important to consider the budgets for those two types of expense as part of the overall sales budget.

Assume that the sales budget is prepared on an annual basis. This is the most usual situation, but it is possible that the planning process might be carried on more frequently. Even when the overall budgeting is done annually, sales forecasting and market planning may be accelerated to quarterly intervals in some industries. Where this is done, procedures will be much the same as when the process is carried out for the year as a whole. The responsibility for preparing the sales budget rests, of course, with the chief sales officer. The budget director provides technical assistance and

EXHIBIT 18   FLASH PROFIT PROJECTION

Responsibility	CONSUMER PRODUCTS COMPANY				
President—J. J. Ames	YEAR ENDED DECEMBER 31, 19—				
	(in thousands of dollars)				

Better (Worse) Than Last Year Actual		Total Sales	Divisions		
			Biscuit	Dry Cereal	Packaged Food
$1,700	Net sales	$34,400	$14,700	$12,600	$7,100
	Cost of sales:				
($ 140)	Variable expenses (standard)	$22,360	$10,290	$ 7,810	$4,260
$1,560	Contribution	$12,040	$ 4,410	$ 4,790	$2,840
3%	% of sales	35%	30%	38%	40%
($ 165)	Fixed expenses (standard)	$ 3,440			
$1,395	Gross profit	$ 8,600			
5.9%	% of sales	25%			
($ 903)	Selling, General and Administrative costs	$ 5,160			
$ 492	Profit before taxes	$ 3,440			
1%	% of sales	10%			
($ 246)	Provision for taxes	$ 1,720			
$ 246	Net profit	$ 1,720			
.05%	% of sales	5%			

assures that the budget process follows an established timetable and format, but the proposed sales budget must be the work of the sales department. This is a fundamental part of the responsibility concept. How the top sales officer carries out this responsibility depends on the organization of his department and on the type of business and its scope of operations. Except in the smallest of companies, the budgeting effort can involve many people; and careful planning is necessary to assure a proper meshing of marketing talents.

Most companies are organized either by function, where all company sales activities report to a vice president of sales or marketing, or by division, where each division has its own sales department. In the latter case, budgeting follows divisional lines: A sales budget, including a marketing plan, is prepared by each division. In this sense the division is like a company organized functionally.

Within the sales or marketing department, there may be an organizational split between product management and field sales management. Where this is the case, specific responsibility for each of the four steps of sales budget preparation must be identified. Perhaps the most usual situation is (1) to charge product managers with the requirement of developing the marketing plans and the advertising and promotional budgets and (2) to secure field sales management coordination in developing sales forecasts and in preparing selling expense budgets.

Senior sales management must submit marketing objectives and policies to the president for his approval. Coordination with other parts of the business is important. Particularly important is the review of production capabilities and of any manufacturing problems that may exist. It would serve little purpose to suggest a dramatic increase in sales of product X if manufacturing is having difficulty making product X in even limited quantities.

Because the marketing plan is a key document for budgeting other phases of the business, sales budgeting occurs early in the overall budget timetable. The sales forecast, for example, may be started as early as August or September in a large company to allow sufficient budget lead time on a calendar-year basis.

When the sales budget is completed, sales management submits it for tentative approval. This step of securing tentative approval differentiates the sales budget from other budgets that fit into the overall corporate budget. No budget can be considered as finally approved by the president until the entire corporate budget has been put together and accepted. Nevertheless the marketing plan must receive early approval (usually on a tentative basis) so that other departments know the activity level expected and can plan accordingly. As explained in the next chapter, production and inventory planning are contingent on the marketing plan.

To facilitate this tentative approval, which is usually based in large measure on the adequacy of the indicated profit, sales management should develop with the budget department a flash report summary showing the indicated level of profitability represented by the proposed marketing plan. Exhibit 18 is an example of a flash report summary based on standard gross profit rates and historical averages for sales deductions and expenses.

The sales forecast is itself the product of reconciling a number of separate and, to varying degrees, independent estimates based on a variety of data sources and diverse logical structures. It is usually helpful to consider the forecast as built up of three elements: (1) sales of present products to present customers; (2) sales of present products to new customers; (3) sales of new products to both present and new customers.

Methods of sales forecasting may be classified into four types which apply in varying degree to these three components. The first and most common method is *statistical* forecasting which involves the projection of historical trends for the economy, for the market or class of trade, for the product group, for individual items, or for some combination. This category of forecasting includes *correlation analysis,* which uses leading indicators and economic indexes obtained from government sources, commercial banks, or private economists and statistical services. Correlation analyses may be

The Sales Forecast

39

particularly useful in such areas as construction materials or major appliances, which may be sensitive to specific identifiable and forecastable economic indicators. The backbone of most modern statistical forecasting systems, however, is *exponential smoothing* (running averages, with relatively higher weights given to the more recent data, and with additional adjustments for trends and seasonal movements).

The second basic forecasting method uses *marketing research* studies aimed at analysis of technological, legislative, and style considerations which may not be reflected fully or even partially in historical data. Normally, these tend to become more important over longer time periods, but their impact can often be felt significantly within a year. Some of the factors may relate, for example, to new and cheaper competitive products, impending legislation regarding labeling requirements, restrictions in raw materials availability, public concern for pollution control, or changes in apparel styles. It is relatively easy to identify these factors, but much more difficult to establish quantitatively their impact on sales of specific products—existing or new. To obtain specific information that can be acted upon, market research may be based on published information sources or statistics or may use surveys at the wholesaler, retailer, or consumer level. Sometimes substantial information can be collected through contacts between the sales organization and the company's own customers. Where surveys are planned to cover representative samples of a customer or user group, they may be more easily extrapolated or projected to the market as a whole. Special techniques of input-output analysis, econometric analysis, or various forms of probability analysis fall in this category of forecasting techniques.

A third forecasting method, widely used particularly in industrial products operations, involves grass-roots forecasts developed by the sales organization. This technique aims at examination of the current and potential needs of individual customers. Information is collected and recorded by individual salesmen using prescribed customer profile forms. The analysis of this information usually requires close involvement by district-level and headquarters sales management. Sometimes the salesmen may provide the required information, but usually some direct discussion with authoritative personnel in the customer organization is necessary. To keep this job at a manageable level, complete data collection is normally limited to selected customers whose purchases are individually significant (historically or potentially) and who collectively account for a major portion of total sales. The remainder may be projected on a statistical basis only.

Generally, historical sales records on individual customers are provided as background information to the sales people who are preparing customer profiles and analyzing customer potential. It must be emphasized, however, that sales personnel should not use these historical records to make statistical projections. Those are almost always better made on a centralized basis. The real purpose of the grass-roots approach is to examine possible ways of changing historical sales patterns and expanding sales with individual customers and groups of customers—or sometimes to identify problem situations where sales must be expected to diminish.

Special statistical analyses can be very helpful in identifying customers who have not regularly bought specific major products or items or in examining the number of sales visits or calls which have been made, their apparent sales results, and their coordination in timing with other promotional efforts.

A fourth forecasting method gaining increasing attention—*market simulation*—is based on a model or explicit description of the market and of the cause-and-effect relationships which influence it. This technique is relatively new and, because of its inherent complexity, used most often by larger companies that can apply the necessary resources. Market research, computer, and operations research skills are normally involved in developing the computer programs and data collection programs by which the model operates. The primary prerequisite in developing a successful market simulation procedure, however, is the active participation of senior marketing personnel who can provide the essential know-how as to the structure of a particular market. To be credible and useful, the model must incorporate an expression of how marketing management (not operations researchers or systems analysts) sees its consumers, distributors, and competitors and how it believes them to act in response to changes in such elements as price, advertising expenditures, and delivery lead times.

For example, a market simulation program may incorporate data regarding the average frequency of purchase by individual consumers and the fraction of these consumers who are expected to switch from one brand to another on successive purchases according to the relative weight of advertising expenditure for the different brands. The brand manager can specify various levels of advertising expenditure and, by processing these through the program, can estimate or forecast the corresponding expected levels of sales for his brand. He may also specify various levels of competitors' expenditures on advertising and use the model to estimate their effect on his brand.

Development of Sales Data Base

In order to carry out the necessary analysis and projections routinely and efficiently—not just once a year but periodically and as conditions change and forecasts must be revised—information has to be properly organized, taking advantage of available data processing facilities and techniques.

Sales analysis data are taken from customer invoices during the accounting process. The way in which the information is captured and presented depends upon the system's design and the provision for coding. Since budgetary planning and control are major users of sales analysis, marketing and sales have a primary interest in invoice coding. In businesses where the time interval between order entry and invoicing is long—because of custom manufacturing, for example—sales analysis may be done on the basis of orders entered rather than invoices issued. In such situations, the same principles apply to coding and summarizing of orders.

Modern sales analysis has been greatly facilitated by the development of high-speed data processing equipment, which has made it possible to obtain a great variety of data quickly and at reasonable cost. Most companies of significant size have such equipment, and sales management should participate actively in structuring the information so it will be useful in budgeting. The key to doing this is to consider how products and product lines are identified, how customers are classified and assigned for sales coverage, how territories or trading areas are established, what distribution channels are used, and what product price classes or pricing distinctions are made. One additional consideration is vital because of the coordinating aspect of the sales budget: the location of manufacturing or customer-service facilities (inventory stocking points).

Invoice coding for sales analysis may involve customer identification (billing location and shipping destination); customer class; salesman and branch office identification; product identification (group, style, size, color, price class); territory or trading area; customer industry; product end-use; quantity sold; and unit price. Obviously, the more detailed the coding, the greater the cost of data processing. However, necessary information for the marketing plan (a breakdown of product styles by color, for example) can frequently be provided far more easily, accurately, and cheaply by applying formulas on the basis of experience than by requiring sales personnel to project such breakdowns on the basis of judgment. A sales analysis such as that for the New York branch (Exhibit 19) is useful for branch-management sales planning, particularly in the development of a field sales forecast.

Despite the passive nature of the sales forecast, it is a document of great importance—so much so that considerably more effort should be expended in its preparation than many managements choose to apply. The format, frequency, and manner in which the sales forecast is prepared depends, of course, on the type of business. Two extreme examples will illustrate the contrast in possible methods. The president or other key officers of a highly skilled machine shop operation producing custom-engineered precision parts for a relatively few large accounts may prepare the sales forecast by simply asking each customer to develop a forecast of his expected requirements. On the other hand, a large consumer goods manufacturer selling a broad product line to millions of homeowners may forecast most accurately by developing share-of-market expectations applied to economic indexes or statistical indexes of consumer buying.

In the salesman's forecast form for Consumer Products Company (Exhibit 20), note that unit sales for the prior year have been summarized as background data for the salesman. This information is supplemented by regular sales analysis reports giving further detail to the extent necessary. In addition, salesmen preparing forecasts normally receive instructions relating to changes in marketing policy or objectives and to changes in predictions about general economic conditions. An important feature of any grass-roots approach is the provision of space on the forms for salesmen's comments so that management does not overlook significant marketing factors.

Where external data such as economic indexes, syndicated market research reports, trade association statistics, or census statistics are routinely used, they also can be made more accessible through incorporation in a mechanized data base. It serves little purpose, of course, to simply accumulate data banks on computer tapes or disks unless there are established systems and procedures for using them. For this reason, the development of an integrated marketing information system should precede the development of data banks.

Assembling the Sales Forecast

In order for the diverse elements of the sales forecast to flow together properly, a schedule and timetable should be established, together with identification of specific responsibility for individual segments. Normally the major steps are:

1. Establishment of basic assumptions to be used in forecast development.
   (*a.*) Overall economic trends.
   (*b.*) Product line changes—introduction of new products and phasing out of older products.

Branch	New York
Responsibility Head	P. Bradbury

CONSUMER PRODUCTS COMPANY
YEAR ENDED DECEMBER 31, 19—

Customer Classification	Month Cases	Month Dollars	Year to Date Cases	Year to Date Dollars	% of Quota
CHAIN STORES					
A & J Stores					
Biscuit					
Jumbo	40	$ 1,208	484	$ 14,500	82
Minipak	51	1,542	616	18,500	110
Cookies	59	1,750	700	21,000	90
	150	$ 4,500	1,800	$ 54,000	96
Cereal					
Crunchies	97	$ 2,925	1,170	$ 35,100	92
Korn Krisps	112	3,333	1,333	40,000	102
Rice Flakes	91	2,742	1,097	32,900	86
	300	$ 9,000	3,600	$ 108,000	94
Packaged food					
Peas	167	$ 5,021	2,008	$ 60,250	104
Corn	150	4,500	1,800	54,000	98
Beans	133	3,979	1,592	47,750	87
	450	$13,500	5,400	$ 162,000	98
Subtotal	900	$27,000	10,800	$ 324,000	96
Peter B's Markets					
Biscuit					
Jumbo	18	$ 542	217	$ 6,500	90
Minipak	34	1,021	408	12,250	98
Cookies	29	868	347	10,416	84
	81	$ 2,431	972	$ 29,166	89
Cereal					
Crunchies	55	$ 1,644	658	$ 19,722	94
Korn Krisps	68	2,034	814	24,411	115
Rice Flakes	39	1,175	470	14,100	91
	162	$ 4,853	1,942	$ 58,233	99
Packaged food					
Peas	91	$ 2,742	1,097	$ 32,900	95
Corn	80	2,383	953	28,598	90
Beans	44	1,333	534	16,000	85
	215	$ 6,458	2,584	$ 77,498	87
Subtotal	458	$13,742	5,498	$ 164,897	91
Other Chains	1,028	$30,821	12,328	$ 369,853	97
Total	2,386	$71,563	28,626	$ 858,750	92
INDEPENDENT STORES	279	$ 8,353	3,341	$ 100,250	97
SPECIALTY STORES	113	$ 3,417	1,367	$ 41,000	91
Grand total	2,778	$83,333	33,334	$1,000,000	95

EXHIBIT 20

SAMPLE OF SALESMAN'S SALES FORECAST

(*In Cases*)

Branch	New York
Division	Dry Cereal
Product	Crunchies
Salesman	P. J. O'Hara

CONSUMER PRODUCTS COMPANY
MONTH—DECEMBER 19—

Last Year Total	Current Customers:	19— Total	1st Quarter Jan.	Feb.	March	1st Quarter Total	2nd	Quarters 3rd	4th	Comments
	Chain Stores:									
1,170	A & J Stores	1,230	75	95	105	275	310	350	295	(1) J. Schmidt has indicated that he will take on our dry cereals line, beginning the first quarter, on a conservative-order basis. If line sells, he indicated increase in orders after 1st quarter sales.
658	Peter B's Markets	690	35	45	60	140	190	210	150	
1,522	Other chains	1,500	90	100	110	300	400	450	350	
3,350	Total	3,420	200	240	275	715	900	1,010	795	
341	Independent Stores	360	20	25	30	75	95	115	75	
137	Specialty Stores	145	5	10	15	30	40	45	30	
3,828	Total (current)	505	25	35	45	105	135	160	105	
	New Customers:									(2) R. B. Gamble indicates that he will begin to order our dry cereal line the first part of the spring quarter.
	J. Schmidt Supers	200	5	15	20	40	50	60	50	
	R. B. Gamble Markets	75	—	—	—	—	25	30	20	
	Total (new)	275	5	15	20	40	75	90	70	
	Grand Total	4,200	230	290	340	860	1,110	1,260	970	

(*c.*) Distribution changes—addition of new geographic areas or classes of customers to be served.

(*d.*) Competitive products or marketing actions (such as price changes) to be anticipated.

2. Execution of marketing research studies and market simulations dealing with specific areas of potential change.

3. Distribution of necessary background information to sales personnel as a basis for their analysis of individual customer needs.

4. Collection and summarization of grass-roots forecasts developed by sales personnel.

5. Refinement of basic assumptions on the basis of new studies, analyses, and management objectives.

6. Execution of statistical projections.

7. Merging and reconciliation into combined forecast.

Since the forecast is to be the basis for further analysis of marketing plans and budgets, it needs to be available well in advance of the date of budget submission. The budget, in turn, requires considerable effort in preparation. As a result, the steps just outlined may be put in motion some six months prior to the target date for budget completion.

In view of the extended time periods, it is of course necessary for forecast information to be periodically updated. The analysis of individual customers is usually the most complex and time-consuming element of the job and is normally done in depth only once a year, although sales personnel may be asked to recommend adjustments on an exception basis each quarter. Similarly, any significant forecast adjustments arising out of new information collected through market research study should be incorporated in quarterly revisions.

Economic analysis and statistical projections, when properly systematized, can be updated more frequently—generally monthly. Thus a final budget submitted, let us say, on the first of December for the ensuing year would typically be based on a forecast issued in late September, incorporating customer analysis carried out during August, but reflecting updated statistical projections and other adjustments that are based on data collected up to the first of November.

The Marketing Plan

The next step of sales budget preparation involves the development of a marketing plan—

· To establish marketing goals in terms of expected unit and dollar sales.

· To provide production management and other departments with detailed product requirements for setting the level of activity.

The goals of a properly prepared marketing plan should be achievable, because all departments of the company will be geared to execute the plan. If it is unduly optimistic or pessimistic, the heavy costs of unplanned expansion or contraction will occur. Obviously no plan can be guaranteed for accuracy, but solid business judgment is required in preparing the marketing plan.

For this reason, the marketing plan is prepared generally on a far more centralized basis than the sales forecast—usually by senior product managers or general sales managers. Its preparation commences with a comparison of the external and internal sales forecasts. Additional data considered include the following:

1. Overall sales objectives, such as increasing or decreasing market shares, expanding or contracting product lines, price changes, and so on.
2. Expected competitive strategy.
3. Product characteristics, including profitability, competitive strengths and weaknesses, stage in product life cycle, and so on.
4. Prior sales trends.
5. Expected relationship of promotional and sales effort to changes in volume.

By factoring in these considerations, product and sales management will develop the marketing plan. Because this process is more a matter of judgment than of routine, procedural technique is not too important in this phase of budgeting. The only requirements are that the plan show units and dollars of sales revenue by products, usually month by month or quarter by quarter, and that the plan be stated in sufficient detail to make review by top management meaningful. Generally, to fulfill this latter requirement, the marketing plan will include narrative commentary detailing justification of assumptions, policies to be implemented, and supporting promotional programs.

The marketing plan is of course the sales department's basic job, and the budget director can be of only limited help. However, he should be prepared to work with sales management in furnishing past statistics and developing profitability analyses as required. A good budget director also will question the marketing plan if it appears to contain unsound economics. For example, in one company the planned sales growth for a given product line showed a trend toward marginal accounts, where the distribution channel provided for lower profit per unit sold. Sales management, upon recognizing the trend, changed its plan to improve the profitability of the mix.

Once the marketing plan is completed, it should be compared with the prior year's performance and an analysis and explanation of changes prepared. This will permit top management to evaluate the plan on a more intelligent basis. Exhibit 21 is an example of a marketing plan summary for one product line.

The Advertising and Promotion Budget

The completed marketing plan is based on an adequate level of advertising and promotional support. Furthermore, by product line it will assume the use and cost of certain promotional programs or media advertising. In preparing the overall budget for these expenses, the third step of sales budget preparation, the amounts are generally summarized by type of expense; for example, advertising by type of media —network TV, trade magazines, and so on. Obviously this permits management to review and coordinate all types of advertising and promotion programs. Also, in most larger companies, the advertising department may be a separate staff department whose function is to get maximum results for the company as a whole from the combined programs.

Nevertheless, the grouping of expenses by media and promotions should not obscure the relationship of the individual programs to the product lines. This is so because spending will be controlled and marketing results watched on a program basis. In effect, these expenses are best controlled by program budgets. Program budgeting will be described in a later chapter, but in simplified terms it means that the expense is approved once the program is approved; and the program is assigned a budget code for purposes of accumulating costs assigned to that program. By and large, control of program costs is exercised by approving or rejecting the program to start with rather than by checking the disbursements monthly.

The Selling Expense Budget

The selling expense budget—the fourth element of sales budget preparation—includes all expenses of the sales department and its various subdivisions, such as branch offices, except the costs of advertising and sales promotion described previously. We need not belabor the process of establishing these budgets, because the subject of expense budgeting is detailed in Chapter 6, "The General and Administrative Budget." Since selling expenses primarily involve "people costs," the normal techniques of developing manning tables, used for controlling general and administrative expenses, are also applicable. However, it is necessary to dwell on budgetary planning and control for one category of selling expense—field salesmen or sales engineers or account representatives—because in this case the management planning and control problem is somewhat different than in areas of administrative expense.

MARKETING PLAN SUMMARY
(*In Cases*)

EXHIBIT 21

Division	Biscuit
Responsibility Head	Product Manager

CONSUMER PRODUCTS COMPANY
BISCUIT DIVISION
YEAR ENDED DECEMBER 31, 19—

Prior Three Years			Case Sales by Customer Classification	Total 19—	Quarters			
19X1	*19X2*	*19X3*			*1st*	*2nd*	*3rd*	*4th*
			Chain Stores					
98,600	110,000	123,000	Jumbo	127,700	29,000	33,000	33,700	32,000
140,500	142,000	141,000	Minipak	148,200	35,300	37,000	38,500	37,400
125,400	133,000	136,000	Cookies	137,700	33,000	34,500	35,300	34,900
364,500	385,000	400,000	*Total*	413,600	97,300	104,500	107,500	104,300
44,000	47,000	46,700	Independent Stores	51,000	12,000	13,000	13,500	12,500
21,500	18,000	14,100	Specialty Stores	25,400	5,700	6,500	7,000	6,200
430,000	450,000	460,800	*Grand total*	490,000	115,000	124,000	128,000	123,000
4%	4.7%	5.2%	Market Share %	6%				
15,000	20,000	10,800	Increase (Decrease) from Last Year	29,200				

Field salesmen and the like are the personnel who actually make customer calls and generate orders. Because of their salary or commission level or both and because of their greater requirements for travel and entertainment expenses, the cost of the sales force is often the major part of selling expense. Thus it is evident why a little extra effort in the budgetary planning and control system is warranted in this area in many companies.

Salesmen are employed, of course, for a very specific purpose—to make sales. Sales management therefore finds an easily understood relationship, at least on the surface, between sales revenue and number of salesmen or costs of salesmen. In fact many sales managers use such rules of thumb as (1) sales revenue should be about $300,000 per sales representative or (2) the cost of a salesman, including salary and out-of-pocket expenses, should not exceed 3 percent of his sales volume.

These rules of thumb are perfect examples of what is called variable or flexible budgeting (see Chapter 5). Variable budgeting provides budget allowances which increase or decrease on the basis of some measure of activity—in this case sales revenue. Therefore, under a simple variable budgeting system, salesmen's expenses could be budgeted as X dollars per $100 of sales, and the budget would change with the level of sales. The advantage of variable budgeting is that it relates budgets or expenses to effort or output. This is a potentially powerful motivating force. Furthermore, field selling is a good example of an area of the business where costs can be related to output or results.

If this is true, why isn't sales expense budgeting done more frequently on a flexible basis, at least insofar as field sales effort is concerned? The answer lies in the difficulty of averaging. While it may be true in a given case that sales revenue per salesman averages $300,000, probably some salesmen are selling $600,000 per year and others, justifiably, only $100,000. Therefore, a variable budget plan for field sales must take into account the factors that management expects will cause sales variations among salesmen or branch offices. Such a plan is called a "factored sales value" plan. It can be developed if management can identify the factors that affect field sales performance.

There are basically five factors that affect selling effort in terms of the sales and profits made:

1. Customer density—that is, the number and concentration of customers in a given territory.
2. Customer size. When calling on small companies, a salesman may have to spend considerable time even to secure relatively few orders.
3. Product profitability. Different product lines have different profit margins.
4. Product popularity. Some products are far easier to sell than others because of their competitive position or a particular demand fad.
5. General economic conditions. The level of general business conditions can have a large impact on sales performance, particularly when a business is heavily influenced by the business cycle, as is the machine tools industry, for example.

The first step in developing the budget under a variable budget plan when using a factored-sales-value approach is to prepare a manning table and expense budget, based on the marketing plan, for each branch office. Exhibit 22 is an example of such a budget for the Bridgeport office of Consumer Products Company. Note that each significant element of expense is shown in total dollars, and for the total of all variable expenses (those other than rent, utilities, and branch manager expense) the budget is expressed in dollars per $100 of sales indicated by the marketing plan. This is the base variable budget rate for that office.

From past experience and in consultation with the branch manager, sales management appraises each of the five selling-effort factors as applied to the company as a whole and to the Bridgeport office. Let's assume that Bridgeport is the perfect example of average density so that no factoring is required. We shall also assume that no factoring is required for general economic conditions.

Based on past experience, sales management groups customers by average order size. Exhibit 23 shows this distribution and the application of a customer-size factor

SAMPLE BRANCH OFFICE BUDGET   **EXHIBIT 22**

Branch	Bridgeport
Responsibility Head	R. Brown

CONSUMER PRODUCTS COMPANY
YEAR ENDED DECEMBER 31, 19—

	This Year's Budget		*Last Year's Actual*	
	($000 omitted)	*Budget Rate Per $100 of Sales*	($000 omitted)	*Budget Rate Per $100 of Sales*
Branch Sales	$1,845.0		$1,634.9	
Expense Classification:				
Variable expenses				
Salesmen's salaries (including fringe benefits)	$ 49.8	$2.70	$ 43.3	$ 2.60
Salesmen's commissions	36.9	2.00	33.4	2.00
Travel & entertainment	44.3	2.40	38.6	2.40
Telephone & telegraph	5.5	.30	5.7	.30
Miscellaneous	1.9	.10	1.5	.10
Total variable expenses	$138.4	$7.50	$122.5	$ 7.40
Fixed expenses:				
Branch manager expense	$ 33.6	$1.82	$ 33.0	$ 2.00
Rent	6.0	.32	6.0	.40
Utilities	3.0	.16	3.0	.20
Total fixed expenses	$ 42.6	$2.30	$ 42.0	$ 2.60
Total branch expenses	$181.0	$9.80	$164.5	$10.00

No. of Personnel:	*Personnel*	*Personnel*
Manager	1	1
Salesmen	5	4
Secretaries	1	1
Total personnel	7	6

to each grouping. Note that where the order size gets smaller and smaller the factor is not increased beyond 1.4, because management has decided that to budget for additional selling cost would be unprofitable. Exhibit 24 shows factoring rates based on the profitability of each product line.

The measure of product popularity can be assumed to be the relationship of actual sales to budgeted sales in accordance with the profit plan. Thus in this case the popularity factor for any given month will be the budgeted sales divided by the actual sales on an overall basis by product line. The result of this, of course, is to exert pressure to bring actual sales into line with the marketing plan; this is important for many companies because production is closely coordinated with the marketing plan. Exhibit 25 is a budget control report for the Bridgeport office for October. The exhibit includes the calculation of the total budget factor for the month and year to date. The total rate factor is the average of the five indices recognized as influencing the sales effort within the branch sales territory. These indices are determined each month from published tables and from calculations made from the various sales invoices. The total rate factor of 1.06 for October is multiplied by the actual sales for that month to determine the factored sales value. This in turn is used to generate the earned variable expense budget.

From month to month the earned variable expense budget will differ from the fixed budget for these expenses. The use of the earned-budget concept at the branch level of reporting is to establish operating control of expenses according to an achieved level of effort or activity. In this example, the higher the level of factored sales value achieved, the higher the earned budget. Since the factored sales value is influenced by the level of monthly sales and the calculated budget factor, the achievement of a satisfactory sales volume together with favorable selling-effort indices will provide higher budget allowances. In this way, selling expense control is achieved by making the size of the budget allowance dependent upon the level of effort exerted.

Although we have presented a broad range of considerations that could be used by most companies to assist management in its budgetary control system, simpler factored sales plans could be developed to control the major items of selling expense. The alternative to a plan for an earned sales-expense budget is a fixed budget, which most sales managers recognize as having very limited usefulness.

Preparing Sales Budget Reports

A substantial part of the value of any budgeting system depends on proper reporting. The reports prepared should provide a basis of control and, as discussed in Chapter 1, such a basis exists in the responsibility accounting framework. Thus the reports for marketing, selling, and product management should be prepared to reflect the way the organization assigns those responsibilities. Every manager can then review his performance on the basis of the revenues and expenses he controls.

Budgetary reporting should also provide a basis for replanning, including taking advantage of economic opportunity as it develops. This is particularly true in the sales area because of the impact on profits of external events which are not shaped by management and which can be "controlled" only in terms of management reaction to such events. In selling, control can be as opportunistic as it can be restrictive.

DEVELOPMENT OF CUSTOMER-SIZE FACTORS—
CONSUMER PRODUCTS COMPANY

EXHIBIT 23

(*Year Ended December 31, 19—*)

Average Sales Order Ranges	Actual Sales	Number of Customers	Customer-Size Factor*
$ 1–$ 50	$ 110,000	135	1.4
51– 100	200,000	95	1.4
101– 200	270,800	80	1.1
201– 300	400,000	70	.8
301– 500	195,000	60	.7
501– 1,000	159,100	30	.5
1,001+	300,000	15	.2
	$1,634,900	485	

* Customer-size factor for each sales-order range was based on a study of the average number of salesman calls required in each range to obtain $100 of sales.

DEVELOPMENT OF PRODUCT-LINE PROFITABILITY FACTOR—
CONSUMER PRODUCTS COMPANY

EXHIBIT 24

(*Year Ended December 31, 19—*)

	Branch Sales (Market Plan)	Percentage of Total Branch Sales	Standard Mfg. Contribution Margin (% to Sales)	Profitability Factor*
Biscuit Division				
Product Line A	$ 475,000	26%	25 %	1.0
Product Line B	313,000	17%	30 %	1.2
Total	$ 788,000	43%	27 %	1.1
Dry Cereal Division				
Product Line A	$ 236,000	13%	15 %	.6
Product Line B	440,000	24%	20 %	.8
Total	$ 676,000	37%	18 %	.7
Packaged Foods Division				
Product Line A	$ 191,000	10%	40 %	1.6
Product Line B	80,000	4%	20 %	.8
Product Line C	110,000	6%	25 %	1.0
Total	$ 381,000	20%	31 %	1.3
Total branch	$1,845,000	100%	24.7%	1.0

* Product-line contribution margin % ÷ Total branch-contribution margin %.

EXHIBIT 25

SAMPLE OF BUDGET CONTROL REPORT—CONSUMER PRODUCTS COMPANY: OCTOBER 31, 19—

Branch:	Bridgeport
Responsibility Head:	Branch Manager

	Current Period ($000 omitted)				Year-to-Date ($000 omitted)			
	Better (Worse) Than Budget	*Budget*	*Actual*	*Budget Rate*	*Budget Rate*	*Actual*	*Budget*	*Better (Worse) Than Budget*
Sales	($25.0)	$150.0	$125.0	—	—	$1,250.0	$1,500.0	($250.0)
Budget rate factor	—	—	1.06	—	—	1.12	—	—
Factored sales value	—	—	$132.5	—	—	$1,400.0	—	—
Variable Expenses								
Salesmen's salaries (incl. fringe)	($ .4)	3.6	$ 4.0	$2.70	$2.70	$ 40.0	$ 37.8	($ 2.2)
Salesmen's commissions	(.4)	2.6	3.0	2.00	2.00	30.0	28.0	(2.0)
Travel and entertainment	.2	3.2	3.0	2.40	2.40	30.0	33.6	3.6
Telephone and telegraph	(.6)	.4	1.0	.30	.30	10.0	4.2	(5.8)
Miscellaneous	(.1)	.1	.2	.10	.10	2.0	1.4	(.6)
Total variable expenses	($ 1.3)	$ 9.9	$ 11.2	$7.50	$7.50	$ 112.0	$ 105.0	($ 7.0)
Fixed Expenses								
Branch-manager expense	$ .1	$ 2.8	$ 2.7			$ 25.0	$ 28.0	$ 3.0
Rent	—	.5	.5			5.0	5.0	—
Utilities	(.1)	.2	.3			2.1	2.0	(.1)
Total fixed expenses	$—	$ 3.5	$ 3.5			$ 32.1	$ 35.0	$ 2.9
Total branch expenses	($ 1.3)	$ 13.4	$ 14.7			$ 144.1	$ 140.0	($ 4.1)
Personnel Count								
Manager	—	1	1					
Salesmen	—	5	5					
Secretaries	—	1	1					

Calculation of Budget Rate Factor	*Customer Density*	*Customer Order Size*	*Product Profitability*	*Product Popularity*	*General Economic Conditions*	*Total Factor*
Month	1.0	0.8	1.3	1.2	1.0	1.06
Year to Date	1.0	1.0	1.3	1.3	1.0	1.12

52

Budgetary reporting must therefore facilitate control and replanning. The key to accomplishing this is good structure in terms of reporting by responsibility and good variance analysis in terms of explaining deviations from planned performance. The ability to explain such deviations by cause and to identify opportunities and problems at an early stage is a key ingredient in management control.

To illustrate the way in which budgetary reporting can be developed for sales and product management, we can review some examples from our hypothetical Consumer Products Company. This company manufacturers and sells food products, grouped in three broad product lines: biscuit products, dry cereal products, and packaged prepared foods. Exhibit 26 is an organization chart of Consumer Products Company. Note that among the sales executives reporting to the president are three product managers and a sales vice president.

Under the plan of organization established, the three product managers are viewed as being in charge of profit centers. In other words each is responsible to the president for producing a profit contribution, after deducting on a standard or predetermined basis the variable manufacturing cost of products sold. The standard cost is used because the product manager has no responsibility for manufacturing cost performance.

The sales vice president is responsible for field sales performance and marketing services, such as advertising, packaging, and market research. Other executives reporting to the president include the manufacturing vice president, the controller, and the directors of Research and Development and of Personnel. As evident from the organization chart, the basic subdivision of responsibilities is along functional lines.

ORGANIZATION CHART—CONSUMER PRODUCTS COMPANY   **EXHIBIT 26**

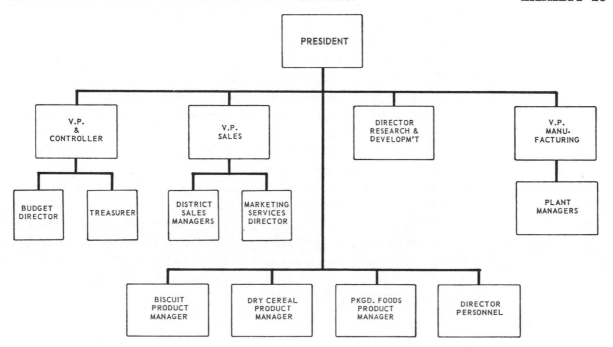

In order to follow the use of the budget reports, we will trace sample reports, starting with the president's profit and loss statement for December (Exhibit 27). The president's responsibility, of course, is total, and the final result of business performance is the net profit of $520,000 for the year to date shown on the bottom line. By referring to the column which compares this result with the budget, one can see that there is a favorable variance of $250,000. This favorable variance is $550,000 on a before-tax basis. The president can quickly review the performance of various managers by scanning each line of his report and referring to supporting reports. Where deviations are large, whether favorable or unfavorable, he will naturally ask for explanatory comment.

It is evident from scanning Exhibit 27 that the Biscuit Division is responsible for substantial gains in sales and in profit contribution; reference to Exhibit 28, the product manager's summary responsibility report, reveals the composition of those favorable results. It does not explain the results, but shows a general pattern of what happened. As indicated by Exhibit 28, highlights of this pattern are as follows for the year to date:

- Sales volume showed a significant increase—almost 15 percent in dollars.
- Marginal profit as a percent of sales was worse than budget because of product mix or price changes.
- Variable distribution expenses were higher than budget, as would have been expected.
- Greater sales produced greater factory production and a favorable variance from the use of facilities. It should be noted that the manufacturing volume variance is assigned to product management because of the profit-center concept at that level of responsibility. The product manager in this case is responsible for using certain manufacturing capacity in accordance with the marketing plan; fixed overhead rates are set accordingly. In some companies this variance is charged to manufacturing management, despite the fact that control of volume is in the sales department.
- Sales promotion expense was substantially in excess of budget but partly offset by a favorable advertising variance.
- Market research costs significantly exceeded the planned level.

A further analysis of how these results were achieved is shown in Exhibit 29, a variance report. Note that the improved profit contribution is the result of a combination of factors, including marketing strategy growing out of detailed market research work. The net effect was to increase case shipments substantially while maintaining competitive prices and changing the product mix by apparently promoting smaller packages (with lower margins) at check-out counters, for example.

Obviously, to make this kind of analysis of the business reasons behind the financial results requires considerable participation of operating management in the budgetary reporting process as well as in the planning process. This participation fosters dynamic control. Budget personnel can display the financial facts, but sales management must provide the answers.

ILLUSTRATIVE PROFIT AND LOSS STATEMENT

EXHIBIT 27

Responsibility Head	R. Crane President				

CONSUMER PRODUCTS COMPANY
MONTH—DECEMBER 19—

Current Month			*Year to Date*	
Actual	*Better (Worse) Than Budget*		*Better (Worse) Than Budget*	*Actual*
		Sales:		
$1,166,667	$166,667	Biscuit division	$2,000,000	$14,000,000
1,000,000	(20,833)	Dry cereal division	(250,000)	12,000,000
562,500	83,333	Packaged food division	1,000,000	6,750,000
$2,729,167	$229,167	*Total*	$2,750,000	$32,750,000
		Product Profit Contribution:		
$ 225,000	$ 26,667	Biscuit division	$ 320,000	$ 2,700,000
155,000	8,333	Dry cereal division	100,000	1,860,000
141,667	4,167	Packaged food division	50,000	1,700,000
$ 521,667	$ 39,167	*Total*	$ 470,000	$ 6,260,000
		Standard Fixed Manufacturing		
$ 125,000	—	Cost	—	$ 1,500,000
		Expenses:		
$ 175,000	$ 3,667	Sales department	$ 44,000	$ 2,100,000
833	(833)	Manufacturing dept.	(10,000)	10,000
		Service departments—		
—	—	Advertising	—	—
8,333	—	Market research	—	100,000
8,333	(333)	Packaging	(4,000)	100,000
		Corporate departments—		
25,000	2,500	General management	30,000	300,000
20,834	—	Personnel	—	250,000
37,500	1,667	Finance	20,000	450,000
		Research and development		
33,334	—	ment	—	400,000
$ 434,167	$ 6,668	*Total*	$ 80,000	$ 5,210,000
$ 87,500	$ 45,835	Operating Profit	$ 550,000	$ 1,050,000
(44,166)	(25,000)	Provision for Income Taxes	(300,000)	530,000
$ 43,334	$ 20,835	Net profit	$ 250,000	$ 520,000

EXHIBIT 28   SAMPLE RESPONSIBILITY REPORT

Division	Biscuit
Responsibility Head	Product Manager

CONSUMER PRODUCTS COMPANY
MONTH—DECEMBER 19—

Current Month			Year to Date	
Actual	Better (Worse) Than Budget		Better (Worse) Than Budget	Actual
$1,166,667	$166,667	Sales	$2,000,000	$14,000,000
583,333	—	Variable Standard Cost of Sales	—	7,000,000
$ 583,334	$ 83,333	Standard marginal profit	$1,000,000	$ 7,000,000
50.0%	(5.0%)	% of sales	(5.0%)	50.0%
		Variable Distribution Expense:		
$ 26,667	($ 3,917)	Freight	($ 47,000)	$ 320,000
31,667	(4,833)	Sales commissions	(58,000)	380,000
$ 58,334	($ 8,750)	Total	($ 105,000)	$ 700,000
$ 525,000	$ 74,583	Variable product margin	$ 895,000	$ 6,300,000
45.0%	(5.0%)	% of sales	(5.0%)	45.0%
		Manufacturing Volume Variance		
$ 8,333	$ 8,333		$ 100,000	$ 100,000
		Managed Expenses:		
		Product management—		
		No. of personnel	1	14
$ 12,917	$ 458	Salaries	$ 5,500	$ 155,000
5,417	(375)	Travel	(4,500)	65,000
2,500	—	Space cost	—	30,000
4,167	(167)	Other	(2,000)	50,000
120,833	9,167	Advertising	110,000	1,450,000
135,833	(55,333)	Sales promotion	(664,000)	1,630,000
$ 281,667	($ 46,250)	Total	($ 555,000)	$ 3,380,000
		Service Department Charges:		
$ 8,333	($ 833)	Advertising	($ 10,000)	$ 100,000
13,333	(10,000)	Market research	(120,000)	160,000
1,667	2,500	Packaging	30,000	20,000
3,333	(1,667)	Product research	(20,000)	40,000
$ 26,666	($ 10,000)	Total	($ 120,000)	$ 320,000
$ 308,333	($ 56,250)	Total expenses and charges	($ 675,000)	$ 3,700,000
$ 225,000	$ 26,666	Product profit contribution	$ 320,000	$ 2,700,000
19.3%	(2.4%)	% of sales	(2.4%)	19.3%

Division	Biscuit
Responsibility Head	Product Manager

CONSUMER PRODUCTS COMPANY
YEAR TO DATE ENDING—DECEMBER 19—
(*$000 omitted*)

	Better (Worse) Than Budget		
Sales	$2,000	(1) Case volume up 1,500,000.	$1,650
Standard Marginal Profit	$1,000	(2) Price reduction averaging 11.9¢ per case on product C to meet new Dolly brand.	(277.3)
%	(5.0%)	(3) Product mix—unfavorable. Pushed product D—"MINI-SIZE."	(372.7)
Volume Variance	100	Marginal profit	$1,000.0
Freight	(47)	(1) Increased tonnage volume.	($ 80)
		(2) Better distribution pattern.	40
		(3) Increased warehouse cost.	(7)
		Recommend consideration of two more warehouse stock points—Dallas & Denver.	($ 47)
Sales Commissions	(58)	Increased sales export.	
Advertising	110	Shift to TV spots from network show; less magazine space.	
Sales Promotion	(664)	Substantial success in store deal programs to get shelf space & check-out counter display.	
Market Research	(120)	Did exhaustive study of shopper habits. Found competitor advertising promoting biscuits & cookies generally and shopper buying on impulse & accessibility.	
Other	(1)		
Product Profit Contribution	$ 320	Promoted displays (MINISIZE) at check-out counter & shelf space.	

EXHIBIT 30   SAMPLE OF DEPARTMENT RESPONSIBILITY REPORT

Department	Sales Vice President
Responsibility Head	A. Colin

CONSUMER PRODUCTS COMPANY
MONTH—DECEMBER 19—

Current Month				Year to Date	
	Better (Worse)			Better (Worse)	
Actual	*Than Budget*			*Than Budget*	*Actual*
		Sales:			
$ 466,667	($ 41,667)	District 1		($ 500,000)	$ 5,600,000
325,000	62,500	District 2		750,000	3,900,000
375,000	83,333	District 3		1,000,000	4,500,000
458,333	145,833	District 4		1,750,000	5,500,000
270,833	(20,833)	District 5		(250,000)	3,250,000
$1,895,833	$229,166	Total		$2,750,000	$22,750,000
		Operating Expenses:			
$ 26,667	($ 1,250)	District 1		($ 15,000)	$ 320,000
15,000	417	District 2		5,000	180,000
16,667	—	District 3		—	200,000
19,166	1,667	District 4		20,000	230,000
12,500	666	District 5		8,000	150,000
$ 90,000	$ 1,500	Total		$ 18,000	$ 1,080,000
		Sales Management Expenses:			
		Number of personnel		1	7
$ 58,333	$ 3,500	Salaries		$ 42,000	$ 700,000
16,667	(1,750)	Travel		(21,000)	200,000
2,917	—	Space cost		—	35,000
7,083	417	Other		5,000	85,000
$ 85,000	$ 2,167	Total		$ 26,000	$ 1,020,000
$ 175,000	$ 3,667	Department total		$ 44,000	$ 2,100,000

Continuing with the reporting sequence, let's look at a responsibility report for the sales vice president (Exhibit 30). Although the sales department performance was favorable overall, it is apparent that District 1 is not performing in accordance with the plan. Therefore, we could expect a review of District 1 in more depth. The district manager's report is shown as Exhibit 31. The district manager is 9 percent under his planned sales volume, despite the fact that his expenses are running

SAMPLE SALES DISTRICT RESPONSIBILITY REPORT   **EXHIBIT 31**

District	1
District Head	B. Prime

CONSUMER PRODUCTS COMPANY
MONTH—DECEMBER 19—

Current Month				Year to Date	
	Better (Worse)			Better (Worse)	
Actual	Than Budget			Than Budget	Actual
		No. of Personnel		(2)	60
		Salaries (including commissions charged to products)			
$ 41,667	($ 833)	Travel, etc.		($ 10,000)	$ 500,000
3,333	(167)	Rent		(2,000)	40,000
1,000	—	Telephone and Telegraph		—	12,000
667	(125)	Supplies		(1,500)	8,000
166	(42)	Other		(500)	2,000
250	(83)			(1,000)	3,000
$ 47,083	($ 1,250)			($ 15,000)	$ 565,000
		Deduct: Commissions charged to products			
20,417	—			—	245,000
$ 26,666	($ 1,250)	Net district cost		($ 15,000)	$ 320,000
		Statistical Summary:			
		Sales (by customer class):			
$409,583	($48,750)	Chains		($585,000)	$4,915,000
50,000	8,333	Independents		100,000	600,000
7,083	(1,250)	Specialty stores		(15,000)	85,000
$466,666	($41,667)	Total		($500,000)	$5,600,000
		No. of calls:			
250	21	Chains		250	3,000
500	83	Independents		1,000	6,000
354	21	Specialty stores		250	4,250
		Sales value per call:			
$ 1,638	($ 302)	Chains		($ 3,620)	$ 1,638
100	(8)	Independents		(100)	100
20	(4)	Specialty stores		(50)	20
$ 77,778		Sales value per employee			$ 933,333

$15,000 (5 percent) over budget. From the sales management point of view, with a result such as this, obviously questions would be raised about the application of selling effort. To assist in directing attention to this area, the bottom half of the report includes a summary of certain statistical information. By covering types of distribution channels, the report shows sales to chain stores are lagging. However, coverage in terms of number of calls is greater than planned in the marketing plan (favorable), but the order value per call is substantially below what it was expected to average. Possibly there is some change in the purchasing pattern of chain-store buyers, such as a change in inventory policy, that has not been met by replanning of district sales effort. In any event further investigation would be required.

Our purpose, of course, in reviewing these reports is to demonstrate the vitality of budget reporting when properly designed to facilitate management planning and control. The formats depicted throughout are not intended to be rigid models prescribed for all situations but are merely illustrative of techniques presently used by a number of progressive companies. Purposely avoided are the technical calculations required for variance analysis; the emphasis has been on the usefulness of this key tool of control and replanning. In summary, sales budgeting is an important contribution enabling management to deal more effectively with the basic problems of anticipating, coordinating, controlling, and of evaluating payout. The importance of a well-conceived marketing plan as the key budget has been stressed. By and large, the quality of the firm's entire budget depends on the quality of the sales budget.

4

Inventory Budgeting

WHILE IT IS OFTEN CONVENIENT in budgeting to assume that production over a three months' period, or whatever, will equal sales and that inventories will remain at—or return to—a constant level, this is seldom a good assumption. Inventory levels can change for a variety of reasons; perhaps they *should* be changed. In the course of budget preparation the need for, or the likelihood of, changes in inventory levels should be explored. Almost invariably this brings to light operating problems which can significantly affect other phases of the overall budget.

Because inventories serve a great variety of purposes, it is hard to generalize about them. However, one can identify the basic reasons for having inventories and outline some general approaches to their budgetary control. It is useful to think of inventories in terms of layers, starting with a relatively permanent base level or minimum. Other inventory layers or fluctuations are added for various specific purposes at various times. As a minimum it is normally necessary to retain possession of goods for the length of time required to carry out whatever manufacturing, packaging, or distribution processes are involved. The amount of work-in-process inventory is directly related not only to the time during which the material is actually being worked on, tested, or transported but also to the waiting time between operations. In multistep manufacturing—for example, in a job shop or a complex chemical synthesis operation—waiting time may substantially exceed operation time, and the overall in-process time will run into weeks or months. Material in process but not being worked on represents an inventory to guard against unforeseen equipment or process failures, quality or scheduling problems, and manpower or equipment under-utilization. But, through poor control, the amount of in-process inventory may exceed what is really needed. This is particularly serious when goods are produced on a made-to-order basis, because excessive in-process inventories plug the pipeline and lead to delays in delivery.

Distribution or merchandising operations require very little process time. Only a few days are normally needed to receive goods, store them, and subsequently to move them out of storage or off the shelf for delivery to the customer. The inventories involved are generally not even classified as work-in-process but rather as finished goods. They serve primarily to assure availability for customer service. It is not unusual, however, to have both a high level of finished goods inventory and inadequate customer service because of stock imbalances—that is, too much of some items and too little of others. This again is a result of poor control.

Work-in-process inventories and minimum finished goods requirements to maintain customer service are two elements of the base inventory level. Another element results from the intermittent nature of most production processes. Fabrication and packaging operations often use the same equipment for producing in succession a variety of different products (or different varieties, colors, or sizes of the same product). Any one item is therefore produced intermittently, and sufficient inventory must be built up during each run to serve the customers while the equipment is turning out other items.

It is necessary in intermittent production to strike a balance between the costs of changing over from one item to the next and the costs of accumulating inventory. The shorter the individual runs, the greater is the number of equipment change-overs and therefore the greater the cost associated with down time and setting up. The inventory buildup, on the other hand, is less on a shorter run, and consequently the costs associated with storage and financing may be less. The proper balance for any individual item is generally determined by an economic-production-quantity formula.

Inventories controlled by economic-production-quantity formulas (usually finished goods inventories) fluctuate between a minimum and a maximum level. The minimum is often called safety stock and represents the average stock on hand just before each new production lot is received. The maximum level is the amount on hand just after receipt of a new lot. The average inventory over a period of time falls half way between the minimum and maximum levels, an amount corresponding to the safety stock (minimum) plus one-half the economic production quantity. When no seasonal or promotional inventory peaks are involved, the aggregate inventory level for a group of intermittently produced items controlled by economic-production-quantity formulas is equal to the sum of the safety stock levels of the various items in the group plus half the sum of the production quantities of those items.

The same principles can be applied to raw materials, purchased parts, and maintenance stores. But we are concerned with economics of purchasing, not of production. Some items are procured one at a time as needed, but, more commonly, procurement involves periodic purchases of lot quantities. Again, the most economic amount to be ordered at one time is determined by striking a balance between ordering costs and inventory carrying costs. In principle, the ordering costs in purchasing are analogous to set-up costs in production and include those elements which increase in direct proportion to the number of orders written per year, such as the cost of preparing and processing the orders and of handling accounts payable. Economic-order-quantity formulas, however, fail to take into account quantity price discounts or freight savings which can be obtained by ordering in larger quantities than the formula suggests or by combining several items on a single order. When these factors apply, appropriate adjustments must be made.

There are special situations which do not lend themselves to the use of simple formulas. In chemical processing, for example, inventory is dependent upon batch sizes, which in turn are often fixed or limited by equipment capacity. In textile operations, production rates, and therefore inventory accumulation of individual items, can vary substantially depending on the number of spindles and looms assigned to an item. Many other special situations could be named.

Up to this point we have discussed inventory elements which make up only the base level. Let us briefly consider factors which lead to major fluctuations above the base level. One basic cause of such fluctuations is seasonality or, more precisely, a difference in seasonality between demand for product and ability to purchase or produce. Many manufacturers of such highly seasonal items as toys, textiles, or garden supplies generally find it desirable to produce substantial quantities in advance of the seasonal sales peak rather than try to maintain a production capacity sufficient to meet the demand on a current basis or to provide manpower for the seasonal peak through costly overtime or expensive-to-train temporary help.

Processors of food and other agricultural commodities, on the other hand, may enjoy relatively stable year-round demand for their products but must accumulate large quantities of raw materials at harvest time to assure their availability. For certain agricultural products, as well as for some metals and minerals, expectation of commodity price fluctuations may lead to accelerated purchases and inventory accumulation in excess of real requirements. These purchases may in turn be hedged through the futures market, an operation too specialized to be treated here.

Fluctuations in demand are often self-imposed—for example, by the soap manufacturer who periodically gives his customers a limited-time "deal" of two cents off the retail price of each cake of soap. All products for this deal must be specially labeled and distributed over a brief period. This necessitates a prior inventory buildup and is generally followed by a period of depressed sales because of overbuying while the deal was in effect. The time during which the effects on inventory are apparent may be weeks or perhaps months.

A similar situation occurs during the introduction of a new product, particularly when it is widely advertised. A substantial initial inventory must be provided in order to assure that the distribution pipeline is filled and that the demand generated when the product is put on the market will be met.

It is clear that no single formula or method for budgeting inventory requirements will work in all cases. Nevertheless there are some basic approaches to inventory analysis that merit consideration. We will focus attention not on controlling inventories but on budgeting for them. There is a relationship, of course, between budgetary control and physical control in that the analysis by which budgets are established will raise questions about the adequacy of management controls, just as analysis of expenses or of sales will lead to questions about management controls in these areas.

The usual first step in analyzing any inventory situation is to segregate total inventories into—

- Raw materials—procured from others.
- Work in process and intermediate products.

EXHIBIT 32   INVENTORY ANALYSIS—PAPER MILL

Sales: $1,400,000/year   20,000 tons/year

Inventories:	Dollars		Tons Equiv.		Weeks Equiv.	
	High	Low	High	Low	High	Low
Pulpwood	$288,000	$ 74,400	9,600	2,480	24.0	6.2
Work in process	48,000	32,000	1,200	800	3.0	2.0
Finished paper	30,000	20,000	600	400	1.5	1.0
Stores materials	225,000	175,000	—	—	—	—

· Finished goods—available for shipment.
· Maintenance and supply stores.

Vertically integrated companies may make intermediate products both for sale to outside customers and for further processing internally. For example, a textile mill may provide yarn both to the weaving operation, which constitutes the next step in the process, and to outside mills. In such a case, it is useful to consider the yarn not as an intermediate product but as finished goods for which there are external and internal customers, the former being the outside mills and the latter being the weaving operation. However, the weaving operation is considered a customer that does not maintain an inventory of the basic raw material (yarn).

In long and complex manufacturing processes it is also sometimes convenient to treat major stages of a process as separate operations, even though none of the intermediate product is sold to outside customers. It is possible, in principle, to treat every step in the production process as a seperate operation and every item as a separate product. This is seldom practical, however, and for inventory budgeting purposes not necessary. What degree of detail is necessary will vary substantially and is difficult to define without reference to a specific situation. The best way of getting to know and understand an inventory budget is to look at inventory components in terms of turnover or, even better, in terms of number of weeks of production or sales they represent. This will generally suggest where more detail is needed.

For example consider the statistics in Exhibit 32 for a New England paper mill producing a single product, newsprint. The bulk of the inventory is comprised of pulpwood, which must be cut and transported to the mill from a relatively wide area. Because of the highly seasonal nature of these operations, a substantial stockpile is accumulated prior to the winter freeze, resulting in a wide inventory fluctuation. This is an area which requires further detail in terms of the different varieties and sources of this basic raw material and in terms of the length of time required to get wood to the mill at different times of the year. The analysis becomes quite complex; it may require use of linear programing or related techniques.

Work-in-process and finished paper inventory, when converted to equivalent weeks of production, are found to be relatively low: Physical capacity to store material is limited. The amount of work in process in this instance is almost completely determined by the duration of the paper-making process; quite properly,

INVENTORY ANALYSIS—JOB SHOP **EXHIBIT 33**

Annual cost of sales of manufactured parts = $4,800,000

Work-in-process inventory of manufactured parts = $ 800,000

Converted to finished parts cost (divide by 59%) = $1,356,000

Inventory-to-sales ratio = $1,356,000/$4,800,000 = 0.282 years
or 14.7 weeks

therefore, the work-in-process budget is prepared on this basis. Once processing begins, there is virtually no way for any appreciable quantity of material to be held aside while other material passes through.

This is in distinct contrast to multistep fabrication or packaging operations (1) where a large number of lots or batches of unfinished product may be set aside to expedite high priority orders and (2) where unfinished lots may accumulate at one production station because of imbalances in capacity among the different stations.

When dealing with the work-in-process inventory of, for example, a machine tool manufacturer, it is desirable to separate the inventory into that pertaining to parts production and that relating to assembly operations. Let us focus on the manufactured parts portion. At any one time the work-in-process inventory of manufactured parts is composed of several hundred production lots for nearly as many different items. This makes it more difficult to determine how many weeks of production this inventory represents. It can be established, by experience or by sampling, that the inventory costs of finished parts are made up, on the average, of 30 percent for purchased components and materials and 70 percent for value added in manufacturing. The average lot in process is half finished and therefore can reasonably be assumed to have been charged with 50 percent of the ultimate cost of the value added. However, most of the purchased components are charged to the process at an early stage, and the average lot in process contains 80 percent of the ultimate cost of purchased components and materials. Thus the average lot in process represents approximately 59 percent (80 percent of 30 percent plus 50 percent of 70 percent) of finished parts cost. Armed with this information, we can now estimate the inventory-to-sales ratio as shown in Exhibit 33.

This ratio can be checked by dividing the number of lots in process by the total number released in a year. Another method of estimating the same ratio is to determine the average length of time individual lots are in process, from the date of their release to production to the date of completion. Whenever sampling is used in estimating such ratios, care must be taken to insure that the samples are representative so that sample results can be properly extrapolated.

With an average work-in-process inventory of 14.7 weeks, some lots probably will be in process substantially longer and some less than the average figure. To understand the significance of the inventory-to-sales ratio, one must know what portion of the total time in process represents working time and what portion waiting time. Again we may have to resort to sampling to get a rough answer. In our example, working time averages about two weeks with an average of six successive work stations or machines per lot. This means that material, on the average, waits a total of twelve weeks—two weeks per station. This information suggests an overload condition. The periodic determination of these statistics in the course of budget analysis provides a means for taking remedial action.

Correcting such an overload condition may require increasing the capacity of bottleneck operations. (From a budgeting viewpoint this suggests a close look at capital budgets and overtime budgets.) Or correction may require improved scheduling. As mentioned earlier, excessive work in process is damaging not only because of the financial implications but also because of the longer delivery lead times that result. While large inventories of finished goods may permit better delivery service to the customer, high work-in-process inventories often have the opposite effect.

Using our analysis up to this point, we might attempt a budget estimate of work-in-process inventories for the parts fabrication shop by converting the cost-of-sales budget for manufactured parts into a weekly rate and multiplying that weekly budget rate by 14.7 (weeks) and then by 0.59 (59 percent). Often this may prove to be an adequate estimate.

However, the implied assumption is that shop capacity will be utilized to about the same degree during the period being budgeted as it was during the period of analysis. But shop utilization or loading will change if equipment capacity is changed or if the total workload to be processed changes; this, in turn, will affect the need for overtime and for subcontracting. An increase in the utilization of shop capacity will usually result in increased scheduling problems and delays, accompanied by lengthened in-process time and by larger work-in-process inventories that are out of proportion to the increase in output. In this situation, our simple formulas will not do the job; a more detailed analysis is necessary. Some companies have employed computer simulation to make this analysis practicable.

Getting back to the newsprint mill example (Exhibit 32), note that the inventory of stores materials represents a sizable dollar investment and merits study in further detail. Because of the diversity of this inventory, analysis is possible only on an item-by-item basis. We shall not go into the technicalities of demand forecasting and inventory economics. For budgeting purposes it is necessary to recognize that a minimum and maximum stock quantity should be defined, in units and in dollars, for each item. Generally, the absence of such limits denotes a weakness in inventory control procedure and therefore in inventory budgets.

Usually, inventory controls are established not in terms of minimums and maximums but in terms of reorder points and reorder quantities, or order-up-to quantities. Thus to calculate the minimum and maximum levels, it is necessary to know the reorder lead time for each item (the time required from inventory depletion below the reorder point level to receipt of replenishment). Exhibit 34 shows the basic formulas that apply. (Minimum stock quantity is synonymous with safety stock quantity.) To obtain an overall inventory budget, the average expected inventory levels for each individual item must be added up. If inventory minimums and maximums are revised or changed seasonally, the inventory budget should be adjusted correspondingly.

The formulas in Exhibit 34 cannot be strictly applied to items with a very low unit usage rate, such as a rate of only four to six per year. For example, consider a special gear which is normally replaced about once a year. Such items may not be

INVENTORY CONVERSION FORMULAS   **EXHIBIT 34**

Lead time quantity	=	Lead time (weeks)
	×	Weekly usage (units/week)
Reorder point quantity	=	Lead time quantity
	+	Minimum stock quantity
Order-up-to quantity	=	Reorder point quantity
	+	Reorder quantity
Maximum stock quantity	=	Order-up-to quantity
	−	Lead time quantity
Average expected inventory level	=	½ (Min. stock quantity
or		+ Max. stock quantity)
Average expected inventory level	=	Reorder point quantity
	−	Lead time quantity
	+	½ (reorder quantity)

stored at all if they can be obtained on sufficiently short notice from a supplier who can be relied on to keep them in stock. If the gear is stocked, only a single unit need be kept, unless two failures in quick succession are likely. Since this unit must be reordered as soon as it is withdrawn from stock, the maximum is, for all practical purposes, the same as the minimum—one unit.

It is generally good practice, in establishing budgets for the stores, to review a listing of items in stock and to place them into three categories:

1. Items which should not be stocked because of insufficient usage, ready availability from others, or high likelihood of obsolescence. These have no budgeted quantities, and stocks on hand should be reviewed for possible disposal.

2. Items which are stocked but have very low unit usage. For these, the budget may be taken as equal to the maximum on-hand units.

3. Other items, for which minimums and maximums must be specified. The budget is the average of the minimums and maximums.

In arriving at a budget, we may be faced with clerical problems of tabulating and extending hundreds and perhaps thousands of individual items. This is not too difficult where records are kept in a form suitable for computer or tabulating-machine processing. If there are manual records or exceptionally large inventories (in terms of number of items), sampling methods are very effectively used. These require the talents of a trained statistician, however.

The approach to inventory analysis just described for a maintenance-parts and supply inventory will generally apply equally well to inventories of purchased parts, raw materials, or finished goods whenever stock is controlled by a reorder-point/re-order-quantity procedure.

The preceding discussion deals with determination of inventory budgets once stock limits have been specified. In preparing a budget it is equally appropriate to question whether these limits have been properly determined in the first place and are being appropriately updated. Statistical procedures for setting such limits are

EXHIBIT 35   Pʀᴏᴅᴜᴄᴛ Gʀᴏᴜᴘs

Category	Typical Items	Percent of Sales in 2nd Half (July–December Period)
I	Bread box, fry pan, funnel, fuse, pie pan.	53%
II	Cake decorator, cooky cutter, giftware, roaster.	64%
III	Corn poppers, snow shovel, Christmas items.	88%

gaining increasing acceptance. These inventory control procedures are based on operations research or statistical methods and have two basic advantages. The first is that they enable management to calculate the probability of out-of-stock occurrences based on predetermined levels of individual items or groups of items. (Provisions are usually made for routine reporting of stock-out performance to verify that specified levels are maintained.) The second advantage of the inventory control procedures is that they enable management to maintain the total "administrative" costs of inventories at the minimum consistent with the specified out-of-stock probability level. Administrative costs include the costs of purchasing, handling accounts payable, financing, and storing—as well as costs relating to deterioration and obsolescence and, when applicable, to production setups or change-overs. From a budgetary control viewpoint, these expense elements are therefore interrelated with inventory budgets. For any specified set of minimum and maximum stock levels, there is a corresponding number of production setups or purchase requisitions per year; and there is a predictable requirement for storage space, resulting in occupancy charges.

Let us now take up the question of seasonal inventory requirements. A seasonal item may exhibit some demand throughout the year but has significantly higher-than-average sales within a limited period that occurs consistently at about the same time each year. It is possible to develop separate seasonal demand patterns for each individual item in the inventory, but it is usually more practical to group items according to seasonal patterns. For example, Exhibit 35 indicates how a manufacturer of aluminum housewares and implements might group his products. The first category is, for all practical purposes, nonseasonal. The other two classifications have their seasonal peaks in late fall. Such peaks can, of course, occur at any time of year and occasionally occur twice a year—as is the case with fountain pens, which are popular gift items both at graduation time and at Christmas.

Items are fitted into groups according to historical patterns or on the basis of judgment when no records exist. For each group there is a standard table showing percentage of annual sales by month (see Exhibit 36). The standard table provides a basis for a month-by-month breakdown of the annual sales forecast or budget. This must be translated into inventory requirements. Here again there is no simple formula. Total inventory requirements as well as types of inventory (raw

MONTHLY SALES: CATEGORY III **EXHIBIT 36**

Month	% of Yearly Sales	Month	% of Yearly Sales
January	2.8	July	6.0
February	1.5	August	16.2
March	1.0	September	20.1
April	1.8	October	24.5
May	1.9	November	16.3
June	3.3	December	4.6

materials, work in process, or finished goods) depend on the company's method of operation.

In the case of a *distributor,* where items are purchased from an outside source rather than manufactured internally, only the finished goods inventory is involved. And the same basic control procedures described for nonseasonal inventories can be equally applied to seasonal items. Inventory control by a reorder point and by an economic-order-quantity procedure will work effectively. In fact, if the seasonal fluctuations are relatively minor, they can be ignored with relatively little risk. The result will be more frequent ordering during the peak period and somewhat greater risk of running out of stock at, or directly after, the peak. Inventory levels would, however, be relatively unaffected.

With a strong pattern of seasonality, it is necessary to build up the inventory in anticipation of the seasonal demand. This involves the following steps, which are relatively typical of inventory budgeting procedure in wholesale and retail operations:

1. Identify the "season" as the time span comprised of consecutive periods (months) with above-average sales demand, average monthly demand being 8.33 percent of total annual demand.
2. Determine the total season demand for these periods.
3. Establish the purchasing procedure. If the season is short—two or three months—it is common practice to order the required quantity in a single shipment or in two shipments, of which the first is the larger; the second order may be reduced or omitted if the seasonal requirement proves to have been overestimated. In many situations, there is not enough time to place a second order after the sales picture crystallizes.

Once the magnitude of planned orders and their probable timing have been established, the projected inventory balances can be calculated, using the month-by-month sales forecast. Safety stock requirements are determined separately and must be added on.

The determination of safety stock requirements is particularly critical for style- or fashion-oriented products, which are not only seasonal but also subject to a high degree of obsolescence. Because of the substantial costs which may be incurred in disposing of leftover merchandise after the end of the season, it may be economical

EXHIBIT 37   CALCULATION OF SEASONAL INVENTORY BUILDUP

(In Thousands of Direct Labor Hours)

Month	Sales Demand	Sales Less Max. Capacity of 1,000	Inventory Cumulation
January	280	−720	negative
February	150	−850	negative
March	100	−900	110
April	180	−820	1,010
May	190	−810	1,830
June	330	−670	2,640
July	600	−400	3,310
August	1,620	620	3,710
September	2,010	1,010	3,090
October	2,450	1,450	2,080
November	1,630	630	630
December	460	−540	negative
	10,000		

to accept a relatively high risk of stock-outs by providing little or no safety stock.

Returning to our example of a manufacturer of aluminum utensils, let us next consider the consequences of having to produce seasonal goods internally. The basic approach in establishing finished goods requirements is similar to that for a distributor, as described above. If the manufacturer acts as his own distributor, with the same seasonal demand pattern and safety stock requirements, the budgeted inventory levels might, in fact, be the same. These inventory levels must be increased, however, to the degree that the manufacturer wishes to spread the production of these goods over a longer period. This may be necessary because of limited equipment capacity or limited availability of manpower. Productive labor can, when necessary, be increased through temporary help, subcontracting, or overtime; but, in any case, there is a limit to the rate at which production can be carried on. To establish this limit generally requires a study of the relative economics, availability, and quality performance of these alternative means of temporarily expanding capacity. Prudent management usually avoids planning production at the maximum possible rate, thereby allowing some cushion in the event of an unusually good season or unforeseen breakdowns, strikes, or other calamities. The development of the inventory budget, in any case, requires the establishment of a maximum practical operating rate for planning purposes. The proper level depends on the relative cost of increasing the production rate over a short period in contrast to increasing inventories in anticipation of seasonal demand.

In order to work out the interrelationship between sales demand (actually, the projected schedule of shipments) and production capacity, it is necessary that both be expressed in terms of the same units. In a multiproduct facility, direct labor manhours may provide a convenient common unit, as shown in Exhibit 37.

The next step is to determine the amount by which sales demand in each period exceeds production capacity—that is, the maximum operating rate to be planned for.

Month-to-month seasonal inventory requirements are calculated by cumulating this difference, starting with the last period in which demand exceeds capacity and working backward in time until the cumulative difference becomes negative. Exhibit 37 shows the inventory cumulation calculation as follows:

1. Select last period in which demand exceeds capacity (November).
2. Enter inventory requirement (630) in cumulation column.
3. Add inventory requirements (1450) of preceding month (October), and so on. Inventory cumulation is increased until capacity exceeds sales (July), at which point inventory cumulation begins to decrease.
4. Discontinue cumulation when cumulative inventory requirement becomes negative (February).

Safety stock must be determined separately and added on. In establishing safety stock levels for items for which a seasonal inventory buildup is planned because of limited capacity, it should be remembered that this safety stock must be carried throughout the season in order to have it on hand at the end of the season when it may be needed. The risk of exhausting the safety stock exists only once, however— at the end of the season. As a consequence, a relatively high inventory carrying cost is incurred for relatively little payoff in avoidance of lost sales. Economics generally favor little or no safety stock under these conditions. By providing a safety cushion of "emergency" production capacity in excess of the maximum level used for planning purposes, as mentioned earlier, additional products can be made later in the season should the demand materialize. Proper planning depends on a careful economic evaluation of the relative advantages of providing for unexpected demand through inventory or through reserve capacity.

For budgeting purposes, the seasonal inventory buildup, expressed here in direct labor hours, must of course be translated into dollars of inventory cost, including materials and overhead. Standard conversion factors based on experience will generally serve this purpose. In addition to the finished goods inventory buildup, seasonal changes in production level will also result in fluctuations of work-in-process inventories, roughly in proportion to the production rate. Raw material inventories may be similarly affected.

One other area of inventory budgeting worthy of brief discussion relates to the question of centralized versus decentralized stock. When inventory is maintained to service many customers over a wide geographic area, it is desirable—and often necessary because of competitive pressures—to disperse this inventory among several branch warehouse locations from which it can be delivered to the customers more quickly. In establishing inventory budgets, it is necessary, at least in principle, to determine minimum and maximum levels for each item by location. The total inventory level required to support a given level of overall sales will generally increase with the number of different locations in which any item is stocked, but the relationship is rather complex. The question of how many different locations are appropriate involves, of course, not only inventory considerations but also shipping methods, freight costs, and customer service requirements.

To summarize briefly, increasing competitive pressure for rapid distribution and service to customers has made the control of inventories, particularly those of finished goods, an increasingly important aspect of budgetary procedures. It is common practice to exercise overall control of finished goods inventories by comparing current investments both with those of prior years and with the sales volume they support. It is not valid, however, to assume performance to be satisfactory when sales-to-inventory ratios (inventory turnover) remain relatively constant. This may reflect only the perpetuation of improper levels. Frequently, apparent satisfactory overall ratios hide imbalances of individual items, with excessive stocks in some areas and repeated shortages in others. In comparing historical ratios in a growing company, it is also necessary to remember that greater sales volume should generally lead to higher inventory turnover, except where the additional sales are derived primarily from new items.

To overcome the shortcomings of historical comparisons of aggregate inventories, it is necessary to segregate inventories not only by major components of raw material, work in process, and finished goods but also by individual product lines and major stages of the manufacturing process. For effective analysis, particularly in the area of finished goods, it is often necessary to provide objective inventory standards for each individual item. Since each item and location in a multiproduct and multilocation inventory would have a different standard level, the determination of such levels can be a very sizable job. With the widening adoption of statistical reorder point systems, such individual standards are coming into common usage and, when available, can and should be tied into the budgeting process.

When comprehensive systems are not used, sampling approaches can be employed. The required sample size is not necessarily greater for an inventory of 10,000 items than for one of 1,000 items. Standards established for the sample items can be used to estimate what total inventories should be. Comparison of this estimate with actual inventory levels often provides a basis for management decision as to the need for improved forecasting and control procedures.

The Manufacturing Manager's Budget

THE MANUFACTURING MANAGER'S BUDGET is a very important step in the financial plan because of the amount of money involved. The manufacturing manager usually controls the greatest number of personnel and the greatest amount of equipment, not to mention his control over raw material and in-process inventories. He establishes a base for the purchasing budget and evaluates the required level of production. All these factors must be carefully planned, because a poor manufacturing plan can create an unfavorable overall profit picture.

The manufacturing manager's work begins when he receives the annual budget timetable or schedule. The receipt of this schedule should serve as a reminder that it is time to lay the necessary groundwork: Past history can be summarized (by the accounting department) and nonrepetitive costs extracted; standard raw material costs and average wage rates can be brought up to date; material quantity standards, direct labor and machine-time standards, and scrap allowances can be reviewed and revised.

When the marketing plan and finished goods inventory requirements are received, they must be translated into a production plan. This plan, among other things, must achieve an optimum balance between sales, inventory, and production. Achieving this balance is difficult because of the many factors which must be considered and the opposing viewpoints which must be arbitrated. For example, the sales department, in establishing the marketing plan, assumes that it will be able to quote a delivery schedule as well as a price that will be competitive. To the extent that the production department cannot complete its entire cycle within this time, inventories of parts or subassemblies must be maintained. The cost of carrying inventories can be a significant financial burden; and since there is a direct relationship between delivery policy and inventory, the cost of supporting various delivery policies must be compared to the income potential of each policy.

If sales fluctuate from period to period or are seasonal, the cost and other implications of "hiring and firing" must be compared with the alternate cost or desirability of periodically building inventory to maintain a level workforce. Consequently, certain policy matters must be decided before the production plan can be formulated. These include determining the following:

- The delivery-time objective of the company.
- The restrictions, if any, governing the delivery objective established. For example, a salesman should not book an order for an unusually large quantity and also promise normal delivery.
- The desired level of delivery schedule performance. The cost of a no-stock-out policy can be exorbitant, and moving upward from a delivery effectiveness of, say, 98 percent can have substantial cost implications.
- The maximum acceptable fluctuation in employment level.
- The cost of carrying inventory. The elements and amounts to be included in the computation should be agreed upon, such as cost of money, occupancy, obsolescence, and so on.

Since the foregoing decisions not only directly affect the production plan but have ramifications throughout the company, it is important that they be reached as a result of a mutual effort of the management team. The budget director or committee should play a prominent role in arriving at these decisions. Thereafter, the production department can take the next step of developing the production plan.

The units required by the marketing plan must be compared with available inventory to determine *when* and *how many* additional units must be produced. Both decisions must be made within the policy limitations imposed by management. *When* a product is manufactured is governed by the delivery policy and desired delivery performance level; *how much* will be produced is determined by balancing the costs of carrying inventory with the costs of acquiring inventory. The production plan or schedule is developed within the framework of these decision rules to meet anticipated demand during the coming year.

The tentative production plan so developed by the production department should be returned to the budget director or committee for approval. The production department should highlight instances where the production plan will not support the marketing plan as originally conceived; the reasons for such departures must be given. Executive management must resolve differences, and the production plan or marketing plan is modified as required. Once approved, the production plan should be treated as the master plan from which raw material, manpower, equipment, cash requirements, and sales commitments are projected.

Manufacturing budgets are concerned with three elements of cost: *direct materials, direct labor,* and *manufacturing expense (overhead)*. The remaining portion of this chapter will explain the principles behind, and the development of, the manufacturing cost budget.

Preparing the Direct Materials Budget

In order to prepare the direct materials budget, raw material requirements must be determined. This step is important because the purchasing budget, the production cost budget, and the cash budgets depend on it. Determining raw material requirements is not difficult when the quantity of each type of raw material for all production units is known. It can be time consuming, however, depending upon the complexity of the product and the degree of record mechanization (by punched card or computer equipment) existing in the company. For example, a manufacturer who draws (reduces the size of) wire does not have a difficult chore because his raw material is his end product. His only problem is determining the amount of scrap generated at each operation. The problem becomes more complex when the same manufacturer plates or coats the wire with varying thicknesses of different materials. Here he must determine the quantities of coating materials as well. Probably the most complex situation is one in which a manufacturer fabricates parts from a raw material for assembly with other purchased parts into a piece of equipment. When this situation exists, raw material, fabricated parts, and sub-assemblies could be purchased or produced for stock to reduce customer lead time as well as to realize manufacturing economies. The problem then is not only one of determining requirements for the end product but also one of determining requirements for the various stages of subassemblies. It is in this latter area that record mechanization can be of the greatest assistance.

When the material quantity per unit of production is known, requirements are computed by multiplying the units to be produced by the quantity of each type of material comprising the unit. It should be determined whether a normal allowance for scrap or rejects has been included in this computation. If not, the allowance can be added at this time or included as an overall figure when the requirements for all units are summarized. When unit material quantities are not known or cannot be developed as a practical matter, historical ratios can be resorted to. Such ratios include the following:

- Ratio of material cost to direct labor cost.
- Ratio of material cost to direct labor or machine hours.
- Ratio of the quantity of each type of material used to direct labor or machine hours.
- Ratio of the quantity of each type of material used to the number of units produced.

Exhibit 38 is part of a materials requirement schedule—when quantities are known —for Reliable, Inc., a hypothetical toy manufacturer.

Once the individual requirements for each unit have been computed they must be summarized to determine the total requirement for each type of material and to serve as the basis for the purchased materials budget. As is well known by all production managers, the timing of the receipt of purchased materials is most important. In Exhibit 38, total requirements were computed based on the completion date of each unit. Fabrication or assembly lead time was not considered. When the factory processing time is relatively short, the timing of the materials required for the finished units could perhaps be determined in this way. If the processing time is much longer than the purchasing lead time, materials will be needed much sooner than indicated by Exhibit 38. In the latter situation, the required date is determined as indicated by Exhibit 39.

Another factor that must be considered is management's inventory policy. The requirements computed in Exhibits 38 and 39 do not consider beginning and ending inventories for raw materials or component parts. Therefore, the requirements for

EXHIBIT 38
Materials Requirement Schedule for 19——: Reliable, Inc.
(Units of Material Required: 000's Omitted)

Materials Required	Department	Material Quantity Per 100 Units	Total Required (In Units)	1st Quarter January	1st Quarter February	1st Quarter March	Quarters 1st	Quarters 2nd	Quarters 3rd	Quarters 4th
Bearcat—Units to be produced			5,115	322	322	401	1,045	880	1,410	1,780
ABC Luxtrex—clear	Molding	50 lbs.	2,558	161	161	201	523	440	705	890
XP164 Unicolor (1:10)	Molding	5 lbs.	256	16	16	20	52	44	71	89
Instructions—Bearcat	Assembly	100 ea.	5,115	322	322	401	1,045	880	1,410	1,780
Glass eye—green #1045	Assembly	200 ea.	10,230	644	644	802	2,090	1,760	2,820	3,560
Carton—Bearcat	Assembly	100 ea.	5,115	322	322	401	1,045	880	1,410	1,780
Teddy Bear—Units to be produced			1,815	116	116	147	379	231	813	392
DEF polyethylene—natural 2002	Molding	80 lbs.	1,452	93	93	117	303	185	650	314
XP175 Unicolor (1:19)	Molding	4.2 lbs.	76	5	5	6	16	10	34	16
Tin slugs—1/16" × 2" × 2"	Fabrication	200 ea.	3,630	232	232	294	758	462	1,626	784
Glass eye—gray #1490	Assembly	200 ea.	3,630	232	232	294	758	462	1,626	784
Paws—black #595	Assembly	200 ea.	3,630	232	232	294	758	462	1,626	784
Instructions—Teddy Bear	Assembly	100 ea.	1,815	116	116	147	379	231	813	392
Carton—Teddy Bear	Assembly	100 ea.	1,815	116	116	147	379	231	813	392

EXHIBIT 38
(*concluded*)

Materials Required	Department	Material Quantity Per 100 Units	Total Required (In Units)	January	February	March	1st	2nd	3rd	4th
				1st Quarter			*Quarters*			
B-58—Units to be produced			2,735	223	223	279	725	515	735	760
DEF polyethylene—natural 6009	Molding	98 lbs.	2,681	219	219	273	711	505	720	745
XP184 Unicolor (1:49)	Molding	2 lbs.	55	4	4	7	15	10	15	15
Tin slugs—1⁄16″ × 1½″ × 1½″	Fabrication	200 ea.	5,470	446	446	558	1,450	1,030	1,470	1,520
Steel rod #303—3⁄16″ dia.	Fabrication	54.17 ft.	1,481	121	121	151	393	279	398	411
Rubber wheels—black 2″	Assembly	200 ea.	5,470	446	446	558	1,450	1,030	1,470	1,520
Rubber wheels—black 1″	Assembly	100 ea.	2,735	223	223	279	725	515	735	760
Cockpit—Luxtrex clear	Assembly	100 ea.	2,735	223	223	279	725	515	735	760
Insignia—paper #914	Assembly	200 ea.	5,470	446	446	558	1,450	1,030	1,470	1,520
Instructions—B-58	Assembly	100 ea.	2,735	223	223	279	725	515	735	760
Carton—B-58	Assembly	100 ea.	2,735	223	223	279	725	515	735	760
Ant Farm—Units to be produced			1,091	43	43	54	140	323	283	345
ABC Lustran—clear	Molding	100 lbs.	1,091	43	43	54	140	323	283	345
Stainless steel "V" strip ⅛″ × ½″ × ½″	Fabrication	1,200 ft.	13,092	516	516	648	1,680	3,876	3,396	4,140
Flat head screws—S/S 9⁄16″	Assembly	2,500 ea.	27,275	1,075	1,075	1,350	3,500	8,075	7,075	8,625
Envelope—manila 5″ × 3″	Assembly	100 ea.	1,091	43	43	54	140	323	283	345
Instructions—Ant Farm	Assembly	100 ea.	1,091	43	43	54	140	323	283	345
Carton—Ant Farm	Assembly	100 ea.	1,091	43	43	54	140	323	283	345

EXHIBIT 39 COMPUTING MATERIALS REQUIREMENT DATES

	Working Days
Finished Unit *A*—date required:	Day 110 (June 15)
Days of assembly time:	20
Date components required (110–20):	Day 90
Part *X* (fabricated from raw material— two days required):	2
Part *Y* (purchased—no fabrication time required):	0
Date raw material for Part *X* required:	Day 88
Date purchased parts required:	Day 90

EXHIBIT 40 PURCHASED MATERIALS BUDGET FOR 19——: RELIABLE, INC.

(000's *Omitted*)

	Units			Purchases	
	Required for Production	*Add— Ending Inventory*	*Less— Beginning Inventory*	*Units*	*Total Cost*
Bearcat:					
ABC Luxtrex—clear		(Unit cost $.2018)			
January	161	161	150	172	$ 35
February	161	201	161	201	41
March	201	147	201	147	30
2nd quarter	440	235	147	528	106
3rd quarter	705	297	235	767	154
4th quarter	890	175	297	768	155
Total budget for year	2,558	175	150	2,583	$521
XP164 Unicolor (1:10)		(Unit cost $.72)			
January	16	16	20	12	$ 9
February	16	20	16	20	15
March	20	15	20	15	11
2nd quarter	44	24	15	53	38
3rd quarter	71	30	24	77	55
4th quarter	89	18	30	77	55
Total budget for year	256	18	20	254	$183
Instructions—Bearcat		(Unit cost $.01)			
January	322	322	300	344	$ 4
February	322	401	322	401	4
March	401	293	401	293	3
2nd quarter	880	470	293	1,057	11
3rd quarter	1,410	593	470	1,533	15
4th quarter	1,780	350	593	1,537	15
Total budget for year	5,115	350	300	5,165	$ 52

	Units			Purchases	
	Required for Production	Add— Ending Inventory	Less— Beginning Inventory	Units	Total Cost
Glass eye—green #1045		(Unit cost $.0854)			
January	644	644	650	638	$ 55
February	644	802	644	802	69
March	802	587	802	587	50
2nd quarter	1,760	940	587	2,113	180
3rd quarter	2,820	1,187	940	3,067	262
4th quarter	3,560	700	1,187	3,073	262
Total budget for year	10,230	700	650	10,280	$878
Carton—Bearcat		(Unit cost $.045)			
January	322	322	322	322	$ 14
February	322	401	322	401	18
March	401	293	401	293	13
2nd quarter	880	470	293	1,057	48
3rd quarter	1,410	593	470	1,533	69
4th quarter	1,780	350	593	1,537	69
Total budget for year	5,115	350	322	5,143	$231

EXHIBIT 40
(*concluded*)

manufacturing are not necessarily the same as those for purchasing. For simplicity let us say that inventory policy requires sufficient raw material on hand to equal the next month's production requirements. Estimated production requirements for the next two months are 75,000 and 100,000 pounds, respectively; the inventory balance at the beginning of the first month is 70,000 pounds. This means that the purchase requirement for the first month is 105,000 pounds, computed as follows:

Inventory required at end of first month	100,000 lbs.
Plus production requirements	75,000
Minus beginning inventory	70,000
Purchase requirements for first month	105,000 lbs.

When the purchase quantities have been determined, the purchasing manager should estimate prices. For high-volume materials, firm blanket prices could be negotiated. In other cases, volume discounts could be negotiated with suppliers, based on total annual purchases. When raw material prices have been estimated, the purchased materials budget can be prepared (Exhibit 40).

When and *how much* to buy are decided by management-approved rules which should be related to return-on-investment objectives and budget policy. Two such rules are:

1. *Economic-order-quantity* (*EOQ*) *rule.* This is a mathematical technique that provides an order quantity that will produce the lowest possible total cost.

EXHIBIT 41   PORTION OF DIRECT LABOR SCHEDULE: RELIABLE, INC.

(*Direct Labor Budget for 19—*)

	Labor Rate	Total* Labor Hours	Total* Labor Cost	Bearcat Units To Be Produced (In 000's)	Labor Hrs. Per 100 Units	Direct Labor Hours	Direct Labor Cost
January:				322			
Molding	$3.00	27,109	$ 81,327		3.025	9,741	$ 29,223
Fabrication	2.75	17,945	49,349		—	—	—
Assembly	2.00	98,191	196,382		7.000	22,540	45,080
Total		143,245	$ 327,058			32,281	$ 74,303
February:				322			
Molding	3.00	27,109	$ 81,327		3.025	9,741	$ 29,223
Fabrication	2.75	17,945	49,349		—	—	—
Assembly	2.00	98,191	196,382		7.000	22,540	45,080
Total		143,245	$ 327,058			32,281	$ 74,303
March:				401			
Molding	3.00	33,935	$ 101,805		3.025	12,130	$ 36,390
Fabrication	2.75	22,503	61,883		—	—	—
Assembly	2.00	123,021	246,042		7.000	28,070	56,140
Total		179,459	$ 409,730			40,200	$ 92,530
2nd Quarter:				880			
Molding	3.00	74,650	$ 223,950		3.025	26,620	$ 79,860
Fabrication	2.75	47,239	129,907		—	—	—
Assembly	2.00	269,051	538,102		7.000	61,600	123,200
Total		390,940	$ 891,959			88,220	$ 203,060
3rd Quarter:				1,410			
Molding	3.00	120,992	$ 362,976		3.025	42,652	$ 127,956
Fabrication	2.75	74,060	203,665		—	—	—
Assembly	2.00	433,774	867,548		7.000	98,700	197,400
Total		628,826	$1,434,189			141,352	$ 325,356
4th Quarter:				1,780			
Molding	3.00	121,105	$ 363,315		3.025	53,845	$ 161,535
Fabrication	2.75	67,028	184,327		—	—	—
Assembly	2.00	415,683	831,366		7.000	124,600	249,200
Total		603,816	$1,379,008			178,445	$ 410,735
Total Year:				5,115			
Molding	3.00	404,900	$1,214,700		3.025	154,729	$ 464,187
Fabrication	2.75	246,720	678,480		—	—	—
Assembly	2.00	1,437,911	2,875,822		7.000	358,050	716,100
Total		2,089,531	$4,769,002			512,779	$1,180,287

* For brevity, direct labor for Teddy Bear, B-58, and Ant Farm, included in total, has not been shown.

Under this method the cost of acquiring inventory is related to inventory carrying costs. Assume the following facts:

(*a*) Annual usage of Part *A* is 2,000 units.

(*b*) Procurement cost for each order is $10.

(*c*) Unit cost of Part *A* is $5, excluding procurement.

(*d*) Inventory carrying cost is 20 percent per year ($0.20 for every dollar in inventory).

Using a conventional EOQ formula, one finds that the economic order quantity is 200 units;* therefore, Part *A* would be ordered ten times per year. To prove that a lot of 200 units is the most economical order size, let us analyze the cost involved. If the order cost is $10 per order and if there are ten orders per year, the annual order cost is $100. Based on an order quantity of 200 units, the average inventory is 100 units. Therefore, 100 units at $5 per unit is equivalent to an average inventory investment of $500. The $500 investment multiplied by the 20 percent carrying cost results in an annual carrying cost of $100. As can be seen, order costs balance carrying costs. Order sizes of any other quantity will upset that balance and result in higher total costs.

2. *Reorder point* (*ROP*) *rule.* The reorder point is reached when existing inventory can sustain production or shipments for a period no longer than the time needed to order and receive replenishments. Generally, replenishment time includes paperwork processing, receiving, manufacturing, and inspection. If replenishment time is 30 days, a reorder point inventory of 100 units means that, under normal circumstances, 100 units will sustain operations 30 days. Customarily, the reorder point inventory also includes a safety quantity to accommodate fluctuations in demand. There are several techniques available for developing and evaluating safety stocks, some being more sophisticated and elaborate than others. No matter how these quantities are determined, it is important to recognize that this represents a fixed portion of the total inventory investment, and the cost of carrying this inventory is the price paid for delivery performance.

Preparing the Direct Labor Budget

The direct labor budget is a projection of manpower requirements in dollars, or in hours and dollars, for the execution of the production plan. This projection is prepared to estimate the cost of production, to provide data for the cash budgets, to determine manning requirements by labor classification for use as a hiring aid, and to assist management in forecasting overtime requirements, reducing peak loads, and stabilizing employment.

In most companies, records of the labor hours needed for producing a finished unit are available in one form or another. When they are available, projecting total time is simply a matter of multiplying the number of units to be produced by the labor time per unit. Exhibit 41 illustrates a portion of a typical direct labor schedule.

* $$\sqrt{\frac{2 \times 2000 \text{ units} \times \$10 \text{ order}}{\$5 \text{ unit cost} \times \$0.20 \text{ carrying cost}}} = 200 \text{ units}$$

EXHIBIT 42   THE FIXED ANNUAL AND QUARTERLY BUDGET

DEPT. *A*—FIXED ANNUAL BUDGET

	Annual Budget	*Monthly Budget*
Salaries	$120,000	$10,000
Overtime	6,000	500
Supplies	72,000	6,000
Utilities	12,000	1,000
Depreciation	24,000	2,000
	$234,000	$19,500

DEPT. *A*—FIXED QUARTERLY BUDGET

	Annual Budget	*1st Qtr.* 3 Mos.	1 Mo.	*2nd Qtr.* 3 Mos.	1 Mo.	*3rd Qtr.* 3 Mos.	1 Mo.	*4th Qtr.* 3 Mos.	1 Mo.
Salaries	$120,000	24,000	8,000	27,000	9,000	33,000	11,000	36,000	12,000
Overtime	6,000	1,200	400	1,500	500	1,800	600	1,500	500
Supplies	72,000	18,000	6,000	24,000	8,000	21,000	7,000	9,000	3,000
Utilities	12,000	4,200	1,400	1,800	600	1,800	600	4,200	1,400
Depreciation	24,000	6,000	2,000	6,000	2,000	6,000	2,000	6,000	2,000
Total Budget	$234,000	53,400	17,800	60,300	20,100	63,600	21,200	56,700	18,900

When computing labor cost, the average labor rate to be used depends on the wage plan in effect. For hourly rated employees not on incentive, an overall plant rate may be sufficient. In other cases, departmental or labor-grade rates may be used. When a straight piece-rate plan is in effect, the labor cost is the amount paid per unit produced. When other types of incentive plans are used, average labor rates that include an estimated amount for bonus payments must be computed.

In companies where standard costs are used, cost accounting records can be very useful in determining budget requirements for nonproductive direct labor. Many cost accounting systems are sophisticated enough to indicate the extent to which direct labor is nonproductive because of machine down time, waiting time, change-over or set-up time, and so on.

Very often, labor requirements are related directly to equipment usage. In such cases, the determination of equipment operation—in terms of hours—is based on processing rates or production rates. A crew, comprised of a fixed number of persons with given job classifications, is usually required to operate major facilities. The information obtained from the crew schedules, often known as manning tables, combined with the anticipated number of hours of equipment operation will enable management to relate labor requirements directly to equipment usage.

Preparing the Manufacturing Expense Budget

The budgeting of manufacturing expenses (often called overhead or burden) is the third important segment of the manufacturing manager's task after the direct materials and direct labor budgets have been completed. Fixed budgets for manufacturing expenses are actually the simplest type; budget amounts are constant for a period or periods of time. Although this budget has some application in a manufacturing operation, it does not consider fluctuations in the level of activity. Exhibit 42 illustrates two methods of fixed budgeting. These two methods illustrate the basic principle behind fixed budgets. Notice, however, the restrictions being imposed. In either method, would the budget be a realistic one if the activity dropped considerably below the level (8,000 hours) assumed in the budget? The answer would be yes for depreciation, which is the only true fixed cost. It may or may not be yes for salaries, depending on the situation. And it would be no for all other expense categories.

A step budget (Exhibit 43) is a variable means of budgeting. When this technique is used, predetermined levels of activity are selected, and budgets are computed for each level. This budget gives some recognition to the variability of the different manufacturing expenses at varying levels of activity; however, several budgets must be prepared to do so. It is also unrealistic to assume that such expenses as supplies and utilities would change in the magnitude illustrated with a difference of just one hour between activity levels.

A fully variable budget (Exhibit 44) is actually the more sophisticated and probably the most realistic because it considers both fixed and variable costs at any level of activity. When this technique is used, the annual budget is split between its fixed and variable elements of expense. The variable elements are then divided by

DEPARTMENT *A*—STEP BUDGET   **EXHIBIT 43**

	Annual Budget	Monthly Budget Ranges				
Level of Budgetary Activity in Hours:		11,000 to	9,000 to	7,000 to	5,000 to	3,000 to
	96,000	12,999	10,999	8,999	6,999	4,999
Normal level (hours):				8,000		
Salaries	$120,000	$12,000	$12,000	$10,000	$ 8,000	$ 8,000
Overtime	6,000	800	600	500	300	200
Supplies	72,000	8,000	7,000	6,000	5,000	4,000
Utilities	12,000	1,400	1,200	1,000	800	600
Depreciation	24,000	2,000	2,000	2,000	2,000	2,000
Total	$234,000	$24,200	$22,800	$19,500	$16,100	$14,800

DEPARTMENT *A*—VARIABLE BUDGET   **EXHIBIT 44**
   (*Level of Activity: 96,000 Hours*)

	Annual Amount			Variable Rate Per Hour	Fixed Amount Per Month
	Total	Fixed	Variable		
Salaries	$120,000	$ 96,000	$ 24,000	$ .250	$ 8,000
Overtime	6,000	—	6,000	.063	—
Supplies	72,000	12,000	60,000	.625	1,000
Utilities	12,000	—	12,000	.125	—
Depreciation	24,000	24,000	—	—	2,000
Total	$234,000	$132,000	$102,000	$1.063*	$11,000

* $102,000 ÷ 96,000 hours

EXHIBIT 45

DEPARTMENT *A*—COMPARISON OF BUDGETING TECHNIQUES
(*Operating Level of 9,000 Hours*)

	Fixed Budget		Step Budget	Fully Variable Budget
	Annual	Quarterly		
Salaries	$10,000	$ 8,000	$12,000	$10,250
Overtime	500	400	600	567
Supplies	6,000	6,000	7,000	6,625
Utilities	1,000	1,400	1,200	1,125
Depreciation	2,000	2,000	2,000	2,000
Total	$19,500	$17,800	$22,800	$20,567

the level of activity (expressed in hours) to determine an hourly dollar rate for each unit of activity.

This method takes into account even minor changes of activity in the factory, thereby providing a more realistic budget. To compute the monthly budget allowance, the variable rates are multiplied by the level of activity for the period. The fixed amount is then added to the calculated variable amount.

Exhibit 45 is a comparison of the three techniques and illustrates the differences in budget amounts at a monthly operating level of 9,000 hours; the figures are for the month of January. As can be seen, each technique produced a different result. The fixed budgets did not recognize a change in volume above 8,000 hours; the step budget was forced into the next level of activity, which produced a budget amount for approximately 10,000 hours; the fully variable budget was sensitive to the change in activity.

The remainder of this chapter will illustrate variable budgeting in order to acquaint you with the principles and also to explain its integration with the accounting and reporting systems.

Manufacturing overhead can be defined as consisting of elements of manufacturing cost that cannot be readily identified with a specific product or unit of production. From that definition many such costs should come to mind—such as supervisory and clerical salaries, equipment maintenance, general supplies, utilities, depreciation, insurance, and so forth. Manufacturing overhead budgeting is made difficult because these costs contrast sharply with direct material and direct labor in that each overhead cost is usually of small consequence at the point of application. Each originates from a different source, and each requires control by a different method and at a different time.

As indicated in the preceding example, manufacturing overhead can be classified as a fixed, variable, or semivariable expense:

· Fixed expenses are those that do not fluctuate with volume.
· Variable expenses generally vary in direct proportion to volume.
· Semivariable expenses contain both fixed and variable elements.

A typical instance of the semivariable or step type of expense occurs when, by union contract, a set-up man (treated as indirect labor) is limited to four machines.

GRAPHIC CORRELATION   **EXHIBIT 46**

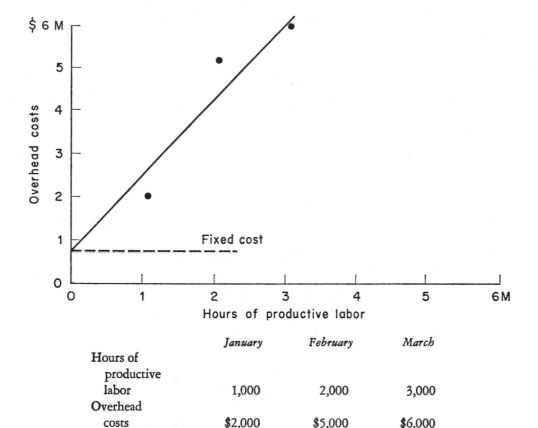

	January	*February*	*March*
Hours of productive labor	1,000	2,000	3,000
Overhead costs	$2,000	$5,000	$6,000

Variable Rate Computation:

Total cost $6,000 at 3,000 hours
Total cost $750 at zero hours (fixed cost)
Variable cost $5,250 for 3,000 hours = $1.75 per hour

A second set-up man would be required if five machines were being used; however, a third man would not be required until a ninth machine was put into operation.

Although these or any other definitions give the appearance of firm rules for classifying expenses, arguments persist today, and probably always will, as to which expenses are fixed and which variable. This cannot be settled until the level of activity on which the fixed costs are based has been agreed upon and until management's policy for termination of salaried personnel as a result of reductions in volume has been defined. For instance, salaried personnel may be considered as a fixed expense if the level of activity on which fixed costs are based approximates normal operating conditions. In this situation, it is assumed that business will maintain an activity level that will require no changes in personnel. If the activity base were assumed to be zero volume, it is likely that many salaries would be treated as a variable cost because at zero volume many salaried personnel would not be required. Each company is different and must be treated individually according to

EXHIBIT 47

BUDGET WORKSHEET—DEVELOPMENT OF NIGHT SHIFT PREMIUM

☒ Hourly
☐ Salary

Description	Key	501	502	503	504	505	506	507	508	509	Total Plant
Total budgeted second-shift hours	A	6,000	8,000	20,000	15,000	30,000	24,000	18,000	10,000	12,000	XXX
Average budget wage rate	B	$ 3.40	$ 4.00	$ 2.80	$ 2.50	$ 2.40	$ 2.40	$ 2.50	$ 3.00	$ 3.40	XXX
Total (A × B)	C	$20,400	$32,000	$56,000	$37,500	$72,000	$57,600	$45,000	$30,000	$40,800	XXX
Second-shift premium percent	D	5%	5%	5%	5%	5%	5%	5%	5%	5%	XXX
Second-shift premium dollars	E	$ 1,020	$ 1,600	$ 2,800	$ 1,875	$ 3,600	$ 2,880	$ 2,250	$ 1,500	$ 2,040	$19,565
Total budget third-shift hours	F	5,000	7,000	18,000	12,000	24,000	20,000	15,000	8,000	10,000	XXX
Average budget wage rate	G	$ 3.40	$ 4.00	$ 2.80	$ 2.50	$ 2.40	$ 2.40	$ 2.50	$ 3.00	$ 3.40	XXX
Total (F × G)	H	$17,000	$28,000	$50,400	$30,000	$57,600	$48,000	$37,500	$24,000	$34,000	XXX
Third-shift premium percent	J	10%	10%	10%	10%	10%	10%	10%	10%	10%	XXX
Third-shift premium dollars	K	$ 1,700	$ 2,800	$ 5,040	$ 3,000	$ 5,760	$ 4,800	$ 3,750	$ 2,400	$ 3,400	$32,650
Total hourly night shift premium (Line E & line K)	L	$ 2,720	$ 4,400	$ 7,840	$ 4,875	$ 9,360	$ 7,680	$ 6,000	$ 3,900	$ 5,440	$52,215

Departments

management's short-term needs for fixed and variable information for dynamic cost control, breakeven analyses, marginal cost analyses, or idle-plant cost analyses.

Once a base level has been determined, expenses can easily be categorized as fixed, variable, or semivariable. The next step is to separate the fixed and variable portions of semivariable expenses. There are several techniques that may be used, most relying on historical data. *Engineering studies* attempt to determine what costs should be, rather than what they actually are at varying levels of activity. Although this method is probably the most scientific, it is usually time consuming and expensive. When step budgets are used, *direct estimates* are made at several levels of activity. This technique was discussed earlier in the chapter. Under the *standby cost method,* the fixed amounts would be those costs still incurred if the plant or department experienced a temporary shutdown of short duration, say less than one week.

When a *scatter chart* or *graphic correlation* (Exhibit 46) is used, historical costs (usually monthly) are plotted on a graph for the appropriate level of activity. A line is drawn through the dots and extended to zero volume. The amount at zero volume represents the fixed cost. One of the fallacies of this technique is that one cannot be sure that the visual line of fit is the best line. Different people may well draw lines of different slopes, even though the identical situation is being plotted. When employing the *least squares* (*mathematical correlation*) technique, one uses the same historical data as for the scatter chart; however, mathematics are relied on to provide a line of *best* fit. That is, the amount of variation from the line to each dot will be the smallest possible. The technique is relatively simple and the formulas can be found in any text on statistics.

In order to make budgets more meaningful and to control costs more effectively, manufacturing overhead is usually departmentalized. As a result, costs can be budgeted more accurately and each supervisor and foreman is able to participate. Departments may be divided into three classes: producing, service, and general. Producing departments are those that contribute something to the improvement and value of the product, such as fabrication and assembly. Service departments perform a service for producing and other departments, such as maintenance and power. General departments are those that provide a general service not necessarily related to a particular product or department, such as purchasing and administration.

In variable budgeting, as implied earlier, some means must be found for relating the budgets of manufacturing departments to a proper level of activity. The selection of an appropriate level of activity for budgeting purposes is important for three reasons:

- The assumed level provides a basis for planning expenditures.
- Standard or estimated product costs, which are the result of volume and total costs, will vary depending on the level adopted. If an incorrect level is assumed, product costs can be distorted, which in turn can misdirect sales efforts.
- Variances developed in comparing actual costs of operation with budget allowances will vary under different assumptions of volume. If such assumptions are not realistic, variances will prove meaningless and confidence in the cost-control aspect of budgets will be undermined.

All persons concerned with the preparation and use of the budget must understand

EXHIBIT 48   MANUFACTURING EXPENSE BUDGET

Group/Division ABC		*Plant* XYZ/R/501		*Dept.* XYZ/R/501		
Line A	Account Name B	No. C	Budget Variable Rate D	Fixed & Non- Variable E	Variable F	Total G
	MAINTENANCE, CAPITAL EXPENSE, AND REPAIRS—MATERIAL					
	Buildings and Grounds	3310				
	Machinery and Equipment	3320				
	Mach. and Equip.—Capital Exp.	3321				
	Furniture and Fixtures	3330				
	Fur. and Fixt.—Capital Exp.	3331				
	Special Tools	3340				
	Perishable Tools	3350				
	Plant Rearrangement	3360				
30	Total Maintenance	3300				
	PERISHABLE TOOLS—MATERIAL					
	Abrasives (Tools)	3402	$ .30	$ 10,000	$ 15,000	$ 25,000
	Die Accessories and Punches	3419	.25	12,000	12,500	24,500
	Die and Die Casting Details	3420	.20	8,000	10,000	18,000
	Jig and Fixture Parts	3442	.25	20,000	12,500	32,500
	Jig and Fixture Details	3443	.23	10,000	11,500	21,500
	Tools—Cutting	3486	.18	40,000	9,000	49,000
	Tools—Air and Elect. Portable	3487	.06	25,000	3,000	28,000
	Tools—Cutting Machine	3489	.50	18,000	25,000	43,000
	Tools—Hand	3490	.10	9,000	5,000	14,000
	Tools—Group Stds.—Weld.—Resist.	3491	.04	12,000	2,000	14,000
	Tools—Machine Power—("H")	3492	.06	8,000	3,000	11,000
	Tools—Machine Powered	3493	.12	14,000	6,000	20,000
	Tools—Precision—("G" and "R")	3494	.08	15,000	4,000	19,000
	Tools—Precision	3495	.10	10,000	5,000	15,000
31	Total Perishable Tools	3400	$2.47	$211,000	$123,500	$334,500
	SPOILAGE AND REWORK—MATERIAL					
	Material Spoilage	3560				
	Rework Material	3580				
32	Total Spoilage and Rework	3500				

the assumptions inherent in the budget and product cost computations. Expected sales volume in the budget year, average historical sales volume, and practical plant capacity are examples of levels of activity which are frequently used.

Some commonly accepted bases for measuring overhead in producing departments are direct labor hours, machine hours, pounds of material consumed, and units of production. The characteristics of each industry and of each department will determine which yardsticks are appropriate. For example, pounds of material consumed or units of production would be a poor measurement for a diversified plastic blow-molding operation, because the amount of consumption and production depends on mold cooling time or on machine limitations. Overhead costs, therefore, would be more appropriately related to time; that is, direct labor or machine hours. Listed below are several characteristics of a good measurement base:

1. It must be a direct measure of the cost-incurring activity.
2. It must be affected only by volume.
3. It must be sensitive to changes in the activity level.
4. It must be applicable to all products in a department.
5. It must be understood and accepted by those using the budget.

Measurement bases for service and general departments are determined in much the same manner as for producing departments. Some acceptable measures of activity are as follows:

- *Service departments.* Maintenance—direct maintenance hours. Salvage—pounds salvaged or salvage hours.
- *General departments.* Purchasing—number of purchase orders or purchase dollars. Administration—total number of personnel or total direct labor hours.

Whenever possible, individual departmental expenses should be budgeted first in nondollar terms—indirect labor hours, quantities of supplies, and so forth. These can then be converted into the dollar equivalent. In larger companies, separate forms may be required for this application. Exhibit 47 is a form used by a large corporation to compute budgeted shift premiums. The dollar amounts are posted to budget summaries. Exhibit 48 is a portion of a departmental budget also used by the same corporation. Because of the large dollar amounts involved, as in the "perishable tools—material" category, considerable refinement is needed. Many smaller companies would not require as much detail. It should be remembered that dollars can be fragmentized to the point where they appear to be insignificant. On the other hand, very large amounts can practically defy analysis.

The dollars represented on budget summaries are annual amounts, based on the budgeted level of activity for the entire year. Service and general department costs can now be allocated to producing and other service departments. This is done primarily to determine an overhead rate which can be applied to product costs.

Service department costs are allocated on the basis of service required by other departments. For costs of general departments, the allocation is based on the units of activity assigned to other departments, such as square feet occupied or direct labor hours. When costs have been allocated, overhead rates can be computed merely by dividing the budgeted dollars by the level of activity. Exhibit 49 illustrates the allocation and computation of overhead rates for Reliable, Inc., whose direct material and direct labor budgets were illustrated earlier in this chapter.

It will be useful to elaborate briefly on techniques of budgetary control with respect to service departments. In the departmental structure of most manufacturing plants, service departments are organized not only to provide service to production and other departments but also to improve the effectiveness of control over the cost of the service provided. In the budget development described earlier it is necessary to estimate the requirements for a given service in order to develop the portion of the manufacturing expense budget related to that service. In addition, of course, the expenses of providing that level of service must be budgeted on a basis that assumes efficient operation of the service department.

EXHIBIT 49
MANUFACTURING EXPENSE BUDGET FOR 19—: NORMAL LEVEL
(Reliable, Inc.)

Expense Class	Molding Fixed Amount	Molding Variable Rate Per Machine Hour	Fabrication Fixed Amount	Fabrication Variable Rate Per Machine Hour	Assembly Fixed Amount	Assembly Variable Rate Per Direct Labor Hour	Repairs and Maintenance Fixed Amount	Repairs and Maintenance Variable Amount	Repairs and Maintenance Percent of Total	Purchasing Fixed Amount	Purchasing Variable Amount	Purchasing Percent of Total	General Factory Fixed Amount	General Factory Variable Amount	General Factory Percent of Total
Indirect labor	$36,000	$.483	$80,000	$2.200	$ —	$ —	$ —	$280,000	46.5	$ —	$ —		$100,000	$600,000	42.6
Supervisory and clerical	—	—	—	—	—	—	64,000	—		52,000	—		540,000	—	
Employee benefits	11,900	1.247	26,400	3.449	—	.660	21,100	92,400	15.3	17,200	—		211,200	198,000	14.1
Repairs:															
Machinery	—	1.550	—	2.450	—	—	—	—		—	—		—	—	
Molds	—	1.300	—	—	—	—	—	—		—	—		—	—	
Other	—	.220	—	.300	—	.015	—	30,000	5.0	—	500	1.3	—	145,000	10.3
Supplies	162,000	1.514	70,000	.800	15,000	.020	—	100,000	16.6	—	5,000	12.5	—	150,000	10.6
Utilities	43,200	.620	10,000	.502	4,000	.018	500	19,500	3.3	100	2,400	6.0	100,000	260,000	18.5
Telephone and telegraph	—	—	—	—	—	—	1,000	5,000	.8	1,200	6,000	15.0	5,000	25,000	1.8
Inventory adjustment	—	—	—	—	—	—	—	—		—	—		—	—	
Travel	—	—	—	—	—	—	—	—		—	4,000	10.0	—	18,000	1.3
Miscellaneous	—	.250	—	.110	—	.012	—	4,000	.7	—	1,000	2.5	—	12,000	.8
Depreciation	220,000	—	175,000	—	15,000	—	12,000	—		2,200	—		248,000	—	
General taxes	—	—	—	—	—	—	—	—		—	—		55,000	—	
Insurance	—	—	—	—	—	—	—	—		—	—		28,000	—	
Total direct fixed	$473,100		$361,400		$ 34,000		$ 98,600			$72,700			$1,287,200		
Total direct variable		$7.184		$9.811		$.725		$530,900	88.2		$18,900	47.3		$1,408,000	100.0

90

EXHIBIT 49
(concluded)

Expense Class	Molding Fixed Amount	Molding Variable Rate Per Machine Hour	Fabrication Fixed Amount	Fabrication Variable Rate Per Machine Hour	Assembly Fixed Amount	Assembly Variable Rate Per Direct Labor Hour	Repairs and Maintenance Fixed Amount	Repairs and Maintenance Variable Amount	Repairs and Maintenance Percent of Total	Purchasing Fixed Amount	Purchasing Variable Amount	Purchasing Percent of Total	General Factory Fixed Amount	General Factory Variable Amount	General Factory Percent of Total
Allocated expenses:															
General factory	$467,300	$ 511,100	$292,200	$319,600	$444,100	$485,800	64,300	70,400	11.7	19,300	21,100	52.7	(1,287,200)	(1,408,000)	
Purchasing	66,400	28,900	10,600	4,600	12,900	5,600	2,100	900	.1	(92,000)	(40,000)	100.0	—	—	
Repair and maintenance	135,100	493,200	26,400	96,400	3,500	12,600	(165,000)	(602,200)	100.0	—	—		—	—	
Total allocated	$668,800	$1,033,200	$329,200	$420,600	$460,500	$504,000	$ —	$ —		$ —	$ —		$ —	$ —	
Budget year operating hours	396,000		80,000		1,500,000										
Overhead rate per hour:															
Direct fixed	$ 1.195		$ 4.518		$ .023										
Direct variable	7.184		9.811		.725										
Allocated fixed	1.689		4.115		.307										
Allocated variable:															
General factory	1.291		3.995		.324										
Purchasing	.073		.058		.004										
Repair and maintenance	1.245		1.205		.008										
Overhead rate—budget year	$12.677		$23.702		$1.391										
Overhead rate—prior year	$13.200		$24.770		$1.330										

A dynamic control environment for the subsequent control of that service expense will improve the effectiveness of budgetary management. The maintenance department is used as an example of providing that control through the "sold service" concept. The adoption of this concept in the maintenance department permits the earning of budget, or the variable budgeting technique, to be applied to the foreman of the maintenance function. This concept also reflects the basic operating characteristics of a maintenance activity in that the maintenance department is required to provide a certain number of hours of maintenance labor to production departments for efficient operation.

There are basically two points of control over these service costs. The first is the quantity of services rendered or sold—the requirement for maintenance labor hours, for example, which is primarily the responsibility of recipient departments such as production cost centers. The second point of control is the cost of providing an hour of maintenance service, which is the responsibility of the service department foreman such as the maintenance superintendent. Typically, maintenance services are provided to other cost centers on the basis of work order authorizations, and the charge for actual maintenance labor is distributed to work orders and then is distributed to the using cost center on the basis of the work order accumulation and assignment. In the budgeting process, production cost centers will estimate the requirements for work order maintenance on the basis of both preventive maintenance programs and historical experience for emergency maintenance service. The preventive maintenance program will be approved at a high level of manufacturing management since it involves policy considerations with regard to the age and operating efficiency of machinery and equipment, as well as the general physical condition desired in the plant. The demand for direct maintenance hours projected is accumulated to determine the requirements for maintenance labor by craft as a basis for establishing the manning table and the support cost budgets for the maintenance activity.

The determination of effective cost control in the maintenance department then requires a continuing reporting of the effective utilization and performance of direct maintenance labor. This is where the sold service concept can be particularly useful. Maintenance management may have decided that an efficient operating plan would call for each direct maintenance man to be utilized on work order maintenance for an average of 95 percent of his available clock hours. Establishing this level of utilization has direct implications on the staffing level required for each type of maintenance labor. It also provides the basis for accumulating the cost of the maintenance function and developing a budgeted rate for charging work orders that will, at that level of utilization, cover all costs of maintenance labor and overhead for the maintenance department. Typically, maintenance materials are charged to a separate cost code by type of material and are budgeted separately from the sold service charging rate.

Under this approach it is then possible in each accounting period to reflect in the maintenance department cost report the value of services sold at the budget rate for all work order work performed during the month and to create what is in effect an earned budget or an earned variable budget for each maintenance cost center. When the actual cost differs from the earned budget, management can analyze whether the cause was related to the level of service required and thus the utilization of maintenance personnel or was related to the control over spending to support the maintenance man in the plant. In addition, in certain cases the charging rate may be refined by establishing for certain predetermined types of preventive maintenance a standard time allowance for completion of work order work so that an efficiency percentage can also be calculated and reviewed in terms of dollar cost variance.

This concept of budgetary control is introduced into the cost reporting for a service center to assist manufacturing management in determining the level of staffing and utilization of services so that excessive costs of service departments do not creep into the manufacturing cost structure. It should also have the continuing advantage of insuring better communication between service department foremen, such as the maintenance foreman, and production department foremen who are causing the cost. One of the great difficulties in manufacturing control arises when production foremen are charged differing rates for a service where in fact the difference in the rate reflects the level of utilization of a fixed complement of personnel in the service center. The use of budgeted charging rates eliminates this difficulty and also should improve the precision of control over the cost of services rendered.

When the annual overhead budget is complete and variable rates have been determined, the monthly budgets must be computed. This is a matter of simple multiplication and division. The variable rates must be multiplied by the budgeted monthly level of activity, and the fixed costs must be divided by 12. A completed overhead budget is illustrated in Exhibits 50 and 51.

At this point, the manufacturing manager's budget is complete. He has combined the sales forecast with inventory policies and developed a well-balanced production plan. The production plan was translated into material, labor, and equipment requirements. These requirements were then converted into budgeted dollars.

To complete the process, the cost accounting department will extract required information and compute standard product costs. The standard costs will be used to cost monthly production and sales. Monthly production will be used to determine the budgeted level of activity for the month, and this will be used to compute the monthly budget allowances. Actual performance is then compared with the budget allowances, and variances are reported for analysis and control (see Chapter 10). Exhibit 52 is a simplified flow diagram of this integrated manufacturing budgetary system.

* * *

To summarize, we have explained the principles behind the manufacturing manager's budget. We have taken you through the various steps involved in preparing the budget:

1. Developing the production plan.
2. Determining material, labor, and machine quantity requirements.
3. Developing the purchasing budget.
4. Computing direct material and direct labor requirements.
5. Developing the manufacturing expense budget.

In addition, we've illustrated the means by which manufacturing budgets are integrated into the inventory control and accounting systems. At this point it should be clear why the manufacturing manager's budget is regarded as a vital element in the management planning and control system.

EXHIBIT 50   Manufacturing Expense Budget for 19—: Producing Departments

(*Reliable, Inc.*)

	Prior Year		Budget Year			
		Total Year				
Expense Class	Total Actual	Total Budget	Fixed Budget	Variable Budget	January
Molding (machine hours)	321,000	396,000			28,500
Indirect labor	$ 190,700	$ 227,300	$ 36,000	$ 191,300	$ 18,900
Employee benefits	441,000	505,700	11,900	493,800	35,000
Repairs—					
Machinery	486,000	613,800	—	613,800	41,000
Molds	421,000	514,800	—	514,800	35,400
Other	65,000	87,100	—	87,100	5,800
Supplies	648,000	761,600	162,000	599,600	64,700
Utilities	242,000	288,700	43,200	245,500	23,000
Miscellaneous	81,000	99,000	—	99,000	6,700
Depreciation	213,000	220,000	220,000	—	18,300
Total	$2,787,700	$3,318,000	$473,100	$2,844,900	$248,800
Fabrication (machine hours)	65,000	80,000			5,750
Indirect labor	$ 239,600	$ 256,000	$ 80,000	$ 176,000	
Employee benefits	288,900	302,300	26,400	275,900	
Repairs—					
Machinery	149,800	196,000	—	196,000	(Detail
Other	19,600	24,000	—	24,000	not illus-
Supplies	118,000	134,000	70,000	64,000	trated)
Utilities	43,300	50,200	10,000	40,200	
Miscellaneous	7,800	8,800	—	8,800	
Depreciation	173,700	175,000	175,000	—	
Total	$1,040,700	$1,146,300	$361,400	$ 784,900	$ 87,300
Assembly (direct labor hours)	1,188,000	1,500,000			102,400
Employee benefits	$ 744,600	$ 990,000	$ —	$ 990,000	
Repairs—other	13,000	22,500	—	22,500	
Supplies	39,000	45,000	15,000	30,000	(Detail
Utilities	26,000	31,000	4,000	27,000	not illus-
Miscellaneous	13,000	18,000	—	18,000	trated)
Depreciation	9,100	15,000	15,000	—	
Total	$ 844,700	$1,121,500	$ 34,000	$1,087,500	$ 77,300

February	March	2nd Quarter	3rd Quarter	4th Quarter	Expense Class
26,500	33,200	71,000	118,300	118,500	Molding (machine hours)
$ 18,900	$ 22,400	$ 41,700	$ 62,600	$ 62,800	Indirect labor
35,000	43,300	93,100	149,600	149,700	Employee benefits
					Repairs—
41,000	51,600	113,200	183,400	183,600	Machinery
35,400	43,200	95,000	152,800	153,000	Molds
5,800	7,300	16,100	26,000	26,100	Other
64,700	80,000	139,300	206,200	206,700	Supplies
23,000	27,500	52,800	81,000	81,400	Utilities
6,700	8,100	18,100	29,700	29,700	Miscellaneous
18,300	18,300	55,000	55,000	55,100	Depreciation
$248,800	$301,700	$624,300	$946,300	$948,100	*Total*
5,750	7,300	15,300	24,100	21,800	Fabrication (machine hours)
					Indirect labor
					Employee benefits
					Repairs—
					Machinery
					Other
					Supplies
					Utilities
					Miscellaneous
					Depreciation
	(Detail not illustrated)				
$ 87,300	$101,900	$239,900	$326,400	$303,500	*Total*
102,400	128,300	280,600	452,500	433,800	Assembly (direct labor hours)
					Employee benefits
					Repairs—other
					Supplies
					Utilities
					Miscellaneous
					Depreciation
	(Detail not illustrated)				
$ 77,300	$ 95,900	$211,700	$336,400	$322,900	*Total*

95

EXHIBIT 51 MANUFACTURING EXPENSE BUDGET—SERVICE AND
GENERAL DEPARTMENTS

(Reliable, Inc.: 19—)

| | Total Year | | | | |
| | Prior Year | Budget Year | | | |
Expense Class	Total Actual	Total Budget	Fixed Budget	Variable Budget	January
Repairs and Maintenance:					
Indirect labor	$ 265,000	$ 280,000	$ —	$ 280,000	$ 18,900
Supervisory & clerical	63,000	64,000	64,000	—	5,300
Employee benefits	88,000	113,500	21,100	92,400	8,000
Repairs—other	—	30,000	—	30,000	2,000
Supplies	88,000	100,000	—	100,000	6,700
Utilities	15,800	20,000	500	19,500	1,400
Telephone & telegraph	5,000	6,000	1,000	5,000	500
Miscellaneous	3,000	4,000	—	4,000	400
Depreciation	12,000	12,000	12,000	—	1,000
Total	$ 539,800	$ 629,500	$ 98,600	$ 530,900	$ 44,200
Purchasing:					
Supervisory & clerical	$ 40,200	$ 52,000	$ 52,000	$ —	
Employee benefits	14,800	17,200	17,200	—	
Repairs—other	400	500	—	500	
Supplies	3,500	5,000	—	5,000	(Detail
Utilities	2,000	2,500	100	2,400	not illus-
Telephone & telegraph	4,600	7,200	1,200	6,000	trated)
Travel	2,500	4,000	—	4,000	
Miscellaneous	700	1,000	—	1,000	
Depreciation	2,100	2,200	2,200	—	
Total	$ 70,800	$ 91,600	$ 72,700	$ 18,900	$ 7,300
General Factory:					
Indirect labor	$ 602,100	$ 700,000	$ 100,000	$ 600,000	
Supervisory & clerical	530,800	540,000	540,000	—	
Employee benefits	386,800	409,200	211,200	198,000	
Repairs—other	118,100	145,000	—	145,000	
Supplies	124,000	150,000	—	150,000	(Detail
Utilities	314,200	360,000	100,000	260,000	not illus-
Telephone & telegraph	17,200	30,000	5,000	25,000	trated)
Travel	11,600	18,000	—	18,000	
Miscellaneous	10,100	12,000	—	12,000	
Depreciation	219,100	248,000	248,000	—	
General taxes	50,000	55,000	55,000	—	
Insurance	25,000	28,000	28,000	—	
Total	$2,409,000	$2,695,200	$1,287,200	$1,408,000	$207,600
Grand total *(Exh. 50 + 51)*	$7,692,700	$9,002,100	$2,327,000	$6,675,100	

February	March	2nd Quarter	3rd Quarter	4th Quarter	Expense Class
					Repairs and Maintenance:
$18,900	$24,000	$ 52,100	$ 83,900	$ 82,200	Indirect labor
5,300	5,300	16,000	16,000	16,100	Supervisory & clerical
8,000	9,500	22,400	33,200	32,400	Employee benefits
2,000	2,500	5,700	8,900	8,900	Repairs—other
6,700	8,700	18,500	29,900	29,500	Supplies
1,400	1,600	3,900	5,800	5,900	Utilities
500	600	1,100	1,900	1,400	Telephone & telegraph
400	500	700	1,000	1,000	Miscellaneous
1,000	1,000	3,000	3,000	3,000	Depreciation
$44,200	$53,700	$123,400	$183,600	$180,400	*Total*
					Purchasing:
					Supervisory & clerical
					Employee benefits
					Repairs—other
					Supplies
					Utilities
	(Detail not illustrated)				Telephone & telegraph
					Travel
					Miscellaneous
					Depreciation
$ 7,400	$ 7,700	$ 21,600	$ 23,800	$ 23,800	*Total*
					General Factory:
					Indirect labor
					Supervisory & clerical
					Employee benefits
					Repairs—other
					Supplies
	(Detail not illustrated)				Utilities
					Telephone & telegraph
					Travel
					Miscellaneous
					Depreciation
					General taxes
					Insurance
$207,600	$232,200	$587,000	$738,100	$722,700	*Total*

EXHIBIT 52   FLOW DIAGRAM—INTEGRATED BUDGETING SYSTEM

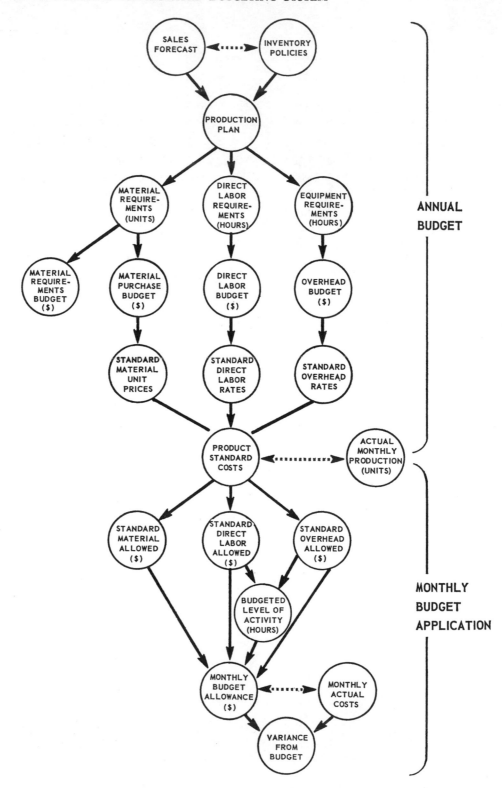

6

The General
and Administrative Budget

Until now we have focused on those expenses directly connected with the manufacturing and distribution processes. This chapter concentrates on expenses connected with running the top offices in the company and with providing the necessary legal, secretarial, financial, and related services. This is an area of importance not only because most businesses have experienced increases in such expenses in recent years but also because the control of these costs is sometimes an elusive process.

Considerable attention has been devoted to new concepts of control relating to general and administrative (G&A) expenses. New techniques are being developed to insure effective utilization of personnel in the G&A area; these techniques are related to those used by the industrial engineer in the factory. Some of those techniques are mentioned later in the chapter, as they are fundamental to the concept of budgeting.

For purposes of analysis, we will identify three types of work whose costs comprise G&A expenses:

1. *Administrative work,* which includes all the positions that exist because of the organization structure; for example, the administrative activity of a manager of a function.

2. *Measurable work,* which includes all jobs where a relatively repetitive and often routine type of work is performed and where the number of required personnel can be related to some measure of activity. The handling of bills for payment or the processing of invoices are examples of such jobs.

3. *Program work,* which includes research-related or other technically oriented jobs where the workload is related to programs undertaken by the company rather than to repetitive activity. Examples of such jobs are found in the areas of commercial and scientific research.

This breakdown is useful, because each type of work involves different techniques of cost control. For example, control of measurable activity may be exercised through the application of manning tables and flexible budgeting whereas control of administrative activity is dependent on the type of organizational structure that exists. Program work is subject to still another control technique—a technique related to the use of program budgets, which state concrete objectives of the program and include (1) lists of tasks required to complete the program and (2) budgeted manpower and timing for each task. The three types of work just described are not restricted to the G&A area. Actually, this same classification can be made of manufacturing and distribution activities. However, we shall concentrate on how the three categories of work relate to the G&A budget.

The expenses associated with G&A work are largely personnel costs, including not only salaries, wages, and fringe benefits but also space costs associated with personnel. Equipment costs can be another sizable item in a company with extensive data processing machinery. This fact takes on added importance because, while personnel costs may be somewhat variable, equipment costs are relatively fixed for the life of the lease or the contract. This shifts a substantial part of the control of equipment costs from a day-to-day or month-to-month basis to a longer-range basis—that is, control is effected largely when the commitment is made or renewed. Some cost control exists, of course, in the day-to-day utilization rates of such equipment.

There are generally three problem areas associated with G&A expenses:

- Control of such expenses, including control of overtime and other "hidden" extras.
- Maintenance of some balance between G&A expenses and other factors in the organization, such as sales or total costs. Some managers use a rule of thumb that G&A expenses should never exceed, say, 5 percent or 10 percent of sales.
- Identification of G&A expenditures with an appropriate activity, such as a corporate subdivision (in the case of headquarters expenses) or a product line. Examples of the latter are the application of underwriting and claims-service costs to various lines of insurance of a multiline carrier and the association of financial or statistical costs with a particular report produced.

The reason that those areas present problems is precisely that they are separate and distinct, and the answers to the problems associated with one area do not necessarily apply to those of the other areas. Yet many businesses do not keep the three distinct. Thus one executive may feel that he is controlling G&A because it represents only 6 percent of total sales and has never been any higher. Or an accountant may feel that he is rendering a valuable service to his management by allocating all G&A to various product lines (on a completely arbitrary basis), even though he does not report the total amount for each area of responsibility. In the case of the executive, the *relative* amount of G&A provides no assurance that the *total* amount is under control. The nature of the business may be such that normal relationships do not apply; 6 percent may actually be too high a figure. In any event, the danger of this approach is that it perpetuates all prior operating inefficiencies and ignores the planning function of management.

In the case of the allocating accountant, a basic principle of cost control is that all costs incurred must be grouped and reported by areas of responsibility before any distribution or allocation is made. Otherwise there is no guarantee that the activity receiving the allocation is responsible for the incurrence of the cost or, in many cases, even for the amount allocated. Therefore, it is meaningless to expect those who have no responsibility for certain costs to exercise control over them. Secondly, the dissipation of a pool of costs puts the one responsible for that pool of costs in a diffused light rather than in the spotlight of accountability. For example, there is an engineering firm that accounts for various support activities by charging actual costs of these activities to job numbers; thus the total costs incurred in any one area of responsibility or office are not reported but only the total charges to each number from every source. Such a procedure makes it impossible to exercise cost control at the source, which is the home department of each of the support personnel who devotes his time to assigned jobs. In this particular firm it is also virtually impossible for the man controlling the job number to police charges to it effectively, since in many cases he does not even know some of the people charging the number (let alone approve in advance the charging of time to the job).

Until now we have not spoken specifically of budgeting G&A expenses. This is because, while budgeting is an effective tool for cost control, its effectiveness is limited by other general types of control already in existence. Conversely, the existence of these other controls, which we are about to discuss, greatly facilitates the implementation of budgetary controls and increases the possibilities for truly effective controls through the planning and budgetary process. For this reason, we will touch upon some of these other control tools before discussing specific budgetary techniques.

The key to control in any business is organization—the process by which resources are allocated, responsibilities and authorities defined, and relationships established. True organization descends to the lowest levels of authority in the business. Thus, in the G&A area, it is not enough to outline the broad framework of authority. Sufficient detail must be added to insure that every group and section know what their responsibilities are and to whom they report.

It is possible in many instances to economize on clerical costs by establishing pools or by shifting personnel to different departments on a temporary basis. Even in these cases, the organization must be clearly established so that there are no gray areas which will permit a breakdown in control through overlapping responsibilities. Numerous examples could be cited of administrative areas where this concept of organization was entirely lacking and where any type of effective cost control was impossible. In one case, not only was it impossible to evaluate performance of the groups in a certain administrative category (a difficult enough task in itself), but it was equally impossible to find out who was responsible for what activity, what output should be expected of a particular group, or what level of staffing was realistic. Budgetary control in such a situation could result in nothing more than a perpetuation of past ways of setting the initial budget and of determining how much of the budget allowance was truly earned in a given period. Conversely, the establishment of an organizational framework incorporating position descriptions and tables of approval makes it possible to answer all such basic questions and provides realistic budgets to insure tighter controls on costs and performance.

The second element of basic control in the G&A area is the establishment of proper systems for performing the necessary work at reasonable cost. A critical review of a company often reveals startlingly poor methods, which slow down the progress of work and involve excessive overhead costs. In one company which exercised good control of methods in the factory, very poor methods were used in the office—for example, complete retyping of the same information several times in the processing of an order, detailed checking of every $5 and $10 item on a vendor's invoice, and meaningless paper shuffling and duplication of effort. All of this was taking its toll in poor customer service and excessive overhead costs. Upon the completion of elementary methods work and upon the use of new techniques, better customer service at lower cost resulted.

Closely related to methods work are the techniques of work measurement; that is, the determination of what a fair day's output should be. While the most obvious area of application is what was previously defined as measurable work, we should not overlook the fact that administrative work and program work can also be measured, although less formally. Management should ask itself how many functional managers—for that matter, how many separate functions—are required to accomplish the company's objectives. Does it make sense, for instance, to establish within the legal department separate sections for patents, real estate, antitrust, and so forth when the job really requires the attention of only one or two men? To a great extent this type of work measurement is a part of general organization work—the basic question of both is, What is the best way to get the job done? The proper answer to this question involves an appraisal of what the job really is and how many people are required to do it the best way.

In measurable work, the measurement techniques involve a breakdown of work into basic functions—sorting, calculating, filing, and the like—and a measurement of each basic function. The purpose of such a measurement is to determine how much effort is required to handle a given workload. One can then determine what the proper staffing should be and what budget allowance should be credited for a particular period, given the level of productivity.

Work measurement can take one of several forms. It is possible to derive an engineered standard based on actual time studies. Or it is possible that predetermined standards are appropriate. But, generally speaking, the most satisfactory way of measuring work is to use historical data, if available, or to sample various batches of current work. While the latter method may be less exact, it has the advantages of being simple and of measuring work being performed at the accustomed rate. Of course, work measurement will not make sense if the basic systems for processing work are unsound.

The final step is to express in dollars the standards developed; this is done by applying average wage or salary rates, to which are added benefits and overhead. One then has, in effect, a standard cost system for the office which provides a powerful productivity-related tool for cost control and a means of equitably charging other groups and product lines for services actually rendered. Such a system is also an excellent vehicle for installing budgetary control, since the same rates used in costing are used in computing budget allowances. This procedure is described at the end of the chapter.

Another basic feature of control is good supervision. It can be regarded as organization in action, since good supervision is just that—bringing to life the organizational relationships which exist on paper. Supervision is necessary, especially in the area of measurable work, to insure that productivity is maintained at the required level. During the normal processing of work, imbalances in departmental workload are bound to occur, and supervisors must be there to restore balance through shifting the workload or personnel. Even in the same department, peaks and valleys will occur in the day-to-day workload. In the mail order business, for instance, Monday may be the most busy day of the week because of the accumulation of two days' mail. Or Tuesday may be the most busy day because of newspaper advertising on Sunday. Or it may not be possible to anticipate high-volume days, so variable is the workload. In any case, there must be good supervisors to level the peaks and valleys and to insure that each employee has enough work in front of him to maintain overall productivity. Otherwise, the staff may work overtime on Tuesday to "finish up" and yet be practically idle on Thursday.

While some of the controls previously described are more applicable to large administrative departments than to smaller ones, one should not overlook the opportunity to apply some or all of them in a manner that will keep overhead costs under control without, at the same time, jeopardizing corporate objectives. For example, periodic reviews of work methods and the effectiveness or value of the output of organization units should be a continuing part of the control process.

Everything we have said until now provides a necessary backdrop for the discussion of budgeting G&A expenses. In the ideal situation, budgeting proceeds as a natural outgrowth of the other control techniques described earlier. In fact budgeting and rate setting are, to some degree, inseparable, because to establish hourly rates for fixed or partially fixed costs, an assumption must be made about the level of activity. This assumption is very much like the one used for budgeting. The difference is that in addition to using rates to generate cost data, budgeting supplies a bench mark against which actual expenditures can be compared.

The fundamental step in preparing a departmental budget is to determine the level of operations. In the G&A area this level will largely be determined by the expected activity in other areas. For instance, in the accounting department the number of invoices prepared will vary to some degree with the level of sales, and the number of vendors' invoices paid will vary with the production and inventory plan. Similar correlations can be made for such departments as tabulating, credit, and office services. It is not true that administrative activity in research departments will vary directly with the level of sales or production; instead, the level of activity in these departments will be set by a management decision based on what management can afford and what it feels will make the most important contribution to overall progress. Upon establishing the general level of activity, one should then proceed to a more precise statement of plans for the coming period. For administrative work and program work the most common planning vehicle is a manning table, which indicates the positions needed (with a statement of justification, including a description of duties to be performed and expected workloads) together with the planned staffing and the salary for each position. Additional costs, such as those of overtime, space, and equipment, should be included in the same budget.

While this may seem like a lot of detail, it is the only sure way of keeping overhead costs from continually creeping upward through the addition of "a person here and there" and too-generous salary adjustments. Some of the largest U.S. corporations apply this technique down to the lowest levels at the most far-flung locations. The paperwork involved is easily systematized, and the little effort involved pays rich dividends in helping supervisors at all levels to keep their costs under control.

For measurable work, the manning table just described is also appropriate, but when work measurement has been performed it becomes a secondary step. The basic step is a projection of the units of work expected for the period, based on such activity measures as are appropriate for the department. This forms the basis of a projection of the hours to be worked in a department during the budget period. This projection, in turn, is translated into a manning table, which reflects such factors as schedule requirements, overtime estimates, peak loads, and vacation periods. The manning table should be used in the same way as that for administrative and program work, with the work-measurement calculations added as supporting detail.

As with all budgets, the G&A budget should be built up from the grass roots. The first-line supervisors and others who will have to make the budget work should have a voice in it and should budget only expenses which they can control. The overall budget should then be assembled and reviewed at each higher level of responsibility. When revisions are necessary, they should be made in such a way that lower-level supervisors still feel it is *their* budget. Finally, when the finished budget is assembled, it should be structured in a way to facilitate the reporting of actual results. All of the responsibility-reporting concepts discussed in earlier chapters should be employed, and the completed budget statements should look exactly like the monthly report formats illustrated in Chapter 1. Budget reports should be prepared each month, comparing actual results with those budgeted for the period. With variable budgeting, the budget allowance will vary not with time but with the level of activity. The application of this technique requires an understanding of the nature of costs and the way in which they vary.

Few costs are completely fixed, but it may be convenient to talk of certain ones—such as supervisory salaries, space and equipment costs, and certain overhead allocations—as fixed for purposes of this analysis. Budgeting for these is just a matter of prorating the total year's cost over the months or over other budget periods and of providing an equal budget allowance for each period. As with fixed costs, few costs are truly variable with any measure of time or activity; but when flexible budgeting is used, it is helpful to make certain assumptions about variability. Where to draw the line between fixed and variable costs can be a difficult question. Generally it can be done only by assuming a normal level of activity and deciding what costs will be fixed, even at the bottom of the normal range. Where gray areas still exist, it is generally better to consider questionable items as variable, rather than go through a detailed analysis of semifixed and semivariable (or "step") costs.

Costs which are determined variable should receive a budget allowance equivalent to the activity level actually attained. In simplest terms, if salaries and wages vary directly with hours worked (as in the case of an hourly office payroll), the budget for any period should relate to either the hours actually worked or the hours earned, based on physical production (converted through work-measurement units into hours). Using the second choice, hours earned, makes it possible to identify an efficiency variance (where actual hours are more or less than earned hours) as well as a rate variance (where the amount spent for hourly wages differs from the budget allowance). For fixed expenses it is also possible to develop a volume variance (where the number of hours worked or earned is more or less than those budgeted for the period), which will indicate whether fixed costs have been overabsorbed or underabsorbed.

We will conclude the chapter with a simplified case study which illustrates many of the points previously discussed. The Able Insurance Company had a large typing pool of 17 girls (including two supervisors), which handled all typing done in the company, except for a small amount of secretarial and confidential work. In effect, the typing pool provided services to all other departments. The problems this presented were—

1. How to control and budget costs in the typing pool.
2. How to make a reasonable charge for typing services to other departments, since those department managers were on a bonus-sharing plan.
3. How to charge typing services to a particular insurance plan, since the company wanted to develop data on "product" profitability; and this required an allocation of all costs—such as underwriting, claims, and office services—to individual policy classes.

Able attacked these problems in several ways. First, it organized the typing pool as a cost or budget center so that its costs of operation could be clearly segregated from other costs. Second, it reviewed the workflow in the typing pool, to be sure that it was satisfactory. Third, Able made a rather simple work-measurement study to determine what the basic units of work were and what a normal time allowance for each unit should be.

For purposes of simplicity, all typing was divided into three categories—based on observation of the workload:

1. Small sheets—8.5 inches wide, or less.
2. Large sheets—over 8.5 inches wide.
3. Preprinted forms on which typed information was entered.

The next step was to sample enough batches of each type of work to arrive at a proper time allowance, the relative complexity and density (or words on a page) of the work having been taken into consideration. To do this, the supervisors gave each girl a log sheet to keep for two weeks. On this sheet each girl indicated the proper category of each piece of work she completed, along with the time she began the work and the time she finished it, including any coffee or personal breaks which occurred during the work.

On the basis of this sample, the following time standards evolved: small page—23.5 minutes (.39 hours); large page—42.75 minutes (.71 hours); form—15 minutes (.25 hours). Normal monthly volumes were also established by using the

EXHIBIT 53   COMPUTATION OF EARNED HOURS

	Quantity		Time Allowance		Earned Hours	Actual Available Hours
Small page	2,050	×	.39	=	800	
Large page	1,100	×	.71	=	781	
Form	2,200	×	.25	=	550	
					2,131	2,250*

* 15 typists (excluding 2 supervisors) × 7½ hours a day × 20 working days. Sickness and other absences were about equal to overtime.

sample and other historical data. Earned hours were then computed (Exhibit 53). The difference between earned and actual hours (about 6 percent) was determined to be normal lost time. To cover this, 6 percent was added to each time allowance, making them .41, .75, and .27 hours, respectively.

Since this work measurement was done near the beginning of the budget year, it was decided to develop the cost rates and the budget rates at the same time. The first step was to set the planned level of activity. After consultation with the various departments providing work for the typing pool, it appeared as though monthly activity would increase to 2,300 small pages, 1,250 large pages, and 2,350 forms. On the basis of historical experience, this would require 2,515 available hours per month. Seasonality did not seem to be a factor, and Able planned to use overtime when necessary to make up for sick time and vacations.

On the basis of the workload projections, the indicated staffing for the department was 17 typists. Of the present force, two were known to be leaving in March, but no other changes were expected. It was budgeted to increase the force by two girls as of January 1 to handle the increased workload. However, in March the workload and productivity would again be reviewed before arbitrarily replacing either of the resigning girls. Therefore, 17 girls were budgeted for only the first quarter; hopefully, productivity increases would hold the workforce down to 15 typists when the two girls left. This staffing policy was reflected in the manning table, along with the two supervisory positions.

The budget for next year is shown in Exhibit 54. It was supported by detailed worksheets showing all of the calculations described, was approved by the budget committee, and was included in the company's budget on November 20. The budget form also served as the worksheet for calculating the hourly rates. For purposes of comparison, last year's "rates" were also computed (using estimated total dollars and hours), although the cost and budget system was not to be installed until January 1.

The procedures followed under the new cost system are as follows. *First,* any department requesting the services of the typing pool fills out a two-part standard work request (Exhibit 55). The left half is reserved for instructions to the typist; the right half (a detachable stub) goes to the accounting department to serve as the basis for the charge to the department, to the appropriate insurance policy, or to

EXHIBIT 54

TYPING DEPARTMENT BUDGET

	ACTUAL LAST YEAR	TOTAL YEAR	BUDGET — NEXT YEAR							COMMENTS
			FIRST QUARTER				SECOND QUARTER	THIRD QUARTER	FOURTH QUARTER	
			JAN.	FEB.	MAR.	TOTAL				
DIRECT HOURS	22,600	23,445	2,115	2,115	2,115	6,345	5,700	5,700	5,700	2 ADDITIONAL PEOPLE IN 1st QTR.
OVERTIME HOURS	2,156	2,340	180	180	180	540	600	600	600	EXPECT INCREASE WHEN EXTRA PEOPLE LEAVE
VARIABLE EXPENSES:										
HOURLY PAYROLL	32,205	37,512	3,384	3,384	3,384	10,152	9,120	9,120	9,120	EXPECT AVG. WAGE INCREASE OF 17 1/2¢
OVERTIME PAY	4,377	5,148	396	396	396	1,188	1,320	1,320	1,320	PER HR. (TO 1.60) IN JANUARY
EMPLOYEE BENEFITS	10,211	12,000	1,100	1,100	1,100	3,300	2,900	2,900	2,900	INCREASE IN PROPORTION TO WAGES
TEMPORARY HELP	1,725	1,500	100	100	100	300	400	400	400	INCREASE IN WORKLOAD EXPECTED
SUPPLIES	2,126	2,400	200	200	200	600	600	600	600	
GENERAL EXPENSE	1,305	1,000	80	80	90	250	250	250	250	
TOTAL	51,949	59,560	5,260	5,260	5,270	15,790	14,590	14,590	14,590	
FIXED & ALLOCATED EXP.										
SUPERVISORY SALARIES	12,500	12,800	1,065	1,065	1,070	3,200	3,200	3,200	3,200	$300 RAISE AUTHORIZED FOR 1/1
EQUIPT. SERV. CONTRACT	2,300	2,400	200	200	200	600	600	600	600	
BUILDING COSTS	5,280	5,400	450	450	450	1,350	1,350	1,350	1,350	
DEPRECIATION	1,750	1,750	145	145	148	438	438	437	437	
MANAGEMENT FEE	2,300	2,400	200	200	200	600	600	600	600	
TOTAL FIXED	24,130	24,750	2,060	2,060	2,068	6,188	6,188	6,187	6,187	
TOTAL EXPENSES	76,079	84,310	7,320	7,320	7,338	21,978	20,778	20,777	20,777	
HOURLY RATE —										
VARIABLE	2.10	2.31								
FIXED	.97	.96								
TOTAL	3.07	3.27								

EXHIBIT 55   TYPING REQUISITION FORM

No. <u>0001</u>	THE ABLE INSURANCE CO. TYPING REQUISITION	No. <u>0001</u>

Department _____

Policy (Job) _____

From: _____ Dept.: _____

Date _____

Typist _____

Policy (Job) No. _____

ITEM	QUAN.	STD. HOURS	TOTAL EARN HOURS	TOTAL ACTUAL HOURS
SMALL PG.		.41		
LARGE PG.		.75		
FORM		.27		
TOTAL HOURS				
RATE		$3.27		
TOTAL CHARGE $				

Date Given: _____

Date Wanted: _____

Instructions: _____

_____

_____

_____

other "product" codes. Those typing jobs not identified with a product are charged against the general budget of the requesting department.

Second, the accounting department computes the charge by converting units produced to hours (at standard), accumulating total hours, and converting total hours into dollars at the departmental rate. The amount charged to the requesting department serves as a credit to the typing pool. Ideally, all the costs of the typing pool are absorbed in this manner. We say "ideally" because changes in the amount spent, in the volume of work, or in productivity could create variances which would not be absorbed by the rate. In that event, a change in the rate might be in order.

Third, the variable rate developed for costing purposes serves as the budget rate for providing budget allowances based on activity (measured in terms of total standard hours of work produced). For this purpose the rate is split into its component parts (Exhibit 56). This means that for every productive hour worked

EXHIBIT 56   BUDGET RATE COMPONENTS

	Variable Expense	÷ *Total Hours* =	*Budget Rate*
Hourly payroll	$37,512		$1.45
Overtime pay	5,148		.20
Employee benefits	12,000		.47
Temporary help	1,500	25,785	.06
Supplies	2,400		.09
General	1,000		.04
Total	$59,560		$2.31

DISTRIBUTION OF TYPING-POOL CHARGES   **EXHIBIT 57**

Underwriting department:
Policy A	$ 302.11
Policy B	1,096.14
↓	↓
Policy K	12.85
General	72.84
	$1,587.39

Claims department:
Policy A	$ 875.26
Policy B	1,782.66
↓	↓
General	84.09
	$4,892.98

Research department:
Project 1	$ 15.27
Project 2	327.56
General	87.36
	$ 430.19

Accounting department:
General	$ 125.00

Administrative department:
General	$ 250.00
Total	$7,285.56

(applying hourly standards) a budget allowance of $1.45 is earned for the hourly payroll, 20 cents is earned for overtime pay, and so on. For fixed expenses, the monthly budget allowance is one-twelfth of the total year's budget, since the level of activity is not expected to increase or decrease these expenses.

On January 1 the conversion to the new system was made. The supervisors logged in each piece of work and prepared requisition tickets. The tickets helped in work-flow control because if the supervisor assigned twelve small pages and five forms to a typist, the supervisor knew that the standard time allowance would be about six hours; and she would make a note on her control sheet to check with the typist when six hours had elapsed.

At the end of January, the accounting department tabulated all of the tickets, which showed the production of the typing department to be 2,178 small pages, totaling 893 standard earned hours; 1,032 large pages, totaling 774 standard earned hours; and 2,076 forms, totaling 561 standard earned hours. The total of 2,228 earned hours multiplied by $3.27 (the departmental rate after including monthly budgeted fixed charges) resulted in a charge of $7,285.56, distributed as indicated by Exhibit 57 (per the individual work orders).

These charges, along with the standard hourly charges for each department's time, were used for product profitability analyses and as a measure of the true costs of operating each of the other departments. The same amount was credited to the typing pool as expenses absorbed by its production. Exhibit 58 is a copy of the typing pool's performance statement for January. This statement was distributed to Miss Sparks, head of the typing pool, and to Mr. Davis, manager of office services, who was Miss Sparks' department head.

At the monthly performance review meeting, Mr. Grant, controller, explained the significance of the statement and the meaning of its variances to Miss Sparks and Mr. Davis. The first point he made was that the typing pool had logged 2,376 hours but had earned only 2,228 hours on the basis of production. This indicated a slippage in efficiency from the established standards. Upon reflection, Miss Sparks recalled that a number of smaller jobs had been done without filling out a ticket and that the pace had been somewhat slower than usual. Mr. Grant pointed out that this was so, since 2,295 earned hours would have been the normal activity for the month. But he further pointed out that there had been 150 overtime hours worked and $100 spent for temporary help. Mr. Davis said that while both of those expenditures were below budget, he questioned the necessity of as much overtime and outside assistance as there had been.

Miss Sparks said that some overtime was always unavoidable because of sickness and other absences. She added that during the month she had received several requests for rush work and next-day service, which meant working overtime even though the overall workload was lighter. Mr. Grant said that this would help to explain the efficiency loss, since the girls who were working overtime one night were probably not fully occupied the next day. Mr. Davis agreed to review the rush procedures and to help screen requests for rush work, if such action would facilitate controlling the cost of this work.

Before the meeting ended, Miss Sparks asked Mr. Grant to explain what the variances meant and how they were computed. He replied that, in the variable cost area, hourly payroll data provided both the pay rate and the efficiency variance. The pay rate used for budget and rate making had been $1.60 per hour for straight time and $2.20 for overtime. However, in January the actual hourly pay had averaged $1.64 for straight time and $2.18 for overtime. The differences in both cases, multiplied by the hours worked, made up the rate variance of $86. The efficiency variance, he said, related to the difference between total straight time and overtime budgeted and the amount actually spent (less what had already been identified as the rate variance), or $216. The other-spending variance of $181, he explained, was the net effect of all other variable expenses. Together, the variances totaled $483, the same amount which was unabsorbed, since the budget and absorption rates were the same.

Mr. Grant explained that in the fixed cost area there were three variances—a planned overabsorption variance (the difference between the amount of fixed expenses we planned to absorb and the amount of expenses we planned to spend), the spending variance (the sum of all variations of actual expenses from the budget) and the volume variance (caused by deviations from the planned level of activity). He pointed out that, even though in January there had been an overabsorption of expenses, there had still been a negative volume variance because an even greater over-

TYPING DEPARTMENT OPERATING REPORT

EXHIBIT 58

YEAR TO DATE			THIS MONTH	
BETTER OR (WORSE) THAN BUDGET	AMOUNT	ITEM	AMOUNT	BETTER OR (WORSE) THAN BUDGET
		CONTROLLABLE (VARIABLE) EXPENSES		
(421)	3651	HOURLY PAYROLL (ACTUAL RATE 1.64)	3651	(421)
119	327	OVERTIME PAY (ACTUAL RATE 2.18)	327	119
(215)	1262	EMPLOYEE BENEFITS	1262	(215)
34	100	TEMPORARY HELP	100	34
(14)	215	SUPPLIES	215	(14)
14	75	GENERAL EXPENSE	75	14
(483)	5630	TOTAL	5630	(483)
	5147	LESS EXPENSES ABSORBED BY PRODUCTIVE WORK	5147	
(483)	483	UNABSORBED	483	(483)
		ANALYSIS OF UNABSORBED EXPENSES		
(86)	86	PAY RATE VARIANCE	86	(86)
(181)	204	OTHER SPENDING VARIANCE	204	(181)
(216)	193	EFFICIENCY VARIANCE	193	(216)
(483)	483	TOTAL	483	(483)
		FIXED AND ALLOCATED EXPENSES		
--	1065	SUPERVISORY SALARIES	1065	--
(20)	220	EQUIPMENT SERVICE CONTRACT COSTS	220	(20)
(33)	483	BUILDING COSTS	483	(33)
--	145	DEPRECIATION	145	--
--	200	MANAGEMENT FEE	200	--
(53)	2113	TOTAL	2113	(53)
	2139	LESS EXPENSES ABSORBED BY PRODUCTION	2139	
	26	OVER-ABSORBED	26	
		ANALYSIS OF OVER-ABSORBED EXPENSES		
(143)	143	PLANNED OVER-ABSORPTION VARIANCE	143	(143)
53	(53)	SPENDING VARIANCE	(53)	53
64	(64)	VOLUME VARIANCE	(64)	64
(26)	26	TOTAL	26	(26)
		--- STATISTICAL DATA ---		
(67)	2228	PRODUCTIVE HOURS EARNED AT STANDARD	2228	(67)
		ACTUAL HOURS WORKED		
(111)	2226	STRAIGHT TIME (BUDGET RATE 1.60)	2226	(111)
30	150	OVERTIME (BUDGET RATE 2.20)	150	30
(81)	2376	TOTAL	2376	(81)

absorption had been budgeted. Both Miss Sparks and Mr. Davis were puzzled by this, until Mr. Grant explained that the budget of fixed expenses had been spread evenly over the year but that productive hours were not equally distributed, since two girls would be leaving in March and the budget did not provide for their replacement. Therefore, although it was budgeted to absorb all fixed costs by the end of the year, the pattern of absorption would be a little irregular, with the first three months being overabsorbed and the last nine being slightly underabsorbed.

He calculated the planned overabsorption variance for the month of January to be $143—the difference between the budgeted expenses of $2,060 and the planned 2,295 hours times the fixed expense absorption rate of $0.96 [(2,295 × .96) − $2,060 = $143]. He added that the volume variance was computed by comparing budgeted hours with those actually earned and multiplying the difference by the fixed absorption rate [(2,295 − 2,228) × .96 = $64].

At the conclusion of the meeting, it was agreed that the rate and budget structure appeared reasonable for the present but that it might be revised later in the year if volume continued at low level or if any revisions in cost budgets appeared necessary.

7

Program Budgets

A PROGRAM BUDGET REPRESENTS the appropriation of a fixed sum of money to achieve a specific objective or set of objectives. This budgetary approach is most common in the "programed" activities of a business such as research and development, marketing, engineering, preventive maintenance, training, and public relations. The program or appropriation budget in these areas represents the total cost of undertaking a series of individual projects.

As in most budgeting processes there is a top-down and bottom-up approach taken to establish the cost and content of these programs. In some organizations, management will specify an overall investment limitation which may relate to past spending, such as a percentage of sales. This upper limit may be derived from management's judgment as to a total amount necessary to remain competitive or to keep in step with current growth rates and future expectations.

On the other hand, there are those companies that arrive at a total budget based on a buildup of individual projects "sold" to management by the respective department or functional managers. In these cases, since the company cannot financially support an infinite number of projects, a budget limitation probably exists, but it is not preset in the same manner as in the top-down approach.

In both approaches to program budgeting, there is a distinct need to provide some mechanism to assist management in identifying a preferred choice among possible alternatives. Where a total budget is established initially, management must decide how to allocate the funds to individual project efforts. Where many projects are first being proposed at department levels, management must decide how to screen and select the projects to be worked on.

In recent years, considerable attention has been given to cost-effectiveness analysis as a basis for this sort of management action. This analysis involves a comparison of alternative courses of action (which projects to work on) in terms of their cost and their effectiveness (output of the project effort) in attaining specific goals. Cost-effectiveness analysis in program budgeting generally consists of an attempt to minimize the dollar appropriation required to meet a corporate mission (which may not be explicitly measurable in dollars) or, conversely, to maximize the output of the program (for example, number of new products from R&D) subject to an overall budget constraint.

Cost-effectiveness analysis requires looking at the relationship among a number of factors present in every analysis of choice. The overall framework for this analysis is management's objectives, since the rest of the process boils down to measuring the extent to which the objectives are being met by the *selected* alternatives. Then, of course, there must be alternatives, which might be a set of project proposals. The projects need not be direct substitutes for one another since there can be numerous alternatives which direct themselves to management's objectives.

Choosing a particular project means that the resources needed for that project can no longer be used for other purposes. Thus, for a given project, these are the costs to be considered in evaluating the proposal. The evaluation itself entails the use of an appropriate model to abstract the information relevant to reaching a decision to include a project in the program. An example of such a model might be a return-on-investment formula which abstracts and relates the project costs to the project output (its measured economic payoff).

Having evaluated each alternative, it is then necessary to weigh costs against effectiveness. This is accomplished by applying a criterion or standard by which the evaluated projects can be ranked in order of desirability (for example, descending order of return on investment). This permits a selection of the most promising projects up to the overall budget limitation.

The quantitative nature of cost-effectiveness analysis often leads to a number of questions pertinent to its usefulness in decision making. These questions relate to (1) the ability to identify the right company objectives, (2) the clear-cut specification of these objectives, (3) the influence of nondollar factors, and (4) the determination of an appropriate measure of project performance. The last point is, of course, the cost-effectiveness measure, which must be relevant and measurable.

There are many examples of the problems in choosing effectiveness measures and the effects of maximizing on such measures. Consider, as an extreme example, the plant manager of a nail factory whose initial measure of performance was stated in terms of the *total weight* of the factory's output. He then proceeded to maximize this explicitly stated objective, with the result that the plant turned out only huge railroad spikes. Seeing a surplus of railroad spikes for which there was no demand, management revised the measure of the merit of the plant's output to the *number of nails* produced, whereupon the plant manager switched entirely to producing tacks, brads, and staples. Management's measure of effectiveness in physical terms and its failure to evaluate the production output by market criteria led to activity and costs which obviously were inconsistent with long-range corporate interests.

The difficulties in making meaningful use of cost-effectiveness analysis do not, however, negate the role that budgeting can play in establishing program goals and controlling performance. The discussion in this chapter will demonstrate the need for and the usefulness of qualitative measures of performance evaluation as a supplement to the quantitative approach of the cost-effectiveness analysis in program-budget areas.

The research manager plays an increasingly vital role in the success of business in our fast-moving economy. Product obsolescence takes place at a rapid rate as a result of competitive action and technological advance. The research and development (R&D) function has to answer this challenge by developing products which will meet or beat those of competitors. Realizing this, as most businessmen do, one would assume that the R&D manager would have a relatively easy time obtaining and managing budget funds. Such is not the case, however, because of the intangible nature of much R&D effort. Even though great progress may be made in a particular year in developing a new product, the results may not be impressive until a new product is turned over to the marketing people for market testing. Accordingly, when there is pressure on management to increase earnings, there may be a temptation to cut the R&D appropriations in the mistaken notion that essentials are not being neglected. This condition points up the importance of an R&D budgeting system which will permit management to make rational decisions about such expenditures.

The research function, regardless of its position within the organizational structure of a firm, may be viewed as a system wherein an input of money results in an output from various projects and as a system having a control mechanism to divert the flow of money from the less-promising projects to those of greater potential. This viewpoint emphasizes the importance of considering the following interrelationships in any discussion of the R&D budgeting process:

1. Company policies and long-range plans to provide the framework for decisions regarding the potential of a technical program or project.
2. Methods of project evaluation to relate the potential of one project to that of others under consideration.
3. Budgets or planned-cost estimates to control the overall flow of money to program and project activity.
4. Means for measuring and reviewing project performance to serve as a basis for decisions about the continuation, rechanneling, or termination of effort.

We will illustrate these interrelationships by reference to the planning and control process at the research laboratories of Consumer Products Company (see Exhibit 59). These interrelationships exist in an actual firm, but they have been altered slightly to avoid disclosure of proprietary information.

Consumer Products Company includes three divisions engaged in the production and marketing of diverse product lines. Total annual sales amount to slightly more than $350 million. The R&D laboratories conduct product- and process-oriented research for each division in addition to corporate research (primarily basic research). The existing procedures and organizational structure make it possible for division general managers to exercise control of the research activities that are financially supported by their divisions. At the same time, the vice president of research—a corporate officer—has the responsibility of reviewing all research activity in the company.

The final R&D budget (Exhibit 60) of Consumer Products Company is the culminating result of several phases of planning and evaluation. Initially, the president and the R&D vice president establish the general level of spending to be

EXHIBIT 59

R&D Planning and Control Process

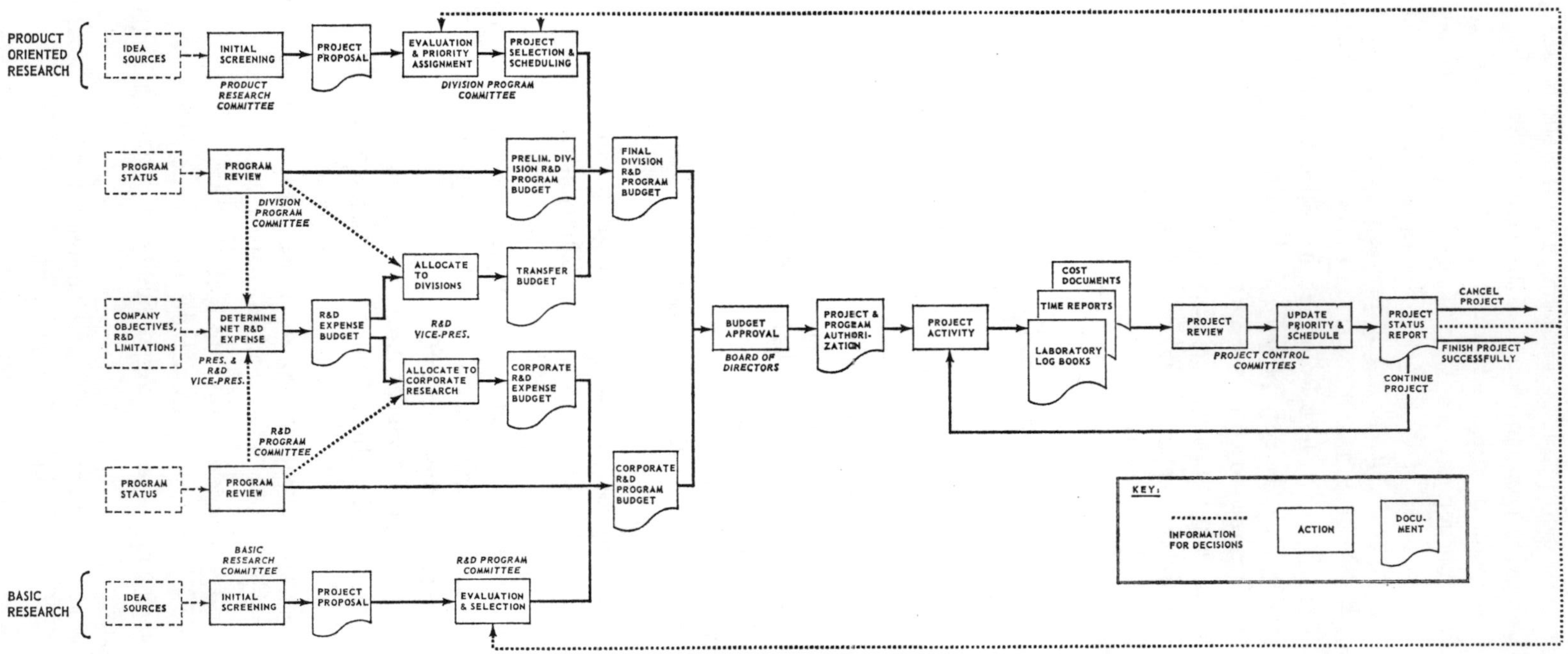

permitted for manpower, contracted research, supplies and equipment, facilities, and a variety of other expenses of operating the laboratories.

In a sense, this budget is "backed into," because the bottom line, net R&D expense, is decided upon first. This represents the financial limits on research activity and evolves from discussions and agreements between the president and the R&D vice president. Budget preparation involves a four-step procedure. First, the president reviews company policies covering such factors as product line diversification, expansion of existing product lines, and entrance into new markets. He also reviews the current technical programs and related costs, which have been established to meet the objectives defined by company policies. Second, the R&D vice president evaluates the technical limits of the research staff, in terms of its ability to conduct the necessary work in relation to existing projects and in relation to the expected demand for additional work. Also, he specifies—as is his responsibility—the nature and magnitude of the research effort that should be undertaken presently in order to safeguard Consumer's future position in the marketplace. Third, rough cost estimates are established on the basis of the foregoing considerations. These estimates are totaled and compared with the dollar level the president wants to maintain and feels the company can afford. (In this case, he uses as a bench mark a fairly consistent percentage of net sales, running between 10 and 15 percent.) Fourth, if proposed R&D expenditures appear too high, a further evaluation is made to determine which existing programs might be held to their current levels without sacrificing company objectives.

The details of the R&D expense budget, as shown in Exhibit 60, are worked out by the R&D vice president to conform to the agreed-upon net R&D expense. Many other companies employ a similar approach—that is, the details of expense budgets are developed after totals are derived from historical expense relationships, rather than built up from independent estimates of the cost of individual projects.

The R&D vice president then prepares a transfer budget (Exhibit 61), which is that part of the R&D expense budget to be charged to the marketing divisions. The transfer amounts are the R&D vice president's estimates of the future needs of the divisions regarding their respective programs; that is, the amounts represent the hours of professional manpower at a standard rate (where the rate is a weighted average for different levels of engineers and scientists) plus factory labor (pilot plant, sample production, and so on) plus outside research.

The difference between the net R&D expense ($5.08 million) and the transfer budget ($3.2 million) is the budgeted gross cost of corporate research ($1.88 million). However, only a part of this amount is considered in subsequent phases of budgeting corporate R&D expense (basic research). The following are deducted from the gross cost of corporate research to arrive at the total available for basic research:

1. Unallocated contracted research. This is an amount usually set aside for the president's use so that a specific effort he may desire can be initiated without detracting from existing project work.
2. Uncontrollable charges. This is a catchall of charges for which no project number is available. Experience indicates that mischarges will occur and must be deducted to arrive at a realistic corporate R&D budget.

117

EXHIBIT 60   19X5 R&D Expense Budget—Consumer Products Company

(*000's Omitted*)

Expense Category	Actual 19X1	Actual 19X2	Actual 19X3	Latest Estimate 19X4	Budget 19X5	19X5 Increase (Decrease) Over 19X4
Salaries						
Professional	910	1,100	1,200	1,660	1,960	300
Nonprofessional	350	370	480	510	590	80
College recruits	20	30	50	50	50	—
Factory labor	170	150	130	140	150	10
Personnel services	50	50	40	40	50	10
Total payroll costs	1,500	1,700	1,900	2,400	2,800	400
Contracted Research						
Consultants	60	70	50	30	30	—
Private laboratories	100	280	140	160	200	40
Universities	110	120	80	130	170	40
Clinical tests	30	30	80	200	210	10
Unallocated	—	—	50	80	90	10
Total contracted research	300	500	400	600	700	100
Operating Expenses						
Overtime premium	3	5	10	9	10	1
Experiment materials	80	95	90	120	120	—
Laboratory chemicals, etc.	100	130	150	140	150	10
Office supplies	15	17	16	20	20	—
Towels and laundry	10	7	8	8	8	—
Scientific literature	9	15	22	20	20	—
Professional society dues	1	1	2	2	2	—
Conventions	10	12	16	10	10	—
Traveling expenses	40	50	45	75	60	(15)
Scientific exhibits	6	4	3	3	—	(3)
Miscellaneous	26	64	88	73	80	7
Total operating expenses	300	400	450	480	480	—

3. Supporting programs. The R&D organization has a computer facility and several analytical laboratories that service all corporate and divisional research activity. These centers do not charge to specific projects.

The resulting corporate R&D expense budget (Exhibit 62) and the transfer budget represent overall dollar estimates of the cost of performing basic research and of product-oriented research, respectively. There are, of course, two distinct phases in the continuation of the research-planning process which must be completed before budgets can be considered as part of a planning and control system. These phases are programing and project selection. Programing translates company objectives into relatively precise definitions of the fields that should be investigated and of the emphases that should be placed on different kinds of research activity within each field. Project selection involves choosing those technical endeavors—within the framework of the programs—which bear most closely on the short- and long-range profits of the company. Consumer Products Company serves as an excellent example of an approach that encompasses these two phases in the areas of both product-oriented research for the marketing divisions and basic research on the corporate

EXHIBIT 60
(*concluded*)

Expense Category	Actual 19X1	Actual 19X2	Actual 19X3	Latest Estimate 19X4	Budget 19X5	19X5 Increase (Decrease) Over 19X4
Building and Equipment						
Depreciation	210	260	380	390	380	(10)
Building rental	315	205	120	160	170	10
Utilities	40	50	80	80	90	10
Provision for alterations	60	100	35	50	70	20
Fuel	—	5	15	15	20	5
Purchased services	—	25	100	160	140	(20)
Outside equipment rental	5	30	40	50	80	30
Mechanical services	5	10	25	10	30	20
Wire and telephone service	15	15	15	20	25	5
Property and liability insurance	—	—	10	15	20	5
Taxes	—	—	110	150	175	25
Total building and equipment costs	650	700	930	1,100	1,200	100
Total direct expenses	2,750	3,300	3,680	4,580	5,180	600
Nonresearch Transfers to R&D						
Wire and telephone service	5	5	10	5	5	—
General service	80	60	40	50	50	—
Employee benefits	130	140	160	160	190	30
Office space	10	5	10	5	5	—
Total nonresearch transfers	225	210	220	220	250	30
Nonresearch Services to Divisions						
Materials storage	20	20	30	40	60	20
Quality control	—	5	10	30	30	—
Space rental	90	90	80	140	160	20
Computer usage	—	—	40	70	100	30
Total nonresearch service to divisions	110	115	160	280	350	70
Net R&D expense	2,865	3,395	3,740	4,520	5,080	560

level. We shall discuss the programing and product-selection sequence as it relates to the divisions.

In each division a committee is set up to decide which brand categories require continuing research to meet the company's short- and long-range objectives. This committee consists of the R&D vice president, division general manager, division director of marketing, and division manager of long-range planning. As the R&D vice president prepares the transfer budget, this committee concurrently develops a recommended level of research spending for the selected brand categories. In this manner the sum of the division's R&D program budgets will equal the transfer budget, which we know ties into the company's overall R&D expense budget.

The recommendations of this committee are passed on to a product-planning committee, which in turn establishes the approved level of research activity for types of work within each brand category. This committee has as its members the appropriate R&D research director and manager(s), a division research coordinator, and the various division product managers. The result of their initial decisions is a preliminary R&D program budget for the division, Exhibit 63.

EXHIBIT 61 19X5 R&D Transfer Budget—Consumer Products Company

(000's Omitted)

	Actual			Latest Estimate	Budget	19X5 Increase (Decrease)
	19X1	19X2	19X3	19X4	19X5	Over 19X4
Division A	1,040	1,380	1,400	1,980	2,000	20
Division B	500	400	600	950	1,000	50
Division C	140	170	150	170	200	30
Total service to divisions	1,680	1,950	2,150	3,100	3,200	100

EXHIBIT 62 Determination of Corporate R&D Expense Budget
Consumer Products Company

(000's Omitted)

		Budget 19X5
Budgeted Net R & D Expense		$5,080
Less: estimated transfers to divisions		3,200
Budgeted Gross Cost of Corporate Research		$1,880
Other Deductions:		
Unallocated contracted research	$ 90	
Estimated nonproject charges	7	
Cost of computer facility not transferred	100	
Analytical laboratory A	30	
Analytical laboratory B	20	
Total Deductions		247
Budgeted Corporate R & D Expenses		$1,633

The final R&D program budget for the division has the individual programs scheduled, at least to the extent of indicating the rate of spending by calendar quarters. This scheduling is possible because the types of projects that comprise these programs have identifiable bench marks by which to gauge the completion of the programs; to progress from one bench mark to another requires a certain amount of staff time, which, on the basis of experience, can be accurately estimated. While other cost factors enter the picture, staff time generally accounts for 70 to 80 percent of the total cost in product-oriented projects; consequently, staff time is the key consideration in scheduling projects and programs and in estimating their costs.

Obviously, the ability to schedule the flow of money to individual programs, as indicated by the final division R&D program budget, implies a preceding step:

EXHIBIT 63

Division Preliminary R&D Program Budget

Brand Category	Maintenance			Cost Reduction			Product Improvement			New Products			Total			Category Per Cent of Total	
	19X4	19X5	Change	19X4	19X5	Change	19X4	19X5	Change	19X4	19X5	Change	19X4	19X5	Change	19X4	19X5
A	$ 49	$ 45	($ 4)	$ -	$ 3	$ 3	$ 44	$ 40	($ 4)	$ 210	$ 158	($ 52)	$ 303	$ 246	($ 57)	15.3	12.3
B	87	73	(14)	7	20	13	129	82	(47)	157	169	12	380	344	(36)	19.2	17.2
C	43	38	(5)	-	12	12	59	37	(22)	56	109	53	158	196	38	8.0	9.8
D	27	31	4	-	3	3	38	34	(4)	26	26	-	91	94	3	4.6	4.7
E	27	40	13	-	3	3	75	34	(41)	35	37	2	137	114	(23)	6.9	5.7
F	35	31	(4)	59	34	(25)	-	-	-	100	85	(15)	194	150	(44)	9.8	7.5
G	27	18	(9)	9	-	(9)	13	10	(3)	18	36	18	67	64	(3)	3.4	3.2
H	14	14	-	-	-	-	10	10	-	160	192	32	184	216	32	9.3	10.8
I	13	13	-	-	-	-	1	7	6	-	-	-	14	20	6	0.7	1.0
J	-	-	-	-	-	-	-	-	-	48	10	(38)	48	10	(38)	2.4	0.5
K	-	7	7	-	-	-	-	-	-	20	5	(15)	20	12	(8)	1.0	0.6
L	-	7	7	-	-	-	-	14	14	34	45	11	34	66	32	1.7	3.3
M	-	8	8	-	-	-	-	12	12	40	40	-	40	60	20	2.0	3.0
N	-	-	-	-	-	-	-	-	-	254	254	-	254	254	-	12.9	12.7
O	-	-	-	-	-	-	26	-	(26)	30	154	124	56	154	98	2.8	7.7
TOTAL	$322	$325	$ 3	$75	$75	$ -	$395	$280	($115)	$1,188	$1,320	$132	$1,980	$2,000	$20	100.0	100.0

TYPE OF ACTIVITY

defining and scheduling specific research tasks in even greater detail. The specific tasks essential to the success of each program are decided upon in the project-selection phase, of which the review and re-evaluation of projects in process is an integral part.

Referring to Exhibit 59, you will see a continuing selection process in which—

- Current projects are being reselected; that is, the original decision to work on a given project is reaffirmed or rejected on the basis of a review and evaluation of up-to-date information on expenditures, profit potential, and technical problems. (We will discuss this procedure as it relates to control in a later section of this chapter.)
- New ideas are communicated and coordinated to form project proposals, which are then evaluated in terms of their potential for being introduced into existing programs.

New proposals and existing projects have certain priorities assigned to them, which are initially arrived at in the following sequence. First, after adequate communication between the division and R&D, the division research coordinator prepares a project proposal consisting of a statement of objectives; supporting marketing information, including estimates of payoff expected; and supporting technical information, including an estimate of the total R&D cost. Second, the division reviews each project and assigns one of three possible priorities. Priority *A* means the project is essential to the short- or long-range sales and profit plans of the division. Priority *B* indicates that the project is valuable to the short- or long-range sales and profit plans of the division. Priority *C* designates the project as desirable to investigate, but its value to the division is not as clear cut as *A* or *B*. Third, cognizant of division priorities, R&D assigns a priority representing its ability to commit itself to the project in light of existing projects and existing R&D technical skill. Priority I indicates R&D's ability to fit the project into a program within the next month and to adhere to a specific timetable. Priority II means that R&D is able to spend minor effort on a regular basis for the next three months and to work thereafter on the basis of a probable timetable. Priority III indicates R&D's inability to schedule a project at this time and to commit itself to a future timetable.

You can readily see that this process, while enabling the marketing division to introduce new projects for consideration, allows the R&D organization veto power when too many projects are rated *A* or *B* and when available R&D resources are limited by the existing R&D program budget and by current effort on projects previously ranked *A* or *B*. This check forces the marketing division to re-evaluate priorities of existing projects. (In practice the marketing division reviews and rates new proposals at the same time it is evaluating progress on current work.)

The integration of this continuing procedure with budget preparation is accomplished after a division's preliminary R&D program budget is completed. At that time, all authorized projects (whether currently being worked on or scheduled for the future) and all new proposals available are evaluated on an accelerated basis. Existing priorities are reviewed; new ones are assigned. R&D timetables are included for any that may fall in the R&D rating of I or II. The complete package is then submitted to the product-planning committee (comprised of essentially the same persons involved in the review of existing projects and of new proposals), which selects projects to be undertaken (or continued, in many cases) so as to conform to the totals of the programs in the division's preliminary R&D program budget and to provide for a reasonably level utilization of manpower on a month-to-month basis in the various R&D process centers.

It is the practice of Consumer Products Company, as is the case in many organizations, to set aside part of the budget for the third and fourth quarters in order to build in flexibility for later budget revisions and to accommodate the possible introduction of accelerated programs which otherwise could be handled only by halting efforts on projects in progress. Of course, the amount set aside reduces the total to be supported by projects selected during the initial budgeting. Consequently, very few of the projects with a low marketing priority and not already scheduled by R&D will be included initially in the budget, since there are generally many more projects of greater interest that will be considered first and that will more than account for the dollars available.

To recap, the final R&D program budget of a division represents the dollar limits of R&D activity by brand category and by type of research within each category. For the first and second quarters these limits are accounted for by selected projects with agreed-upon timetables for their completion. For the third and fourth quarters, the dollar limit is comprised of projects previously begun and of lower-priority projects selected for possible work. The balance of the budget is unsupported by detailed projects and is left open to accommodate the introduction of new, high-priority projects and shifts in program emphasis.

The program development and project selection to support the corporate R&D expense budget in Consumer Products Company follow much the same procedure as that followed on the divisional level. The responsibility for the development of the corporate R&D program budget rests completely with the R&D organization, although division research coordinators are consulted with regard to the long-range plans of the marketing divisions. The evaluation of the individual projects of the programs (broad product categories) is more subjective than the priority system used by the divisions. In addition, project schedules are not prepared; consequently, the corporate R&D program budget represents an arbitrary breakdown of total estimated costs into four equal quarters.

In Chapter 1 we described the principles of responsibility accounting as the basis for cost measurement and reporting. We further elaborated on the control phase of budgeting in Chapter 2. When an R&D budget is split in accordance with the organizational structure of a company, these same principles of accounting, reporting, and variance evaluation hold true. However, reporting against budgets as we have discussed them in this chapter is another matter. First, the variance between actual and budgeted expenses by organizational unit becomes a minor issue; more important is the kind of program and type of research for which the actual money was spent. Second, the comparison of actual expenditures with budget produces a figure representing the dollar progress of the technical work. Yet this dollar progress may or may not have a direct relationship to the technical progress of the research activity. Thus the reporting and control of R&D expenditures require an approach that adequately relates the technical and financial aspects of project and program activity. This latter requirement is most often met through the use of project status reports (Exhibit 64). This single document represents the project's status in terms of

EXHIBIT 64   PROJECT STATUS REPORT

PROJECT STATUS REPORT

PROJECT TITLE A. B. C. Maintenance

CHARGE NUMBER 30120

START DATE Nov., 19X4   ESTIMATED COMPLETION DATE Dec., 19X5

INITIAL PRIORITY B-II   TOTAL ESTIMATED PROJECT COST $21,025

BUDGET 19 X5 $ 21,025
19 ____ $ -
TO COMPLETE $ 21,025

REVIEW DATE Dec. 15, 19X4   Month   Year—to-Date   As of

BUDGET: MAN-HOURS 137.7 $ 1,430 $ 1,430

ACTUAL: MAN-HOURS 223.5   2,438   2,438   Nov. 30, 19X4

ACCOMPLISHED TO DATE X Y Z Solvent/hydrocarbon composition developed. New formulation decreases usage 25 per cent due to increase in spray rate, compensated by coarser particles. Meets flammability requirements.

CURRENT PRIORITY A-I   ACTION TAKEN Accelerate under new approach

COMMENTS 25% decrease in usage would increase total units sold by estimated 600,000 cases ($2,800,000). New approach undertaken to develop water-based formulation to retain present usage rate. Estimated cost savings $1,000,000 per year. (Four fold)

REVIEW DATE _____

ACCOMPLISHED SINCE LAST REVIEW _____

dollars expended, accomplishment of interim technical objectives, schedule, and assessed potential (priority). Timely and concise reports of this type (and those integrated for use at various levels of management) permit the kind of reappraisal that will help avoid costly continuation of work that drifts outside specified objectives or that becomes barren of results.

A management review of such technical-financial status reports—conducted as frequently as dictated by the company's marketing and technological characteristics —will tend toward the inclusion of the "best" possible projects, given the limitations of manpower and facilities. This review also provides a basis for decision: If only high-priority projects are being worked on and if the professional staff is fully utilized, management may want to increase its research capacity (revise the budget) to permit the inclusion of a greater number of projects. Similarly, if the lower-priority projects are filling the program, management may cut back research funds.

We have covered the three basic phases of the budgeting process as they apply to the R&D function. The *preplanning phase* is, in essence, the continuing activity of project evaluation and broad program review, coupled with a current appraisal of long- and short-range company plans and R&D limitations. As we have seen in Consumer Products Company, this preplanning culminates in an overall financial limit on research activity set by the president and the R&D vice president.

The *budget-preparation phase* involves the reconciliation of the estimated costs of various research programs with the total projected expense of running the R&D laboratories. This second phase also recognizes the direct tie-in of project review and evaluation which provide the list of individual efforts to which funds will ultimately be allocated.

The *control phase* of R&D operations requires a timely and adequate tie-in of the technical and financial progress of project activity. This permits a review and re-evaluation of projects as a basis for decisions to continue or abandon further effort and affords an opportunity to introduce new projects believed to have a greater potential for attaining company objectives.

For Consumer Products Company, these three phases and their interrelationship were shown in Exhibit 59. This company uses only one of a wide variety of planning, programing, and selection techniques employed by industry today. There is, in fact, a continuing program of research on the management of R&D being conducted throughout industry and the academic field. There is no unique combination of approaches which has been demonstrated and tested as giving the best possible results. Rather, based on the growing contribution of R&D activity to the survival of a company in our free, competitive economy, one must recognize the need to improve continually information and methods for administering and controlling a research program. This continuing effort must be concentrated on the research decision problems inherent in the basic elements of the budgeting process presented in this chapter.

The public relations function, by its very nature, affects all areas of communication within the company. It has no definitive set of ground rules and might better be described as an art rather than as a science. This does not mean, however, | *The Public Relations Budget* that there is no sensible way to measure the activities associated with this function. It does mean that a greater effort must be made to define its activities and projects, along with the objectives and costs to accomplish them, so that there is no doubt about what is to be done and how performance and results will be measured.

Performance evaluation is one of the most important factors in the preparation of a budget. Current methods of evaluating performance in the public relations area have fallen far short of what might be considered as a desirable level of control. The most common method used today to measure the success or failure of public relations activities is the monthly or quarterly report comparing actual expenses with budget. (See Exhibit 65.) The question then is, Are these performance measures enough?

One should readily see from Exhibit 65 that it would be impossible to determine from an expense report alone whether the department's performance was good or

EXHIBIT 65   ILLUSTRATIVE DEPARTMENT EXPENSE REPORT
(Consumer Products Company)

Department: Public Relations
Supervisor: R. Stone
Period: Month ended 12/31/—

Current Month				*Year-to-Date*	
Better (Worse) Than Budget	*Actual*			*Actual*	*Better (Worse) Than Budget*
		Controllable Expenses:			
($400)	$ 5,000	Salaries		$ 60,000	($3,300)
100	400	Overtime premium		4,000	1,300
(200)	1,000	Travel and entertainment		10,000	(1,000)
(100)	600	Telephone and telegraph		5,000	(1,000)
—	400	Contracted services		10,000	1,000
50	600	Stationery and office supplies		4,000	(300)
50	800	Dues and subscriptions		2,000	(1,000)
($500)	$ 8,800	*Total* controllable		$ 95,000	($4,300)
		Transfers from Other Departments:			
($100)	$ 700	Employee benefits		$ 7,000	($ 600)
100	150	Switchboard service		1,000	(100)
—	550	Office space		7,000	—
$—	$ 1,400	*Total* transfers		$ 15,000	($ 700)
($500)	$10,200	*Total* department		$110,000	($5,000)
—	1,200	Less: services charged to divisions		(10,000)	—
($500)	$ 9,000	Net department expense		$100,000	($5,000)*

* The total department variances were determined by comparing the actual expenses with the budgeted expenses shown in Exhibit 67.

ILLUSTRATIVE PROGRAM BUDGET

EXHIBIT 66

(*Consumer Products Company*)

Program: Customer Public
Responsibility: A. Jones
Period: Year Ended 12/31/—

| | *Budgeted Dollars* | | |
	Total	*Project A*	*Project B*
Controllable Expenses:			
Salaries	$20,000	$ 5,000	$15,000
Overtime premium	1,000	200	800
Travel and entertainment	5,000	3,000	2,000
Telephone and telegraph	2,500	2,300	200
Contracted services	1,000	—	1,000
Stationery and office supplies	400	100	300
Dues and subscriptions	100	—	100
Total	$30,000*	$10,600	$19,400

Project *A:* Preparation and publication of a series of articles on the new and improved line of consumer products recently developed.

Project *B:* Preparation of text material for new TV documentary on company's research and development programs.

* This total also appears on Exhibit 67. The "customer public" program budget shows two major projects contemplated for the coming year. Each of these projects is described above. When specific quantitative measures of performance can be agreed upon, they would also be included as a part of the project descriptions.

bad. The reason, of course, is that there is no basis for performance measurement other than the dollar variances by expense account. With reference to Exhibit 65, it is possible that one might reach a favorable decision as to performance if all of the factors were known, even though actual expenses exceed budgeted expenses. In what other way, then, can we measure performance in order to bring to light other factors which influence the level of spending for a particular reporting period?

Before proceeding to answer this question, let us first discuss the initial step necessary to establish a realistic framework for budgeting the public relations activity. The first prerequisite, as in any good budgeting program, is to define the various projects or programs currently under way or to be undertaken by the department. Each program should have a stated objective in terms of its expected achievements, and each should be related to current short- and long-range management objectives. Because of the myriad of activities associated with the public relations function, one should be careful to avoid breaking down the programs into too much detail or stating too narrow an objective.

One way in which these objectives might be stated would be to relate them to

EXHIBIT 67   ILLUSTRATIVE DEPARTMENT BUDGET
(Consumer Products Company)

Area: Public Relations
Responsibility: R. Stone
Period: Year Ended 12/31/—

	Total Budget	Program Budgets		
		Customers	Employees	Government
Controllable Expenses:				
Salaries	$ 56,700	$20,000	$21,700	$15,000
Overtime premium	5,300	1,000	3,600	700
Travel and entertainment	9,000	5,000	1,000	3,000
Telephone and telegraph	4,000	2,500	1,400	100
Contracted services	11,000	1,000	2,500	7,500
Stationery and office supplies	3,700	400	1,700	1,600
Dues and subscriptions	1,000	100	600	300
Total controllable	$ 90,700	$30,000*	$32,500	$28,200
Transfers from Other Departments:				
Employee benefits	6,400			
Switchboard service	900			
Office space	7,000			
Total transfers	$ 14,300			
Total department	$105,000			
Less—services charged to divisions	(10,000)			
Net department expense	$ 95,000			

* The detail for this total is shown in Exhibit 66. The total expense budget for the department is summarized by the various program expense budgets. The budgets would be shown by month or quarter depending on the period established for reporting progress. Exhibit 68 illustrates a quarterly progress report for the "customer public" program.

the various "publics" which the company might be trying to influence. Within this framework, the various activities or projects needed to attain these objectives might also be shown. Among the possible publics of a company are the press, government, financial community, employees, customers, and competitors. Among the potential activities and projects that can be used to achieve specific objectives are articles, speeches, reports, surveys, legislation, trade associations, and internal communications. These, of course, are only illustrative and should not be viewed as the only classifications which might be useful in establishing public relations objectives. For example, the customer public might be stated in terms of the company's male and female publics or even in terms of the age categories within each, if these distinctions are necessary to describe more accurately the specific objectives for the various activities or projects contemplated. Stating company objectives in terms of the various programs, however, is the only realistic way to facilitate the preparation of progress reporting and to evaluate the attainment of the goals.

Once the objectives have been determined, the next step is to budget the expenses for each of the programs. This can be accomplished by first allocating the controllable expenses of the public relations department to the various projects associated with each of the programs. The extent to which these expenses should be budgeted on a project basis should depend on the materiality of the expenditure, the degree of control that can be exercised at the project level, and the degree of difficulty in obtaining actual cost information for comparing results. An illustration of a specific program budget is shown in Exhibit 66. The total public relations budget is shown in Exhibit 67.

We are now ready to answer this question: What other means of performance measurement should be used to help management evaluate the stated program and project objectives? In addition to the comparison of actual expenditures with budgets, there are other quantitative and qualitative measures which can be used to evaluate performance:

Quantitative Goals	*Selected Bases for Measurement or Evaluation*
Receive favorable comments in at least 80 percent of all customer letters received.	Percentage of favorable letters received.
Increase attendance at stockholders' meetings to a minimum of 300 people.	Attendance at stockholders' meetings.
Obtain between three and five hours of public-service time on television and a minimum of ten hours on radio.	Number of hours on television and radio.

Qualitative Goals	*Selected Bases for Measurement or Evaluation*
Make more effective use of our in-company publications.	Review of comments received from the employee suggestion box; solicitation of opinions from department managers.
Increase public awareness of our company by submitting articles to magazines on our history and future growth.	Evaluation of editors' acceptance of articles submitted for publication. Review of opinion polls conducted by the market research department.
Improve the quality of our advertising and press releases.	Evaluation of awards or recognition of achievement by advertising, press, or other groups. Review results of special opinion survey conducted by the market research department.

129

EXHIBIT 68 ILLUSTRATIVE PROGRAM PROGRESS REPORT
(Consumer Products Company)

Program: Customer Public
Responsibility: A. Jones
Period: Quarter Ended 12/31/—

Current Quarter			Year-to-Date	
Better (Worse) Than Budget	Actual	Controllable Expenses	Actual	Better (Worse) Than Budget
$ 500	$4,000	Salaries	$ 16,000	$4,000
50	200	Overtime premium	1,000	—
300	1,100	Travel & entertainment	5,500	(500)
200	500	Telephone & telegraph	2,000	500
—	—	Contracted services	—	1,000
(50)	200	Stationery & office supplies	400	0
—	—	Dues & subscriptions	100	(0
$1,000	$6,000	Total	$ 25,000	$5,000 *
(10%)	70%	% of favorable customer letters received	85%	5%
—	—	No. of lawsuits	2	—
—	—	Potential liability	$100,000	—

Report: The plan to develop a series of articles on the Company's improved line of consumer products is moving slower than we had hoped. So far, editors have not been sold on the superiority of our new product line, but a new project is being worked on which shows promise. This project is to develop a TV documentary on the Company's research and development program for consumer products. On the basis of trial runs, the film looks very promising.

* The total program variances were determined by comparing the actual expenses with the budgeted expenses shown in Exhibit 67. Variances would also be determined by project by comparing actual project expenses to the project budgets shown in Exhibit 66.

Even though the established measures may not be the only ones that could be used to evaluate the results of a given program or project, it must be understood that in today's complex business climate some agreed-upon standards of measurement are better than none at all.

In deciding on what we want to measure, we will seldom be able to identify conclusively the causes of changes in the attitudes of the various company publics. Not only does the public relations communication effort influence public response but so also do other factors, such as product quality, service, and management strategy. The important thing, therefore, is to obtain management acceptance of these standards in advance. Once the standards for performance measurement are agreed upon, they should be incorporated into periodic progress reports. These reports should be prepared and submitted to management no less than once each quarter.

An example of a progress report for the company's customer-public program is shown in Exhibit 68. Note that in addition to the reporting of controllable expenses and certain quantitative standards, there is a written statement of how well the program is achieving its objectives. This written statement of performance is essential to the control of the program. Too often there is a reluctance to put in writing the failures and accomplishments for a given activity. One failure does not negate an entire program. Conversely, one clearly written success is worth several "vocal" stories. The reason for this is simple. If the results are worthwhile talking about, then certainly they should be formally communicated to management. How else will management be able to relate the various public relations success stories to the programs which helped to bring them about?

In the final analysis, the use of written program objectives and reports will help the public relations director sell his programs to management. At the same time, management will become more aware of the various program successes and failures and will be able to make more qualified judgments as to where its "investment" will accomplish the best results.

8

The Capital Expenditure Budget

As was pointed out in Chapter 2, planning is generally in terms of long-range objectives—say, over the next five years. This sets the stage for the detailed planning for the first year, which is part of the budget-preparation process. Long-range objectives usually provide for expansion of plants, distribution facilities, sources of raw materials, and other resources which require capital expenditures financed by retained earnings, by equity, or by debt secured from outside sources.

Because the commitment of funds in capital projects is irrevocable, plans and proposals for these expenditures are carefully examined by management and the directors. A faulty decision to enlarge the staff for a particular function may be corrected by cutting back, thereby terminating the effects of the decision. But funds put into brick and mortar represent sunk or fixed costs and cannot generally be terminated or retrieved without considerable financial sacrifice. The more important evaluation and control techniques in this field are discussed in this chapter.

An essential starting point in capital expenditures planning and control is the identification of proposals with corporate long-range objectives. This requires a definition and a rather complete description of both the objectives and the capital expenditures proposals. Company objectives are often organized as follows: present nature of the business and products and planned changes; volume and profitability policies; marketing plans; manufacturing plans; financing plans; relocations; industrial relations; and public relations. Capital expenditure proposals must then be sufficiently specific to permit their identification with objectives for expansion and change or to permit their justification on the basis of cost-reduction improvements or necessary replacements.

To be sure that operating and divisional managers give adequate consideration to the need for generating sound and profitable capital expenditure proposals, top management usually establishes capital expenditure targets or goals. For example, as a part of overall budget objectives, the president may say that, in light of business trends and general economic forecasts, each division is expected to generate capital investment opportunities equivalent to 150 percent of its annual depreciation charges and that such investments are expected to yield a return on investment of 10 percent or better. While such targets are always guidelines rather than rigid requirements, and while operating men should know that the amount of capital available to them will be based ultimately on specific projects, it is nevertheless true that top management must stimulate forward thinking and planning. The fact that the president puts a premium on the long-range planning associated with the capital budgeting program will help instill in operating managers a desire to pursue profitable investment opportunities. This is more important than one might at first imagine, because in many companies the reason for a lack of sound capital expenditure requests is probably a corresponding lack of adequate long-range planning.

Generally, evaluation and approval involves (1) the technical feasibility and validity of assumptions about production volumes, market potentials, and engineering consequences and (2) the business wisdom of making the expenditures under the assumed conditions and expected results. The flow of a proposal through the evaluation and approval process is illustrated in Exhibit 69.

The technical-evaluation phase must be accomplished by subjecting a capital expenditure proposal to a review by all departments capable of passing judgment on the technical aspects. In many cases, outside consultation is sought to bolster company judgments on advanced processes and market potentials. Forms and procedures are provided for the processing of proposals in a formal way and for the accumulation of supporting data and approvals. Selectivity must be built into this procedure to permit decisions at lower levels of management for limited amounts.

The second phase of the evaluation process is economic in nature and is done in many ways. Management may find that it has more investment opportunities than capital to invest or more investable capital than investment opportunities. Whichever situation exists, management must have some economic criteria for selecting or rejecting investment proposals. Its decision is in either case likely to be based largely on certain measures of financial return. Let us consider three common methods of economically evaluating return:

1. Years to payback.
2. Average rate of return.
3. Discounted-cash-flow rate of return.

All three methods determine in one way or another a return on investment (ROI). To evaluate whether a project is yielding a good or bad return, ROI must be compared with a standard acceptable level of profit the company wishes to maintain. This internal cutoff rate is the *cost of capital*.

There is no substantial agreement as to precisely how management should calculate cost of capital. One thing is clear: Management must set an objective by which all investment opportunities are monitored. The company must recognize that few investment proposals are financed solely from debt or equity; most are made up of some combination of the two. Hence calculating the cost of capital should include the cost of borrowed funds as well as the cost of equity financing.

Suppose management has determined that the cost of borrowing is 9 percent at current loan rates. Furthermore, the growth potential illustrated in the financial state-

EXHIBIT 69
CAPITAL EXPENDITURE PROJECT EVALUATION PROCESS

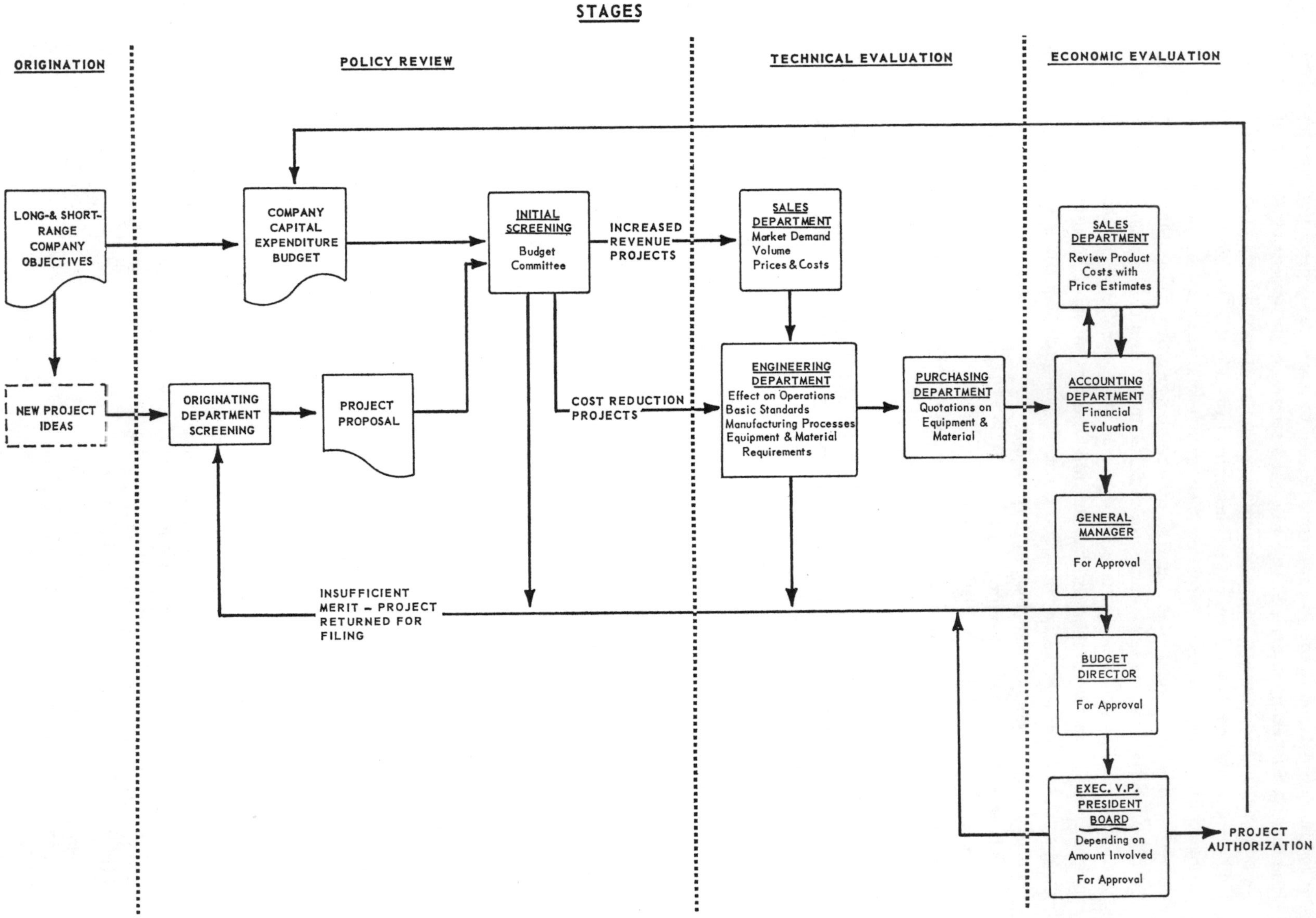

ments indicates after-tax earnings per share of $5. This will cover the cost of equity financing through stockholder dividends and also provide a sufficient amount for retained earnings. With a book value of $25 per share, the earnings would represent a 20 percent return on equity. It might be assumed that cost of capital is simply the addition of the cost of borrowing, with the cost of equity financing yielding 29 percent; however, the capital base with which management invests is proportioned between debt and equity. If debt represents 40 percent and equity represents 60 percent of the capital base, the cost of capital must reflect this debt-to-equity ratio and be the weighted average of the costs of each type of capital. The calculation would be performed in the following manner.

	(A) Cost (Percent)	(B) Percent of Total Capital	(A × B) Cost of Capital (Percent)
Debt	9	40	3.6
Equity	20	60	12.0
			15.6

The cost of capital for this company would thus be approximately 15 percent.

Having derived the company's cost of capital, management can compare the costs with those of major companies in the industry as illustrated in Exhibit 17. This information is available through various governmental statistical reports. Such a comparison will act as a guideline in the development of management's own objectives.

Every company has to consider that certain investments will not yield a measurable corporate profit because they are needed to improve employee goodwill or to meet legal requirements. Investments in equipment to reduce air pollutants and investments in the social well-being of the community may not contribute dollars to the bottom line. Management must increase the cost of capital accordingly so that the portfolio of profit and nonprofit investments taken together yield a sufficient overall return. Suppose the company has calculated its cost of capital to be approximately 15 percent; however, 25 percent of its investments are nonprofit or necessity projects. To cover such investments, the cost of capital will have to be approximately 20 percent (15 percent ÷ 75 percent).

The result of such an effort to determine a cost of investing the company's capital enables management to monitor various proposals within the confines of the following three methods.

Years to Payback

The years-to-payback method determines the number of years for the earnings on a project to pay back the original outlay. It is probably the most widely used measure of investment worth. The normal method for calculating payback when aggregate return and depreciation are roughly equal from year to year is the following:

$$\frac{\text{Total investment for capital expenditure}}{\text{Annual savings} + \text{annual depreciation}} = \text{Years to payback}$$

Generally, companies using this method adopt decision rules for approval of projects in terms of the number of years required to recover the investment. By setting a limit on the number of years, management can screen out high-profit projects that are so clearly desirable as to require no refined rate-of-return estimates; and at the same time it can quickly reject projects showing such poor promise that they do not merit thorough economic analysis. Such a decision rule could provide for the approval of cost reduction projects only if they paid back in three years or less, and for the approval of major capital expenditures if they paid back in eight years or less.

Here is an example of two investment alternatives with their corresponding years to payback.

		Investment A	*Investment B*
1.	Investment outlay	$1,500	$1,500
2.	Project life	6 years	10 years
3.	Average annual depreciation	$250	$150
4.	Average annual savings	$250	$300
5.	Annual savings and depreciation	$500	$450
6.	Years to payback	3 years	3⅓ years

From this example management might select Investment A since it requires fewer years to recover the investment outlay. However, upon further analysis of the two alternatives we find that Investment A indicates a cash flow of $500 per year for only three additional years after payback, while Investment B maintains a cash flow of $450 per year for six and two-thirds more years after payback has been achieved.

In effect, after payback Investment A will return an additional $1,500 while Investment B will return an additional $3,000 (6⅔ years × $450 per year). Whether Investment A or B is really more profitable is not known from the payback period analysis. Hence applying the years-to-payback method to the evaluation of investment alternatives weights near-year earnings heavily and distant earnings not at all. A drawback to the years-to-payback method is that it does not consider earnings of a project after the initial outlay has been paid back. However, if the company places emphasis on the liquidity value of the investment, this method offers some value.

Average Rate of Return

As compared with years to payback, the average rate of return measures capital productivity over the whole life of the investment. The method permits management to measure the profitability of the investment as compared with a standard of acceptable profitability: the company's cost of capital. The return is computed as the average profit or cost savings per year, after taxes, throughout the life of the project divided by one-half the investment. Considering our example:

	Investment A	*Investment B*
Investment outlay	$1,500	$1,500
Average annual savings	250	300
Project life	6 years	10 years
Average annual rate of return	$250/$750 = 33%	$300/$750 = 40%

Based on this method, management would select Investment B since it yields a higher return. However, since aggregate savings and investment are averaged over the life of·the project, the method does not take into account the time pattern of earnings and investments. Earnings in the early stages of the project's life are more valuable to management than later returns. Hence, to evaluate complex investment alternatives, it becomes necessary to weight near earnings more heavily than distant earnings, yet still be influenced by future returns. Such an approach combines the best of both methods previously discussed and is called discounted-cash-flow rate of return.

The discounted-cash-flow method, like the previous methods, enables management to measure the productivity of capital in terms of a rate of return on investment. This approach provides three distinct advantages over the years-to-payback and the average rate of return methods.

1. The timing of investment and cash flows is weighted so as to reflect the differences in the value of near and distant dollars.
2. It is recognized that cash flows are the essential ingredient; capitalization policy and the resulting book costs are irrelevant to capital decision making except where income taxes are affected.
3. Since income taxes have an important effect upon cash flows, they are figured into the analysis of project worth.

The first step of this technique is to multiply the net cash flow (inflow minus outflow) for the project for any time period by the discount factor for that period. The discounted cash flows are then accumulated for the entire life of the project, yielding the present value of the investment alternative.

There are, however, two variations of the discounted-cash-flow method. The first is to discount the cash flows at a rate of return that results in a present value equal to the investment outlay. With this approach, whether a project is accepted or rejected depends on whether the discounted rate of return is greater or less than the company's cost of capital. The second variation is to discount the cash flows using the company's cost of capital, then compare the resulting present value with the investment outlay. If the present value exceeds it, the project is accepted; if it falls below, the project is rejected. In addition projects can be ranked by various kinds of profitability indexes which reflect the amount or ratio of excess of present value over investment outlay.

Management has decided to evaluate Investment A and Investment B by means of the discounted-cash-flow method. As previously described, both investments have an initial expenditure of $1,500; however, Investment A yields a cash flow of $500 per year for only six years. Investment B, on the other hand yields a cash flow of $450 per year throughout its ten-year life. Management would like to determine which investment yields the larger present value using the company's cost of capital of 20 percent to discount the resulting cash flows. A table of discount factors was used to prepare the evaluation manually, with the result shown in Exhibit 70.

EXHIBIT 70   DISCOUNTED CASH FLOW, INVESTMENTS A AND B

	Investment A				*Investment B*		
Year	*Net Cash Flow*	*Discount Factor at 20%*	*Discounted Cash Flow*	*Year*	*Net Cash Flow*	*Discount Factor at 20%*	*Discounted Cash Flow*
0	($1,500)	1.000	($1,500)	0	($1,500)	1.000	($1,500)
1	500	.906	453	1	450	.906	408
2	500	.742	371	2	450	.742	327
3	500	.608	304	3	450	.608	274
4	500	.497	248	4	450	.497	223
5	500	.407	204	5	450	.407	183
6	500	.333	166	6	450	.333	150
	Present value		$ 246	7	450	.273	123
				8	450	.224	101
				9	450	.183	82
				10	450	.150	68
					Present value		$ 439

The analysis indicates that Investment B yields a greater excess of present value over the project cost and is therefore preferable to Investment A. This agrees with the selection made by the average rate of return method.

Having determined that Investment B is more profitable, management would like to calculate what the rate of return is for this project. This is the rate at which the sum of the discounted cash flows is equal to the $1,500 project cost (the present value will be $0). Since management does not have a computer to determine this rate of return, it has decided to manually calculate the discounted cash flow at a rate of 30 percent, as was done for 20 percent. (See Exhibit 71.) By plotting the present

EXHIBIT 71   DISCOUNTED CASH FLOW, INVESTMENT B, AT 30 PERCENT

Year	Net Cash Flow	Discount Factor at 30%	Discounted Cash Flow
0	($1,500)	1.000	($1,500)
1	450	.864	389
2	450	.640	288
3	450	.474	213
4	450	.351	158
5	450	.260	112
6	450	.193	87
7	450	.143	64
8	450	.106	48
9	450	.078	35
10	450	.058	26
	Present value		($ 80)

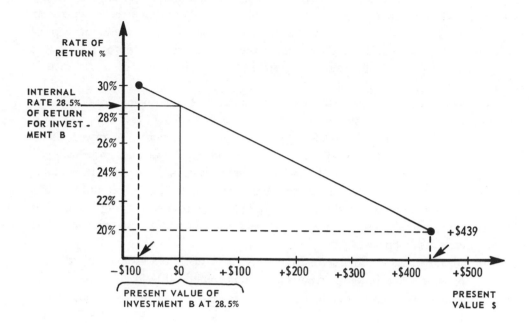

values for both rates of return and drawing a straight line between these two points, management can determine at approximately what rate the present value is equal to $0, as shown in Exhibit 72.

Using the graph in Exhibit 72, management has determined that the rate of return on this investment is approximately 28.5 percent; this yields a present value of the cash inflows (project income) and cash outflows (project cost) of $0. This return on investment is greater than the company's cost of capital and is acceptable to management. However, as compared with the average rate of return method, with which a 40 percent return was calculated for Investment B, the project does not seem as lucrative.

The discounted-cash-flow method does have certain limitations. Management is not as familiar with it as with years to payback and average rate of return and must therefore be educated in its use. Although the method appears initially to be complex, once the basic concept is understood the technique is easy to apply. Because of the computational nature of the method, a systematic procedure becomes necessary. Finally, because the cash flows do not correspond precisely to accounting concepts of costs and revenues, a special analysis may be needed for post-completion auditing of earnings on prior investments.

The underlying assumption in all three methods for evaluating capital investments is that the anticipated earnings will in fact be realized. The shortcomings of such an assumption are obvious. Since the return on a capital investment occurs in the future after the outlay has been made, there is a degree of uncertainty in achieving these returns. Moreover, the longer the period of return, the more uncertain management is as to what the future holds. A natural extension of the economic analysis is to consider the riskiness of the investment.

Risk Analysis in Capital Investment Decisions

The term *risk* as applied to capital investment decisions involves management's determination of the chances of achieving a certain level of earnings over time. There are several ways to introduce the concept of risk. By setting a very high cost of capital cutoff or a low years-to-payback limit, management can exclude many projects that do not have such a high liquidity value. Using such an approach, management is thus faced with the problem of establishing a reasonable rate of return that considers risk.

Another approach to introducing risk in the capital investment decision is for management to determine the chances of achieving the revenues and costs associated with the project. By relying on historical experience in previous investments or on management's judgment of a new venture, certain probability factors can be assigned to the cash inflows and outflows. Considering the analysis of Investment B, management had determined that the expected revenue would be $500 per year and the costs associated with the project would be $200 per year; the resultant saving being $300 per year. With a depreciation of $150 per year, management's best estimate of the investment's cash inflow was $450 per year.

The sales manager has had second thoughts about his initial estimate of revenue. After having surveyed historical reports on income generated by similar projects, the sales manager has noted that annual revenues have ranged between $350 and $600. Of the ten projects surveyed, five generated revenues between $350 and $450, three ranged between $450 and $550, and two ranged between $550 and $600. As a result of the review, management has decided to assign probabilities to the middle of the range of revenues surveyed; they expect there is a 50 percent chance that revenue will be approximately $400, a 30 percent chance that it will be $500, and a 20 percent chance that it will be $575. Having introduced the concept of risk, their next step was to determine the rate of return for this investment on the basis of the specified ranges of revenue and an assumed constant cost of $200. The following were the results:

Revenues	Percent of Probability	Rate of Return (Percent)
$400	50	20.0
500	30	28.5
575	20	34.1

This analysis illustrates that rate of return for Investment B covered a range from 20.0 to 34.1 percent. Moreover, there seems to be an equal chance that the investment's rate of return will be less than, equal to, or greater than 28.5 percent as indicated by the probability distribution. It is also important to note how sensitive the investment's rate of return is to changes in the project's revenues; a decrease in revenues from $500 to $425 results in an 8.5 percent drop in the rate of return (from 28.5 to 20.0 percent).

As compared with the results demonstrated in the discounted-cash-flow method, in which a single value of return of 28.5 percent was calculated, the risk analysis approach provides management with a view of the variability of returns and the chances of achieving these returns. Management can also evaluate how sensitive the project return is to certain cash flow ingredients (revenues and costs). On the other hand, risk analysis seems to be a complex tool to apply. The approach becomes extremely computational when there is an increase in the number of different revenue, cost, and investment factors associated with the project. Also as probabilities may or may not be interdependent, computer processing is necessary for an accurate evaluation of risk. For example, the quantity of physical product sold (such as tons) from a new plant is interdependent with the variable cost of production, but the price of such shipments is not interdependent with cost.

Regardless of the method or approach used, much analyst and management time is wasted in considering and debating the relative merits of the economic evaluation methods. Each highlights a particular feature of the evaluation, such as the time within which an investment will be recovered or the rate of return on the money invested. What is needed is a composite evaluation that shows all these factors. Once the procedures are established and incorporated into a manual, computations on more than one basis can be made in an hour or so; it is therefore recommended that this procedure be followed.

The department requesting the capital appropriation usually prepares the basic computations, generally with the assistance of the budget director or other staff officers, and completes a request-for-appropriation form in accordance with prescribed rules. This form then circulates to the various approving officers and to the directors for authorization or modification. Thereafter, each approved project is entered in a project status report and is reported on periodically as a means of keeping expenditures in line with budget objectives and authorized appropriations (see Exhibit 73). The total amount of projected authorized expenditures forms the basis for the capital expenditure budget for the ensuing year and, when supplemented by estimates of anticipated future appropriations, provides the basis for the long-range plan.

The annual capital expenditure budget summarizes the total appropriations budgeted by project, by the projected return on investment, and by the forecast expenditures in the current year and in subsequent years. Exhibit 74 illustrates such a summarized budget. Class A projects are presented on the basis of return on investment, and class B are considered necessary replacements not subject to a return evaluation. Note, however, that the total budget shows a return on investment for all capital projects, including class B, of 21 percent. This is shown so that management can be assured of having an adequate balance of return-producing projects and "necessity" projects.

The process of budgeting capital expenditures and controlling performance in accordance with authorized objectives must be formalized to insure an understanding of the requirements and compliance with management desires in this area. This can best be accomplished by means of a manual.

The best tests of a planning and control system are the results achieved. In the case of capital budgeting this involves a comparison of actual costs with the projected costs of the facility and a comparison of actual benefits and savings with those anticipated. Cost comparisons are generally made in any formalized system.

Benefits or savings comparisons, however, are usually not made, but they add the much-needed finishing touch to a capital budgeting system. This phase is sometimes referred to as the postcompletion audit and requires careful planning if it is to achieve the expected results. Very often, after-the-fact judgments are difficult to render be-

EXHIBIT 73

SAMPLE PAGE OF PROJECT STATUS REPORT

CONVEYOR EQUIPMENT COMPANY

PROJECT STATUS REPORT

Month ___May 19XX___

DIVISION ___Western___ LOCATION ___Los Angeles___ PROJECT NUMBER ___XX-8___

TITLE ___Revised Processing -- Line 1___

CLASS ___A___ PAYBACK PERIOD ___4___ YRS.

CATEGORY ___V___ RETURN ___24___ %

PROJECT APPROPRIATION AND INVESTMENT:

($ 000 OMITTED)	APPROVED AMOUNT		EXPENDED TO DATE	ESTIMATE TO COMPLETE	FORECAST (OVERRUN)/ UNDERRUN
	ORIGINAL	REVISED			
1. CAPITAL FACILITIES:					
LAND	$ --	--	--	--	--
BUILDINGS	--	--	--	--	--
MACHINERY & EQUIP.	$380,000	--	$218,315	$160,000	$ 1,685
OTHER: Leasehold Improvements	40,000	--	46,220	2,000	(8,220)
TOTAL	$420,000	--	$264,535	$162,000	$(6,535)
2. RELATED EXPENSES:					
SITE PREPARATION	$ 15,000	--	$ 17,500	$ 2,500	$(5,000)
REARRANGEMENT	5,000	--	3,200	1,000	800
TESTING	30,000	--	5,100	20,000	4,900
OTHER:					
TOTAL	$ 50,000	--	$ 25,800	$ 23,500	$ 700
3. WORKING CAPITAL	$ 8,000	--	--	$ 8,000	--
GRAND TOTAL	$478,000	0	$290,335	$193,500	$(5,835)

COMMENTS (OVERRUNS AND UNDERRUNS THAT ARE SIGNIFICANT MUST BE EXPLAINED AS TO CAUSE AND CORRECTIVE ACTION IN COMPLETE DETAIL) :

Installation has experienced difficulty with electrical system and power fluctuation which was unanticipated in project proposal. Problem has now been solved with the help of the Power Co. Request for revised budget is in process.

SIGNED: DIVISION MANAGER ___[signature]___ DIVISION CONTROLLER ___[signature]___

EXHIBIT 74   ILLUSTRATION OF ANNUAL CAPITAL EXPENDITURE BUDGET

(*Conveyor Equipment Company*)

Investment Request

Class	Category 19— Budget Year	Project No.	Project Title	Capital	Related Expenses	Total Appropriation	Net Working Capital	Total	Project Life (Yrs.)
A	II	X–1	New England Gear & Machinery Plant	$ 4,861,000	$420,000	$ 5,281,000	$ 290,000	$ 5,571,000	15
A	III	X–4	Facilities-Contract Y	9,400,000	—	9,400,000	6,200,000	15,600,000	3
A	V	X–2	Casting Reamer and Polishers	50,000	2,000	52,000	—	52,000	5
A	*Total*			$14,311,000	$422,000	$14,733,000	$6,490,000	$21,223,000	—
B	IX	X–3	Lubrication and Painting Facility	102,600	7,000	109,600	—	109,600	7
A + B			Total Budget	$14,413,600	$429,000	$14,842,600	$6,490,000	$21,332,600	—

Forecast Expenditures

Class	Category 19— Budget Year	Project No.	Project Title	Return on Investment	Annual Capital Cost	Current Year First Half	Current Year Second Half	Next Year	Subsequent Years
A	II	X–1	New England Gear & Machinery Plant	12.6%	$ —	$2,100,000	$ 1,315,000	$ 511,000	$1,645,000
A	III	X–4	Facilities-Contract Y	22.4%	—	1,000,000	14,100,000	500,000	—
A	V	X–2	Casting Reamer and Polishers	9.8%	—	52,000	—	—	—
A	*Total*			21.1%*	$ —	$3,152,000	$15,415,000	$1,011,000	$1,645,000
B	IX	X–3	Lubrication and Painting Facility	—	28,673	62,600	47,000	—	—
A + B			Total Budget	21.0%*	$28,673	$3,214,600	$15,462,000	$1,011,000	$1,645,000

* Composite rate.

cause the necessary data have not been accumulated in the period between activation of the facility and date of the audit. For example, if a piece of equipment is installed this year to achieve savings in certain costs over its ten-year life, an effective post-completion audit after the first three years or other prescribed period for such audits would not be possible if the pertinent costs were not accumulated in a meaningful way from the date of operation. These audit requirements should also be spelled out in a manual and should prove to be the most effective deterrent to a continuing optimistic bias in capital appropriation and budgeting.

Capital Expenditures Budget Manual

In this chapter we have referred to the value of a capital expenditures budget manual. To assist those who wish to formalize the capital expenditures process, the following sample manual for the hypothetical Conveyor Equipment Company concludes the chapter. This manual is divided into three parts. Part I is the introduction, which discusses the determination of a capital budget, the authorization to expend funds, the definition of "project," and the classifications and categories of expenditures. Part II deals with general procedures, such as those pertinent to the preparation and submission of the capital expenditures budget, the authorization to expend funds, the capital budget and expenditures status report, the evaluation of capital expenditures, and the postcompletion review. Part III contains the following forms and tables, along with detailed instructions regarding their use:

- Form 1—Capital Expenditure Request.
- Form 2—Return on Investment and Payback Calculation.
- Form 3—Schedule of Investment and Depreciation.
- Form 4—Description of Economic Factors and Justification.
- Form 5—Calculation of Computed Annual Cost.
- Table A—Continuous Interest and Discount Table.
- Table B—Cumulative Discount Table.

The sample manual for Conveyor Equipment Company is not meant to serve as a model that all businesses should rigidly adopt; rather, it is a model that companies should mold to fit their particular needs.

CAPITAL EXPENDITURES MANUAL

PART I: INTRODUCTION

Proper control of expenditures for capital facilities requires consideration of:

1. The relationship of the expenditures to the long-range plans of the Company.
2. The Company's financial position and the availability of funds for capital facilities.
3. The coordination and integration of the proposed expenditures with the annual profit plan and balance sheet budget.
4. The careful examination of the economic justification and business need for the proposed capital expenditures.
5. The coordination and review of capital expenditures to assure minimum duplication of operating effort and maximum utilization of facilities among all divisions.
6. The effect of the expenditures on the overall profitability of each Division and the Company.

Determination of Capital Budget

Annually each Division shall submit a capital expenditure budget for the ensuing year, prepared in accordance with procedures and timing established by the Budget Director, who shall prepare a consolidated budget proposal for review by the President and for submission to the Board of Directors. Based on this report and on consideration of the financial position of the Company, the Chairman of the Board shall recommend to the Board of Directors for its consideration an aggregate amount which can be expended for capital facilities during the ensuing year. The President shall then designate an aggregate amount for each Division. Transfers of amounts between Divisions shall be made on approval of the President.

If changes in circumstances make it advisable to increase or decrease the aggregate amount authorized for the year, the President shall submit his recommendation to the Board of Directors for its action.

The approval of an aggregate amount for the year indicates the willingness of the Board of Directors to allocate a given amount for the purpose of acquiring capital facilities as a necessary part of the Company's overall budget planning but does not constitute approval actually to commit or expend funds for specific projects or for the acquisition of equipment.

Authorization to Expend Funds

Authorization to expend funds for specific capital facilities projects shall be obtained by submission of individual capital expenditure requests in accordance with procedures outlined by the Budget Director. Individual capital expenditure requests provided for in the annual budget shall require the approval of the Chairman of the Board for requests of $50,000 or more, of the President for requests of $10,000–$50,000, and of the appropriate Division Manager for requests of less than $10,000. For individual capital expenditure requests not included in the annual budget, Board-of-Directors approval is required in addition to the above approval if either of the following applies:

  · The overall budgeted amount for the Company is increased or decreased.
  · The amount exceeds the established amount for specific identification in the annual budget presentation.

The President may delegate to Corporate Officers authority to approve individual capital expenditure requests up to specified amounts, which shall vary depending upon the size of the project and other factors.

Definition of a Project

A project is an integral unit which would logically be considered for the investment of Company funds. Therefore, a project should include all expenditures required for a specific business purpose; for example, a project for construction of a storage facility must include not only the expenditure for land and building but also all equipment and other items necessary to place the facility in operation for its intended business purpose. However, a project will not be construed to be a consolidation of purchases or investments which are independent; that is, any one of which could be acquired separately, both with respect to serving a business purpose and complying with sound purchasing practices regarding economic order quantities.

In connection with a contract proposal involving a capital expenditure request, the term "project" shall encompass the overall contract proposal and all capital expenditures which will be required to complete performance of the contract.

Classification and Categories of Capital Expenditures

Capital expenditures are either for necessary projects or for optional projects. Necessary projects include those required by law, for safety, or for replacement of nonoperative equipment. Optional projects arise in connection with plant expansion, new ventures, changed techniques, and replacement of still-operative equipment. In the case of necessary projects, the capital expenditure should be kept at the minimum possible consistent with sound economics. In the case of optional projects, an important consideration shall be the predicted return on investment; and, all other things being equal, preference shall be given to those projects demonstrating the best rate of return on investment.

Every capital expenditure request shall be classified according to its economic consequence and category of investment as follows:

- Class *A*—profit producing through additional revenues or cost savings. This class refers to expenditures for plant and facilities for the purpose of producing and marketing a new product (Category 1), expanding the production or marketing of an existing product (Category 2), producing and delivering under proposed contracts (Category 3), improving the quality of product or customer services (Category 4), or replacing or improving existing facilities or equipment to reduce costs (Category 5).
- Class *B*—cost in terms of profit reduction. This class refers to expenditures for facilities and equipment for the purpose of meeting the requirement of local ordinances (Category 6), improving or maintaining employee morale or safety (Category 7), replacing nonoperative equipment (Category 8), improving capability in research and engineering (Category 9), improving capability in other areas (Category 10), or meeting requirements under previously approved projects or contracts which do not produce additional revenues for that project or contract or result in cost savings (Category 11).

Expenditures for capital facilities usually include costs which for accounting and tax purposes are expensed rather than capitalized. All capital expenditure requests shall include information with respect to both categories of disbursements, and the total of both shall determine the approval required.

PART II: GENERAL PROCEDURES

The purpose of these procedures is as follows: to establish sound administrative procedures for Conveyor Equipment Company and its Divisions governing the appropriation of funds for the acquisition of capital facilities; to establish uniform practices governing the preparation and the submission of the annual capital expenditure budget and revisions thereof for approval by the Board of Directors; to establish a uniform system for the preparation, submission, and approval of capital expenditure requests, including the evaluation thereof; to establish a uniform system for postcompletion review of the operating results obtained as a result of approved capital expenditures.

Section 1: Definitions

Appropriated amount. The appropriated amount consists of the sum to be expended for the capital facilities as defined below plus the related expenses required in connection with rearrangement and installation of such facilities.

Capital facilities. Capital facilities are defined as permanent or semipermanent items in the following classifications as determined by the Chart of Accounts in use by the Company:

1. Land and improvements.
2. Buildings and improvements.
3. Machinery and equipment.
4. Office furniture, fixtures, and equipment.
5. Automotive equipment.
6. Engineering and technical equipment.
7. Research and development equipment.
8. Leasehold improvements.

Annual capital expenditure budget. This budget is defined as the proposed amount to be expended for capital facilities and related expenses during the ensuing year as finally approved by the President and the Board of Directors.

Capital expenditure request. This is the document used to obtain approval for the actual expenditure of the funds as provided in the budget or to obtain approval of projects not covered by the budget.

Capital budget and expenditure status report. This is a periodic report required to indicate the status of each budget and each approved capital expenditure request.

Evaluation of capital expenditure requests. Each expenditure shall be evaluated in terms of its economic consequences, which (1) for profit-producing projects is based upon the discounted-cash-flow and payout methods of return evaluation and (2) for nonprofit-producing projects, upon the annual cost of capital. Each capital expenditure request shall be supported in accordance with the instructions under Section 5.

Section 2: Preparation and Submission of Annual Capital Expenditure Budget

Annually, at dates to be established by the Budget Director, each Division shall submit its contemplated capital expenditure budget requirements for the ensuing year, including spending plans for subsequent years for projects which will take more than one year to complete.

The capital expenditure budget shall be submitted by operating division or major location, and the projects contemplated shall be arranged by class and category (see Part I of this manual). The capital expenditure budget shall be integrated with each Division's annual profit plan and balance sheet budget.

The contemplated capital expenditures shall be summarized in accordance with the following format:

1. *General.* Individual projects in excess of the limitation established for each Division shall be listed separately by class and category. All other projects shall be summarized by class and category and shown in total for each class and category.
2. *Budget format.* The budget format shall include columns as follows:
   (*a*) Class and category.
   (*b*) Project number.
   (*c*) Project title.

(*d*) Investment request.
    (1) Capital.
    (2) Related expenses.
    (3) Total appropriation.
    (4) Maximum net working capital requirements, if any.
    (5) Total investment.
(*e*) Project life.
(*f*) Return-on-investment percent.
(*g*) Annual capital cost.
(*h*) Forecast expenditures.
    (1) Current year—first half, second half.
    (2) Next year.
    (3) Subsequent years.

The Budget Director shall advise the Division Controllers of the approved budget amounts.

The approval of the capital expenditure budget indicates the willingness of the Board of Directors to allocate a given amount for the purpose of acquiring capital facilities but does not constitute approval to actually commit or expend funds for specific projects. Authorization to expend funds is conferred by the approval of a capital expenditure request under procedures outlined in Section 3, immediately following.

Section 3: Authorization to Expend Funds

General. Authorization to expend funds for specific capital facilities projects shall be obtained by submission of Form 1, Capital Expenditure Request. The instructions for preparing Form 1, including supporting data and the form itself, are set forth in Part III, Section 1, of this manual.

Requirements for submission and approval. Form 1 shall be prepared for each project. Requests for projects approved in the capital expenditure budget shall be submitted as follows: to Budget Director for all expenditures in excess of the amount established for each Division; to the Division General Manager for projects having expenditures less than the amount established for headquarters' approval.

Request for expenditures for projects not included in the capital expenditure budget shall be submitted as follows:

1. When the Division capital expenditure budget is increased thereby, submit the request to the Budget Director for approval of the President and Board of Directors.
2. When the Division capital expenditure budget is not increased thereby, and if—
    (*a*) The appropriated amount exceeds the amount established for specific identification in the annual capital expenditure budget, submit the request to the Budget Director for approval by the President and the Board of Directors.
    (*b*) The appropriated amount does not exceed the amount established for specific identification, submit the request to the Division General Manager.

Requests for additional expenditures to cover overruns on previously approved projects shall be submitted as follows: to the Budget Director for overruns in excess of 5 percent of the originally approved amount or $100,000, whichever is smaller; to the Division General Manager for all others.

Authorization to cancel a previously approved project will be obtained from the same executives who were originally required to approve the project.

The Budget Director will advise Operating Divisions and Department Heads of approval or disapproval of capital expenditure requests as applicable.

Section 4: Capital Budget and Expenditure Status Report

A monthly report reflecting the current status of the capital expenditure budget and of approved capital expenditure requests shall be submitted by project in substantially the following format.

General. (1) Individual projects in excess of the limitation established for each Division shall be listed separately by class and category. (2) All other projects shall be summarized by class and category and shown in total for each class and category. (3) Projects carried forward from prior years shall be summarized as required by (1) and (2) above.

Specific format. The following format will be prepared by budget year:

1. Class and category.
2. Project number.
3. Project title.
4. Approved budget. Original—amount approved at annual review by Board of Directors. Revised—amount subsequently approved, if any.
5. Approved capital expenditure requests. Original—amounts approved at initial submission of request. Revised—the sum of the originally approved request and any additional approved amounts.
6. Actual expenditures—year to date and total to date.
7. Unappropriated budget. Represents the amount of budget for which capital expenditure requests have not been approved.
8. Unexpended appropriation. Represents the amount by which approved capital expenditure requests exceed total expenditures to date.
9. Estimated cost to complete. Best estimate of the remaining expenditures required to complete the project.
10. Over/under. Difference between unexpended appropriations and estimated cost to complete.

Section 5: The Evaluation of Capital Expenditures

General. The desirability of any capital expenditure must be based in part on an evaluation of its economic consequences. In view of the fact that all requests for capital expenditures must compete for the supply of available funds, requests should be evaluated in terms of a common denominator which sets forth the profitability or capital cost of each request. Such a common denominator will provide management with a yardstick for judging the financial merits of widely differing types of proposals.

Measurement of return on capital expenditures. The method of computing return on investment to be used is the discounted-cash-flow method. Basically, this method takes into account, in addition to the amount of return that will be earned, the timing of disbursements and receipts by the Company. This timing affects the profitability of an investment, because a dollar received today is worth more than a dollar to be received in the future.

The mechanics of the discounted-cash-flow method consist essentially of finding the interest rate that discounts future cash receipts of a project down to a present value equal to the cash disbursements required by the project. This interest rate is the rate of return on that investment.

It should be noted that this method of computing a percentage return deals with cash flows as opposed to the more conventional financial concepts of net income and book value of investment. The flow of cash involves both outflow and inflow. The cash flowing

EVALUA-
TION 1

PROPOSAL *A*

Year	Investment	Income Before Taxes and Depreciation	Net Income	Depreciation	Cash Flow	Disc. Factor 20%	Discounted Cash Flow
0	($1,000)	$ —	$ —	$ —	($1,000)	1.000	($1,000)
1	—	400	33	333	366	.906	332
2	—	400	67	267	334	.742	248
3	—	400	100	200	300	.608	182
4	—	400	133	133	266	.497	132
5	—	400	167	67	234	.407	95
		$2,000	$500	$1,000	$ 500		($ 11)

By interpolation, it can be found that the discounted cash flow would total zero when the rate of return is 19.5 percent.

EVALUA-
TION 2

PROPOSAL *B*

Year	Investment	Income Before Taxes and Depreciation	Net Income	Depreciation	Cash Flow	Disc. Factor 15%	Discounted Cash Flow
0	($1,000)	$ —	$ —	$ —	($1,000)	1.000	($1,000)
1	—	200	(67)	333	266	.929	247
2	—	300	16	267	283	.799	226
3	—	400	100	200	300	.688	206
4	—	500	184	133	317	.592	188
5	—	600	267	67	334	.510	170
		$2,000	$500	$1,000	$ 500		$ 37

By interpolation, the correct rate of return equals 16.7 percent.

EVALUA-
TION 3

PROPOSAL *C*

Year	Investment	Income Before Taxes and Depreciation	Net Income	Depreciation	Cash Flow	Disc. Factor 25%	Discounted Cash Flow
0	($1,000)	$ —	$ —	$ —	($1,000)	1.000	($1,000)
1	—	600	134	333	467	.885	413
2	—	500	116	267	383	.689	264
3	—	400	100	200	300	.537	161
4	—	300	84	133	217	.418	91
5	—	200	66	67	133	.326	43
		$2,000	$500	$1,000	$ 500		($ 28)

By interpolation, the correct rate of return equals 23.2 percent.

PAYBACK PERIOD

Year	*Cash Flow*		
	A	B	C
0	($1,000)	($1,000)	($1,000)
1	366	266	467
2	334	283	383
3	300	300	300
4		317	
5			
Payback period:	3 yrs.	3.52 yrs.	2.50 yrs.

out is represented by the disbursements (including capital, related expenses, and working capital additions) required by the project. The cash flowing in is the net profit (after taxes) or "saving" plus the depreciation produced by capitalized disbursements over the life of the project.

To illustrate the mechanics, consider Proposal A. This proposal involves a project having a five-year life and requiring a capital expenditure of $1,000. If this expenditure is made, it is estimated that the return or additional profit to the Company before taxes and depreciation will be $400 per year. Using the sum of the digits depreciation and a 50-percent tax rate, the resulting net income would be as shown in Evaluation 1. The annual cash inflow would be the net income plus the annual depreciation. In order to compute the return on investment for this project, it is necessary to use a discount table. Such a table simply shows the value today of a dollar received in each of five subsequent years, assuming a given rate of yield or return. In Evaluation 1, the assumed rate of return is 20 percent; a discount table would indicate that, at the 20 percent rate, $366 (the cash flow for Year 1) to be received one year hence is equivalent to $332 in hand today ($336 × .906).

It can be seen from Evaluation 1 that the net cash flow over the life of the project ($500) is equal to the net income over the life of the project, reflecting the recoupment, through depreciation, of the original cash disbursement. It should also be noted that when the net cash flow is discounted at the proper return rate, the total over the life of the project is zero, reflecting the fact that the net income is "consumed" by application of the correct return rate. Therefore, the return on the investment is that discount rate, found by trial and error, which equates the cash outflow with the cash inflow at the end of the project's life.

This illustration also reflects the inadequacy, when one evaluates a project, of relying on a percentage return computed by dividing the annual net income by the gross investment or by net book value of the investment. Such a ratio either fails to reflect the recovery of capital or changes radically as the book value decreases, and it does not give consideration to annual fluctuations in net income of the project.

As discussed earlier, the discounted-cash-flow method takes into account the timing of cash flows and therefore is a reliable yardstick for comparative evaluation of projects with widely different characteristics. As an illustration, it can be assumed that Proposal A is one of three possible alternatives, each requiring a $1,000 investment. The other two alternatives produce the same net cash flow ($500), but the income under Proposal B increases over the life of the project while the income under Proposal C declines. On the basis of economic evaluation (Evaluations 2 and 3), it is clear that Proposal *C* is the most profitable. Its cash flow returns more money in the early years.

It is useful to consider a measure of the risk involved in a capital expenditure—the payback period. This is defined as the length of time required to recover through cash inflow the amount of the original investment or cash outflow. Since this capital recovery period is the time when a portion of the expenditure is still "at risk," it's a rough guide of the degree of risk assumed. However, it cannot be considered a measure of the profitability of a project, because it is concerned only with the recovery of the amounts originally expended.

For example, regarding Proposals *A, B,* and *C,* the calculation of the payback period is as indicated by Evaluation 4.

Measurement of the computed annual capital cost of Class B *projects.* It is necessary to measure the financial impact of investments in facilities which are not specifically profit producing. This economic impact or cost of such a project can be considered as the amount of cash return that would have been achieved had the same expenditure been invested in a profit-producing project at a given rate of return.

Basic considerations. In order to evaluate a capital expenditure under prescribed Company procedure, it is necessary to develop estimates of the factors or components involved in computing the return on investment. The following components must be considered and are discussed here in general terms:

1. Investment.
2. Project life.
3. Additional revenue and cost saving.
4. Depreciation and income taxes.
5. Time characteristics.

The specific application of these concepts to a given proposal involves, in addition to an understanding of the concepts, good judgment and the proper coordination of specialized knowledge.

Regarding the *investment* component, a capital expenditure request will normally involve a commitment of Company funds through one or more of three types of disbursements: Type *A*—expenditures capitalized as part of the Company's property accounts; Type *B*—expenditures required for expenses incident to and necessary for placing capital equipment in operation; Type *C*—expenditures required for net working capital.

All three types of expenditures taken together represent the investment in a given project. Since all cash outlays must share the burden of earning a return, the failure to include expenditure requirements in any of the disbursement categories would understate the investment and overstate the projected return. To categorize expenditures by type is necessary to the evaluation, because each type has a different impact on the return calculation. To illustrate:

  · Type *A* expenditures determine the depreciation and thereby affect the timing of income tax payments and the cash flow.
  · Type *B* expenditures produce immediate income tax benefits which affect cash flow.
  · Type *C* expenditures are normally substantially recovered at the end of the project life rather than during the project life.

Regarding the second component of computing return on investment, *project life,* the revenue-producing life of a capital expenditure is a determinant of its profitability. Its life will normally be limited by one of three factors:

1. Its physical life; that is, the length of time it will operate at the projected operating rate before being worn out. In this connection, significant replacement parts, which are required to keep equipment operating and which are capitalized, should be con-

sidered as part of the investment to be acquired (cash outlay) in the year of replacement.

2. Its technological life; that is, the service life of equipment before obsolescence makes the procurement of new equipment necessary.

3. Its economic life for the intended use; that is, the period of intended use in the application specified.

Project life will normally be determined by the shortest of the three factors described, since any one limits the ability of the capital expenditure to continue to earn a return. When the economic life for the intended use is the limiting factor, however, the physical and technological lives may well have a bearing on the salvage value assumed.

When determining the return on a capital investment, one must estimate the *additional revenue or cost saving* that will result from making the investment. Since the return, in terms of revenue or savings, can result only from making the investment as opposed to not making it, the forecast additional revenue and cost saving should include only the incremental amounts directly associated with the proposed project. For example, under many proposals, fixed overhead expense will neither increase nor decrease as a result of accepting the proposal. To allocate a portion of such overhead to this kind of proposal would be unrealistic and fail to follow the economic facts.

On the other hand, any out-of-pocket expenses resulting from accepting the proposal must be considered in full, since if the proposal were not approved these costs would be avoided entirely. The process of forecasting additional revenue and cost savings for computing return on investment should be directed at estimating the net profit before income taxes and depreciation for each year of the project's life. Many factors have to be considered, only some of which are mentioned here for general guidance:

· The pricing and market potential of additional product units.

· The operating capacity and percent utilization of requested equipment and facilities.

· The cost of recurring maintenance and repair associated with such facilities.

· The manpower increase or decrease that would result from accepting the project.

· The need for or elimination of incremental supporting services.

· The increases or decreases in insurance cost, property taxes, and so on.

With reference to the fourth component of computing return on investment, *depreciation and income taxes,* depreciation must be considered separately, because it is both an element of cash inflow and a reduction of income before taxes. The interrelationship of this dual role is readily understood by reference to the concept of cash flow. The depreciation charge does not involve an outlay of cash but does reduce the cash outlay for income taxes. The depreciation rates used and the method of application with respect to any capital investment must be those prescribed by Company policy because they produce the amount of allowable depreciation for income tax purposes.

The fifth component of computing return on investment involves *timing.* Determination of the economic consequences of a project requires that careful consideration be given to the timing of the related expenditures and income. As pointed out earlier, the use of the discount factors in the return calculation gives greater weight to cash flow in the near future than in the distant future. It is apparent, therefore, that the failure to consider the time factor carefully will distort the calculated return.

Section 6: Postcompletion Review Performance

General. A postcompletion review of performance will be made annually by Division Controllers, covering all completed projects involving actual capital expenditures in excess of $10,000. These reviews will consist of comparisons of (1) actual expenditures for all elements of the investment with the forecast and approved amounts and (2) actual profit produced through added net revenues or cost savings with the forecast profit.

Reporting. The Division Controllers will transmit a copy of each postcompletion re-

FORM 1   CAPITAL EXPENDITURE REQUEST—CONVEYOR EQUIPMENT COMPANY

☐ Initial   ☐ Supplemental

(1) Division ——————— (2) Location ——————— (3) Date ————
(4) Project Title ————————————————— (5) Project No. ————
(6) Appropriated Amount ————————————— (7) Budget Year ————
(8) Is This Request Included in Annual Capital Expenditure Budget?   Yes   No

(9) Description of Project:	Summary of Economic Data:
	(10) Class ——— (11) Category ———
	(12) Project Life ——— Years
	(13) Request Based on Profitability ☐
	(14) Request Based on Business Need ☐
	(15) Return on Investment ——— %
	(16) Payback Period ——— Years
	(17) Computed Annual Cost $ ———

(18) Scheduled: Starting Date ——————— Completion Date ———————

(19) Description of Facilities to Be Retired or Replaced:	(20) Retirements (Item 19):
	Gross Book Value ———————
	Reserved ———————
	Net Book Value ———————
	Recovery Value ———————
	Gain or (Loss) ———————

(21) Estimated Cost of Project: (Must agree with Col. 1, Form 3)	(22) Expenditure Schedule:
Capital ———	Current Year— 1st Half ———
Related Expense ———	2nd Half ———
Total Appropriation (Enter as Item 6) ———	Next Year ———
Maximum Net Working Capital ———	Subsequent Years ———
Total Investment ———	Total ———

(23) Supporting Forms Attached: 2 ☐   3 ☐   4 ☐   5 ☐

(24) Requested By ————————————— Date ————
(25) Approved By and Date

Division Comptroller	Division General Manager
Controller	Budget Director
President	Chairman of Board

154

view to the Budget Director and to the Controller when the review discloses either of the following conditions: actual expenditures exceed the originally appropriated amount; actual return on investment is less than the forecast return.

PART III: INSTRUCTIONS

Instructions for the preparation of five forms are detailed in the following paragraphs. In addition to line-by-line instructions regarding the preparation of the forms, an explanation of their applicability and purpose is included.

Form 1: Capital Expenditure Request

Applicability. Form 1 will be completed for each project, regardless of the amount of funds requested. As supporting data, Forms 2–5 will be attached when appropriate. For every project in excess of prescribed limits, Form 1 and supporting forms, after their approval by the Division Controller and Division General Manager, will be submitted to the Budget Director for Company approval. For projects involving a total appropriation of less than prescribed limits, Form 1 and supporting forms will be retained at the Division level and will not be submitted to Company Headquarters except upon the specific request of the Budget Director.

Purpose. Form 1 summarizes pertinent information with respect to each project involving a capital expenditure. In addition, it serves as the record of management approval or disapproval of a capital expenditure request and thereby provides the authority to commit or expend Company funds.

Preparation. Form 1 should be completed in accordance with the following instructions, keyed to the numbered captions on the form:

1. Enter the name of the Division.
2. Enter the principal location submitting the request.
3. Enter the date on which Form 1 and supporting forms are completed by requesting location.
4. Enter the title of the project.
5. Enter a project number assigned by principal location in sequential order. The first two digits of the project number will indicate the budget year for which the appropriation is requested and will be separated from the remainder of the number by a dash (for example, 66-1, 66-2, and so on).
6. Enter the total amount of the appropriation requested, as shown in caption (21).
7. Enter budget year.
8. Indicate by a check mark whether the request was included in the annual capital expenditure budget. If the request was not included in the budget, refer to Part II of this manual.
9. Enter a brief description of the project. If this is a supplemental request, show the amount and project number of the original request.
10. Enter class of project.
11. Enter category of project.
12. Enter project life as shown on Form 4.
13. Check this box if this is an optional project submitted on the basis of producing added profit. This box will be checked for all Class *A* projects that are not mandatory for continued operation. Do not check this box for Class *B* projects.

FORM 2

CLASS *A* PROJECT—RETURN ON INVESTMENT AND PAYBACK CALCULATION

(*Conveyor Equipment Company*)

Division _____

Location _____

Project Title _____

Project Number _____

(1)	(2)	(3) Cash Outflow	(4) Cash Inflow	(5)	(6)	(7)	(8)	(9)	(10)	(11)	(12)
Calendar Year	Reference Year	Total Investment (Form 3, Column 6)	Operating Profit Before Depreciation and Income Tax (Form 4)	Depreciation and Related Expenses (Form 3, Column 8)	Total (Columns 4 + 5)	Total Cash Return (Col. 6 × 50%)	Net Cash Flow (Column 7 minus Column 3)	Discount Factors @ %	Discounted Cash Flow (Col. 8 × 9)	Discount Factors @ %	Discounted Cash Flow (Col. 8 × 11)
	−3										
	−2										
	−1										
	Reference Year										
	1										
	2										
	3										
	4										
	5										
	6										
	7										

Return on Investment _____ %

Payback Year _____

14. Check this box if this project represents either a mandatory expenditure for continued operation, whether or not it will produce added profit, or a desirable expenditure that is nonprofit producing. This box will always be checked for Class *B* projects and may be checked for a Class *A* project. The significance of "Business Need"—for example, desirability versus mandatory for continued operation—must be explained on Form 4.

15. Enter from Form 2 for Class *A* projects. If a Class *B* project, leave blank.

16. Enter from Form 2 for Class *A* projects. If a Class *B* project, leave blank.

17. Enter from Form 5, Line 6, for Class *B* projects. If a Class *A* project, leave blank.

18. Enter an estimate of starting and completion dates. The completion date is the date on which the project will be operative.

19. Enter a brief description of facilities which will be replaced or retired as a result of the project's approval.

20. Self-explanatory. The recovery value should be the net cash to be received upon disposal.

21. Self-explanatory.

22. Enter the timing of fund requirements for the total appropriation as shown in caption (6).

23. Self-explanatory.

24. Signature of requesting department head.

25. Self-explanatory. Division approvals must be completed *before* submission to the Budget Director.

Form 2: Return on Investment and Payback Calculation

Applicability. Form 2 will be completed to determine the return on investment and payback year for all Class *A* projects (that is, projects which are expected to produce profits through additional revenue or cost savings). This Form should be prepared after completion of Forms 3 and 4.

Purpose. The purpose of Form 2 is to summarize the information affecting the cash flow and to determine what rate of return will discount the net cash flow to zero. To accomplish this, it is necessary to reflect the cash outflow or total cash investment by year of expenditure and the cash inflow or total cash return by year of receipt. The total cash return is the net profit after income taxes plus the annual depreciation. To facilitate the forecasting of the total cash return, its elements are presented in a different format on Form 2, which accomplishes the same result, assuming an effective income tax rate of 50 percent. In other words, the net profit after income taxes plus the depreciation equals, assuming a 50 percent tax rate, one-half of the operating profit before depreciation plus the tax benefit of the depreciation provision (one-half of the depreciation).

As a result of this different format, the forecasting of the cash inflow for any project breaks down into two elements: (1) the operating profit, which is the profit or savings before deducting the depreciation, the related expenses, and the income taxes (the operating profit will be forecast by year on Form 4); (2) the depreciation and related expenses (to be scheduled by year on Form 3).

Preparation. To complete Form 2, proceed as follows:

1. Enter the appropriate calendar year in Column (1) on the line designated "Reference Year" in Column (2). The appropriate calendar year will be the year immediately preceding the first year in which the project will earn revenue as shown

TABLE A   CONTINUOUS INTEREST AND DISCOUNT TABLE

Years in Which Dollar Will Be Expended or Received	Percentage Return									
	5%	10%	15%	20%	25%	30%	40%	50%	60%	70%
Before Reference Point										
3	1.079	1.166	1.263	1.370	1.489	1.622	1.933	2.321	2.805	3.413
2	1.052	1.107	1.166	1.230	1.297	1.370	1.532	1.718	1.933	2.182
1	1.025	1.052	1.079	1.107	1.136	1.166	1.230	1.297	1.370	1.448
Reference Point	1.000	1.000	1.000	1.000	1.000	1.000	1.000	1.000	1.000	1.000
After Reference Point										
1	.975	.952	.929	.906	.885	.864	.824	.787	.752	.719
2	.928	.861	.799	.742	.689	.640	.553	.477	.413	.357
3	.883	.779	.688	.608	.537	.474	.370	.290	.227	.177
4	.840	.705	.592	.497	.418	.351	.248	.176	.124	.088
5	.799	.638	.510	.407	.326	.260	.166	.107	.068	.044
6	.760	.577	.439	.333	.254	.193	.112	.065	.037	.022
7	.723	.522	.378	.273	.197	.143	.075	.039	.021	.011
8	.687	.473	.325	.224	.154	.106	.050	.024	.011	.005
9	.654	.428	.280	.183	.120	.078	.034	.014	.006	.003
10	.622	.387	.241	.150	.093	.058	.023	.009	.003	.001
11	.592	.350	.207	.123	.073	.043	.015	.005	.002	.001
12	.563	.317	.178	.100	.057	.032	.010	.003	.001	Nil
13	.535	.287	.154	.082	.044	.024	.007	.002	.001	Nil
14	.509	.259	.132	.067	.034	.018	.005	.001	Nil	Nil
15	.484	.235	.114	.055	.027	.013	.003	.001	Nil	Nil

Reference point is the year immediately preceding the first year in which income or savings will be realized.

on Form 4. Complete the sequence of calendar years for the life of the project in Column (1).

2. Enter in Column (3) the information shown in Column (6), Form 3. Note: In entering information from other forms, be sure amounts are entered opposite the proper calendar years as shown in Column (1).

3. Enter in Column (4) the operating profit by year during the project's life.

4. Enter in Column (5) the information shown in Column (8), Form 3. •

5. Complete Columns (6) and (7), which are self-explanatory.

6. Enter in Column (8) the excess of Column (7) over Column (3) as a positive figure or the excess of Column (3) over Column (7) as a negative or bracketed ( ) figure.

7. Enter in Column (9) the discount factors from Table *A* (Continuous Interest and Discount Table) on a trial basis, at the return rate expected. The discount factor for the reference year will always be 1.000.

8. Enter in Column (10), for each year, the product of the amount in Column (8) multiplied by the discount factor in Column (9). Total Column (10). If the total is a minus figure, the discount factors from Table *A* represent a return rate that is too high. Select a lower return rate and repeat the procedure using Columns (11) and (12). If the total is a plus figure, the return rate selected is too low. Repeat procedure with a higher return rate. The correct rate of return, which may have to be found by interpolation, will produce a total in Column (10) of zero.

9. The correct return rate is to be stated on Form 2 and carried forward to Form 1.

10. Add, cumulatively, Column (8) to that point where the positive figures equal the negative figures and determine the year in Column (2) at that point. This year represents the payback year and should be entered on Form 2 and carried forward to Form 1.

Form 3: Schedule of Investment and Depreciation

Applicability. Form 3 will be prepared for both Class *A* and *B* projects; however, Columns (2) through (8) will not be completed for Class *B* projects.

Purpose. This form represents a schedule for determining the amount of the total Company investment required by the proposed project and, in the case of Class *A* projects, for determining the timing of expenditures, capital recovery, and depreciation. Form 3 is also used for the determination of the total depreciation and related expenses required for the return-on-investment calculation on Form 2.

It is important to recognize that, irrespective of the amount requested for capital expenditures, the commitment of funds may be required for expenses incident to placing capital facilities in operation and for net working capital necessary to support the operation. Such commitments must be completely anticipated and included in the investment base.

Preparation. Form 3 should be prepared as follows:

1. Column (1). Include the total Company investment required by the proposed project. Sections I, II, and III represent the total required cash outlay. For Section I, Capital Facilities, enter data as indicated. In "Other," include all capital facilities not designated, such as automotive equipment, leasehold improvements, research and development equipment, and so on. For Section II, Related Expense, enter all costs which will be charged as expenses in the accounts and which are required to place the capital facilities in operation. Do not include ordinary operating expenses, which will be considered in the projected annual profit or savings associated with the project and presented on Form 4. For Section III, Maximum Net Working Capital, enter the amount of additional net working capital that would be required by the project. The maximum net working capital shall represent the investment required by the project in current assets, net of any amounts which may be financed by suppliers and others. When the nature of the project requires an investment in net working capital, it must be remembered that such an investment normally builds up during the early years of the project and can be recovered in full at the end of the project's life.

2. Column (2). Summarize by year the expected timing of expenditures, capital recovery, and depreciation. Enter the calendar years for the period beginning with the year expenditures are made or the year salvage revenue is obtained for facilities retired or replaced, whichever is earlier, and terminating with the end of the project's life.

3. Columns (3), (4), and (5). Enter as a positive figure by year the capital expenditures for capital facilities, related expenses, and net working capital. Enter as a negative figure, in the appropriate year and column, the salvage value to be obtained for facilities being retired or replaced (Form 1, Item 20); and enter the amount of salvage value or working capital which is expected to be recovered in

FORM 3

SCHEDULE OF INVESTMENT AND DEPRECIATION—CONVEYOR EQUIPMENT COMPANY

Division ———————
Location ———————

Project Title ———————
Project Number ———————

	(1)	(2)	Timing of Expenditures, Capital Recovery, and Depreciation					
			(3)	(4)	(5)	(6)	(7)	(8)
Investment	*Total*	*Year*	*Capital Facilities*	*Related Expense*	*Net Working Capital*	*Total (Cols. 3 − 5)*	*Depreciation*	*Depreciation and Related Expenses (Col. 4 + 7)*
I. Capital Facilities								
Land								
Buildings								
Machinery & equipment								
Other								
Total capital facilities								
II. Related Expense								
Site preparation								
Rearrangement								
Testing								
Other								
Total expense								
III. Maximum Net Working Capital	——							
Total investment	══							

cash, all of which normally occur in the year following the final year of the project's life.

4. Column (6). Total by year Columns (3) through (5).
5. Column (7). This column will include in total by year the depreciation on capital facilities during the life of the project. It is necessary, therefore, to compute the annual depreciation over the depreciable life for each asset category on the basis of depreciation rates prescribed by Company policy. Any difference at the end of the economic life of the project between the net book value and the expected salvage value should be considered additional depreciation in the year of disposal or salvage (normally the year following the final year of the project's life).
6. Column (8). Total by year Columns (4) and (7).

Form 4: Description of Economic Factors and Justification

Applicability. Form 4 will be prepared for all capital expenditure requests, regardless of the project class or amount of funds requested. This form will specifically support Form 1, the Capital Expenditure Request.

Purpose. The purposes of Form 4 are as follows:

1. To describe the purpose, scope, and background of the project and to explain its relationship to the long-range plans of the Division and Company.
2. To describe the capital equipment presently in use that will be disposed of.
3. To discuss what assumptions were considered in determining the amount and timing of the investment of Company funds as scheduled on Form 3.
4. To present a forecast of the project's life, stating assumptions made.
5. To present a forecast of the cash revenue and costs or cost savings attributable to the project over the life of the project, stating the assumptions made.
6. To describe the desirability or need of making the proposed expenditure, relating such narrative justification specifically to the return on investment or computed annual cost as shown on Forms 2 or 5, respectively.
7. To discuss alternative courses of action which might be pursued to accomplish the objective of the project. To the extent that alternatives might be feasible (such as leasing) and to the extent that the rate of return might be better or the computed annual cost lower, such alternatives should be evaluated on Forms 2 or 5, as applicable.
8. To present any other information which should be considered by the approval authority in reviewing the project.

It is important to recognize that all of the economic factors bearing on a capital expenditure request cannot be reduced to measurable quantities. Therefore, it is an important purpose of Form 4 to relate such nonmeasurable factors to the profitability of the project as computed from the economic factors which can be measured.

Preparation. The preparation of Form 4 should conform to the purposes just listed. Depending upon the nature of the project, all or some of the following subjects require development in determining the forecast of operating income, costs, or savings to be derived from the project:

- The pricing and market potential of additional product units.
- The operating capacity and percent utilization of requested equipment and facilities.
- The manpower increase or decrease that would result from accepting the project.

- The cost of recurring maintenance and repair associated with the requested facilities.
- The cost of nonrecurring or special expenses.
- The need for incremental supporting services.
- The increase or decrease in insurance cost, property taxes, and so on.
- The integration of proposed operations with other existing operations.
- The capacity of and impact on present distribution facilities.
- The need for and availability of utilities and services.

In the case of Class *A* projects, the forecast of operating profit should be shown in the form of a profit and loss statement, indicating income and expense accounts affected by the project. In the case of Class *B* projects, the amount of annual out-of-pocket expense (if any) associated with the project should be estimated.

Form 5: Calculation of Computed Annual Cost

Applicability. Form 5 will be completed to determine the computed annual cost of each Class *B* project (that is, projects which are not expected to produce profits through additional revenues or cost savings). This form should be prepared after completion of Forms 3 and 4.

Purpose. The purpose of Form 5 is to present a measure of the economic consequence of expending corporation funds for a Class *B* project. This measure is a computed annual cost, throughout the project life, which represents the amount of forgone return that could have been achieved had the same sum of money been invested in a Class *A* project at a prescribed rate of return. In effect, a dollar invested in a nonprofit-producing

FORM 4   DESCRIPTION OF ECONOMIC FACTORS AND JUSTIFICATION
                (Conveyor Equipment Company)

Division ——————————— Location ——————————— Date ————

Project Title ——————————————————————— Project No. ————

——————————————————————————————————————
——————————————————————————————————————
——————————————————————————————————————
——————————————————————————————————————

FORM 5   CLASS *B* PROJECT—CALCULATION OF COMPUTED ANNUAL COST
                (Conveyor Equipment Company)

Division————————————   Project Title ———————————

Location————————————   Project Number ——————————

1. Total investment $ —————
2. Economic life in years   —————
3. Table factor (at prescribed rate of return)   —————
4. Annual cost (Line 1 ÷ Line 3) $ —————
5. Annual out-of-pocket cost @ 50% $ —————
6. Computed annual cost of project (Line 4 + Line 5) $ —————

CUMULATIVE DISCOUNT TABLE

Percentage Return

Life of Project Year	5%	10%	15%	20%	25%	30%	40%	50%	60%	70%
1	.975	.952	.929	.906	.885	.864	.824	.787	.752	.719
2	1.903	1.813	1.728	1.648	1.574	1.504	1.377	1.264	1.165	1.076
3	2.786	2.592	2.416	2.256	2.111	1.978	1.747	1.554	1.392	1.253
4	3.626	3.297	3.008	2.753	2.529	2.329	1.995	1.730	1.516	1.341
5	4.425	3.935	3.518	3.160	2.855	2.589	2.161	1.837	1.584	1.385
6	5.185	4.512	3.957	3.493	3.109	2.782	2.273	1.902	1.621	1.407
7	5.908	5.034	4.335	3.766	3.306	2.925	2.348	1.941	1.642	1.418
8	6.595	5.507	4.660	3.990	3.460	3.031	2.398	1.965	1.653	1.423
9	7.249	5.935	4.940	4.173	3.580	3.109	2.432	1.979	1.659	1.426
10	7.871	6.322	5.181	4.323	3.673	3.167	2.455	1.988	1.662	1.427
11	8.463	6.672	5.388	4.446	3.746	3.210	2.470	1.993	1.664	1.428
12	9.026	6.989	5.566	4.546	3.803	3.242	2.480	1.996	1.665	—
13	9.561	7.276	5.720	4.628	3.847	3.266	2.487	1.998	1.666	—
14	10.070	7.535	5.852	4.695	3.881	3.284	2.492	1.999	—	—
15	10.554	7.770	5.966	4.750	3.908	3.297	2.495	2.000	—	—

project means one less dollar to invest in a profit-producing project, and the profit given up thereby is the measure of the cost of investing in nonprofit-producing projects.

Preparation. Form 5 is prepared as follows:

1. The total investment to be entered in Line 1 will be computed by subtracting from the total investment, as shown on Form 3, Column (1), 50 percent of the total expenses (if any) shown on Form 3, Column (1), Section II, and the recovery value of replaced or retired facilities (if any) as shown on Form 1, Item 20. The resultant figure will be shown as the total investment. This procedure gives effect to the tax benefit of the immediate expense deduction and to the cash recovery of replaced equipment, if any.

2. Enter on Line 2 the economic life in years as shown on Form 4.

3. Enter on Line 3 the discount factor to be found in Table *B,* Cumulative Discount Table. To find the factor, read down the column under the prescribed rate of return to the year which represents the economic life of the project. The figure in the column opposite that year represents the factor to be entered on Line 3. The prescribed rate of return will be furnished by the Budget Director each year.

4. Complete Line 4 as shown.

5. Enter one-half of any projected annual out-of-pocket costs resulting specifically from the project. Such costs should be described on Form 4.

6. Complete Line 6 as shown.

9

The Treasurer
and the Balance Sheet Budget

MOST BUSINESSMEN probably think of budgeting in terms of operations or in terms of the profit-and-loss statement. The basic purpose of budgetary planning and control, however, is to assist the company to earn an acceptable return on investment. This requires not only budgeting the return or earnings but also planning and controlling the investment.

The level of investment assumes great importance in business, because (1) earnings are not possible without resources and (2) corporate resources are generally limited and must be used for the most profitable opportunities. Therefore, the efficiency with which resources are employed has a significant effect on corporate profitability. While it is basically true that the maintenance of an adequate investment base ultimately depends on reasonable earnings, it is not always true that current profits will insure an adequate investment base. In fact, there have been examples where rapidly growing concerns, even though profitable, have experienced serious cash and working capital shortages. And there have been other companies, with shrinking sales and profits, that experienced the apparently incongruous result of accumulating large cash balances.

What these situations illustrate is that the balance sheet represents the level of net resources available to generate and support a given level of operations. If a business expects to expand its operating activities, as most businesses do, management must plan to increase the level of net resources or to work present resources harder.

Treasurers are generally aware of the importance of sufficient cash to finance operations and of the need for good working capital turnover. Despite these considerations, you will probably agree that many companies fail to include the budgeting of investment as a part of normal profit planning in the annual budget cycle. We suspect that the major reason for this condition may be the superficially correct assumption that the composition of the balance sheet will take care of itself if the planning and control of income and of expenses are properly carried out. Furthermore, as noted in prior chapters, meaningful operational planning requires establishing finished goods inventory levels to coordinate the marketing plan with the production plan; in turn, raw materials and work-in-process requirements will be determined by the production-planning and purchases budgets. The capital expenditure budget will largely determine the level of fixed assets employed. The difficulty with letting the balance sheet or investment levels depend on operational planning is that management may not give adequate attention to what the investment base should be to support the planned amount of profit.

The purpose of balance sheet budgeting is similar to profit-and-loss budgeting: to establish standards of performance and a basis for flexible control, as well as a forecast of future position. In arriving at good investment standards, management may well question the soundness of proposed operating decisions and improve its understanding of the economics of the business. In this chapter, we will discuss budgetary planning and control in terms of the balance sheet and describe the way in which such control is related to management's control of operations.

The corporate officer most closely associated with balance sheet planning is the treasurer or chief financial officer. In a very real sense he is the watchdog of financial policy and takes the lead in assuring sound financial planning. Notwithstanding this fact, much of the planning and control of resources must rest with operating executives. Assets turn over and liabilities arise because of operating decisions. Therefore, financial management must be closely associated with operational planning, and operating management must in turn be held accountable for controlling investment levels.

We have already defined the basic economic mission of every business as earning an acceptable return on investment. This means that the profit earned during the fiscal year must provide a sufficient return on the capital employed to satisfy shareholders and to provide a sound and continuing basis for growth. The rate of return is expressed simply as annual profit divided by average capital employed.

A more meaningful expression of this ratio is reflected by breaking it down into its component parts (Exhibit 75). From the exhibit, you can see that the rate of return can also be expressed as the margin of profitability multiplied by the investment turnover. In a broad economic sense, this formula really equates the business results of a wide range of industries. For example, a supermarket chain will show relatively small profit margins but earns an adequate return through a fast turnover of assets. A steel company, on the other hand, requires a larger margin of profit to compensate for a slower turnover rate. From the standpoint of your own company, the relationship is important as a guide to better results. Profitability can be improved by accelerating the turnover of capital or by using assets more efficiently, just as it can be improved by higher profit margins.

Numerous cases of the businessman's awareness of this fundamental point will occur to you. For example, your customers may ask for extended credit terms or rapid deliveries that require you to carry warehouse inventories. Or you may find competitors running equipment in multiple shifts to get increased facility productivity. While you may recognize such general examples as obvious, specific situations in every company exist which, for one reason or another, are not so obvious. Two examples will illustrate this point and will also serve to point up the need for management to seek out aggressively in the budget process opportunities for improved turnover.

In the first case a manufacturer of branded consumer goods that are sold in supermarkets, independent grocers, and drug stores found itself with excess production capacity because of changing product technology. Manufacturing management questioned whether an unbranded, low-priced product could be manufactured on the equipment and sold in large quantity without advertising support or on attractive discount. Such a program was authorized with a good improvement in profitability. This proposal was sponsored as a result of the plant manager's understanding of turnover and of his search for improvement in his asset turnover. In the second case an industrial products company reappraised its marketing policy of using a number of warehouses to service customer orders rapidly. This reappraisal was caused by the treasurer's concern about whether the apparent competitive advantage was worth the added inventory investment.

The effectiveness of management efforts to improve asset turnover is substantially improved by incorporating balance sheet planning and control as part of the overall budget process. Furthermore, to do so is not an unduly costly planning exercise, because much of the needed information is developed as part of operational planning.

EXHIBIT 75

THE RETURN-ON-INVESTMENT EQUATION

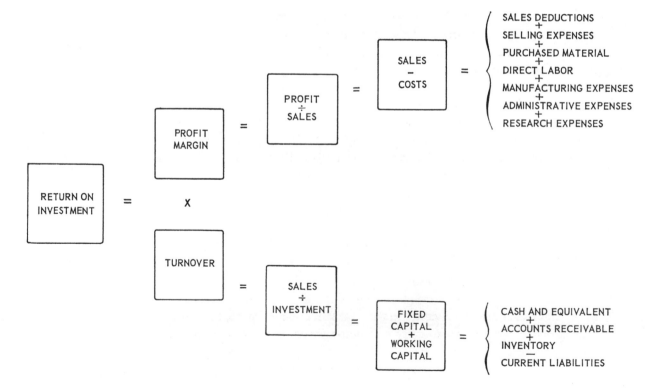

EFFECT OF SALES VOLUME INCREASE ON INVESTMENT—   **EXHIBIT** 76
CONVEYOR EQUIPMENT COMPANY
(Proposed Warehouse Additions and Return on Investment)

	(1)	(2)	(3)	(4)	(5)
			10% Increase In Profit Margin On Added Volume		
		Added Volume At Present Profit Margin		Added Volume Proposed	
	Present Operations				Planned Operations
Net sales	$10,000,000	$2,000,000	—	$2,000,000	$12,000,000
Profit	$800,000	$160,000	$16,000	$176,000	$976,000
Profit margin	8%	8%	0.8%	8.8%	8.13%
Investment	$6,667,000	$1,333,000	$133,000	$1,466,000	$8,133,000
Turnover	1.5	1.5	—	1.36	1.48
Return on investment	12%	12%	12%	12%	12%
Increase in investment					
(as % of Col. 1)		20%	2%	22%	
(as % of Col. 2)			10%		

Essentially, the equation in Exhibit 75 shows the economics of balancing turnover against a change in profit margins. A brief example will illustrate this. Assume that the Conveyor Equipment Company has experienced an annual investment turnover of 1.5 and an annual rate of return of 12 percent before income taxes. This means, of course, a pretax profit margin of 8 percent. Conveyor Equipment Company sales management believes that additional business amounting to 20 percent of present volume can be secured at current list prices by operating two additional field warehouses. The first consideration, of course, is what impact the added volume will have on the profit margin, or, stated another way, what added profit can be planned for because of the added sales.

In this example, profit analysis showed that the profit margin on the planned increase in sales would increase 10 percent as a result of a reduction in fixed cost per dollar of increased sales, partially offset by greater handling and transportation costs. The increase in investment that could be sustained to support the added sales volume would be 20 percent, the same as the increase in sales volume, if the turnover rate remained at 1.5. However, because the profitability of the incremental sales is planned at a 10 percent increase, the incremental investment can also be increased 10 percent without reducing the return on investment.

Exhibit 76 shows the calculations with prospective investment figures boxed in. As is evident, the Conveyor Equipment Company can maintain its rate of return on investment and increase its investment base by 22 percent ($1.466 million), assuming that sales and profit targets are met. Financial officers will make analyses such as this to test proposed courses of action for return-on-investment adequacy. In a

EXHIBIT 77   DIAGRAM OF SOURCES AND USES OF CAPITAL

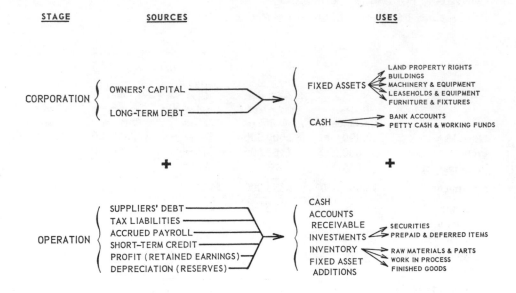

similar way, the development of budget plans should include a review of asset requirements and financing plans. To do so requires an understanding of fundamental financial relationships. We shall illustrate briefly the sources of capital and the flow of cash through a typical manufacturing company.

In any business, the initial sources of capital are the investment of the owners and the capital received from such creditors as bondholders. Creditors' capital secured on a more or less permanent basis is, of course, long-term debt. Exhibit 77 diagrams these sources of capital. Normally the funds derived initially are invested in fixed assets, sometimes called capacity capital, and in cash or working capital. As a business commences operation and progresses, additional sources of capital arise (1) in the form of money owed to suppliers, to employees, to tax authorities, and possibly to banks or other short-term creditors and (2) in the form of retained earnings and depreciation reserves. These funds are used to build inventory, finance receivables, make investments, and add to fixed assets. This is, of course, a continuous process that results in a flow of cash both through the firm and into and out of the firm.

In Exhibit 78, this flow is diagramed to show the working capital cycle. The normal elements of working capital are encompassed within the dotted line. The net increase in total working capital required for growth or expansion can come about only through profit or additions to cash from owners or long-term creditors. Any other changes in working capital flow affect only the relative composition of working capital in terms of the assets and liabilities that comprise working capital. However, it should be noted that—

1. The total amount of working capital is changed only by the profitability of the business and by the decisions or requirements of owners or long-term creditors to alter cash investment through dividends, changes in fixed assets, issuance of stock or bonds, and so on.

2. Management controls the relative composition of working capital and must maintain a proper balance to keep the working capital flow at an acceptable rate.

Each of these points represents an area of budgetary control, and each is important in assuring adequate turnover and, consequently, in assuring adequate return on investment.

To effect good control, a basis for relating the level of investment to operations or to activity must be used. The basis discussed earlier is turnover, which relates activity (sales) with investment (working capital and fixed assets). However, different assets "turn over" in terms of sales dollars at different rates, and these rates cannot be combined by simple addition. Therefore, another basis or another way of expressing turnover should be selected: the number of days of sales represented by total investment and by each element of investment. For example, using a 360-day basis, a company with annual sales of $36 million averages $100,000 of sales per day. If $12 million of working capital is maintained, it represents 120 days of sales or a turnover of three times per year ($360 \div 120$ or $36 million $\div$ $12 million). Assume that the same company has $5 million in accounts receivable and $5.5 million in inventory. These figures represent 50 days of sales in accounts receivable and 55 days of sales in inventory. Accounts receivable turn over better

WORKING CAPITAL FLOW DIAGRAM   EXHIBIT 78

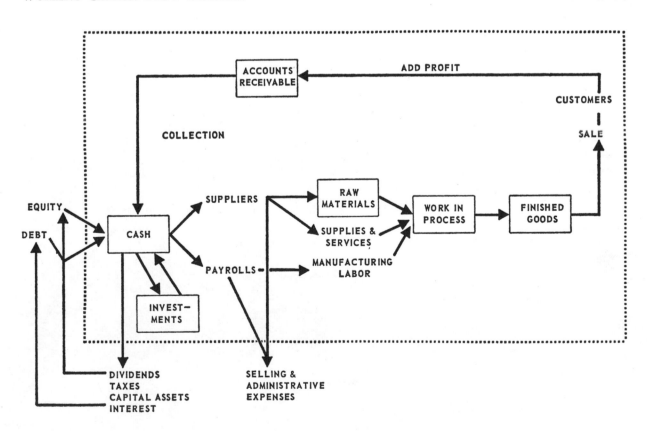

than seven times per year; but this rate of turnover may be inadequate, forcing an imbalance within working capital or an excessive total investment in working capital.

Let us assume, as we have discussed in earlier chapters, that management imposes certain standards on its business performance. Objective standards are vital to dynamic control. In the case of the above company, the credit terms are a simple net 30 days. You can see that if these terms set the standard, 50 days worth of sales in accounts receivable would be excessive. Also, knowing that a sales day represents $100,000 permits an evaluation of the magnitude of off-standard investment levels. Consequently, assuming receivables to be in excess by 20 sales days, this is equivalent to $2 million of excessive accounts in the investment base. At a 5 percent rate of return this "unproductive" investment represents $100,000 of lost profit annually. As treasurers know, the opportunity to earn profit on investment is always available, even if only through the purchase in the money market of short-term Government securities.

The use of the sales-day standard and of several other operating ratios will help demonstrate the relationship of the profit plan to the balance sheet of the Conveyor Equipment Company. This relationship will be discussed in the context of the president's request for a five-year forecast of growth and profitability. This example will illustrate the points discussed so far in the chapter. Exhibit 79 is a summary of the operating and financial-position data of the company as of the

EXHIBIT 79

SUMMARY OF OPERATING AND FINANCIAL DATA—CURRENT YEAR-END
(*Conveyor Equipment Company*)

Balance Sheet

Operating Statement		Balance Sheet	Amount	Days Sales	Return on Investment
Sales	$12,000,000	Cash	$ 300,000	9	Profit margin $= \dfrac{\$12,000,000 - \$11,700,000}{\$12,000,000}$
Marginal profit contribution	$3,600,000	Accounts receivable	1,500,000	45	$= 2.5\%$
		Inventory	3,000,000	90	
%	30%				
		Total	$4,800,000	144	Turnover $= \dfrac{\$12,000,000}{\$9,000,000}$
Fixed cost (includes depreciation of $400,000)	$3,000,000	Current liabilities	1,800,000	54	
		Working capital	$3,000,000	90	$= 1.33$
Taxes	$300,000				ROI $= 2.5\% \times 1.33 = 3.3\%$
		Fixed assets	6,000,000	180	
Profit	$300,000	Stockholders' equity	9,000,000	270	
Profit margin	2.5%				
		Investment turnover	1.33 X		
Equivalent sales/day	$33,333				

current year-end. The president has requested a five-year forecast anticipating a 50 percent increase in sales volume. The following information has been developed by operating managers:

- The sales increase of 50 percent will be achieved in yearly increments of $1.2 million.
- The marginal contribution rate is expected to be maintained at 30 percent despite increased competition.
- The capital additions, net of disposals, will be equal to the annual depreciation provision, except that at the beginning of the third and fifth years an additional $500,000 investment will be required. Depreciation provisions will increase 5 percent per year.
- The fixed costs will increase by $200,000 per year including depreciation.
- The president has indicated that a dividend rate of 50 percent of net income should be maintained.

When such data are summarized on the basis of the income statement and the planned capital investments, the following becomes apparent:

Planned net income (over five years)	$2,700,000
Deduct investments in fixed assets in excess of depreciation provisions	1,000,000
	$1,700,000
Deduct dividends	1,350,000
Increase in working capital	$ 350,000

While at first glance this result may seem acceptable, operating management was asked to indicate whether inventories and accounts receivable could be maintained at the same relative levels and, if not, what increase in sales days could be expected. Operating management indicated that an increase of two sales days per year could be expected in each account, partially offset by an increase of one sales day per year in accounts payable balances. Taking these changes into consideration, the treasurer summarized the projected results (Exhibit 80).

As you can see, notwithstanding a growing return on investment, the company will require additional cash financing by the second year and can look forward to an additional cash requirement in excess of $1.5 million by the fifth year. Even the immediate suspension of dividends would not avoid a cash deficit at the end of the third and fifth years, unless the turnover of receivables and of inventory can be maintained nearer to current standards of 45 and 90 days, respectively. If those standards were maintained throughout and no dividends were paid, the cash balances at the end of the fifth year would amount to $650,000, assuming no stretching-out of accounts payable and no additional financing. This example shows how profit planning and cash and balance sheet planning are interrelated and interdependent. It also demonstrates how important standards can be in the management of investment. You will recognize that the sales-day standard is a variable budget rate in that it reflects changes in asset levels in accordance with changes in sales activity.

EXHIBIT 80

FIVE-YEAR PROJECTION OF CASH, WORKING CAPITAL, AND RETURN ON INVESTMENT—CONVEYOR EQUIPMENT COMPANY

($000's Omitted)

	Year 1	Year 2	Year 3	Year 4	Year 5
Sales	$13,200	$14,400	$15,600	$16,800	$18,000
Marginal contribution ratio	30%	30%	30%	30%	30%
Marginal profit contribution	$ 3,960	$ 4,320	$ 4,680	$ 5,040	$ 5,400
Fixed cost	3,200	3,400	3,600	3,800	4,000
Pretax profit	760	920	1,080	1,240	1,400
Net profit	380	460	540	620	700
Memo—Depreciation	$ 420	$ 442	$ 463	$ 486	$ 510

	Current Year Amount	Sales Days	Year 1 Amount	Sales Days	Year 2 Amount	Sales Days	Year 3 Amount	Sales Days	Year 4 Amount	Sales Days	Year 5 Amount	Sales Days
Cash	$ 300	9	$ 110	3	($ 60)	(2)	($ 710)	(16)	($ 840)	(18)	($ 1,450)	(29)
Accounts receivable	1,500	45	1,723	47	1,960	49	2,210	51	2,473	53	2,750	55
Inventory	3,000	90	3,373	92	3,760	94	4,160	96	4,573	98	5,000	100
Total	$4,800	144	$5,206	142	$5,660	141	$5,660	131	$ 6,206	133	$ 6,300	126
Current liabilities	1,800	54	2,016	55	2,240	56	2,470	57	2,706	58	2,950	59
Working capital	$3,000	90	$3,190	87	$3,420	85	$3,190	74	$ 3,500	75	$ 3,350	67
Fixed assets	6,000	180	6,000	163	6,000	150	6,500	149	6,500	139	7,000	140
Stockholders' equity	$9,000	270	$9,190	250	$9,420	235	$9,690	223	$10,000	214	$10,350	207
Return on investment	3.3%		4.1%		4.9%		5.6%		6.2%		6.8%	

In previous chapters, we have discussed the capital expenditure budget program and the relationship of inventory planning and control to budgeting operations. Therefore, we need not repeat here the specifics of such planning. However, when such budgets are completed, financial management should review them in relation to acceptable turnover standards. Particular attention should be directed to any changes from prior years in the number of stocking points for finished goods and raw materials, in the number of production centers, in the length of the production cycle for product lines, and in the amount of safety stock to be carried. These changes have the greatest impact on inventory standards, because the formulas for average inventory levels recognize those factors as follows:

- Raw material or finished goods inventory $= \text{safety stock} + \dfrac{\text{order quantity}}{2}$.

- Work-in-process inventory (each production center) $= \text{safety stock} + \text{cycle stock} + \dfrac{\text{labor cost}}{2}$.

Planning for accounts receivable and for cash balances will require more effort in the balance sheet budgeting phase, because those two areas are not subject to the same operational planning requirements as inventory and fixed assets.

The level of accounts receivable is determined by the volume of credit sales and by credit and collection policy. From the profit plan, management can determine the amount of credit sales planned. Credit and collection policy will dictate both the credit terms and the aggressiveness with which delinquent accounts are followed up. As indicated earlier in this chapter, credit policy is interrelated with sales and marketing policy. The balance between increased sales objectives and looser credit terms is reflected in the return-on-investment equation.

Once a credit policy has been established and approved by top management, a performance standard can be set. This standard can be tested through an analysis of sales and collection experience. The expression of the standard as a number of sales days in accounts receivable is a convenient technique for controlling performance, although credit management will also generally refer to aged trial balances of accounts in order to specifically identify reasons for off-standard performance when it occurs.

The treasurer will have the direct responsibility for planning and controlling the investment in accounts receivable on the basis of marketing and credit policy approved by the president. In discharging this responsibility, financial management will review the credit standing of all customers periodically and of specific customers, such as new accounts and slow-paying accounts, as sales orders are received. This review can include reference to credit information sources and to bank and trade sources; this review may also include an analysis of customer financial statements.

The budgetary process can facilitate constructive management of credit by assuring that a proper economic balance is struck between receivable investment and potential credit losses on the one hand and profitable incremental sales on the other. If this total planning aspect of budgeting is not used, you can appreciate that sales

173

EXHIBIT 81   ANALYSIS OF COLLECTION TIMING DURING TYPICAL MONTH
(Cents Eliminated)

April Collections By Day	March Sales Total— $650,000	February Sales Total— $700,000	January And Prior Sales	Total Collections $	Total Collections %
April 1	$ 3,100	$ 2,150	$ 1,450	$ 6,700	1.0%
2	2,000	4,200	3,300	9,500	1.4
5	5,000	1,325	910	7,235	1.1
6	10,200	2,575	950	13,725	2.0
7	15,300	500	5,020	20,820	3.1
8	20,900	3,700	3,930	28,530	4.2
9	32,400	6,300	4,010	42,710	6.3
12	80,000	5,450	2,200	87,650	12.9
13	95,100	850	1,000	96,950	14.2
14	103,200	7,200	6,400	116,800	17.1
15	81,500	3,000	3,900	88,400	13.0
16	35,200	1,900	5,000	42,100	6.2
19	17,200	3,900	3,450	24,550	3.6
20	14,300	6,000	2,000	22,300	3.3
21	8,000	2,800	1,800	12,600	1.9
22	9,900	3,800	700	14,400	2.1
23	8,000	2,000	3,800	13,800	2.0
26	3,000	1,600	920	5,520	.8
27	5,100	2,300	4,710	12,110	1.7
28	1,500	4,200	1,580	7,280	1.1
29	500	1,150	150	1,800	.3
30	1,100	3,100	840	5,040	.7
Total	$552,500	$70,000	$58,020	$680,520	100.0%
% of month's sales	85%	10%			

management may feel the treasurer is too restrictive when establishing credit standards.

The level of cash balances in most businesses really represents three types of cash: working cash, accommodation cash, and excess cash. In terms of management planning and control, such a distinction can be highly useful, although financial statements rarely report such categories. By working cash, we mean the amount of cash required to carry on operations. Accommodation cash refers to the amount of cash balances frozen in financial institutions to support services rendered to the business by such institutions. Excess cash represents cash balances in excess of working funds and accommodation cash; generally, management will look for highly liquid and secure temporary investments for such cash so that it will generate income.

Working cash essentially represents a "buffer" in the working capital flow. There are only three operating expenditure routes for working cash: accounts payable, payrolls, and petty cash. From an operating standpoint, cash is generated by collections of accounts receivable and, in some companies, by cash sales. Of course, if the collection of receivables were synchronized with accounts payable expenditures, payroll disbursements, and petty-cash payments, a company would require little or no working cash. This, of course, is entirely theoretical; typically, there are staggered, substantial payments accompanied by receivable collections that bulk large at certain intervals during the month depending upon the credit terms offered. Based on regular analysis of collections, Exhibit 81 shows the receivable collection pattern of *ABC* Company, which sells products under credit terms of 2 percent 10th prox. and net 30 days. Because business activity in *ABC* Company is relatively stable, April collections are considered representative.

Total collections for the month amounted to $680,520, with the heavy concentration of collections in the week of April 12th reflecting customer use of the discounts where offered. Assume that regular payrolls are paid biweekly on the 2nd, 16th, and 30th and that a pattern of disbursements for payables can be determined. With such information, one can calculate the amount of working cash required at the beginning of the month, at the end of the month, and even at the beginning of each week. These amounts are working cash requirements. Management's objective, of course, is to hold the level of working cash to the minimum consistent with good profit planning by reducing costs (taking advantage of suppliers' discount terms, for example) and by adopting sound operating practices.

Our illustration assumes only one business location, but usually multiple locations are the rule; each may require additional buffers of working cash. In planning the working cash standards, however, financial management should consider centralized cash management, made possible in part by the greater speed that today's banking system can transfer money. The advantage of centralized cash management is the opportunity it offers to reduce working cash requirements of multiple locations; thus the business is able to operate with less overall working cash than would be the case on a decentralized basis. Other methods of planning for reductions in working cash include the various possibilities of speeding up the flow of incoming cash; such a speedup can be effected by shortening the time lag between product shipment and invoicing, by using bank lock boxes for collections, and by deferring the flow of outgoing cash by rescheduling payment dates when possible.

The level of accommodation cash required in any business is a function of many factors, including management policy and operating decisions. Basically, such cash represents bank balances maintained to compensate for services rendered by banks. It is probably true that 25 years ago, or even 10 years ago, industry generally carried relatively larger cash balances with banks than is the case today; treasurers now tend to invest cash not required in day-to-day operations in Government securities or commercial paper. At the same time, commercial banks are offering more and more services to the businessman—from processing payrolls to collecting receivables. This trend of service can be expected to continue, although many banks may offer some of their services on a fee basis.

When the fee for services rendered is in the form of compensating balances, such as in the case of a credit line or the handling of checks and deposits, the cash balances so maintained by the businessman can be viewed as accommodation cash.

EXHIBIT 82   WORKSHEET FOR DEVELOPING A BALANCE SHEET BUDGET:
ASSET AND CASH BUDGETING ANALYSIS

(Year-end 19—: 000's Omitted)

	Sales & Variable Costs	Fixed Costs	Purchases and Manufacturing Cost	Cash Receipts	Cash Payments	Net Changes
Cash				$3,805	($4,715)	($ 910)
Accounts receivable	$3,739			(3,805)		(66)
Inventory:						
Raw material and supplies			$1,300			1,300
Work in process						
Finished goods	(2,800)		2,690			(110)
Fixed assets					20	20
Depreciation reserve		($173)				(173)
Total	$ 939	($173)	$3,990	—	($4,695)	$ 61
Accounts payable			$3,000		($2,900)	$ 100
Accrued payroll		$143	852		(985)	10
Accrued expenses	$ 165	109	168		(465)	(23)
Accrued income taxes	162				(345)	(183)
Net worth	612	(425)	(30)			157
Total	$ 939	($173)	$3,990	—	($4,695)	$ 61

Treasurers can and should calculate the required amount of such cash. Thus the amount of accommodation cash in the balance sheet can be included in the budget plan.

Cash levels budgeted over and above planned working and accommodation cash funds is excess cash; one should consider investing the excess in Government securities or in high-grade commercial paper. Almost every business has excess cash available at some time during the year, because cash must normally be accumulated to meet such nonoperating requirements as quarterly dividend payments and capital expenditures as well as certain tax payments. Budgetary planning and control of cash and temporary securities should be the responsibility of the treasurer; he has the obligation to develop justifiable standards for each of the three types of cash.

Basically, the planning and control of cash make use of the same operating data as the planning and control of income and expenses but with two added considerations: (1) the nonoperating sources and uses of cash, such as capital expenditure disbursements, and (2) the effect of differences in timing between the accrual and cash bases of accounting. To plan for these two considerations is the greater part of balance sheet and cash planning.

As a convenient way of summarizing the planned balance sheet levels, we show in Exhibit 82 a worksheet for converting the profit plan into the changes forecast in balance sheet accounts. To complete this worksheet, the budget department will have to bring together sales, production, purchasing, and capital investment plans, as well as such nonoperating decisions as expected dividend action.

This form of worksheet can be prepared at any frequency desired as long as revenues and expenses have been budgeted for the same period. Once the balance sheet has been budgeted, management can plan the return-on-investment and control operations to achieve the planned return. Variances or deviations from the plan should be analyzed and explained in a way similar to variances in operating statements.

As part of a company's regular planning and control of its balance sheet and cash flow, the treasurer should be particularly alert to possibilities for profit improvement through more effective cash management. Today's trend toward centralized cash management in many companies reflects a desire to get greater mileage out of cash, and this trend is likely to continue.

In recent years, economic conditions have resulted in steadily increasing costs of capital, a shortage of reasonable financing, and, in extreme instances, the bankruptcy of corporations that were unable to raise sufficient cash to meet their commitments. It is something of an anomaly for a corporation to see its business growing and its operations apparently profitable, but not be able to secure sufficient cash to continue operations. Yet this situation can and does occur. Because of the serious potential impact of cash problems, every treasurer should put substantial effort into developing a master plan for cash management. The requirements for this plan are a fine-tuned cash forecasting and monitoring system and a regular review—no less frequently than as part of the annual profit-planning program—of the profit opportunities inherent in improving the existing cash management systems. As described earlier, the cash forecasting system will flow from the detailing of the annual operating plan and the profit and loss budget, expressed on a month-by-month basis, with cash receipts and disbursements planned week by week within the month. When cash management is centralized, the forecast of the flow of cash will be accumulated from each decentralized operating entity contributing to the profit plan.

As a treasurer looks for profit improvement in cash management, he will turn his attention to specific techniques designed to speed cash inflows and retard cash outflows. These techniques relate specifically to the way in which cash is generated, received, and marshaled to a central banking point and also to the procedures that surround the disbursement of cash. This review will consider (1) internal procedures such as billing, which controls the timing of invoice release, and (2) procedures which hinge on external systems, such as the way in which the banking system transfers company collections from country banks to major city banks.

The treasurer should review all the systems and procedures that affect his cash flow whether they are internal or external. Some of these procedures stem from operating practices under the direct control of other executives, such as the decision to expand the finished goods inventory. Nevertheless, the treasurer should be prepared to question any internal procedure that affects the rate of working capital turnover and any external procedure that affects the movement of money between his company and customers or suppliers. Aggressiveness by the treasurer is important here because ineffective cash management practices can creep into company operations and become

177

ingrained in day-to-day working habits. Aggressiveness is also warranted because of the profit improvement potential from accelerated cash availability and the increased use of the retained cash.

This profit improvement potential is often measured in terms of the bank loan rate or the incremental cost of borrowed money; in fact, however, a more appropriate measure of improvement is the overall cost of capital, which often will exceed 10 or 15 percent per year. Because a company with $360 million of annual sales has an average daily cash inflow of $1 million, pretax profit improvement potential from making cash available sooner or holding it for, say, three days longer is $300,000 to $450,000 ($3 million times the company's 10 to 15 percent cost of capital). Further, in many companies this profit would be equivalent to additional annual sales of $3 million to $10 million, thus making the three-day improvement very significant. Let us review briefly some techniques which may be employed in the cash receiving and disbursing functions to achieve the desired profit improvement results.

Basically, the timing of cash receipts can be accelerated by the application of cash management techniques in three areas: (1) timing of billing, (2) timing of receipts from customers, and (3) timing of interbank transfers.

Improved billing procedures can facilitate the timely inflow of cash since a delay in billing will cause a delay in the receipt of cash. A number of techniques, including the following, can be employed to reduce billing time:

- *Prebilling.* Invoices can be prepared when orders are received so that they can be mailed immediately upon shipment. A one-write system in which the order, invoice, shipping papers, and other documents are prepared simultaneously when the order is received can be effective in minimizing both processing time and errors.
- *Telecommunications equipment.* This can replace the mail to speed communication between billing offices and shipping points.
- *Decentralized billing.* Invoices are likely to reach the customer sooner if they are prepared at and mailed from the shipping location rather than the home office.

Cash remittances should be deposited in the banking system and made available for company use as soon as possible after the customer mails them. *Lock-box systems* can prove particularly useful in reducing the time between the mailing of the remittance and its receipt by the bank. Under this system, depository accounts are opened in banks at strategic geographic locations selected to reduce the mailing time of the remittance, and customer remittances are sent directly to post office boxes controlled by the banks. The banks credit the company's accounts immediately upon receipt of the cash and forward copies of remittance advices for use in accounts receivable recordkeeping. The funds can then be transferred promptly to central corporate accounts or used locally for payrolls, vendor payments, or other cash needs. This system has the advantages of reducing the remittance mailing time and eliminating the handling of checks by the accounting department.

Sales offices can also be used to process cash receipts. In this case, customers are instructed to mail remittances to the nearest sales office, which deposits the checks in a local bank and advises the home office by wire of the amount of the deposit. On receiving the wire, the home office prepares and deposits a check transferring the funds to the central bank account. These funds become available for disbursement immediately, since the transfer of funds will be complete by the time the disbursement checks are presented for payment.

Other techniques can be set up to facilitate the flow of funds between banks and reduce cash in transit. *Concentration banking* and *depository transfer checks* are useful for collecting large numbers of payments at scattered locations. Local branch offices deposit receipts in local banks and send a depository transfer draft to concentration banks, which then transfer daily deposits to company headquarters. This method allows funds received at the local level to be transferred directly to concentration banks without prior action by the home office.

Where mailing time between banks is long and the funds flow is large, *wire transfers* may be used to speed up the process. At the request of the depositor, the concentration bank transfers funds by telegram to the central bank. Wire transfers are the fastest way to move funds but are more costly than depository transfer checks. Consequently, they should be employed for the movement of larger amounts of funds in situations where the transfer time is reduced significantly. Transfers can be made only in those cases where both banks have wire transfer facilities.

A number of opportunities exist for improving the company's cash position through innovations in the cash disbursing process. *Delay of payments* until the last possible day is a positive and easily implemented technique for slowing cash outflow. This technique requires that the due date of each invoice be identified when it is received and that invoices be filed in a due date file. A payment schedule is developed from the due date file and thus payments are made on the last possible day. A number of companies use such techniques to coordinate the timing of the transfer of funds into disbursing accounts with the clearing of these disbursement checks. In this way they are able to take advantage of the bank "float" and not make funds available until disbursement checks are presented for payment.

Another method of limiting the availability of cash until presentation for payment is the use of *sight drafts*. For example, sight drafts might be issued in place of payroll checks. Employees cash the drafts at their local banks, which forward them to the disbursing banks for payment. The disbursing banks then present the drafts to the issuing company for review and approval to pay. Only at this point does the issuing company make the funds available to cover drafts. This technique can retard the outflow of funds for two to five days.

Centralization of accounts payable systems has the advantage of eliminating divisional working capital funds and making them available for overall corporate use. In addition, such systems allow the corporate cash managers to have up-to-date knowledge about divisional commitments for funds. Companies that employ a centralized payables system normally pay all major bills out of the corporate account and establish small local imprest accounts to handle minor local expenses and petty cash items.

A company can permanently free up significant amounts of cash through the application of these management techniques. The implementation of these techniques in a cash planning and forecasting program that is integrated with the overall corporate budget process can provide dramatic financial results.

10

Making Budgets Work

THE SECRET OF MAKING BUDGETS WORK FOR YOU lies in the effectiveness of the reporting and in the insight into operations provided by variances from budget. What is done about variances is a matter of management judgment which very often makes the difference between a profitable year or a loss year.

The budgeting effort can be effective only if the results are reported in such a manner that they gain the necessary attention from all levels of management. Here are some basic guides which should be followed in preparing budget reports:

1. Only those items of cost which are actually incurred by the individual charged with the responsibility for a particular department should be included in the budget report of that department. Avoid including allocations of general overhead or other items over which the department head has no control.

2. Only that information which is meaningful and necessary should be included in the report.

3. Only the minimum amount of detail appropriate for the organizational level for which the report is intended should be included.

4. Accounting and reporting of expenditures should be in accordance with the principles of responsibility reporting described in Chapter 1.

If those guides are followed, one can gain the acceptability which is required and the attention which is necessary for effective use of budgets.

To illustrate how variances are computed, reported, and used as the basis for management action, we will use selected statements of a heavy machinery company. These statements are taken from an actual case history, after suitable alterations to avoid disclosing confidential information which might be competively injurious. The organizational segments of the business on which we will concentrate are illustrated in the responsibility-reporting diagram, Exhibit 83.

Let's first agree on some of the terms that are used in working with the responsibility-reporting structure. The lowest entity which we recognize in the organization for cost purposes is a *cost center*. For purposes of identification, a cost center is a distinct physical entity; it has physical as well as organizational boundaries; its performance can be measured and its performance responsibility assigned to a specific individual. The next level which we recognize is a collection of cost centers, which we will call a *department*. Several departments make up a functional *group* or an entire *plant*.

Exhibit 84 presents the report of machine-shop expenditures incurred at the cost-center level. Actual expenditures incurred by the foreman are compared with the budget on a monthly and year-to-date basis, and variances from budget are computed for both periods. The term "earnings" is used in this company to denote the amount of budget "allowed" the foreman, based on standards of expenditure related to volume of activity or to the inventoriable value of production for the period at actual cost and standard value. As a basis for comparison, the budget displayed on the responsibility statement is related to the level of activity for the period being reported; that is, it is a variable budget.

To permit the foreman to evaluate in his own terms the validity of his current-month performance report, certain important operating statistics should be shown. Note that in the variance-analysis section, the earned standard hours and the actual

RESPONSIBILITY REPORTING PATH DIAGRAM   EXHIBIT 83

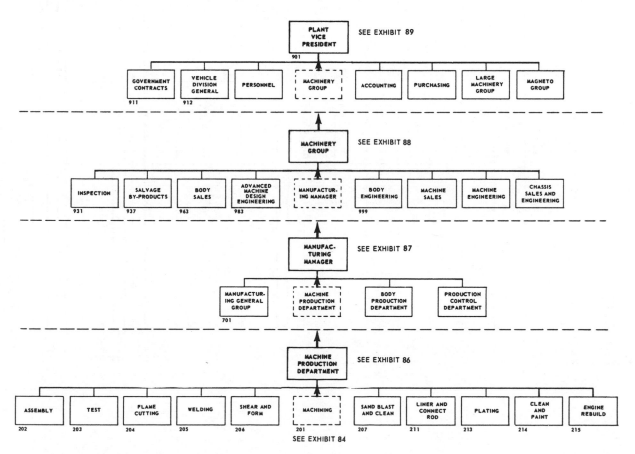

EXHIBIT 84

RESPONSIBILITY REPORT—MACHINING

RESPONSIBILITY OF **MR. FOREMAN** AREA **201 MACHINING** **OCTOBER**

AREA OR ACCT.	DESCRIPTION	CURRENT MONTH BUDGET	CURRENT MONTH ACTUAL	CURRENT MONTH UNDER OR OVER (–) BUDGET	YEAR TO DATE UNDER OR OVER (–) BUDGET	YEAR TO DATE ACTUAL	YEAR TO DATE BUDGET
100	MANAGEMENT	$ 3,568	$ 4,553	985–	$ 2,165–	$ 45,331	$ 43,166
110	CLERICAL	286	285	1	52–	1,750	1,698
120	MATL HANDLING	3,184	3,709	525–	1,691–	33,842	32,151
140	LOST TIME	152	122	30	80	955	1,035
150	PROPY ATTEND	1,943	2,023	80–	411–	19,691	19,280
170	SALABLE LABOR		603	603–	867–	867	
180	SUNDRY LABOR	1,985*	2,059*	74–	420–	16,930	16,510*
	TOTAL INDIRECT LABR	$ 11,118*	$ 13,354*	2,236–*	$ 5,526–*	$ 119,366	$ 113,840
200	VACATION PAY	2,815	3,729	914–	9,140–	37,290	28,150
210	HOLIDAY PAY	2,476	2,004	472	4,720	20,040	24,760
220	FICA	1,738	2,316	578–	5,780–	23,160	17,380
230	UNEMPLOY TAX	934	2,222	1,288–	12,880–	22,220	9,340
240	WORK COMP INS	410	473	63–	430–	4,530	4,100
250	SOCIAL INSUR	1,157	1,661	504–	4,815–	16,517	11,702
260	PENSIONS	1,661	2,362	701–	7,010–	23,620	16,610
270	OVERTIME PREM	929*	1,044*	115–	1,150–	10,440	9,290*
280	SHIFT PREMIUM		37	37–	85–	85	
	TOTAL PAYROLL COSTS	$ 12,120*	$ 15,848*	3,728–*	$ 36,570–*	$ 157,902*	$ 121,332*
300	DURABLE TOOLS	1,579	805	774	5,651	6,218	11,869
800	UTILITIES CO	7,355	5,939	1,416	14,160	59,390	73,550
810	INTRAPLT TRNS	200	434	234–	2,340–	4,340	2,000
820	MFG SERVICES	19,705	18,372	1,333	13,330	183,720	197,050
830	MANPOWR SERV	4,241	4,625	384–	3,840–	46,250	42,410
840	ENG SERVICES	864		864	5,650	3,050	8,700
850	SPECIAL SERV	7,544	6,489	1,055	10,550	64,890	75,440
	SERVICE CHARGES	$ 39,909*	$ 35,859*	4,050*	$ 37,510*	$ 361,640*	$ 399,150*
	UNCONTROLLABLE EXP	$ 9,079*	$ 7,061*	2,018*	$ 15,175*	$ 75,615*	$ 90,790*
	TOTAL OVERHEAD COST	$ 82,256*	$ 84,192*	1,936–*	$ 17,150–*	$ 835,862*	$ 818,712*
10	DIRECT LABOR	45,405	51,512*	6,107–*	49,918–*	509,819*	459,901*
	TOTAL AREA COSTS	$ 127,661*	$ 135,704*	8,043–*	$ 67,068–*	$ 1,345,681*	$ 1,278,613*
	EARN VARIANCE	20,920–		20,920–	171,090–		171,090–
	TOTAL EARNINGS	$ 106,741*	$ 135,704*	28,963–*	$ 238,158–*	$ 1,345,681*	$ 1,107,523*

to Exh. 86 → (TOTAL AREA COSTS)
to Exh. 86 → (TOTAL AREA COSTS)

CURRENT MONTH VARIANCE ANALYSIS

LABOR

CAUSE	STANDARD	ACTUAL	VARIANCE
HOURS	19,321	21,735	$ 2,414–
EFFICIENCY	100%	88.9%	$ 5,673–
RATE	$ 2.35	$ 2.37	$ 434–

OVERHEAD

CAUSE	VARIANCE
LABOR EFFICIENCY	$ 5,214–
SPENDING	$ 1,260
UNCONTROLLABLE BUDGET	$ 2,018

EARNINGS

CAUSE	VARIANCE
PRODUCT MIX	$ 13,391–
VOLUME	$ 7,529–

hours for the machine shop are given. The foreman recognizes that this is the foundation for determining his activity level. He knows that the more standard hours he earns, the more budget he will earn and a greater base he will have to cover his overhead cost. As a result, he will soon come to know the levels at which he performs best. He realizes, too, that he does not have complete control over the number of standard hours he earns. Partially, this is controlled by the amount of production which is scheduled for his cost center. He does, however, have control over the number of actual hours worked to earn the ordered or scheduled standard hours. In many cases, other important statistics, such as equipment, hours, material yields, tons handled, and so on, should appear on the responsibility statement so that on one page the foreman gets a concise view of what his performance is and what major factors have influenced it. The lower section of Exhibit 84 lists, by cause, the monthly variances of total labor, overhead, and earnings.

As indicated by Exhibit 84, direct labor costs for the month varied unfavorably from the budgeted level by $6,107. This was caused by two factors—efficiency and rate. The efficiency factor is a measure of actual hours used (21,735) less standard-hours earned (19,321). The difference of 2,414 hours is valued at the budgeted rate of $2.35 per hour. Thus the efficiency level resulted in an unfavorable variance of $5,673. The other factor in the unfavorable labor performance is labor rate. Labor was budgeted at $2.35 per hour, but the actual departmental average labor rate was $2.37 per hour. The cost of this variance is $434, computed by multiplying the difference between actual and standard rates by the total actual hours worked of 21,735.

Overhead for the month varied unfavorably from the budgeted level by $1,936. This was caused by three factors—labor efficiency, fixed cost deviations from budget (uncontrollable budget), and variable expense deviations from budget (spending). The effect of labor efficiency on overhead is measured by the excessive labor hours expended (2,414) multiplied by the budgeted variable overhead rate ($2.16 per hour), resulting in an unfavorable variance of $5,214.

The uncontrollable budget variance is the difference between the actual and the budgeted uncontrollable costs ($7,061 as compared with $9,079), representing a total favorable variance of $2,018. The remaining overhead factor is the spending variance. This is defined as the difference between the variable overhead budget for the actual hours of operation and the actual variable overhead costs. It can be computed by deducting the algebraic sum of the previously calculated variances of $5,214 (unfavorable) and $2,018 (favorable) from the total unfavorable variance of $1,936.

The difference between the departmental operating budget and the inventoriable value of departmental production for the month is the total earnings variance. This variance is in turn divided into two components—volume and product mix. The volume variance, or the effect of operating at other than the standard volume level established by management, is measured by the difference between the budgeted standard operating hours (27,000) and actual operating hours (21,735), valued at the budgeted fixed cost per hour of $1.43; this results in a total unfavorable variance of $7,529.

The product-mix variance can be calculated by deducting the unfavorable volume variance of $7,529 from the total unfavorable earnings variance of $20,920. In this company, each product has been assigned a standard labor and overhead cost rate for all departments through which it must pass. The departmental production, or standard hours earned, valued at these product standard rates, was compared with the same earned standard hours valued at the departmental standard cost rates. The resultant unfavorable difference is defined as the product-mix variance and reflects a different mix of products going through the cost center than was assumed in the original operating plan and manufacturing budget.

The department foreman is measured only by the "total area cost" line on his responsibility report because he is not in a position to control the earnings variance. But as the management of this company wishes to know the earnings variance at each organizational level, such a variance appears on the foreman's responsibility report.

It must be emphasized at this point that if the responsibility report is to be an effective tool for the foreman to use in controlling and measuring the current performance of his cost center, it must contain accurate information. The accounting department must take the responsibility for providing reliable data in the report and for seeing to it that reliable labor distribution, accounts payable, and stores accounting systems are employed in coding expense information and linking it to the reporting system. In addition, the accounting department must take the responsibility for insuring that reliable information on actual production activity by cost center is provided so that meaningful budgets for direct labor and materials expenses can be presented in the reports. Collection of production data often presents considerable difficulty in the effective operation of a variable budgeting control reporting system, but good information must be provided if the control system is to be useful and dependable.

In the case of the illustration of a machining cost center in Exhibit 84, October's budget of $45,405 for direct labor would be developed by multiplying the actual number of parts completed for the month (in detail by type of part) by the standard direct labor cost per part, then adding the results for all parts produced. Data on actual production would be recorded by machining cost center employees and reported to the accounting department by means of batch tickets, production logs, copies of manufacturing orders, and the like. The same data would also be used for production and inventory reporting and control.

Production reporting based on completion of parts might not be adequate for control and performance measurement if the machining cost center manufactured very large items which required many direct labor hours to complete and which were worked on in the cost center for many weeks. Performance reporting upon completion of the items would be inadequate because an item that was off budget or out of control could not be identified until it was completed; thus it would be too late for management to correct the out-of-control conditions and complete the item at budgeted cost. In such a case, the cost center foreman would have to determine the percentage complete for all items being worked on and report this information to the accounting department regularly. The earned direct labor budgets thus would be calculated by multiplying the percentage complete times the total direct labor budget for the unit. Actual direct labor charged to the unit would be compared to the budgets for both the current period and the year to date, and the variances would pinpoint units requiring management attention.

Accurate production data becomes even more critical, and considerably more difficult to obtain, in the case of such process industries as paper mills, petroleum refineries, and chemical plants. In these industries, raw materials costs typically amount to more than half of total manufacturing costs and thus require careful control and reporting.

Effecting operating and financial control through responsibility reporting in a process industry therefore requires the installation of appropriate measuring devices to record, for each manufacturing cost center, the actual quantities of raw materials consumed, byproducts recovered, and products produced. In the integrated pulp and paper mill illustrated in Exhibit 85, for example, an extensive instrumentation program would be required to provide reliable data on the flows of logs, chips, unbleached and bleached pulp, paper, and other related materials in the manufacturing process. Providing accurate data would entail not only the evaluation and selection of the appropriate measuring device for each point in the flow (rotameters, magnetic flow meters, belt scales, platform scales, and so on), but also the development and implementation of procedures for the reporting of data from the plant floor to the accounting department.

In the wood cooking cost center, for example, establishing effective operating and financial control over operations would require the installation of belt scales to

THE PULP AND PAPER MAKING PROCESS (KRAFT MILL)   **EXHIBIT 85**
AN EXAMPLE OF KEY INSTRUMENTATION POINTS FOR MATERIALS
MEASUREMENT AND REPORTING

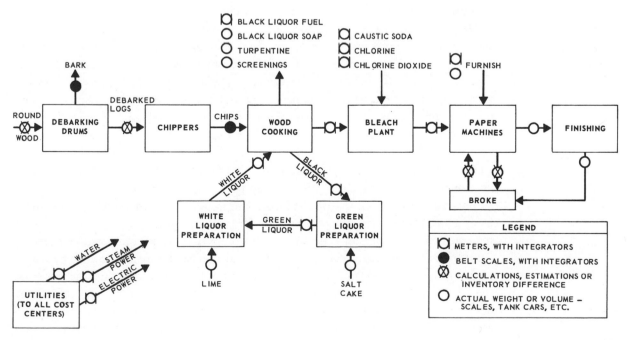

measure the consumption of wood chips and magnetic flow meters to measure white liquor consumed, black liquor recovered, and unbleached pulp produced. Moreover, procedures would have to be installed for reporting the actual weights of truck or rail car shipments to customers for black liquor soap, turpentine, and screenings recovered. Finally, production logs or batch tickets would have to be installed for reporting production activity to the accounting department. Once quantitative raw materials and cost standards were established for all products in the cost center, actual production quantities would be multiplied by the cost standards for each raw material to calculate budgets for comparison against the actual raw materials cost (at standard prices) on the responsibility reports.

The importance of providing the reporting system with accurate data cannot be stressed too highly, whether the application is heavy manufacturing, light manufacturing, or process manufacturing. In all cases, when developing new or modified budgeting and control systems, the measurement and reporting instruments and procedures must be installed concurrently to provide accurate data. It is the responsibility of the budgeting and accounting department to see to it that data achieve an accuracy level suited to the requirements for control.

The next level of reporting and control is reflected in Exhibit 86, which covers all of the cost centers that are the responsibility of the general foreman. The variances shown at the bottom of this exhibit are simply the result of the addition of the individual variances in each of the cost centers listed on the exhibit. The earnings variances are kept separate from the labor and overhead variances, and the general foreman is measured only by the "total area costs" line because he is not in a position to control the earnings variances, just as the cost-center foreman was not. Only the totals are carried forward from the responsibility report of the machining cost center and from other cost centers. The responsibility reports for the other cost centers are not illustrated in this chapter, but they would contain details similar to those shown in Exhibit 84 (machining cost center).

Note that we did not bring forward a summary of the detail accounts in each cost center, since these totals would not be meaningful to the general foreman. He exercises control by determining from the summary information presented in his report (Exhibit 86) how each cost center is performing. This approach illustrates another important principle of management and budget control and of good reporting: management by exception. The general foreman can determine from Exhibit 86 which cost centers are out of control or off budget; he can call for the detail report (similar to Exhibit 84) of only the problem cost centers for further investigation and corrective action. He need not study all of the detailed cost-center reports to determine problem areas.

This same exception approach to observing variances from budget in summary form in terms of managers responsible for various operations is carried up the management chain of command and responsibility. Exhibit 87 presents the variances from budget of all operations under the jurisdiction of the manufacturing manager. Here again, the variances displayed at the bottom of this exhibit are the result of the addition of the individual variances from the responsibility reports of the departments listed. Earnings variances are only listed for management information and are not the responsibility of the manufacturing manager. The figures reflecting

EXHIBIT 86

RESPONSIBILITY REPORT—MACHINE PRODUCTION

AREA — MACHINE PRODUCTION
OCTOBER

RESPONSIBILITY OF
MR GENERAL FOREMAN

Area Costs

CURRENT MONTH — BUDGET	ACTUAL	UNDER OR OVER (-) BUDGET	AREA OR ACCT.	DESCRIPTION	YTD — UNDER OR OVER (-) BUDGET	ACTUAL	BUDGET
$127,661	$135,704	$8,043-	201	MACHINING	$67,068-	$1,345,681	$1,278,613
26,066	29,924	3,858-	202	ASSEMBLY	38,580-	299,240	260,660
22,264	21,741	523	203	TEST	5,230	217,410	222,640
10,143	8,440	1,703	204	FLAME CUTTING	17,030	84,400	101,430
40,539	45,939	5,400-	205	WELDING	54,000-	459,390	405,390
14,243	12,993	1,250	206	SHEAR & FORM	12,500	129,930	142,430
11,379	11,225	154	207	SAND BLAST & CLEAN	1,540	112,250	113,790
36,165	35,581	584	211	LINER & CONNECT ROD	5,840	355,810	361,650
4,297	3,327	970	213	PLATING	9,700	33,020	42,970
8,529	8,902	373-	214	CLEAN & PAINT	3,730-	89,020	85,290
773	1,196	423-	215	ENGINE REBUILD	4,230-	11,960	7,730
$302,059 *	$314,972 *	$12,913- *		TOTAL AREA COSTS	$115,768- *	$3,138,361 *	$3,022,593 *

(from Exh. 84 — to Exh. 87)

Earnings Variance

CURRENT MONTH — BUDGET	ACTUAL	UNDER OR OVER (-) BUDGET	AREA OR ACCT.	DESCRIPTION	YTD — UNDER OR OVER (-) BUDGET	ACTUAL	BUDGET
		20,920-	201	MACHINING	171,090-		171,090-
		4,539	202	ASSEMBLY	45,390		45,390
		5,463-	203	TEST	54,630-		54,630-
		1,858-	204	FLAME CUTTING	18,580-		18,580-
		598-	205	WELDING	5,980-		5,980-
		5,417-	206	SHEAR & FORM	54,170-		54,170-
		467	207	SAND BLAST & CLEAN	4,670		4,670
		4,911-	211	LINER & CONNECT ROD	49,110-		49,110-
		464	213	PLATING	4,640		4,640
		785	214	CLEAN & PAINT	7,850		7,850
		715-	215	ENGINE REBUILD	7,150-		7,150-
		$23,805- *		TOTAL EARN VARIANCE	$199,940- *		$199,940- *
$278,254 *	$314,972 *	$36,718- *		TOTAL EARNINGS	$315,708- *	$3,138,361 *	$2,822,653 *

(from Exh. 84 — to Exh. 87)

CURRENT MONTH VARIANCE ANALYSIS

LABOR

CAUSE	STANDARD	ACTUAL	VARIANCE
HOURS			
EFFICIENCY		%	% $12,426-
RATE		$	$ 674-

OVERHEAD

CAUSE	VARIANCE
LABOR EFFICIENCY	$ 2,094-
SPENDING	6,216
UNCONTROLLABLE BUDGET	3,065

EARNINGS

CAUSE	VARIANCE
PRODUCT MIX	467
VOLUME	$ 24,272-

EXHIBIT 87

RESPONSIBILITY REPORT—MANUFACTURING

RESPONSIBILITY OF
MR MANUFACTURING MANAGER

OCTOBER

AREA
MANUFACTURING

	CURRENT MONTH					YEAR TO DATE		
	BUDGET	ACTUAL	UNDER OR OVER (-) BUDGET	AREA OR ACCT.	DESCRIPTION	UNDER OR OVER (-) BUDGET	ACTUAL	BUDGET
from Exh.86	$ 5,855	$ 14,313	$ 8,458-	701 MFG GENERAL GROUP		$ 84,580-	$ 143,130	$ 58,550
	302,059	314,972	12,913-		MACHINE PRODUCTION	115,768-	3,138,361	3,022,593
	49,959	47,148	2,811-		BODY PRODUCTION	28,110	471,480	499,590
to Exh.88	63,559	72,916	9,357-		PRODUCTION CONTROL	93,570-	729,160	635,590
	$ 421,432 *	$ 449,349 *	$ 27,917-*		TOTAL AREA COSTS	$ 265,808-*	$4,482,131 *	$4,216,323 *
from Exh.86			1,412-	701 MFG GENERAL GROUP		14,120-		14,120-
			23,805-		MACHINE PRODUCTION	199,940-		199,940-
			14,639-		BODY PRODUCTION	146,390-		146,390-
to Exh.88			34,908-		PRODUCTION CONTROL	349,080-		349,080-
			$ 74,764-*		TOTAL EARN VARIANCE	$ 709,530-*		$ 709,530-*
	$ 346,668 *	$ 449,349 *	$ 102,681-*		TOTAL EARNINGS	$ 975,338-*	$4,482,131 *	$3,506,793

CURRENT MONTH VARIANCE ANALYSIS

LABOR

CAUSE	STANDARD	ACTUAL	VARIANCE
HOURS			
EFFICIENCY	%		% $ 17,945-
RATE	$		$ 906-

OVERHEAD

CAUSE	VARIANCE
LABOR EFFICIENCY	$ 15,184 —
SPENDING	$ 2,661
UNCONTROLLABLE BUDGET	$ 3,457

EARNINGS

CAUSE	VARIANCE
PRODUCT MIX	$ 7,854—
VOLUME	$ 66,910—

the performance of the machine production department general foreman against his budget are brought forward from Exhibit 86, in summary form, along with the results of performance of the other general foremen responsible to the manufacturing manager. He reviews and controls his operations by using the same exception principle described previously.

In similar fashion the variances from budget are developed at succeeding higher levels. Exhibit 88 shows the performance of the machinery group general manager as compared with his budget; Exhibit 89 shows how the plant vice president fared in accomplishing his budget objectives in the manufacturing function. The variance figures displayed at the bottom of both these exhibits are again merely the result of the addition of the individual variances from the responsibility reports of the listed groups.

A unique item appears in the lower section of Exhibit 89—a deduction after the earnings line for "selling, general and administrative expenses and recirculated costs." The selling, general and administrative expense deduction is for costs incurred in experimental and bidding work for the sales departments and in effort expended by factory labor against capital appropriations, such effort to be charged off to expense. Recirculated costs refer to the service charges (800 account group) on Exhibit 84. While these charges are shown as expenses for the departments utilizing the services, the same expenses appear on the responsibility reports for the departments providing those services. Thus we must eliminate such charges at the level of Exhibit 89, or we would actually have the same expenses reported twice.

These budget variance reports are then worked into the statement of income through the medium of the cost-of-sales statement shown in Exhibit 90. The totals of the materials, labor, and overhead charges shown in Exhibit 89 are adjusted for changes in inventories and for items capitalized to compute the standard cost of sales and the variance from standard or budget. Through this orderly development and accumulation of variances from budget at all levels of responsibility, we now are in a position to view their effect on the net income of the whole business, as shown in Exhibit 91.

Here we deduct from sales the actual cost of sales computed in Exhibit 90. For the current month, sales were $733,135 less than budget, and cost of sales was $545,308 ($588,206 minus $42,898) less than budget, resulting in an unfavorable budget variance of $102,031 in gross profit. When variances from selling, general and administrative expense budgets are factored in, the net effect is that the company missed its budget for the current month by $77,750. Thus final results of operations of a business can be related to variances from budgets, which in turn can be identified with responsible line managers and department heads.

Two additional points are worth mentioning in connection with these illustrative statements. Although not shown here, the budget system provides budgets and statements of variances, similar to those shown in Exhibits 84 through 89, for selling, general and administrative expense. Also, in this system, the variances are computed and the statements themselves are prepared on conventional punched-card equipment, which is used in the company's accounting operation.

(*text continued on page 194*)

EXHIBIT 88

RESPONSIBILITY REPORT—MACHINERY GROUP

RESPONSIBILITY OF
MR. GENERAL MANAGER OCTOBER AREA MACHINERY GROUP

	CURRENT MONTH		AREA OR ACCT.	DESCRIPTION	YEAR TO DATE		
BUDGET	ACTUAL	UNDER OR OVER (–) BUDGET			UNDER OR OVER (–) BUDGET	ACTUAL	BUDGET
$ 14,786	$ 17,753	$ 2,967–	931	INSPECTION	$ 29,670–	$ 177,530	$ 147,860
4,570–	6,845–	11,415–	937	SALVAGE BY PRODUCTS	114,150–	68,450–	45,700–
7,812	5,112	2,700	963	BODY SALES	27,000	51,120	78,120
9,031	8,358	673	983	ADVAN MACHINE DESIGN ENG	6,730	83,580	90,310
18,188	18,255	67–	999	BODY ENGINEERING	670–	182,550	181,880
168,621	174,350	5,729–		MACHINE SALES	57,290–	1,743,500	1,686,210
59,559	62,070	2,511–		MACHINE ENGINEERING	25,110–	526,700	595,590
52,639	52,667	28–		CHASSIS SALES & ENG	280–	526,390	526,390
421,432 *	449,349 *	27,917– *		MFG MANAGER	265,808– *	4,482,131	4,216,323
$ 747,498– *	$ 794,759 *	$ 47,261– *		TOTAL AREA COSTS	$ 459,248– *	$7,936,231 *	$7,476,983 *
		245–	931	INSPECTION	2,450–		2,450–
		262–	937	SALVAGE BY PRODUCTS	2,620–		2,620–
			963	BODY SALES			
		1,000–	983	ADVAN MACHINE DESIGN ENG	10,000–		10,000–
		16,900–	999	BODY ENGINEERING	169,000–		169,000–
		2,769–		MACHINE SALES	27,690–		27,690–
		133		MACHINE ENGINEERING	1,330		1,330
		13,211–		CHASSIS SALES & ENG	132,110–		132,110–
		74,764–		MFG MANAGER	709,530– *		709,530– *
		$ 109,018– *		TOTAL EARN VARIANCE	$1,052,070– *	$	$1,052,070– *
$ 638,480 *	$ 794,759 *	$ 156,279– *		TOTAL EARNINGS	$1,511,318– *	$7,936,231 *	$6,424,913 *

from Exh. 87
to Exh. 89

CURRENT MONTH VARIANCE ANALYSIS

LABOR

CAUSE	STANDARD	ACTUAL	VARIANCE
HOURS			
EFFICIENCY	%		$ 17,945–
RATE	$	$	906–

OVERHEAD

CAUSE	VARIANCE
LABOR EFFICIENCY	$ 15,184–
SPENDING	$ 16,493–
UNCONTROLLABLE BUDGET	$ 3,267

EARNINGS

CAUSE	VARIANCE
PRODUCT MIX	$ 7,854–
VOLUME	$ 101,164–

EXHIBIT 89

RESPONSIBILITY REPORT—TOTAL PLANT

RESPONSIBILITY OF
MR PLANT VICE PRESIDENT

OCTOBER

AREA
TOTAL PLANT

AREA OR ACCT.	DESCRIPTION	CURRENT MONTH BUDGET	CURRENT MONTH ACTUAL	CURRENT MONTH UNDER OR OVER (-) BUDGET	YEAR TO DATE UNDER OR OVER (-) BUDGET	YEAR TO DATE ACTUAL	YEAR TO DATE BUDGET
901	VICE PRES & GENERAL MGR	$ 17,612	$ 13,941	$ 3,671	$ 36,710	$ 139,410	$ 176,120
911	GOVERNMENT CONTRACTS	4,090	4,164	74-	740-	41,640	40,900
912	VEHICLE DIV GENERAL		11,705	11,705-	117,050-	117,050	
	PERSONNEL	28,464	25,008	3,456	34,560	250,080	284,640
	ACCOUNTING	57,963	63,681	5,718-	57,180-	636,810	579,630
	PURCHASING	22,026	28,053	6,027-	60,270-	280,530	220,260
	MACHINERY GROUP	747,498	794,759	47,261-	459,248-	7,936,231	7,476,983
	LARGE MACHINERY GROUP	1,058,353	1,026,579	31,774	317,740	10,265,790	10,583,530
	MAGNETO GROUP	139,713	149,915	10,202-	102,020-	1,499,150	1,397,130
	TOTAL AREA COSTS	$2,075,719 *	$2,117,805 *	$ 42,086-*	$ 407,498-*	$21,166,691	*$20,759,193
901	VICE PRES & GENERAL MGR						
911	GOVERNMENT CONTRACTS						
912	VEHICLE DIV GENERAL						
	PERSONNEL		5,911-	5,911-	59,210-		59,210-
	ACCOUNTING		14,925-	14,925-	149,250-		149,250-
	PURCHASING		6,566-	6,566-	65,660-		65,660-
	MACHINERY GROUP	109,018-	109,018-		1,052,070-		1,052,070-
	LARGE MACHINERY GROUP	186,474-	186,474-		1,864,740-		1,864,740-
	MAGNETO GROUP	14,292-*	14,292-*		142,920-*		142,920-*
	TOTAL EARN VARIANCE	$ 337,186-*	$ 337,186-*		$3,333,850-*	$	*$ 3,333,850-*
	TOTAL EARNINGS	$1,738,533 *	$2,117,805 *	$ 379,272-*	$3,741,348-*	$21,166,691 *	*$17,425,343 *
	LESS: SELLING, GENERAL AND ADMINISTRATIVE EXPENSES & RECIRCULATED COSTS	100,262	112,432	12,170-	121,700-	1,124,320	1,002,620
	TOTAL MANUFACTURING COSTS	1,638,271 *	2,005,373 *	367,102-*	$3,619,648-*	$20,042,371 *	*$16,422,723 *

from Exh. 88
to Exh. 90

CURRENT MONTH VARIANCE ANALYSIS

LABOR

CAUSE	STANDARD	ACTUAL	VARIANCE
HOURS			
EFFICIENCY	%		$ 31,326-
RATE	$	$	$ 2,108-

OVERHEAD

CAUSE	VARIANCE
LABOR EFFICIENCY	$ 27,670 -
SPENDING	$ 9,445
UNCONTROLLABLE BUDGET	$ 9,573

EARNINGS

CAUSE	VARIANCE
PRODUCT MIX	$ 18,511 -
VOLUME	$ 318,675-

EXHIBIT 90

STATEMENT OF COST OF SALES

OCTOBER

	CURRENT MONTH			DESCRIPTION	YEAR TO DATE		
	BUDGET	ACTUAL	UNDER OR (OVER) BUDGET		UNDER OR (OVER) BUDGET	ACTUAL	BUDGET
				Manufacturing costs			
	912 234	1 187 875	(275 641)	Direct labor and overhead –	(2 761 187)	11 865 725	9 104 538
	726 037	817 498	(91 461)	Standard cost of materials charged to work in process and finished goods	(853 461)	8 176 646	7 318 185
	1 638 271	2 005 373	(367 102)	Total manufacturing costs	(3 619 648)	20 042 371	16 422 723
				Less: Expenses to inventory or plant			
				Inventory increase or (decrease):			
	(9 167)	(9 167)		Finished goods		(90 672)	(90 672)
	(53 514)	(53 514)		Work in process		(508 616)	(508 616)
	(62 681)	(62 681)		Total inventory increase (decrease)		(599 288)	(599 288)
	170 158	170 158		Standard costs expensed and capitalized		906 751	906 751
	107 477	107 477		Total deduction from or (addition) to manufacturing costs		307 463	307 463
	1 530 794	Ⓑ 1 897 896	Ⓑ (367 102)	Cost of sales	Ⓑ (3 619 648)	Ⓐ 19 734 908	16 115 260

from Exh. 89

Ⓐ to Exh. 91
Ⓐ & Ⓑ

192

EXHIBIT 91

STATEMENT OF INCOME

DESCRIPTION	MONTH			OCTOBER — YEAR TO DATE		
	LAST MONTH	THIS MONTH	BETTER OR (WORSE) THAN BUDGET	BETTER OR (WORSE) THAN BUDGET	THIS YEAR	LAST YEAR
Net sales (shipments)						
Net sales	1 570 190	2 008 543	(738 457)	(4 819 630)	20 608 910	17 811 919
Intercompany and Intercompany sales	254 336	165 322	5 322	311 180	1 907 320	1 505 411
Total net sales	1 82_ 526	2 173 865	(733 135)	(4 508 450)	22 516 230	19 317 330
Standard cost of sales	(A)1 232 600	(A)1 530 794	(588 206)	(4 134 780)	(A)16 115 260	14 401 910
Standard gross profit	591 926	643 071	(144 929)	373 570	6 400 970	4 915 420
% sales	32.44%	29.58%			28.43%	25.45%
Favorable or (unfavorable) variances	(B)(370 777)	(B)(367 102)	42 898	91 352	(B)(3 619 648)	(2 924 816)
% sales	20.32%	16.89%			16.08%	15.14%
Gross profit	221 149	275 969	(102 031)	(282 318)	2 781 322	1 990 604
% sales	12.12%	12.69%			12.35%	10.31%
Selling, general and administrative expenses						
Field selling	107 333	117 414	11 586	110 359	1 168 641	1 011 320
Division selling	103 210	105 509	(35 509)	(315 371)	1 054 121	624 589
General and administrative	22 390	26 975	(2 975)	(34 043)	351 357	375 755
Research and development	30 692	9 370	34 630	127 563	311 013	151 183
Total selling, general and administrative	263 625	259 268	7 732	(111 492)	2 885 132	2 162 847
Income (loss) from operations	(42 476)	16 701	(94 299)	(393 810)	(103 810)	(172 243)
Other income and (deductions)	(14 885)	2 549	16 549	167 573	57 573	(134 588)
Net income (loss) before provision for Federal and foreign income taxes	(57 361)	19 250	(77 750)	(226 237)	(46 237)	(306 831)

from Exh. 90 (A)
from Exh. 90 (B)

Once the budget variance reports have been issued, it is important that a communication link be provided to aid in the interpretation and analysis of these reports. The first and most important responsibility of the budget director regarding all regular reporting is to provide an interpretation or a variance analysis for those operating personnel receiving the responsibility statements.

The most routine approach to variance analysis is to identify statistically the causes of variance. Generally speaking, all variances can be reduced to either of two factors—quantity or price. For example, the labor-efficiency variance is simply the difference between earned standard hours and the actual hours incurred at the standard hourly rate. The labor-rate variance is the difference between actual and standard labor rates multiplied by the actual hours. We previously described in connection with Exhibit 84 how variances can be routinely calculated and reflected in the reports.

Further, it is necessary for the budget director to analyze, in some depth, variances such as spending and yields to identify basic causes of unfavorable results. The substitution of materials of varying qualities can actually affect materials yield. This can be confirmed by reviewing the detailed figures for the materials actually consumed and comparing them with those of the standard materials that would have been used for the products actually produced during the accounting period.

The spending variances may be caused by a variety of expenditures. Detailed listings of expenditures for certain overhead items can be reviewed and interpreted; these would originate from accounts payable or from inventory requisitions. This should be reported in narrative form to the foreman or to the cost-center head.

If the foundation for the budget responsibility reports is actually a set of basic standards, then it is possible for the budget director to compare performance with such quantitative standards as hours, pounds of material, and production rates. He can then interpret in some detail the specific causes for variance.

The following example points up how variance analysis of this kind can effectively highlight the problems in an operating area. A company operating a very large machining and assembly operation had, for many years, experienced a fluctuation in the output of individual machining areas. It suspected that a good deal of this was caused by differences in set-up or start-up time caused by varying production runs. In due course, this company installed a responsibility budgeting system which identified as one of the budgeted standards the ratio of allowable set-up time to machining time.

This standard was developed by reviewing a large number of orders of reasonable size and developing the relationship for the various types of equipment. After some time with the new system, the company noted that the actual ratio of set-up to running time exceeded the standard. In reviewing the causes, the budget director found that order size had decreased, although the number of orders had stayed about the same. As a result, the company revised its approach to releasing orders to the shop in order to gain the benefit of spreading the set-up time over larger orders. The analysis was performed by requiring separate reports for set-up time and for running time. As a result, an actual ratio was developed which could be realistically compared, on a regular basis, with the standard or budgeted ratio.

On some occasions it will be necessary for the budget director, in cooperation with the industrial engineering department, to make observations of individual operating areas in an attempt to identify what types of costs are not properly reflected by the budgets or to determine if, in fact, changed operating conditions might have invalidated original budget assumptions. These observations or special studies are a common occurrence in a growing company where operating conditions change frequently.

Once the reporting and analysis have been completed, individual review meetings are held with foremen, line managers, and other department heads by the budget director to explain to them the types and causes of variances. As a result of these meetings, he is able to summarize the reactions and the intended action to be taken. He should then prepare a summary analysis to be presented to the top executive officers. This should be a description of what will be done, rather than simply a recitation on what has happened.

Before line managers can effectively interpret and utilize budget reports, it is important that they understand how variances occur. This understanding begins with an active role in the preparation of the budget. This means that the identification of the units of measure, the bases of variability in expenditures, and the type of expenditures which can be controlled should begin with the line manager. Actually, good budgeting procedure requires that the line manager prepare or approve the request for budgets in his areas. This not only enhances his understanding of the resulting budget allowances and variances but also tends to eliminate possible objections to the resulting budget.

The second factor in understanding budget variances is the control over the incurrence of costs shown on the statements. Charging a manager with items of expense over which he has no control puts him in the position of being responsible for someone else's actions. In order to interpret the meaning of a variance, he must request further information from other managers. In addition, he may feel that if he did have control, he could have prevented the variance in the first place.

If each manager looks upon his responsibility area as though it were his own individual business and as though it were his objective to beat his budget or to make a profit in the business, we would have the ideal atmosphere in which interpretation of budgeting results could take place. With such a viewpoint, the manager looks upon his budget as his own checkbook balance; he can incur expenses against this balance only as long as there is money in his account. After that, in his own personal affairs, he would not write additional checks lest they be returned for insufficient funds. This means, of course, that the most effective control takes place not when vendors' invoices are charged but when the requisition is originally written; not when the payroll is expended but when the individual employee is hired. Thus a proper attitude and an active participation are necessary ingredients for understanding the reasons for and causes of budget variances and for reacting accordingly.

Once this understanding exists, it is possible for the manager to determine the operating causes of individual variances. Every good foreman carries his own black book in which he notes observations of occurrences which he knows are nonstandard or unbudgeted. He also notes those occasions when he exceeds the performance required and can expect a favorable variance. Through observation, he will note the pace set by individuals when they are assigned various types of work. If he is experienced in pacing, he can interpret when their actions and effort will result in favorable or unfavorable performance ratings for himself.

Occasionally, the foreman may suspect the cause of a variance but ask for a special study. These studies can sometimes reveal errors in the budget or in the standards, as well as in the actual cost. For example, a plastic-boat manufacturer suddenly found that his materials costs were completely out of line with the budget allowances. The foreman responsible for molding attempted to determine the cause of the variance by weighing each hull. He found that the total standard weight was being exceeded. But he was conforming to the bills of material. This being the case, he should not have had an unfavorable materials variance. He asked the budget director to review the standards or budget allowances to determine if there might be some error in the budget. In making his study, the budget director found that the individual bills of material listed items that were included in the hull but not considered in the standard. The standard weight should have been developed by actually weighing the total hull and by checking to determine that all materials were included. As a result of the method used, the cost allowance was not sufficient. In this case, action taken was to reduce the weight of the hull by substitute materials and by slight changes in dimensions, since sales prices had been established for the current season's models on the basis of the originally budgeted cost.

In some cases, it may be necessary to run an operation on a controlled basis to determine why variances occur. This is particularly true when complex operations are involved, such as in a refinery or even in an integrated creamery. The following is a case example of the type of control which, while possibly not appropriate for continued use, did help to isolate a variance.

A medium-size dairy, processing a complete line of milk products including ice cream and ice cream specialties, was operating on a standard-cost system using budgeted data as the basis for determining product cost and performance. For several months during the beginning of the ice cream manufacturing season, unfavorable butterfat variances (yields) were noted. Various reviews were made, but the cause for the variance remained a mystery. It was then decided that for several days continuous records would be kept on butterfat consumption at all points. Coincidentally, during this period a particular series of ice cream flavors was being produced. After observations had been made for an entire day, it was noted that to improve the texture for certain flavors of ice cream the machine operator had reduced the overrun from the standard of 100 to about 80. This reduction in overrun improved the texture, but it reduced the butterfat yield to the ice cream manufacturer because the same amount of butterfat was being used in fewer gallons of ice cream. As a result of this revelation, the company changed the ingredients to improve the texture and increased the overrun to standard.

Once the causes of unfavorable variances are determined, the foreman, who now has become aware of the effect that off-standard operations can have on his own scorecard (responsibility report), should be instructed on the proper method for instituting changes. This may be particularly touchy in situations where a union is involved, since a change in work methods may be required. The foreman should take the following steps:

1. Review the method to be changed.
2. Detail each of the individual operations.
3. Question the need or requirement for them.
4. Identify the changes he wishes to make.
5. Instruct individual employees in their role in the revised method.

In cases when changes to correct a variance are required in two or more areas—changes such as those relating to bills of material, log sheets, materials purchases, or inventory levels—the proper lines of communications should be established so that the changes are not made in only one area but in all related functions to assure that there is not a recurrence of the unfavorable condition.

Once the changes have been made, it will be possible for the foreman to follow up by simply reviewing his cost performance reports for the next reporting period. This will save him the trouble of tracing every individual occurrence and will provide him with a composite reporting of all the activities under his supervision.

The ultimate in variance analysis and control concerns the net income of the business, which is the subject of the responsibility report (statement of income) for the president. Reasons for failure to achieve a budgeted profit goal can be found in the following four conditions:

- Level of sales.
- Product (gross profit) mix.
- Pricing level.
- Expense variances.

We have already covered the expense variances; so let us concentrate on the first three conditions, which relate to the total sales dollars. If a sales budget begins with the determination of units to be sold, effective evaluation of why a sales target is missed begins by comparing the number of units expected to be sold with the number actually sold. This points out why it is most important to have a forecast of sales in units as well as in dollars. Further, if the sales budget for units is organized by territory, we can isolate the "miss" in sales level by individual territory and possibly even by individual salesmen. This pinpoints where additional sales effort should be applied.

A comparison of the mix of product units in the budget with the actual mix gives an indication of the effect of changing demands on profit.

Finally, comparison of the prices that were used in forecasting sales with actual prices will indicate the effect of price level changes on profit. This factor is particularly important for a business that must bid for every order and custom-make its products. In developing estimates or bids, cost rates which are based on a budgeted level are often used. A markup is then added in relation to what competitors' prices might be and in relation to what is considered an adequate return on investment. This means, basically, that every order might have a different pricing level. But breaking orders into comparable units and getting a sales price for the average order will provide a better indication of the effects on profit of pricing levels.

Occasionally, an overoptimistic estimate of expected sales is made. When this happens a different approach is required. An actual case study will help to illustrate this point. A company which manufactured and distributed a consumer product on a national basis for the recreation industry had experienced in its prior year a major operating loss. For the current year, the sales vice president had forecast increased sales of about 40 percent and an operating profit. He was able to convince the president that this optimistic viewpoint was valid, and all budgets were based on this expected major increase in sales.

During the first quarter of the budget year, the company experienced an operating loss as a result of sales being considerably below the sales budget. Since this was to be one of the major sales quarters of the year, the president was understandably concerned; but, in internal discussions, he was reassured that the budget would be met. Consultants were called into the picture at about that time, and the president asked them to give him an objective evaluation of what the real conditions for the current year might be. The consultants first discussed the basis of sales forecast with the sales vice president, particularly after they learned of the tremendous increase that the forecast represented over the prior year. He insisted that his forecast was a good one and that it was going to be met.

One of the first places at which the consultants checked the forecast was the association for this particular industry. The industry-association figures projected a similar increase in sales. Of course, the type of industry in which this company was engaged led the consultants to believe that there might be a general air of optimism simply because of its relationship to recreational demands. In searching for another way to test this sales forecast, the consultants went to the industry association of the companies which supplied the basic raw materials and asked if there were forecasts of sales for the current year. The association's data showed a projected increase of only 2 percent over the prior year. Armed with this information, the consultants returned to the client company and suggested that it review the sales forecast with an eye to the fact that one cannot increase sales substantially if an equivalent amount of raw materials is not consumed.

As a result of this and other findings, the forecast was adjusted downward, and the problem of tightening up the spending for the current year was begun. Many positions were eliminated and promotional advertising budgets cut back; the loss for the current year was substantially reduced. As a matter of fact, the sales for the year under discussion actually increased about 5 percent over the prior year.

Another example, which is more in the area of custom-product industries, might also be helpful. A company which deals predominantly in a custom-contract type of business forecast an extension of certain contracts which were in the house at the beginning of the year. However, one of these contracts was suddenly terminated during the fifth month of the budget year, and it took one calendar quarter of substantial loss to make management aware of the fact that it had to retrench because the level of business was substantially lower than had been forecast.

The company went back to its basic budget information, and the president began by requesting cuts in payroll and other costs to balance the loss in sales. He soon found that he could not make heavy payroll reductions since a good deal of the engineering staff was relatively permanent. This then led him to review the types of overhead expenses incurred by the company. As a result, he combined certain functions, and reduced the amount of office space to such an extent that he was able to sublet a building which had been previously occupied by the company. He also reduced the number of telephone extensions and hence telephone costs, and he withdrew credit cards for telephones, auto rentals, airlines, and so on from all persons. (He later reissued certain credit cards to some of the sales people who did extensive traveling.) Through this type of basic approach to reducing costs, he was able to avoid a major disaster and finished the year with a minor profit—a year in which he might have experienced a substantial loss, considering the fact that the terminated contract represented almost 20 percent of annual sales.

Note that in both these examples the middle-of-the year reaction by management depended heavily upon the information available in their budgets. By having specific detailed information as to what constituted its costs at a given level of sales, management was able to react fast enough to turn the company around in a relatively short period of time.

When the annual budget is prepared, it is assumed that a certain product mix, estimated operating levels, and other factors will prevail. If these conditions change during the year, variances are created simply because the original budget did not contain good forecasts. The tendency in many companies is to revise budgets frequently to reflect changing conditions. As a result, the effectiveness of budgetary control may be lost; and if the interim budget revisions are handled loosely, they can in fact be misused by employing them as a method of covering up variances and hiding poor performance. On the other hand, many companies operate under the philosophy that the original budget is the objective for the year. If the budget represents a segment of the long-range plan of the company, it is necessary that variances from the original budget be followed carefully to determine the effect on the overall plan.

From the standpoint of reporting, it is necessary to provide for occasional interim revisions of the budget. In a system where the budgeting is integrated with the accounting and reporting system, these interim revisions should be of sufficient magnitude to justify the effort necessary to revise the budget, product standard cost, and so on. A basic policy should be established to identify the magnitude of a variance which would warrant a budget revision.

There are instances when major factors influence the validity of the original budget and necessitate a complete interim revision. If a new facility is put into operation during the budget period, the effect that it will have on cost performance should be recognized; the budget should be revised accordingly. Whenever there is a major disaster, such as a fire or flood, the original operating budget must be disregarded, obviously, and a revised budget prepared for the recovery period.

Occasionally, a major error is made in forecasts of sales, wage levels, or general economic conditions. If there is a major distortion, it is necessary to provide a budget to identify the actual conditions. In the preparation of their budgets, many companies anticipate what actions would be taken if, for example, the sales forecast is not met. This approach is sometimes called a "downdraft" budget. To prepare a downdraft budget, it is necessary to anticipate the steps which would be taken if business fell off or if a major economic disruption occurred. Such a budget would identify those positions to be eliminated in order to meet costs at various operating levels, and it would provide for an orderly program of reducing expenditures to conform to lower activity levels.

* * *

In summary, the way that budget comparisons and variances are reported is very important. The reporting should provide for identification of responsibility, control over cost incurrence, and control over performance. It should contain interpretation and analysis to increase its usefulness to operating management.

In order to increase the usefulness of the budget for line managers, a coordinated effort in preparing the budgets is necessary. Resulting variances should be understood, analyzed, and corrective action taken where necessary. Avoid revising budgets too frequently, since the relationship of the short-term budget to the long-term objectives of the company might be lost sight of. However, sufficient flexibility in making budget revisions should be provided so that there will be no loss of confidence in the usefulness of the budget as a medium for performance measurement.

The responsibility of the accounting organization to provide accurate information cannot be too heavily stressed: A lack of accuracy in reporting can nullify efforts directed at increasing the usefulness of budget reporting.

11

Use of Budgeting Techniques in Service Companies

Up to this point our discussion has centered almost entirely on the use of budgetary planning and control systems in manufacturing environments. Our discussions of sales planning, inventory and production planning, budgeting of manufacturing costs, and development of general, administrative, and research budgets have all been oriented toward manufacturing businesses. But, of course, there is a large group of businesses engaged in nonmanufacturing activities, and such businesses can benefit greatly from a properly designed budgetary planning and control system.

Many of the budgeting methods and procedures described for manufacturing companies will apply to service businesses, but certain unique features of service-company operations require the emphasis of special budgetary planning and control techniques. In this chapter we intend to develop the budgeting requirements of service businesses and to describe the applicable techniques.

Basically, there are two reasons why special attention should be devoted to budgetary planning and control techniques in nonmanufacturing businesses. First, planning and control are universal functions in all businesses, whether the basic mission of the business is to produce and sell goods or to provide services. You will also recognize, if you are engaged in a service industry, that many service businesses have become more competitive in recent years. This increase in competition can be attributed to many things, such as the growth of the economy, the increase in specialized services, and so on. But the important point is that when competition increases, more of a premium is placed on adequate planning and good control. Second, the art of budgeting is probably not as well developed in many service companies as it is in manufacturing concerns. In manufacturing industries, budgeting is forced upon the businessman to some extent by the need to keep sales and production coordinated—that is, by the need to control inventory levels. In this sense the investment in inventory forces a certain amount of planning. In most service companies, however, the services largely require human effort, and the services are generally performed after the orders are received. The investment in inventory as we know it in manufacturing does not exist, and, consequently, the management of a service company may not see the same need for planning and control.

In the sense that budgeting is a planning and control system, the techniques applied to service companies will be very similar to those applied to manufacturing companies. Consequently, a service company is faced not only with the same problem of developing an overall corporate budget or profit plan for the ensuing year but also with the requirement of establishing good budgetary control that follows a sound plan of organization. The major difference in budgeting nonmanufacturing activities relates to the types of costs incurred and hence to the control techniques applied.

In most service businesses, the major cost element is that of personnel; this is reflected in salaries, wages, commissions, bonuses, and fringe benefits, as well as in lesser costs related to supporting personnel, such as space cost. Because of this fact, budgeting techniques are primarily concerned with planning the use of human resources and with controlling personnel effectiveness. In order to develop such techniques in a meaningful way, we will refer to two specific types of service companies: a casualty insurance company and a firm of professional architects. In some aspects their problems are quite similar, but in others they are not.

The Casualty Insurance Company represents a broad class of businesses providing services that generate a considerable amount of routine paperwork and clerical activity. In fact, insurance companies have sometimes been referred to as large paper-processing factories. By contrast, the architectural firm represents the broad class of professional firms which have increased in great profusion over the past decade and which provide professional services to businessmen and to the general public. Professional work is characterized by the fact that much of the human effort involved is not readily subject to the application of routine standards and routine procedural definition. Despite the fact that the products of these two service companies might be described quite differently, their common denominator is the investment of time on the part of personnel; this is a particularly important point in developing the techniques of budgetary control.

The relationship of budgetary planning and control to organization in service companies is fully as important as in manufacturing companies. Control is exercised by the various department heads, and budgetary reporting should follow the normal responsibility structure found in any good organization. There is a subtle difference, however, in the way in which the organizational structures of many service companies enter into the budgetary planning and control system. That difference becomes evident when we look at the responsibility for and contribution to profit in a service company.

In many service companies, relationships are not clearly defined; that is, all departments contribute to the production of services and hence to the net profit. Thus in a firm of architects the responsibility for poor profits, for example, cannot be attributed to any of the partners or departments involved in the various aspects of the architectural work. Far more likely is the general complaint that "We did not have enough contracts."

A manufacturing company by its nature tends to have a clearer picture of who is responsible for the production and sale of products. Because of inventory accounting requirements, if for no other reason, the manufacturer accumulates his costs of purchasing materials, of converting the materials into end products, and, finally, of selling and delivering products to customers. By using such techniques as standard product cost accounting, product management, and selling expense controls, the manufacturer can determine more quickly how he made or lost money, who was responsible, and to what extent. You can appreciate that this contrast is not meant to be all-inclusive but simply reflects some situations that have been encountered. From the standpoint of service-company management, a premium must be put on defining the operations required to produce a service profitably and on assigning responsibility organizationally for planning and controlling such operations efficiently.

Organizationally, service companies can define their structure in terms of three basic types of departments, and to do so greatly facilitates budgetary planning and control. These departmental classifications are profit centers, service centers, and administrative or corporate centers. Exhibit 92 is a simplified table of this form of organizational breakdown for a casualty insurance company and for a firm of architects. Note that the departments named are really functions (most service companies are organized on a functional basis) but that the functions have been grouped into the three organizational classifications just mentioned.

For The Casualty Insurance Company the Underwriting Department is identified as the profit center. There are four service centers: agency service, branch office services, claims services, and actuarial-statistical services. In addition, there are three administrative centers: administration, actuarial research, and general accounting. For the architect, the profit center is identified as projects management, and service centers include design, drafting, specification writing, and construction supervision; as indicated by Exhibit 92, there is only one administrative center in the firm. In each firm, the administrative center includes various services, such as those provided by personnel departments, and so on.

The logic of identifying underwriting and projects management, respectively, as

SERVICE COMPANY—TABLE OF ORGANIZATION STRUCTURE   EXHIBIT 92

COMPANY   DEPARTMENTAL CLASSIFICATIONS

	Profit Center	*Service Center*	*Corporate Center*
The Casualty Insurance Co.	Underwriting	Agency Service Branch Office Claim Actuarial-Statistical	Administration Actuarial-Research General Accounting
Architects & Associates	Projects Management	Design Drafting Specification Writing Construction Supervision	Administration

profit centers will have to stand on its own merits because there is no specific formula that can be applied. It should not be inferred that the identification of a department as a profit center makes it of greater importance to the overall operation of the business. The real purpose of such identification is to improve budgetary planning and control by assigning responsibility consistent with the way the operations of the business are carried out. Elaboration of this point will help to clarify the reasoning behind it. Let us look at the way the architectural firm conducts business. The architects design new construction and turn over finished blueprints and specifications to a general contractor who does the building. In addition, the architectural firm will generally supervise the construction on behalf of the owner to insure that it is completed in accordance with the architectural design. Each contract entered into by the firm to design a new building becomes a project, and a project manager is put in charge of the project throughout the course of design and construction. If the project manager considers himself assigned to a specific department in the firm (which he may not), it would be a projects-management department.

In the course of managing the project, this man and others like him are in the best position to plan the level of budgeted activity and to control the costs incurred on projects. The project manager will shepherd the job through its design and drafting phases; he will oversee the writing of specifications and supervise the construction; and he will be responsible for all costs incurred through these operations. Because this method of operation is used by the firm, the project manager is the logical profit center. This would not necessarily be the case if the firm's operational method were significantly different.

Applying this logic to The Casualty Insurance Company, the company's operating practice authorizes the underwriter to accept or reject business, to determine the types of coverages that will be sold, and to establish pricing for the various coverages. The actual preparation and issuance of policies and premium notices, the payment of claims, and the processing of policy statistics—as well as the maintenance of agency relations and contact work—are all service-center activities that assist the underwriter in carrying out the mission of the company. This concept of profit-center management in service companies may seem a bit unusual, but it should not be discarded lightly if management wishes to organize for profit planning and control.

One of the great values that a good budgetary planning and control system can offer to a service company is the development of an overall, annual profit plan. When the service company has been operating under a procedure that simply calls for the development of annual expense budgets that are largely related to the actual expenses of the prior year, management forgoes the opportunity to study and approve costs in terms of their revenue-producing capabilities. Furthermore, management in such cases fails to get the benefit of the integrated planning that results when cost and expense levels are directly associated with the revenue budgeted.

In many respects the process of establishing an overall budget for a service business is very similar to that of a manufacturing company. The starting point is the development of a marketing plan. This includes, for the insurance company, projections that identify the number of new and renewal policies by risk category or by policy classification. Past trends and experience can be highly useful in developing this plan. The responsibility for developing the plan falls on the underwriters, although they would probably secure advice and help from the agency service department.

At this point in the planning, management must decide what expenses will be incurred by putting these policies on the books and servicing them. This is very similar to the budgeting procedure for manufacturing companies with respect to determining the sequence of production operations required to make the finished goods. In our mythical insurance company, there are a number of departments, including underwriting and the four service centers, which will contribute to the processing of policies and to the payment of claims. Each of these departments will be subdivided into sections, which perform various routine operations.

To illustrate, let's take a look at the branch-office service department, which is concerned with rating the approved policy application, typing the new or renewed policy, preparing an account card with various policy statistics, and preparing a premium notice to be sent to the agent or policyholder. In addition, when the premium is paid, the branch-office service department will deposit the agent's check, credit the agent's account, and indicate payment on the policy account card. For each of these operations certain costs can be anticipated; such costs can be defined as standard or expected operating cost rates for the various operations. We will call them budgeted cost rates or budget-charging rates.

The marketing plan can be "exploded" into the various types of major operations that pertain to each policy group or product line. By relating those operations to the budgeted cost rates, the insurance company can develop a budget for the profit center and for each of the service centers. A fixed budget can be developed for each of the corporate or administrative centers, and this budget can define the various programs which management has decided to undertake, such as research work. By combining the operations budgets for the profit and service centers with the fixed or program budgets of the administrative centers, the total expenses for the budget year are available. The Underwriting Department will then budget the losses anticipated from predetermined loss ratios developed by the Actuarial Department.

The resulting profit plan gives top management an overall view of the expected profitability of the company, based on the various coverages indicated by the marketing plan. In addition, by calculating profitability according to policy classification —which can be done by projecting premium revenue through the use of historical averages and then subtracting the anticipated losses and operational expenses— management can determine the profit contribution of each type of policy and gain an indication of what the costs of selling and servicing a policy line will be and what the nature of those costs will be. By regrouping budgeted expenses by department, management can decide if the present staffing levels are excessive or inadequate and can investigate the reasons for any misstaffing.

Of course this type of profit planning requires that a service company, in this case the insurance company, have a good knowledge of its cost structure and the way in which operations are sequenced in order to produce the service sold. If these things

EXHIBIT 93

SAMPLE TASK BUDGET—ARCHITECTS & ASSOCIATES

Job: Science Lab—State U. Phase: Drafting Date: Nov. 30, 19— Project Manager: John Smith Partner Approval: H.V.R.

Task/Drawing	Man Days Required				*Per Diem Value*	Accomplishment by Pay Period											
	P.M.	*Supv.*	*Senior*	*Junior*		*1–15*		*1–29*		*2–12*		*2–26*		*3–12*		*3–26*	
						%	*$*	*%*	*$*	*%*	*$*	*%*	*$*	*%*	*$*	*%*	*$*
1. Basement plan	1	2	5	15	$ 1,650												
2. First floor plan	2	4	9	22	2,735												
3. Detail of 1st floor lobby area	1	3	5	8	1,330												
4. Typical floor—2	1	1	1	4	550												
5. Typical floor—3	—	1	1	4	425												
6. Typical floor—4	—	1	1	4	425												
7. Typical floor—5	—	1	1	4	425												
8. Roof & penthouse	1	2	3	7	1,000												
9. Site plan	2	1	4	9	1,230												
10. Riser diagram	1	3	3	10	1,280												
11. Lab service core detail	1	2	7	15	1,820												
12. Interior sketches	2	1	8	8	1,510												
13. General review & discussion	5	3	3	4	1,220												
Total:	17	23	51	114	$15,600												

are not well known to the management, the adoption of the budgetary planning and control system must include a study of these factors. We will discuss this in greater detail later.

With respect to the firm of architects or any other professional firm, the establishment of a marketing plan may be a far more difficult task. From an organizational point of view it might be expected that the project manager, because he is the profit center, would be able to determine the revenue that could be expected during the budget year. This is only partially true, because while any given project manager will be in a position to develop the planned revenue resulting from contracts presently in the house, it may be all but impossible for him to determine what additional contracts will be received during the budget year. The firm never knows when a new property owner will come to them with a request for architectural services. To get around this difficulty, a two-pronged approach to sales planning is used. The purpose of such budgetary planning is not only to establish an overall annual profit plan but also to show management how much new business must be generated during the ensuing year.

The first phase of the two-pronged approach is to consider all contracts presently in the house. Each project manager reviews the status of his contracts in terms of tasks completed and revenue billed in order to determine what tasks remain to be accomplished and what the billing potential is. To do this the project manager will refer to the basic planning document for an individual contract; that is, the task budget. Exhibit 93 shows a sample page from such a task budget. This particular page is taken from the drafting stage of the contract and shows the particular tasks, in this case the number of required drawings, with an allowance in terms of man-days. The man-day allowances are priced by use of a per diem rate for each category of labor involved in the drafting work. The aggregate of all these per diem rates gives the project manager a theoretical value of the contract. For this phase it amounts to $15,600. Any concessions that the firm has given to its clients from this theoretical value are already known regarding work in the house, and the project manager can develop his planned revenue accordingly. After each project manager has developed his planned revenue, the firm will have the total revenue forecast for contracts in progress for the budget year.

The second prong of the dual-pronged approach requires that the top management of the firm calculate the overall revenue expected in the ensuing year, so that management can see how much new business has to be generated. This can be done by making use of certain management policy assumptions. These assumptions also get to the root of how management will exercise control over professional firm activities.

Basically, a professional firm, such as a firm of architects, is selling time and talent. In order to earn an adequate return, management must determine three things:

1. The number of persons to be employed by professional classification, such as designers, draftsmen, field construction supervisors, and so on.
2. The percentage of available working hours during which these people are expected to be productively employed. (This is frequently referred to as the chargeable time ratio.)

EXHIBIT 94

MANNING TABLE AND PER DIEM VALUATION: ARCHITECTS & ASSOCIATES

(*Year 19—*)

Department: Design
Responsibility Head: William Abel

Date Prepared: Nov. 30, 19—
By: W. Abel
Approved: RCA

Column No.:	1	2	3	4	5	6	7	8	9	10
Name	Total Hours	Vacation —Holiday Hours	Available Hours	Budgeted Chargeable Time Ratio	Chargeable Hours	Cost Class	Cost Rate	Total Standard Cost	Per Diem Value (*Hourly Rate*)	Total Billing Value
			(1) − (2)		(3) × (4)			(5) × (7)		(5) × (9)
W. Abel	2,080	170	1,910	60 %	1,146	10	$15.00	$17,190	$25.00	$ 28,650
C. Elliott	2,080	170	1,910	70	1,337	8	12.00	16,044	24.00	32,088
A. McDonald	2,080	130	1,950	80	1,560	7	8.00	12,480	20.00	31,200
G. Stevenson	2,080	90	1,990	90	1,791	6	5.00	8,955	12.50	22,387
R. Abbott	2,080	90	1,990	90	1,791	6	5.00	8,955	12.50	22,387
B. McBride	1,040	85	955	90	860	6	5.00	4,300	12.50	10,750
New hire—1	1,040	5	1,035	90	932	5	4.00	3,728	10.00	9,320
New hire—2	520	3	517	90	465	5	4.00	1,860	10.00	4,650
Department *total*			12,257	80.6%	9,882			$73,512		$161,432

3. The value to the clients and average cost of each group of personnel by professional classification. The value will normally be expressed as the per diem rate and will be related to the man's salary or expected drawings. In addition, it will include a provision for covering various overhead costs and an adequate profit return, assuming the chargeable time ratio established previously.

When management has made a decision on these three policy assumptions, it is possible to calculate the total per diem revenue that will be earned by each departmental group. The aggregate of all the groups then becomes the planned total revenue for the firm as a whole, assuming that management does not intend to allow any planned fee concessions for individual contracts. Exhibit 94 shows an annual manning table and per diem valuation for the design department of the architectural firm. The exhibit shows clearly how each of the three policy decisions discussed previously enters into the calculation.

By comparing the total planned revenue with the projected revenue developed by project managers for contracts in the house, the partners of the firm can determine how much additional business must be generated and can make promotional plans accordingly. One of the advantages of developing planned revenue under the per diem concept is the fact that it also establishes the cost and profit levels, since these factors are built into the per diem rate. Furthermore, budgetary control is facilitated because management can review continuously, as operations progress, what the actual chargeable time ratios are and whether project managers are completing the contracts within the planned per diem prices.

From what has been said previously in this chapter, it is apparent that variable budgeting becomes increasingly significant in the measurable or routine areas of human activity. In the insurance-company illustration, for example, there are a great many routine operations carried on to sell and service policies. By examining each organizational group in each department, one generally finds that a number of people are engaged in activities directed at the achievement of a single objective. Consider the Claim Department; certain operations are required to process each claim, such as:

1. Checking that the coverage is in force.
2. Preparing a claim file.
3. Conducting preliminary investigation.
4. Establishing a tentative reserve requirement (if necessary).
5. Completing investigation.
6. Preparing a claim check.
7. Closing the claim file, including posting of loss to the policyholder record.

For each of these operations standard time allowances could be established and a variable budget determined. However, in a large company this might be quite a cumbersome task in terms of budget administration and reporting. A simplification called "piggybacking" can be applied when the sequence of operations is carried out over a relatively short interval of time and when all of the operations are performed in one organizational unit. Under the simplified procedure, the allowable costs for each of the operations are added together to get a budget rate for the entire processing of a particular type of claim. The categorization of types of claims can be as numerous as necessary so that meaningful budget rates can be established. Then a count of each notice of loss processed in the claim office will give us the activity level for that particular claim office; and by simply extending the activity level, multiplied by the budget rate, we can prepare a statement of earned budget for the claim-office supervisor.

This simplified illustration of variable budgeting is applicable to numerous activities in a service company. It facilitates budgetary control because supervisors know the rates and the work required and can schedule the work to keep employee productivity up.

Of equal importance to management is the way in which budget-charging rates can be used to analyze the structure of operating costs and also to determine product profitability. For the latter purpose it is necessary, as already discussed, for a department charged with profit responsibility to control the amount of service cost incurred. In the case of The Casualty Insurance Company, this role falls to the underwriter. Therefore, when the claim office is paying a claim on a particular policy, it is in effect paying the claim for the underwriter. The underwriter is charged, therefore, with the budget rate for claim cost, multiplied by the number of claims handled by policy type; thus he knows the standard claim cost during the period on all policies in force.

Exhibit 95 shows a page from a schedule of budget-charging rates for the insurance company. Such rates are those that the various operating supervisors earn for each unit of work processed. For example, the supervisor of the registration section of the Claim Department would earn an $8 budget for each Class 1 claim processed and a $12 budget for each Class 2 claim processed. At the same time, the Underwriting Department would be charged $39 and $66, respectively, for every Class 1

EXHIBIT 95   SCHEDULE OF BUDGET CHARGING RATES—SAMPLE PAGE
(*The Casualty Insurance Co.*)

Work Unit	Department	Section		Salary And Benefits	Other	Total
Notice of loss—Class 1	Claim (13)	Registration	(01)	$ 7	$ 1	$ 8
		Investigation	(02)	23	3	26
		Claim payment	(03)	1	—	1
		Files	(04)	3	1	4
		Total		$34	$ 5	$39
Notice of loss—Class 2	Claim (13)	Registration	(01)	$ 9	$ 3	$12
		Investigation	(02)	40	7	47
		Claim payment	(03)	2	1	3
		Files	(04)	3	1	4
		Total		$54	$12	$66

Budget Rates header spans the Salary And Benefits, Other, and Total columns.

BUDGET PERFORMANCE REPORT—CLAIM DEPARTMENT   EXHIBIT 96

(*The Casualty Insurance Co.: June 19—*)

Department: Claim
Responsibility
Head: J. Ault

Better (Worse) Than Earned Budget			Actual Expenses		Year to Date	
Month	Year to Date	Section	Month	Year to Date	Earned Budget	Annual Budget
$ —	$ —	Administration	$ 52,722	$ 372,880	$ —	$ 355,000
(3,211)	(29,947)	Registration	83,216	525,262	495,315	$ 515,000
(825)	16,485	Investigation	394,252	2,348,615	2,365,100	2,250,000
765	6,258	Claim payment	31,020	198,752	205,010	210,000
2,210	14,290	Files	30,224	181,315	195,605	180,000
($1,061)	$ 7,086	*Total*	$591,434	$3,626,824	$3,261,030	$3,510,000
—	—	Earnings charged to underwriting	537,651	3,261,030		
($1,061)	$ 7,086	Net expense	$ 53,783	$ 365,794		

	Units Processed			Earnings	
Total Earnings: Notice of loss—	Month	Year to Date	Rate	Month	Year to Date
Class 1	1,451	8,872	$39	$ 56,589	$ 346,008
2	1,792	10,857	66	118,272	716,562
3	2,106	12,750	80	168,480	1,020,000
4	2,159	13,094	90	194,310	1,178,460
Total	7,508	45,573		$537,651	$3,261,030

and Class 2 claim processed during a reporting period. Changes in rates due to supervisory effort and methods improvement can be identified as they occur.

The use and analysis of reports in service companies is very much like that in manufacturing companies as discussed in Chapter 10. The reports should disclose variances in terms of personnel effectiveness, which can be controlled by the supervisor or department head concerned, and in terms of volume or activity, which can be controlled by the profit-center head or by top management. Exhibit 96 shows a monthly budget performance report for the Claim Department of the insurance company. The annual budget column on the far right shows the budgeted expenses, assuming that Claim Department activities were in accordance with the overall profit plan. The actual expenses, of course, show the expenses that were incurred for the period. The earned-budget allowance shows the amount of earnings based on the claim activity processed, which is detailed in the box shown on the report. The performance variances are shown in the two left-hand columns for month and year to date. These two columns show whether the section supervisors spent more or less than they earned, on the basis of the workload handled. Exhibit 97, monthly budget report for the Underwriting Department, shows the claim cost based on the budgeted charging rates used to develop the earned budget for the Claim Department. Thus the underwriter can tell whether claim activity was in accordance with his overall profit plan and what impact any deviations had on the profitability from insurance operations.

You will note that the claim costs on an earned-budget basis exceeded the amount provided for in the annual profit plan by $106,030 for the year to date. This was so because of greater claim activity. The Underwriting Department can justify the additional activity, and hence the cost, because of the larger volume of business and the larger profit. This budget report then illustrates a profit-center report. From the report you can see that the underwriting profit for the year-to-date period amounted to $3,790,535 at standard loss ratios and commission rates. The actual profit was

EXHIBIT 97

BUDGET PERFORMANCE REPORT—UNDERWRITING DEPARTMENT

(The Casualty Insurance Co.: June 19—)

Department: Underwriting
Responsibility
  Head: H. Wilson

Better (Worse) Than Profit Plan			Actual Revenue Earned Budget		Annual Profit Plan
Month	Year to Date		Month	Year to Date	Year to Date
$758,333	$4,320,500	Premiums earned	$8,725,000	$52,120,500	$47,800,000
(455,000)	(2,592,300)	Losses incurred (standard)	5,235,000	31,272,300	28,680,000
(115,417)	(658,075)	Commissions, taxes (standard)	1,308,750	7,818,075	7,160,000
$187,916	$1,070,125	Profit contribution	$2,181,250	$13,030,125	$11,960,000
		Expense—			
($ 21,120)	($ 121,050)	Underwriting	$ 271,120	$ 1,621,050	$ 1,500,000
(31,050)	(205,000)	Agency service	210,052	1,280,000	1,075,000
(7,393)	4,990	Branch office	375,060	2,195,010	2,200,000
(11,818)	(106,030)	Claim	537,651	3,261,030	3,155,000
(4,210)	(42,500)	Actuarial statistical	144,210	882,500	840,000
($ 75,591)	(469,590)	Total	$1,538,093	$ 9,239,590	$ 8,770,000
		Underwriting profit—			
$112,325	$ 600,535	at Standard	$ 643,157	$ 3,790,535	$ 3,190,000
		Actual	527,347	4,266,715	
		Variance	($ 115,810)	$ 476,180	

Better (Worse) Than Standard or Earned Budget			Actual Expense		Standard or Earned Budget	
Month	Year to Date	Variance due to—	Month	Year to Date	Month	Year to Date
($ 11,600)	$ 689,675	Losses incurred	$5,246,600	$30,582,625	$ 5,235,000	$31,272,300
(99,900)	(214,445)	Commissions, taxes	1,408,650	8,032,520	1,308,750	7,818,075
(4,310)	950	Underwriting expense	275,430	1,620,100	271,120	1,621,050
($115,810)	476,180	Total variance	$6,930,680	$40,235,245	$ 6,814,870	$40,711,425

$4,266,715—$476,180 better than standard. This variance is explained in the bottom half of the report in terms of losses and expenses controlled by the underwriters in accordance with the concept of organization in effect.

Now let us turn to two sample reports of the architectural firm. The first, Exhibit 98, is a monthly budget report for Project X. Furnished to the project manager, this report shows the total actual charges from the various service departments for task work done versus the earned budget for the tasks completed; this gives the project manager an indication of whether he is overrunning or underrunning his project, based on work completed to date.

Exhibit 99 is an operating statement for the firm, comparing actual results with the profit plan. The report clearly shows that the distributable income is less than planned despite billings significantly ahead of the plan, primarily because of overruns in project cost. Reference to job-status reports would show which project managers are responsible. Further departmental summaries would compare actual chargeable ratios with the budgeted ratios as a check on manpower utilization. These reports permit management to take whatever corrective action may be necessary. For example, if chargeable time ratios are not up to the set standards, then management can consider whether to reduce the force or attempt to get more work scheduled for the service departments. With respect to project management, failures to control cost can be reviewed closely as the job is in process rather than after it is completed.

The type of budgetary planning and control system discussed for service companies requires the development of budget-charging rates and operating standards, whether it be on a recurring basis, such as the case of the insurance company for relatively routine operations, or on the basis of planning each individual contract, such as is done through the task budget in an architectural firm. Standards are applicable only where the content of the work is relatively routine or can be predetermined by study or judgment. Basically, there are two methods by which budget rates can be established and the accompanying operating performance set:

1. The first and perhaps the easiest method is to make use of historical experience. This requires a test period during which data must be accumulated, unless the appropriate data are already present in the records. The use of historical experience has the advantage of producing realistic figures, so that operating supervisors know that such rates can be achieved. In addition, the use of historical experience provides supervisors with a realistic bench mark against which to measure their ability to effect subsequent improvement. Such use of historical data can be an effective motivational device.

2. The second method is to establish budget rates based on work measurement and methods study whereby technical experts, usually from a methods and procedure department, go into each section of the company and establish the preferred method of processing and the standard time allowed for a particular method. This technique is obviously a far more costly and time-consuming one to carry out in a company of large size, but it does have the advantage of assuring management that the budget rate will be set on an efficient operating basis.

EXHIBIT 98   MONTHLY PROJECT BUDGET REPORT: ARCHITECTS & ASSOCIATES
(October 31, 19—)

Job Name: Project X   Partner: H. V. Rodney   Project Mgr: John Smith

| | | Amount of Per Diems | | | |
| | Per Diem | | | Job Over* | % |
Phase	Budget	Earned	Spent	Under Budget	Complete
Design	12,350	12,350	12,350	—	100%
Drafting	15,600	2,340	2,750	410*	15%
Specification	5,000	—	—	—	—
Construction	12,000	—	—	—	—
Total	44,950	14,690	15,100	410*	33%
Fee gain or (loss)	(5,950)				
Total negotiated fee	39,000				

EXHIBIT 99   OPERATING STATEMENT—ARCHITECTS & ASSOCIATES
(April 19—)

| This Month | | | Year to Date | |
Better (Worse) Than Profit Plan	Amount		Amount	Better (Worse) Than Profit Plan
$35,050	$312,550	Billings (net of consultant fees)—	$1,213,750	$113,750
($15,020)	$125,020	Less—standard cost of billings	$ 485,500	($ 45,500)
$20,030	$187,530	Standard gross profit	$ 728,250	$ 68,250
676	9,426	Fee gains or losses	37,256	(2,256)
(16,042)	24,792	Project budget variances	99,981	(64,981)
(999)	1,999	Project expenses written off	8,314	(4,314)
$ 3,665	$151,313	Actual gross profit on billings	$ 582,699	($ 3,301)
		Overhead expenses—technical time Cost—		
($ 30)	$ 6,280	Vacation	$ 23,495	$ 1,505
(842)	6,408	Sickness	27,851	(1,149)
500	5,750	Other absences	23,016	2,000
(1,926)	10,926	Promotion	42,811	(7,811)
175	1,875	Professional development	7,496	496
(637)	6,012	Training	24,256	(1,756)
(301)	5,301	Lost time	21,006	(1,006)
($ 3,061)	$ 42,552	*Total*	$ 169,931	($ 7,721)
		Overhead expenses—administrative—		
$ 125	$ 4,500	Office salaries and related costs	$ 18,953	($ 453)
250	8,075	Office services	32,401	1,101
(83)	13,833	Occupancy costs	54,496	504
$ 292	$ 26,408	*Total*	$ 105,850	$ 1,152
$ 896	$ 82,353	Distributable income	$ 306,918	($ 9,870)

EXHIBIT 100 BLOCK CONTROL WORKSHEET

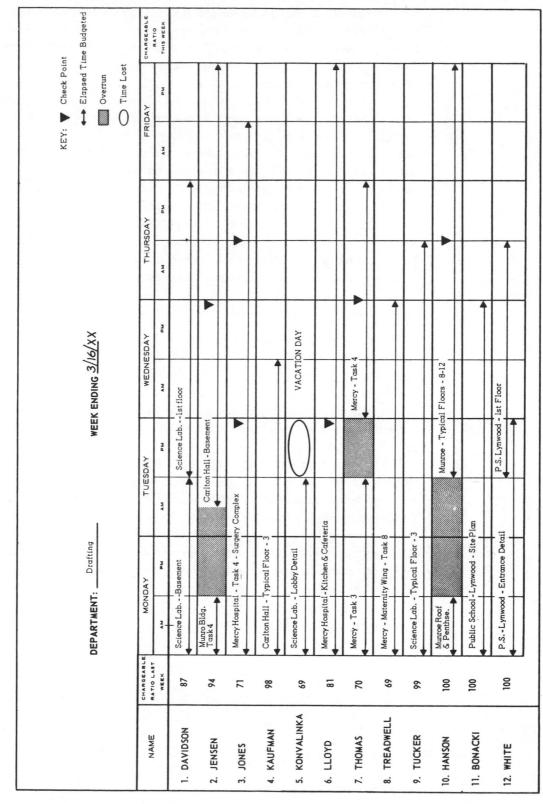

DEPARTMENT: _____ Drafting _____

WEEK ENDING _3/16/XX_

KEY: ▼ Check Point
↕ Elapsed Time Budgeted
▨ Overrun
○ Time Lost

NAME	CHARGEABLE RATIO LAST WEEK	MONDAY AM	MONDAY PM	TUESDAY AM	TUESDAY PM	WEDNESDAY AM	WEDNESDAY PM	THURSDAY AM	THURSDAY PM	FRIDAY AM	FRIDAY PM	CHARGEABLE RATIO THIS WEEK
1. DAVIDSON	87	Science Lab. – Basement		Science Lab. – 1st floor								
2. JENSEN	94	Munro Bldg. Task 4		Carlton Hall - Basement								
3. JONES	71	Mercy Hospital - Task 4 - Surgery Complex										
4. KAUFMAN	98	Carlton Hall - Typical Floor - 3										
5. KONVALINKA	69	Science Lab. - Lobby Detail			VACATION DAY							
6. LLOYD	81	Mercy Hospital - Kitchen & Cafeteria										
7. THOMAS	70	Mercy - Task 3				Mercy - Task 4						
8. TREADWELL	69	Mercy - Maternity Wing - Task 8										
9. TUCKER	99	Science Lab. - Typical Floor - 3										
10. HANSON	100	Munroe Roof & Penthse.				Munroe - Typical Floors - 8-12						
11. BONACKI	100	Public School - Lynwood - Site Plan										
12. WHITE	100	P.S.-Lynwood - Entrance Detail				P.S. Lynwood - 1st Floor						

215

Once standards and budget rates have been established, it is up to the unit supervisors to see that the work is accomplished in accordance with these rates. This aspect of supervisory control is not found to as large an extent in service companies as it is in many manufacturing companies. There are, however, a number of techniques by which supervisors can assure adequate control and thus improve the effectiveness of the overall budgeting system.

One example will illustrate the point with respect to the architectural firm. Exhibit 100 shows a block control worksheet used in the drafting department of Architects & Associates. With this technique the head of the drafting department lists each draftsman in the left column of the worksheet and lists the days of the week across the top. Each day or half-day represents a "block," which is the time interval being controlled. As drafting work is assigned to individual draftsmen, the head of the department inserts the job number in the appropriate block and draws a line to indicate the time when the work should be completed. The illustration shows the job status as of Wednesday morning. From this worksheet he can see how efficiently he is scheduling all draftsmen, and he can check on each job as it is in progress or as the time for completion arrives.

* * *

In summary, we have discussed specific techniques that facilitate good budgetary planning and control in service companies. We have stressed organization because many service businesses have failed to identify profit centers where profit control can be effected. Also, the relationship between service centers and profit centers clarifies the development of standard budget rates. The use of budget rates permits variable budgeting, a powerful tool for performance measurement in the control of human effort.

For many service companies and professional firms, estimating jobs can be a major problem. The use of a good budgetary planning and control system can facilitate better estimating by providing the estimator with budget rates for the various operating requirements of the job. In turn, once the job is secured, the work can be controlled by comparing the cost of actual activities with the budgeted rates.

In general, service companies can benefit enormously by adopting a modern budgetary planning and control system. It may appear that considerable extra effort is required of management to use these budget techniques, but with such a system management has the opportunity to control costs and plan profits in a meaningful way, and with a proper assignment of organizational responsibility.

Special Budget Problems in Retail Merchandising

THE PRINCIPLES OF BUDGETING for costs, expenses, and working and fixed capital which have been discussed and illustrated in previous chapters apply to all industries and business activities. However, the techniques for their application vary according to the particular requirements of the industry involved. Retail merchandising is an important and extremely competitive industry in which continued pressures on profit margins have created a great interest in achieving the planning and control benefits of good budgeting.

Retail merchants have expense control problems, but we will not deal with such problems in this chapter. The principles and techniques in this area are not very different from those in other industries which we have covered. Rather, special emphasis will be given here to the budgeting and control of merchandise when the objective is to provide customers with "the right merchandise, at the right place, at the right time, in the right quantities, and at the right price." Merchandise represents 60 to 70 percent of a merchant's total expenditures. Clearly, then, retail organizations must give considerable attention to planning and maintaining an inventory investment that is reasonably balanced with sales. The principal aspects of this balance are—

1. The range of choice or assortment in merchandise to be offered to the customer when this choice has to do with prices, styles, colors, sizes, materials, and the like within a particular classification or grouping of merchandise.

2. The depth of stock to support the sales of each item in the assortment in such a way as to prevent serious imbalances resulting in out-of-stock situations or in the accumulation of excess goods.

3. The total inventory to be carried so as to attain and maintain a turnover rate consistent with profit objectives and with in-stock or customer-service objectives.

These aspects of balance provide the framework within which the retailer must develop merchandise planning and control tools. Clearly, dollar planning and control are necessary for the accomplishment of total stock balance; the aspects of assortment breadth and supporting-stock depth are related to merchandise planning and control in units.

How formal this planning must be is another question. There is considerable variation, depending on the presence or absence of certain conditions. First, when an organization is large, with many branches and selling departments, there appears to be a greater emphasis on more formal forward planning. Since merchandising responsibility tends to be broadly delegated in large retail organizations, top management requires a plan for each responsible unit (1) as a basis for exercising control of total merchandising operations by controlling at the lower levels and (2) as a means for measuring performance of controllable units.

A second consideration which leads to formal merchandise planning is the extent of seasonal variations in the character of customer demand for products. In the case of so-called staple merchandise, where the same items are available in a store on a year-round basis, major adjustments of the sales-stock balance are limited (except in significant growth areas), and plans may be in effect for longer periods of time. On the other hand, fashion or style merchandise is characterized by wide swings in demand during different seasons (fall, holiday, spring, summer, transitional). Such variations must be anticipated and reflected in current plans in order to maintain turnover objectives.

A third important consideration is vendor lead times. Again, staple merchandise, in continuous demand and therefore replenished frequently, can be obtained from local resources or from a local distribution point of a major vendor. This enables the store to adjust its stock position of such items on a day-to-day basis. Other merchandise, however, involves advance commitments in line with plans for future selling periods. Manufacturers of men's clothing do not even cut garments until after the retailer's order is placed, which may be up to eight or nine months in advance of the selling season. Women's apparel is bought in the New York market; this requires retailers to make forward plans and commitments in other parts of the country. The delivery lead times alone on import goods necessitate formal plans that indicate when dollars must be committed for future selling.

Finally, the formality of merchandise planning—in dollars and in units—depends upon the existence of formal control systems: Without a means of checking progress against plans, there is little value in going through the motions of developing elaborate plans.

We will devote the balance of this chapter to a discussion of the merchandise budgeting process in both retail dollars and units. Emphasis will be on the large retailer, since this will be more indicative of the special budgeting problems confronting retail merchandising organizations; particular attention will be given to the recent developments in unit control for both staple and fashion merchandise.

Dollar Control

Retail dollar budgeting begins with the preparation of what is commonly referred to as a merchandise plan. The typical merchandise plan includes dollar estimates for each major factor that influences gross profit realization: sales, inventories, markdowns and other reductions, purchases, and markups. The merchandise plan shown in Exhibit 101 is the result of departmental dollar planning at a depth that—

1. Focuses upon the profit potential of significant merchandise classifications.
2. Permits realistic planning of sales volume, stock requirements, and buying requirements to reflect seasonal and other variations.
3. Permits measurement of store variations in profit performance.

The depth to which individual retail organizations go in developing merchandise plans varies widely in the industry. Many do not encourage specific profit planning below the department level, since they cannot identify segments of merchandise below this level with a volume large enough to warrant individual attention. Some organizations, dealing primarily in staple merchandise, plan for a three- or six-month period, since there is no need to plan for month-to-month variations. The treatment of separate store locations within an organization depends on the assignment of merchandising responsibilities and can be justified only when subsequent control will be exercised on a store-by-store basis.

Regardless of the detail of the plans, certain fundamental approaches are necessary to achieve effective planning. Foremost, perhaps, is management's communication of total-organization guidelines to set the ground rules for depth planning. These guidelines must include financial plans regarding target sales volume, profit margins, and inventory investment. They should also include certain documentation of broad merchandising policies (change in customer appeal, emphasis on customer service, pricing, and so on); a picture of anticipated growth (economic trends, the competitive situation, and so on); and plans for operational changes (new stores, re-allocation of space, and so forth). Devoid of such guidelines, the depth of the plans may be unrealistic and, in total, completely incompatible with the financial resources and goals of the company.

A second basic element of successful planning is the provision of historical and current performance data that are compatible with the depth of planning involved. The availability and presentation of performance data (1) permit higher levels of merchandising management to make meaningful evaluations of specific departmental operations and (2) highlight areas sufficiently well-defined that corrective action may be incorporated into the new plans—for example, adjusting for overstocked or understocked conditions in a given classification of merchandise.

Finally, there has to be a means of summarizing the detailed merchandise plans to enable comparison with the top-level financial plans and to allow appropriate reconciliation. Assuming the in-depth plans are meaningful, their availability allows the reconciliation to be made on a specific basis rather than on an arbitrary or across-the-board adjustment basis.

The manner in which gross profit factors are actually developed for a merchandise plan is shown in Exhibit 101. First and most important is the forecasting of sales. The usual starting point for estimating sales for the forthcoming budget period is the total dollar sales volume for the corresponding previous period. Initially, it is reasonable to assume that future sales will be near the level of the previous period. Next, one must consider each of the factors that will lead to further adjustments of this estimate.

EXHIBIT 101

A MERCHANDISE PLAN

MERCHANDISE PLAN FOR Jan.- June 19 XX

STORE Downtown DEPARTMENT 86--Men's Furnishgs. CLASSIFICATION White Shirts

	SALES	END OF MONTH INVENTORY	MARKDOWNS		DISCOUNTS & ALLOWANCES		SHRINKAGE		PURCHASES	INITIAL MARKUP PERCENT	GROSS MARGIN	
			DOLLARS	%	DOLLARS	%	DOLLARS	%			DOLLARS	%
LAST YEAR ACTUAL												
JAN JULY	3,200	5,500	163	5.1	32	1.0	26	0.8	3,150	39.5	1,130	35.3
FEB AUG	2,500	5,700	125	5.0	28	1.1	23	0.9	2,876	40.0	895	35.8
MAR SEPT	2,400	5,900	115	4.8	26	1.1	19	0.8	2,760	40.0	864	36.0
APR OCT	2,900	5,500	145	5.0	29	1.0	23	0.8	2,697	40.1	1,044	36.0
MAY NOV	3,200	5,100	166	5.2	38	1.2	29	0.9	3,033	40.1	1,174	36.7
JUNE DEC	3,600	5,000	180	5.0	36	1.0	29	0.8	3,745	40.0	1,292	35.9
TOTAL	17,800	T/O = 3.3	894	5.0	189	1.1	149	0.8	18,261	-	6,399	35.9
CURRENT YEAR PLAN												
JAN JULY	3,600	5,600	180	5.0	36	1.0	29	0.8	3,300	40.0	1,292	35.9
FEB AUG	2,800	5,700	140	5.0	28	1.0	22	0.8	3,090	40.0	1,005	35.9
MAR SEPT	2,700	5,800	135	5.0	27	1.0	21	0.8	2,983	40.0	969	35.9
APR OCT	3,200	5,400	160	5.0	32	1.0	26	0.8	3,018	40.0	1,149	35.9
MAY NOV	3,500	4,900	175	5.0	35	1.0	28	0.8	3,238	40.0	1,256	35.9
JUNE DEC	3,800	4,800	190	5.0	38	1.0	30	0.8	3,958	40.0	1,364	35.9
TOTAL	19,600	T/O = 3.7	980	5.0	196	1.0	156	0.8	19,587	-	7,035	35.9

Prepared by _____

Approved by _____

220

As long as such factors as store location, variety of lines carried, competitive factors, and advertising and promotion stay about the same, sales for the budgeted period may be expected to reflect the most recent trend in sales of the department or of the merchandise classification. Suppose it is October and we are estimating the forthcoming January–June sales for Department *A*. Last January–June sales totaled $500,000. The current trend is indicated by the fact that July–October is 10 percent greater than the previous July–October. Thus, unless unusual circumstances are anticipated, sales during next January–June can be expected to range 10 percent higher (continuing the trend) than the corresponding previous period, or $550,000. There can be no guarantee that a prevailing trend will continue into the future. Consequently, it is essential to review factors outside the store that are likely to influence the dollar sales attainable. Such factors include price trends, consumer buying power, competitive conditions, and so on.

Important to the outlook for probable future sales are top management decisions regarding changes in store operations. It is unlikely that management would reach decisions covering such matters as expansion, increased expenditures for promotion and advertising, or greater emphasis upon credit without an evaluation of the probable effect upon the store and department sales volumes.

The ultimate sales estimate is derived from a careful appraisal of all these factors and from a final exercise of personal judgment by the person responsible for preparing the merchandise plan. The total retail dollar sales for the budgeted period must then be converted into monthly figures on the basis of—

1. Past monthly figures for the classification, department, and store.
2. Trade statistics on the percentage of monthly business represented by a comparable merchandise grouping. (This consideration will help to avoid perpetrating previous errors in merchandising judgment.)
3. Shifting dates of major holidays and the number of selling days in the month.
4. Timing of special events in the store or department.

As indicated, a major objective of merchandise planning is to maintain a well-balanced inventory relative to the month-to-month sales estimates. In practice, the retailer determines the amount of stock to be carried throughout the budget period, based on his idea of a satisfactory stock turnover. This turnover is often an automatic factor generated by the inventory control system(s) being used. (Several such systems will be discussed later in this chapter.)

In order to put the specific dollar level of inventories on a monthly basis, one of two guides is normally used. The first, a stock-sales ratio, is simply the value of the stock at the beginning of the month divided by the sales during that month. Thus if sales had been $15,000 for January and the opening inventory was $30,000 (retail value), then the stock-sales ratio is two. Based on the retailer's past experience and on the experience of other stores similar in nature and in size, as reflected in published trade statistics, these ratios are applied to the monthly sales estimates to determine corresponding planned inventories (Exhibit 102).

An alternate method of planning stocks is to establish goal figures in terms of a given number of weeks' or months' supply. If yearly stock turnover is planned at six, then the stock on hand at any time should be equal to about two months' supply

EXHIBIT 102   COMPUTING INVENTORIES

Month	Stock-Sales Ratio	× Planned Sales	= Planned Beginning-of-Month Stock
January	3.7	$5,000	$18,500
February	3.2	6,700	21,440
March	3.4	5,400	18,360
April	3.4	5,200	17,680
May	4.1	4,400	18,040
June	4.5	3,000	13,500

(twelve months divided by six equals two). The stock at the beginning of each month is then planned at approximately the level of retail sales for the next two months.

These stock-sales relationships are, of course, only an aid to planning. Consideration must be given not only to the expected sales and to the seasonal and monthly variations, but allowances must also be made for the frequency of stock checking and ordering, for lead times, and for the likelihood of unexpected sales or delays in stock procurement. As a check on the planned stocks based on these calculations, Exhibit 103 indicates how the merchant can compute his stock turnover rate (using the figures of Exhibit 102). If the results of these calculations had yielded a rate substantially different from his turnover objective, further revisions to the monthly planned stocks would have been in order.

Essentially the planned purchases (merchandise scheduled for delivery) for each month are those needed to arrive at the target stock position (expressed in dollars at retail value) at the end of that month, after considering the degree to which that month's opening inventory will be reduced by sales during the month. However,

EXHIBIT 103   COMPUTING THE TURNOVER RATE

$$\text{Planned average stock (beginning of month)} = \frac{\text{Total beginning inventories}}{\text{Number of months}}$$

$$= \frac{\$18,500 + \$21,440 + \$18,360 + \$17,680 + \$18,040 + \$13,500}{6}$$

$$= \frac{\$107,520}{6} = \$17,920$$

$$\text{Six-month stock turnover} = \frac{\text{Six months' sales}}{\text{Planned average stock}}$$

$$= \frac{\$29,700}{\$17,920} = 1.65$$

$$\text{Annual stock turnover} = 2 \times 1.65 = 3.3$$

since the retailer is dealing with *dollar* plans, he must anticipate the probable reductions in the retail value of inventories from sources other than sales. These include markdowns, stock shortages or shrinkage, and employee discounts.

In planning markdowns, which account for the major portion of dollar reductions, past experience is an important consideration. The percentage of markdowns (relative to sales) varies widely by type of merchandise but is fairly consistent from season to season or year to year. The key problem is the monthly distribution of the markdown allowance, for there is usually no close relationship between sales and markdowns from one month to the next. This distribution should reflect the anticipated timing of price reductions for season or year-end clearances, for remnants or soiled merchandise, for slow-moving items, and for promotions. The retailer must weigh his own experience and external factors in budgeting sales, inventories, and other reductions to inventories. However, once these factors have been determined, dollar purchases are calculated directly from the following relationship:

$$\text{Planned purchases} = \text{Planned sales} + \text{Planned reductions} + \text{Planned end-of-month stock} - \text{Planned beginning-of-month stock}$$

Perhaps the most complex factor to plan for is the markup percentage on merchandise. The retailer must budget markup so that the dollar gross margin between the cost of goods sold and sales is sufficient to cover all operating expenses plus a reasonable return on invested capital within the limitations imposed by competitive factors. To attain this objective, it is necessary to reflect initial markup, or the difference between the cost of merchandise and original retail price, and the maintained markup or gross margin requirements which identify the cumulative differential between merchandise costs and net sales—after allowances for loss in value due to other reductions. It is beyond the scope of this chapter to delve into the pricing action relating to these goals. It should be pointed out, however, that the budget markup appearing on a department's merchandise plan is the product of separate markup percentages worked out for each product line or type of merchandise, with the expectation that it will yield the specified composite dollar margin sufficient to recover operating costs plus the desired return on invested capital.

At this point, there should be little question that achievement of a meaningful merchandise plan requires a carefully developed plan for balancing inventory investment against expected retail sales. It should be no surprise, then, that the retail merchandiser continually strives to implement effective means of providing a flow of information that will enable management to evaluate whether current operations are in line with plans. Our references to the merchant's use of past experience indicates another reason for his efforts to provide comprehensive control records. While control records are essential to the proper execution of current plans, the same records are also a primary source of data for the detailed planning that must be done in subsequent budget periods.

Dollar control is essentially a top management instrument for the financial con-

EXHIBIT 104 RETAIL DOLLAR CONTROL

Beginning-of-the-period inventory		$30,000
Plus—additions to inventory:		
Purchases	$12,000	
Additional markups	400	
Cancellation of markdowns	200	
Returns from customers	100	
Transfers in	2,000	14,700
Total inventory available		$44,700
Less—deductions from inventory:		
Sales	$ 9,000	
Markdowns	1,000	
Returns to vendors	100	
Discounts	100	
Transfers out	200	10,400
End-of-the-period inventory		$34,300

trol of inventory investment in each unit of the store to which merchandising responsibility has been delegated. It is also used by the buyers, department managers, and store managers as an overall guide for balancing stocks within the range of control limits acceptable to top management. The merchandise units for dollar control are the same as those used for planning purposes. In the example shown in Exhibit 101, the control unit (white shirts) is a classification of merchandise within a given store. This subdivision implies that dollar stock-control records must be maintained for each control unit and is commonly known as classification control.

Exhibit 104 illustrates the nature of retail dollar control. Generally, the merchant's accounting records provide the source of data necessary to generate the retail value of ledger inventories. In contrast to unit controls, retail dollar control is more complicated; as evidenced in Exhibit 104, many factors affect the dollar value of on-hand stock. Modern data processing equipment is becoming increasingly important to the maintenance of the record systems required to provide these data on a timely basis, particularly in light of the expansion of the number of control units in large multiunit retail organizations.

Data from the dollar control records serve as an input to several important management control reports and procedures. We will discuss those procedures and reports that are directly related to the evaluation of actual merchandising performance as compared with the budgeted figures from the merchandise plan: periodic operating reports and open-to-buy reporting and control.

The illustrative calculation of the retail value of on-hand inventories previously given represents the type of information normally included on a store's periodic operating reports. A representative example of the way in which these data are presented for a department is shown in Exhibit 105. Note the following:

1. Comparative data and percentages are given as a guide for proper evaluation of variances from budget.

2. Retail ledger inventory is the basis for extending the reports to include maintained gross margin and gross profit. (This is accomplished through the stock ledger and retail method of accounting.)

3. Forward commitments are used as an input to the regulation of the residual balance of budgeted purchases (open-to-buy control).

Many retailers issue these operating reports as often as once a week on the premise that corrective action can be effective only when performance is reviewed frequently. Other stores, however, provide only monthly merchandise summaries, usually because of an inability to process the needed reports or an inability to effect the necessary cut-off control on inputs other than at month-end. These merchandise reports are generally used as a corrected starting point for open-to-buy control;

DEPARTMENT MERCHANDISE REPORT

EXHIBIT 105

SUMMARY MERCHANDISE REPORT FOR __January__ 19 __XX__

DEPARTMENT __86--Men's Furnishings__

		ALL STORES		STORE 1 DOWNTOWN		STORE 2 CENTRAL PLAZA		STORE 3 ACE STREET		STORE 4 HIGH HILLS	
		MONTH	YTD	MONTH	YTD	MONTH	YTD	MONTH	YTD	MONTH	YTD
NET SALES	TY	108,800	108,800	58,000	58,000	30,000	30,000	12,500	12,500	8,300	8,30
	PLAN	103,400	103,400	57,000	57,000	26,000	26,000	12,000	12,000	8,400	
	LY	96,500	96,500	53,000	53,000	24,000	24,000	11,100	11,100	8,400	300
RETURNS	TY	3,000	3,000	1,950	1,950	750	750	300			
	LY	2,400	2,400	1,680	1,680	500	500	200			
DISC. & ALLOW.	TY	1,135	1,135	637	637	341	341	118			
	PLAN	1,200	1,200	650	650	300	300				
	LY	1,000	1,000	583	583	245	245				
MARKDOWN DOLLARS	TY	5,331	5,331	2,900	2,900	1,380	1,380				
	PLAN	5,070	5,070	2,850	2,850	1,170	1,170				
	LY	4,825	4,825	2,703	2,703	1,128	1,128				
MARKDOWN %	TY	4.9	4.9	5.0	5.0	4.6	4.6				
	PLAN	4.9	4.9	5.0	5.0	4.5					
	LY	5.0	5.0	5.1	5.1	4.7	4.1				
SHRINKAGE %	TY	0.9	0.9	0.8	0.8	1.1	1.1				
	PLAN	1.0	1.0	0.9	0.9	1.1	1				
	LY	1.1	1.1	0.9	0.9	1.2					
MARK ON %	TY	40.0	40.0	40.2	40.2	39.0	3.				
	PLAN	39.5	39.5	40.0	40.0	39.0	3				
	LY	38.9	38.9	39.5	39.5	38.5					
GROSS MARGIN	TY	39,050	39,050	20,880	20,880	10,500	10,50				
	PLAN	36,400	36,400	20,400	20,400	9,100	9,10				
	LY	33,390	33,390	18,650	18,650	8,210	8,21				
GROSS MARGIN %	TY	35.9	35.9	36.0	36.0	35.0	35.				
	PLAN	35.2	35.2	35.8	35.8	35.0	35.0				
	LY	34.6	34.6	35.2	35.2	34.2	34.2				
CASH DISC.	TY	1,800	1,800	1,100	1,100	400	400				
	LY	2,000	2,000	1,300	1,300	600	600				
PURCHASES	TY	114,000	114,000	67,000	67,000	32,000	32,00				
E.O.M. INVENTORY	TY	130,000	-	40,000	-	38,000					
	PLAN	120,000	-	36,000	-	34,000					
ON ORDER	FEB	8,000	-	5,000	-	1,000					
	MAR	3,700	-	2,000	-	1,000					
	APR	1,000	-	600	-	300	-				
	MAY	600	-	500	-	100					
	JUNE	250	-	-	-	100					
	FUT.	1,200	-	700	-	300	-	10			

EXHIBIT 106   OPEN-TO-BUY COMPUTATIONS

FEBRUARY

February opening inventory (actual)		$40,000
On-order for delivery in February		5,000
Total on hand plus on order		$45,000
Less—planned reductions in February:		
Sales	$17,500	
Markdowns	2,100	
Other	400	20,000
February estimated ending inventory		$25,000
February planned ending inventory		37,000
February open-to-buy		$12,000

MARCH

March planned opening inventory		$37,000
On-order for delivery in March		2,000
Total on hand plus on order		$39,000
Less—planned reductions in March:		
Sales	$15,000	
Markdowns	1,800	
Other	300	17,100
March estimated ending inventory		$21,900
March planned ending inventory		35,000
March open-to-buy		$13,100

that is, the control of purchases on a period-to-period basis within the limits of the budget.

We can best describe the open-to-buy control procedure by referring to the situation depicted in Exhibit 105. Given the merchandise report in this exhibit, we know the opening inventory for February and the purchase dollars already committed for delivery in February, March, April, May, and June (the last period covered by the current budget). As of that moment, Exhibit 106 illustrates how the open-to-buy for each of these months can be determined for Store 1. These same steps would be applied for the remaining months. This approach automatically carries forward an overbought situation in January—reflected in the February opening inventory—and reduces the subsequent months' purchase allotments. The open-to-buy figures are posted to a form like the one shown in Exhibit 107. As new orders are written, the total retail value of the order is deducted from the open-to-buy for the month in which delivery of the order is anticipated. This continuous redetermination of the open-to-buy is a device not only to control spending but also to keep inventories in line with the original budget. Of course, until the next merchandise report is prepared, no consideration is given to the effects of variance in sales, markdowns, and all other factors which determine the retail value of on-hand inventories.

There are control units in a retail organization for which sales data and other factors cannot be continuously recorded. In these instances, frequent physical inventory-taking is used to determine the sales-stock relationships for classification dollar control. Estimates of dollar sales are derived from the following type of calculation:

$$\begin{matrix} \text{Derived} \\ \text{sales for} \\ \text{February} \end{matrix} = \begin{matrix} \text{January 31} \\ \text{stock} \\ \text{on-hand} \end{matrix} + \begin{matrix} \text{February} \\ \text{purchases} \end{matrix} - \begin{matrix} \text{February 28} \\ \text{stock} \\ \text{on-hand} \end{matrix}$$

As a financial control device, dollar control is concerned with stock-sales balancing on an overall basis of how much may be spent on merchandise.

Unit Control

Obviously, the retailer cannot begin to concern himself with questions of replenishing the stock of individual items until he has established what items are to be stocked in depth and controlled accordingly. Thus he must decide upon the composition of the merchandise to be offered to the customers. This process is commonly referred to as assortment planning.

Decisions relating to the composition of stocks in terms of assortment factors result from the merchant's consideration of meaningful breakdowns of larger merchandise groupings. The underlying principle of each grouping is that it can be identified with consumer demand so that it has some value in maintaining the

OPEN-TO-BUY CONTROL SHEET

EXHIBIT 107

OPEN-TO-BUY CONTROL SHEET FOR _February_ 19 _X5_

STORE _Downtown_   DEPARTMENT _86 - Men's Furnishings_

MONTH																	
FEBRUARY			MARCH			APRIL			MAY			JUNE			FUTURE ON ORDER		
DATE	AMT.	OTB	DATE	AMT.	OTB	DATE	AMT.	OTB	DATE	AMT.	OTB	DATE	AMT.	OTB	DATE	AMT.	BALANCE
		12,000			13,100			14,000			15,000			16,500			700
2/5	10,000	2,000															
2/16	1,000	1,000	2/16	1,000	12,100	2/16	3,000	11,000									
															2/19	1,000	1,700

227

sales-stock balance. Consequently, assortment factors are expressed in terms of type of merchandise, style, fabric, brand, manufacturer, price line, color, and size.

It is not our intention to array the pros and cons of different assortment factors nor to outline the various combinations that may be used in different stores and departments. We bring them to your attention because unit merchandise plans are expressed formally in terms of assortment factors. Such plans, likely to be found in a large retailing organization, are—

1. Model stock plan. An outline of the composition of stocks in terms of assortment factors, usually specifying the quantities in each assortment the buyer believes will best distribute his budgeted investment. These plans are most often found in fashion merchandise where the period for volume sales of any one item is limited, and consequently the outline of stock must be in terms of assortment factors which have some degree of stability. An example is given in Exhibit 108.

2. Basic stock list. An assortment plan for staple items; that is, those characterized by a greater stability of sales (or at least the seasonal swings are predictable). These lists generally identify specific items to be carried, including a style or vendor number and a basic low quantity to have on hand (see Exhibit 109).

3. Never-out lists. A separate listing of items identified as offering unusual sales

EXHIBIT 108

A MODEL STOCK PLAN

TYPE	COLOR	PRICE LINE	MODEL STOCK		NOTES
			FLOOR	RESERVE	
Sheath with square neck	Black	22.95	1	0	No promotions
		25.98	1	0	
		27.98	2	0	
		32.98	2	1	
		45.98	1	0	
	Blue	22.98	1	0	No promotions
		25.98	1	0	
		27.98	2	0	
		32.98	2	1	
		45.98	1	0	
	Green	22.98	1	0	
Full with tie neck	Black	35.98	1	0	Special display
		37.98	1	0	
		39.98	1	0	
		42.98	1	0	

opportunities and therefore requiring special planning and control efforts. These items are usually of long-term regular demand. Basic low-stock quantities are also specified.

Planning the assortment factors to be included in the regular stock investment does not, in itself, achieve the goals of stock-sales balance or reasonable turnover. Further consideration must be given to the stock depth behind these assortments. In essence, this planning results in the development of criteria for replenishing stocks.

We will deal separately with continuously maintained items and with those which have a limited sales life because of fashion changes.

For continuously maintained items the planned depth of stock involves the following factors:

1. Basic low stock (from the basic list). The lowest on-hand position that can be permitted without losing sales at the lowest demand period of the year.
2. Safety stock or cushion. An additional allowance for protection against stock depletion by an unanticipated increase in demand or unforeseen delays in vendor delivery.
3. Planned minimum stock. The sum of the basic low stock plus the cushion.
4. Review period. The elapsed time between two consecutive reviews of the stock position of an item to determine whether a new order should be placed.
5. Vendor delivery time. The normal time between the placing of an order and the receipt of merchandise.
6. Total lead time (often called buying period). The sum of the review period plus delivery time.
7. Planned coverage or maximum stock. The sum of the expected sales during the total lead time plus the minimum stock.

The criteria for subsequent control thus become the planned minimum and maximum stock levels. These criteria are expressed in both units and number-of-weeks supply. The former requires an updating of the criteria as the trend in unit sales changes, while the latter approach needs no change in the criteria unless one or

A BASIC STOCK LIST   EXHIBIT 109

VENDOR ITEM NUMBER	ITEM DESCRIPTION	RETAIL PRICE	BASIC STOCK	
			FLOOR	WAREHSE.
LP 44162	Wrench Set 4 pc. comb.	1.97 ea	3	4
LP 44163	Wrench Set 5 pc. comb.	2.88 ea.	3	4
LP 44164	Wrench Set 6 pc. comb.	3.73 ea.	3	4
LP 44182	8 inch combnose plier	1.17 ea.	2	4
LP 44183	6 inch side cutn. plier	1.14 ea.	2	4
LP 44154	8 inch Lineman plier	1.21 ea	2	4
LP 7	in Li ma pli	1.45 ea		2
NC 1200	Utility Box	.99	1	2
NC 1501	Tool Box	1.99	1	2

more of the seven factors just listed change. There is an additional advantage to expressing planned minimum and maximum stocks in terms of weeks' supply, in that the buyer is forced to review actual sales performance and make an explicit forecast of future sales in order to convert weeks' supply into equivalent units for ordering purposes.

Given the planned minimum and maximum, one can project a planned turnover since, if control is exercised within these limits, the inventory of an item will fluctuate between the minimum and maximum levels. Over the long run, the average on-hand stock will closely approximate the minimum level plus one-half the amount generally ordered to cover the review period (cycle stock). The following example illustrates this point. Suppose that the minimum stock is planned at five weeks' supply, that stocks are scheduled to be reviewed every four weeks, and that the vendor generally delivers in three weeks. The planned maximum would be 12 weeks' supply. The planned average inventory would be seven weeks' supply, giving a budgeted annual turnover of 7.4. Subsequently, stock replenishment is controlled within these budgeted limits. In Exhibit 110, the average inventory equals 6.85 weeks' supply. The actual annual turnover is equal to:

$$\frac{52 \text{ weeks' sales}}{6.85 \text{ weeks' average inventory}} = 7.6$$

We cannot hope to cover the many facets of the more recent scientific approaches to determining the "best" minimum and maximum stock levels on maintained items. It should be pointed out, however, that the "best" levels are a function of economic considerations and certain management policies. For example, would

EXHIBIT 110

Stock Replenishment Control Rules and Average Inventory Investment

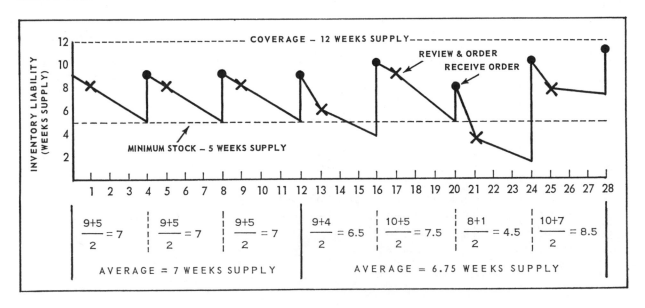

the costs of a more frequent review of stock status be more than offset by the reduction in cycle stock? Is it worth the additional investment in safety stocks to provide for almost any contingency and give the customers practically 100-percent service?

Items characterized by fashion considerations or marked seasonal swings in customer demand are usually planned in terms of broad assortment factors, such as price line or style features; that is, a model-stock plan will be developed. To plan minimum-maximum stock levels for an item would be impossible, since specific items are expected to be in the assortment only for short periods of time. Furthermore, initial ordering must often be considerably in advance of delivery, and the ability to reorder is limited by the cutoff on manufacturing.

The stock depth for each assortment factor is usually established on the basis of an expected beginning inventory (based on advance purchases), the planned sales for the limited selling period, and planned fill-in during the period. Because of the limited selling period, planned sales are often broken down into weeks to establish the proper stock depth to be carried throughout the period. For example, a particular assortment factor—contour body style, for example—may be expected to have an active selling period of about eight weeks. As in most fashion merchandise, heaviest sales will occur in the early weeks (assuming the fashion feature is popular). Consequently, the planned stock depth in the early weeks will be considerably greater than toward the end of the selling period.

Thus it is apparent that for fashion merchandise the criterion for controlling the stock depth of an assortment is a sales-rate/stock-level relationship which is expected to change over the course of the limited selling period. This relationship varies for each of the individual styles comprising the assortment, greater depth being sought for those styles which give an early indication of being the best sellers and an allowed stock depletion for the less-popular or slow-selling styles.

Once the control criteria are established, the planned balance they reflect can only be maintained with some form of unit control system. It must be emphasized that unit control is referred to here as a systematic procedure for maintaining the planned sales-stock balance (turnover) in terms of the physical units of each item. This implies the translation of inventory, sales, and order status into guidelines for the evaluation of what, when, and how much is needed to replenish the inventory of a given item, style, or assortment factor.

There are almost as many different unit control systems as there are major retail establishments in this country. Fundamentally, each represents the company's attempt to develop (1) the best method of collecting the necessary merchandising data, (2) the most suitable format for recording these data, and (3) the meaningful organization of the data for a rapid and intelligent appraisal of the facts. These concepts can best be illustrated by discussing two selected examples: one for maintained or so-called staple items and one for fashion or style merchandise.

Regarding staple items, we will consider a housewares department in a multi-store operation. Each store determines its own stock position, and requisitions additional quantities from a central warehouse. The warehouse, in turn, places consolidated orders with vendors for delivery to the warehouse.

The housewares department in each store takes a periodic stock count to determine the number of units on hand. The counts for a given group of merchandise are taken at four-week intervals. This method of determining stock position is most often found in departments where many of the individual items have a relatively low unit value, where numerous transactions make perpetual records very expensive to maintain, where stock is maintained at about the same depth, and where the rate of sales is reasonably stable from month to month.

A stock count and requisition form, as shown in Exhibit 111, is forwarded to each store with the items prelisted that are scheduled for count. The merchandise on the selling floor and in any reserve location in the store is checked and the on-hand

EXHIBIT 111

STOCK COUNT AND REQUISITION FORM

DEPARTMENT COUNT SHEET

Scheduled count date __January 15__   Page No. __1__

Store __New Plaza__   Department __182--Housewares__

VENDOR ITEM NUMBER	ITEM DESCRIPTION	COLOR	SIZE	RETAIL PRICE	COUNT Floor / Store Reserve	TOTAL ON HAND	RE-QUESTED FILL IN
NES-20	Aluminum Kettle		3 qt	2.79	5 / 2	7	9
NES-22	Aluminum Kettle		4 qt	2.98	2 / 2	4	4
NES-26	Aluminum Kettle		6 qt	3.79	1 / 3	4	4
NES-28	Aluminum Kettle		8 qt	3.98	4 / 0	4	3
NES-30	Aluminum Kettle		10 qt	4.98	1 / 1	2	1
NES-R10	Aluminum Kettle		1 qt	1.95	1 / 2	3	1
NES-R11	Copper Saucepan		2 qt	2.95	2 / 2	4	—
					/		
AL 609	Enamel Pot	Grn	1 qt	1.50	3 / 3	6	—
AL 611	Enamel Pot	Blu	1 qt	1.50	3 / 2	5	—
Al 612	Enamel Pot	Grn	2 qt	2.10	5 / 2	7	2
Al 632	Enamel Pot	Red	6 qt	3.10	3 / 1	4	—

Count taken on __January 17__   by __Eileen Smith__

EXHIBIT 112 ITEM STOCK CONTROL SHEET

STORE __New Plaza__

DEPARTMENT __182 - Houseware__

STOCK CONTROL RECORD

VENDOR __Nesco, Inc.__

ITEM NUMBER	DESCRIPTION	COLOR	SIZE	MIN. PACK	UNIT COST	UNIT RETAIL	COVERAGE (IN WEEKS SUPPLY)
NES-20	Aluminum Kettle	✓	3 qt.	1	1.81	2.79	12

PERIOD	1	2	3	4	5	6	7	8	9
COUNT DATE	12/15	1/17							
ON HAND STORE	8	7							
ORDERED FROM WHSE.	7	9							
SPOT ORDER	2								
QUANTITY RECEIVED	7								
SALES	6	8							
L.Y. SALES	4	4	5	7	4	5	6	4	5
COVERAGE REQUIRE	15	18							

recorded. The count sheet is then turned over to the department manager, who records the on-hand on an item control sheet (Exhibit 112). On the item control sheet the amount to be requisitioned from the central warehouse is determined in the following manner:

1. The number of merchandise units requisitioned on a special or spot order basis (2) is posted.
2. The merchandise units delivered to the store since the last count (7) are determined.
3. The estimated sales since the last count (8) are derived by adding the on-hand at 12/15 (8) to the quantity received (7) and subtracting the on-hand at 1/17 (7). (There is no way of determining how much shortage is included in this figure.)
4. Since the "coverage (in weeks' supply)" is 12 weeks, an estimate of the sales for the next three months is made. This estimate is based on last year's sales $(5 + 7 + 4 = 16)$ and an evaluation of the current rate of sale. The required coverage is estimated at 18 units.
5. The number of units on hand (7) and on order (2)—not indicated in Exhibit 112—is added to determine the total liability.
6. The total liability (9) is subtracted from the required coverage (18) to determine the additional quantity needed. This is then posted to the "ordered from warehouse" line and the requisition form (Exhibit 111) and forwarded to the warehouse to be filled.

We have observed this same procedure carried out differently from an organizational point of view. Many retailers leave all determinations of fill-in requirements to the department buyer, in which case the stock counts would be forwarded to a central location for review. Under any circumstances, the buyer must have access periodically to the item control sheets for an overall review of item performance as a basis for promotions, addition of new items, deletion of items, revisions of coverage requirements, and so on. When the warehouse receives requisitions for fill-ins from the various locations, the quantities delivered to the stores are deducted from the

EXHIBIT 113

WAREHOUSE STOCK CONTROL RECORD

DEPARTMENT		C O L O R	S I Z E	UNIT COST	UNIT RETAIL	MIN. STOCK (WEEKS)	STD. ORDER QTY.	PERIOD	1	2	3
VENDOR								DATE	12/15	1/17	
ITEM NO.	DESCRIPTION										
182-NES-20	Housewares Aluminum Kettle	–	3 qt.	1.81	2.79	2	25	OPENING ON HAND	25	30	
								REGULAR ORDER	25	–	25
								SPOT ORDER	–	–	
								QUANTITY RECEIVED	25	–	
								STORE WITHDRAWAL	20	24	
								BALANCE ON HAND	30	6	
								MINIMUM UNITS	10	12	

234

on-hand inventory balance on the warehouse stock record (Exhibit 113). The balance of undelivered merchandise from vendors is also recorded, and a liability record is maintained on a continuing basis.

The warehouse maintains its stock position on a minimum basis. As its stock is depleted, the quantity on-hand plus on-order is compared to the minimum level noted on the stock record. Once again, the minimum level is in terms of weeks' supply and is converted into units on the basis of a forecast of future unit requirements; this forecast is based on the past rate of withdrawals from stock (which are in essence the sales of the warehouse). When the minimum level is reached, the warehouse informs the buyer that a consolidated replenishment order is required. Orders are placed in quantities determined to be most economical; that is, quantities that minimize the total costs of carrying inventory and processing orders.

You can see from this example that the replenishment of stock in each store and in the warehouse is an organized, systematic procedure. Stock-depth control guidelines are applied to determine when and how much to replenish. Since these guidelines are based on the planned stock-sales balance, which may have been determined at the beginning of the year or selling season, adherence to the procedures will assure attainment of the budgeted performance objectives, assuming the objectives are realistic.

The principles of unit control are the same for both staple and fashion merchandise. As alluded to previously, however, there are difficulties arising from the short selling life of style merchandise. In planning stock depth, the retailer can plan only in terms of broad assortment factors. There is also increased emphasis on planning initial order quantities as a beginning inventory position and on the changing sales-stock relationship throughout the selling period.

Any effective control system for style merchandise must also be geared to this limited sales life and must provide the means for rapidly adjusting upward or downward the stock depth on individual styles within the assortment, depending on customer preferences. The timing of these adjustments cannot be overemphasized. Additions to stock of highly acceptable styles is accomplished through reorders. If the reorders are too late or too small, the retailer's profits will be adversely affected by both an increase in subsequent markdowns and a decrease in potential sales. If the reorders are too early or too large, the incidence of markdowns will again rise; and since the inventory dollars will be invested in potentially unsalable styles, the retailer will be unable to achieve his turnover objective.

Reduction of stock is principally attained through sales. For less popular styles, however, the customer must be further induced to purchase. Markdowns are designed to accomplish this and are an acceptable part of a good merchandising operation. Slow sellers and subsequent markdowns result from the fact that the merchant must test in order to properly determine current tastes, thereby achieving maximum sales. If markdowns are taken too early, profits are reduced. If markdowns are begun too late in the selling period, they are likely to be larger in order to clear stocks before the period ends; profits will suffer, and turnover and return on investment will also be reduced.

Advanced control systems now coming into use incorporate evaluation features

EXHIBIT 114 REORDER AND MARKDOWN EVALUATION

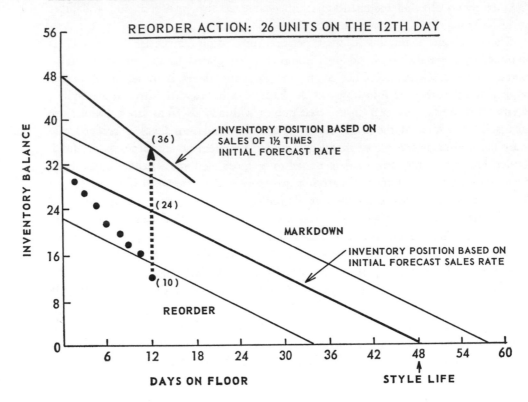

REORDER ACTION: 26 UNITS ON THE 12TH DAY

INVENTORY POSITION BASED ON SALES OF 1½ TIMES INITIAL FORECAST RATE

MARKDOWN

INVENTORY POSITION BASED ON INITIAL FORECAST SALES RATE

REORDER

DAYS ON FLOOR

STYLE LIFE

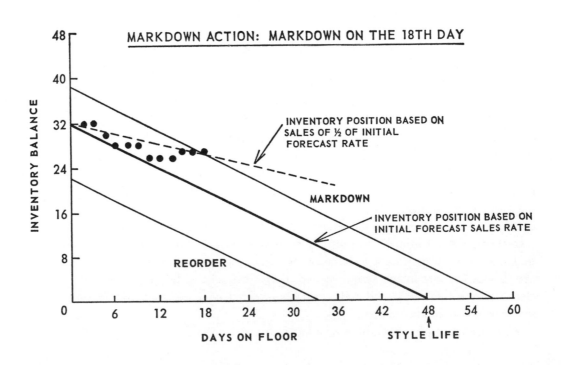

MARKDOWN ACTION: MARKDOWN ON THE 18TH DAY

INVENTORY POSITION BASED ON SALES OF ½ OF INITIAL FORECAST RATE

MARKDOWN

INVENTORY POSITION BASED ON INITIAL FORECAST SALES RATE

REORDER

DAYS ON FLOOR

STYLE LIFE

236

on a style-by-style basis. These evaluation features highlight fast-selling styles rapidly, thus enhancing opportunities for prompt reorders, and spot slow-selling styles, thus permitting timely markdowns or returns to vendors. The evaluation features reflect predetermined sales- and turnover-performance criteria. Such advanced control systems are based on an explicit recognition of the limited selling period of styles in a given assortment factor. This period is commonly referred to as "style life" and is defined as the period of time during which an average style may be expected to sell actively at the full retail price. Style life is reasonably predictable, and the sales rate is relatively constant over the period.

Let us use a specific example, a dress department in a multistore operation, to demonstrate the development of the evaluation criteria and the subsequent operation of the system. All decisions are made on a centralized basis by the buyer. In her planning of initial order quantities, the buyer is essentially forecasting an amount that she expects to sell at full retail value, at least at a normal rate over the selling period. Consequently, if she initially purchases thirty-two units of a dress that has a style life of eight weeks, she expects the normal rate of sales to approximate four per week. The initial quantity (broken down by sizes and colors to provide the necessary breadth of assortment) is distributed to the various stores in accordance with past volumes handled by each store. Once the style is on the selling floor, the buyer must be alerted as to whether the initial purchase was (1) too little to support the normal rate of sale (reorder action), (2) just right (stand pat), or (3) too large (markdown action).

The buyer pre-establishes the evaluation criteria for alerting her to alternate courses of action. As an example, she may wish to detect a fast seller, which she defines as having a sales rate of 1.5 times the initially forecast rate (or six per week in this example). On the basis of her ability to place a reorder within the limited selling period of the style, she would like this indication within 12 days after the style is placed on the selling floor. Conversely, she defines a slow-selling style as one that sells at a rate of one-half the initially forecast rate, or two per week; and she would like to discover this within 18 days after the style goes on the floor. Recognizing that every decision she makes cannot be the right one, she expresses a willingness to accept a certain amount of risk that the course of action she takes will, in fact, be the wrong one. Of course, she cannot afford to be wrong too often, or she will be out of a job; so she indicates that she would like to be right at least 80 percent of the time.

The mathematics involved in converting these ground rules into a set of statistical indicators is demonstrated in Exhibit 114. Given an opening inventory of 32 units, each day's sales are deducted and the stock balance posted to the chart. In the top chart, an example of a reorder action is shown. In this case, the first time the inventory balance falls below the reorder action line, it is assumed that the true rate of sales is six units per week and a reorder should be executed to bring the inventory level up to 1.5 times the "standard" level for this stage of the on-sale period ($1.5 \times 24 = 36$). Since the inventory is at 16, the recommended order quantity is 20 units.

The bottom chart in Exhibit 114 shows a markdown action. Here the residual

EXHIBIT 115

Style Control Record

COMMENTS:

PRICE LINE: THROUGH $17.98

DATE		RECEIPTS	RETURNS	On Hand	O.O.	Cum. Sales	Daily Sales Stores A	B	C	D	E
8-15	1	36		36		—					
-16	2			34		2	1			1	
17	3			33		3				1	
18	4			32		4	1				
20	5			31		5		1			
21	6			28		8	1		2		
22	7			25	21	11		2		1	
23	8			23	21	13	1		1		
24	9			22	21	14		1			
25	10			19	21	17	1		2		
	11										
	12										
29	13		1	20	21	16		(1)			
30	14			19	21	17	1				
31	15			16	21	20	2			1	
	16										
	17										
	18										
9-6	19	21		32		25		2	1	2	
7	20			31		26			1		
8	21			30		27	1				
10	22			29		28	1				
	23										
	24										
	25										
14	26			27		30			1	1	
15	27			24		33	1	2			
	28										
	29										
19	30			21		36	1		1	1	
20	31			20		37				1	
21	32			19		38		1			
22	33			16		41	1		1	1	
	34										
	35										
	36										
27	37			9		48	2	2	2	1	
28	38			8		49		1			
29	39			6		51		2			
	40										
	41										
11-1	42		1	7		50			(1)		
	43										
	44										
	45										
	46										
	47										
	48										
	49										
	50										
	51										

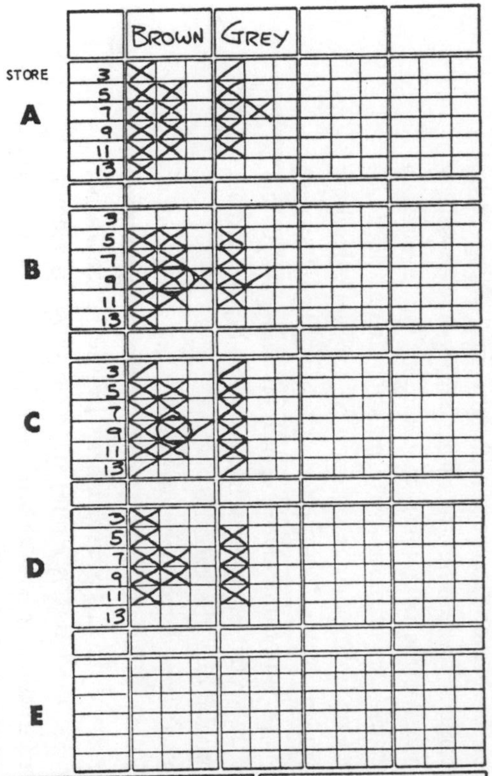

ON ORDER Date	Quan.	DATE DUE	RECEIVED Date	Quan.
8-1	36		8-15	36
8-22	21		9-6	21

MARK DOWNS Date	Quan.	Prev. Price	New Price

FASHION Blouson Sheath Short Sleeve

Stanton Jrs.

FABRIC Wool Salt & Pepper Tweed

TYPE

MFR. No.	STYLE	CLASS
7381	798	41

COST 10 75

SELLING PRICE 17 98

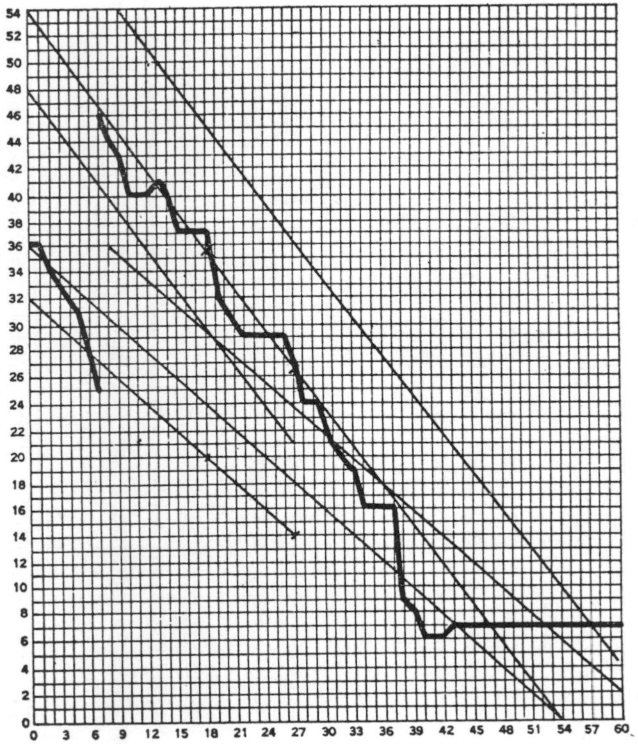

inventory crosses the action line at the end of three weeks. The buyer is alerted to consider marking down the style by an amount considered sufficient to move the slow seller within the style's life. Alternatively, the early-slow-seller signal may enhance the opportunity for returning some of the merchandise to the vendor and avoiding the costly markdown. When neither line is crossed, the sales rate of the style indicates a stand-pat decision. This means that the existing inventory after each posting of sales is about right to support total expected sales for that style for the remainder of the selling period.

Reflecting the control procedures that we have described, Exhibit 115 shows a complete manual record for the unit control of a given style number. You will note this particular style was reordered and new action lines established for the higher rate of sales. Since the action is taken on a style for all stores combined, it is essential to have inventory and sales information by store, size, and color for the proper distribution of the reorder quantity. Also note that the reorder action line ends on the 27th day, since, as a practical matter, even an expedited delivery time would bring merchandise into the store too late to achieve the sale prior to the demise of the style life. Similarly, the markdown action line does not start for a week and a half, since it is advisable to give the style sufficient time for exposure to the buying public.

This system, like most systems in fashion merchandise unit control, requires a perpetual posting of all transactions affecting the stock balance; that is, sales, receipts, customer returns, and returns to vendors. Supporting procedures for gathering this input and making it available to the buyer is a major problem confronting retailers. In the area of sales, for example, stubs of tickets attached to the merchandise are collected by the sales people as each item is sold. As more retailers went into data processing, these stubs were prepunched with identifying information and then subsequently machine-processed for sales reports.

*　*　*

We have seen that the budgeting of merchandise in the retail industry has its unique problems. We have discussed the control aspects of this process in considerable detail because they cannot be separated from planning if good merchandising performance is to be attained. We also found it necessary to distinguish continually between staple and fashion merchandise, which, although handled within the same conceptual framework, require considerably different planning and control procedures.

Historically, dollar control and unit control of merchandise have been regarded by retail organizations as two mutually exclusive methods. As a result, the rigorous application of unit control did not attain the overall dollar objectives of the company. More recently, there has been a trend toward the reconciliation of unit plans with broader dollar plans by merchants who recognize that total company objectives can never be met if both the dollar and the unit plans do not reflect realistically attainable financial and merchandising goals. As more merchants adopt meaningful budgetary planning and control procedures, merchandise budgeting will reflect the coordinated use of both unit and dollar controls.

13

Setting Up
a Profit Improvement Program

IF A BUSINESS FAITHFULLY APPLIED the methods described in the preceding chapters to plan and control its operations, one might assume that it would not need to undertake a separate program to reduce costs or improve profits. However, this is like saying that a person should regularly restrict his food intake to a level which makes rigorous dieting for a limited period of time unnecessary. Every company, sooner or later, is faced with the necessity to mount a cost reduction or profit improvement effort to accomplish results which have not been possible in the normal budgeting routine. A total reappraisal and perhaps severe pruning of the cost and expense structure may occur only once every few years, but it is a needed and healthful part of financial management and completely compatible with a good budget system.

The bulge in costs of doing business may be due to a variety of reasons. Although planning and control of costs and profits should be done in terms of standards or criteria (as explained in earlier chapters), it is sometimes difficult to break with past experience. Thus a high level of expenses in relation to sales may be readily accepted at budget time because of habit and inertia. Costs may get out of line in a business which is subject to volume fluctuations (for example, defense companies) or in those subject to seasonal trends. Although standards and flexible budgetary techniques should be used in these situations, sharp reductions in sales volumes are not always accompanied by a timely reduction of costs. Companies whose products are subject to rapid change because of the results of research also find it necessary to change budget plans rather frequently to meet the needs of new product developments.

One way to increase profit is to sell more goods or services, provided, of course, the selling price more than covers costs. The other way—and this is the one we are concerned with here—is to reduce expenses without diminishing sales or to eliminate sales that do not contribute to profit. This, of course, is what every management strives to do. When efforts to improve profit or to reduce costs fall short of their objectives, it is generally not for lack of trying but only because the proper tools have not been used. Our purpose is to discuss what these tools are and how they can be applied in the form of a profit improvement program.

The need for constant improvement in all areas of operation is one of the basic and continuing responsibilities of management. But because of day-to-day operating problems, too little attention is often given to the need for continual adaptation to changing conditions. Most managements, however, recognize the need for an organized cost reduction and profit improvement program.

Such a program should, in principle, be a permanent function and in many companies is organized as such. On the other hand, to maintain a fully organized profit improvement program requires substantial effort, and there are those who feel that because the point of diminishing returns is soon reached, it is better to disband and reorganize the program periodically. A sustained effort may lose momentum after a while and need a fresh stimulus and a new approach. It is not uncommon, therefore, to find "new" profit improvement programs launched every few years, even where a continuing effort is in effect. This approach, however, has some inherent inefficiencies because of time spent in getting started on each cycle. The best answer may lie in a combined approach, where certain of the features of the program are maintained as a continuing effort and others are applied periodically and for limited duration to restimulate interest and intensify effort.

If regular profit improvement programs are inadequate or special programs are ineffective or delayed too long, management may find itself faced with a sudden need to catch up. This may lead to arbitrary personnel reductions or elimination of entire functions in the overhead area. These methods are effective where there are obvious excesses which are easily recognized. In most companies, however, opportunities for drastic action at reasonable risk are limited, and cost reductions must be effected through painstaking analysis and accumulation of many relatively minor changes. While recognizing the need for an occasional program, we believe that, even when time is short, there is no justification for taking unreasonable risks by omitting necessary analysis. An effective program can be organized and carried through in a matter of months or even weeks.

Some things, of course, cannot be rushed but must await their proper time. With rare exceptions, there is no way to make the customer buy more goods or pay higher prices at a particular time just because the company needs the profits. Increased sales or prices of present products or addition of new products is therefore outside the domain of a profit improvement program. We must also rule out wage rates and related factors involving labor negotiation, or taxes and similar factors involving a branch of government, and concern ourselves only with the things the company buys, including the services of its employees and with the manner in which it operates internally.

In short, the profit improvement program is usually concerned with factors which are completely controlled by management. This is not to say, of course, that these are necessarily under the control of any single individual within management. In fact, reconciliation of conflicting objectives within management—real or apparent—is often a key element in profit improvement.

Internal operation is the proper area for a profit improvement program because decisions on what changes could or should be made can be based on economic considerations of improving profit or return on investment and are not critically dependent on their acceptability to anyone outside the organization. Differentiation between internal and external aspects of the business also tends to separate the areas where decisions are more often delegated to middle management from those requiring top management approval. Changes in methods of operation generally fall in the first category, and changes in company objectives, products, markets, or major facilities in the second.

Thus we broadly define a profit improvement program as an organized effort to promote and to manage the identification and implementation of necessary and worthwhile changes in areas of operation which management controls and where decisions are made largely on the basis of economics.

There are many other aspects of operation which could be made the objects of special improvement programs, such as product quality, customer service, or return on investment. All of these also relate to profit because profit improvement programs invariably generate proposals for changes which will affect—positively or negatively—the appearance or performance of the product, the time required to deliver on a customer's order, the safety of personnel, or the investment in such items as facilities and inventories. In focusing on profit improvement, we normally tend to view these other aspects as side effects which must be taken into consideration in evaluating the desirability of implementing a proposed change but which are not part of the immediate objective. A somewhat broader view, however, should be adopted with respect to investments in inventory and working capital. The consideration of a reduction in such investment falls very properly into the pattern of a cost reduction or profit improvement program. For example, the requisite basic levels of inventories of finished goods and certain semifinished goods are generally dictated by requirements of customer service, which is an external factor only partly within management's control. But the degree to which these requisite levels are exceeded in practice, and the amount of raw material and work-in-process stock provided to back them up, can be controlled by internal methods of ordering, scheduling, expediting, and shipping. Decisions on changes of methods in this area are almost invariably delegated to middle management and can be evaluated in economic terms. Such economic evaluation must consider the costs of owning the inventory—that is, the costs of storage and obsolescence, interest on invested money, property taxes, and insurance. In addition some guidelines are required as to the desirability of freeing invested money. This may be expressed in terms of a percentage return desired over and above the interest cost. The greater this percentage, the more economical it is to adopt procedures which reduce inventory.

To do the profit improvement job effectively, one individual—let us call him the coordinator—must be given responsibility for it, with authority to obtain whatever information is needed and with responsibility to provide overall guidance for the effort. Depending on the magnitude and urgency of the job, this may be a full-time position or part of an established job, involving four steps:

1. Obtaining ideas on how to improve profit and putting these in the form of specific proposals or recommendations.
2. Obtaining the information which is needed for proper evaluation of each proposal.
3. Presenting the proposal to members of management who are in the position to evaluate it and to direct its implementation.
4. Providing necessary follow-through to see whether the expected results have been obtained and reporting overall progress to top management.

Not all proposals need to be handled through this function. Any executive who receives or conceives an idea about how to improve his operation and has or can get the authority to implement it should go ahead on his own. To get credit for having achieved profit improvement, he need only request a change in his budget or his standards. But when the idea originates outside the department—perhaps as a result of a special study by accounting or engineering—or when there is uncertainty as to whom the idea should be addressed, it is useful to have a focal point to coordinate and stimulate the development and submission of ideas.

If the merits of a proposal are not immediately clear, or if it is so complex or extensive as to require clarification on how it can be implemented, or if it requires consideration of which of several alternative means of implementation should be adopted, additional study is necessary. Studies must also be undertaken to generate ideas on profit improvement. Staff specialists—engineers, systems personnel, or accountants—may be called on for this purpose. This raises the question of who shall authorize their time and how it will be controlled.

In some companies the department most directly affected by a proposal authorizes the study, and failure to do so is equivalent to rejection of the proposal. The coordinator can appeal to a higher management level but has no authority to institute a study on his own. This tends to inhibit and delay changes but has the merit of avoiding a proliferation of studies and an excessive buildup of effort on the part of staff departments. A committee of top level executives—at the vice-presidential level or directly under it—may review rejected proposals and direct the department involved to undertake the study.

In other companies the director may authorize studies under a separate budget established for this purpose. In this situation the director must have substantial stature and may be at the level of controller, executive vice president, or administrative vice president—or else work under the immediate direction of such an executive. Under this approach the review committee acts in an advisory capacity and assists the director in obtaining information and gaining acceptance for studies and subsequent implementation. The final decision on implementation always remains with line management.

As an example illustrative of the "coordinator" concept, consider the case of a medium-size manufacturing company which felt itself at a disadvantage in relation to competitors, in part because of high operating costs. Viewing the problem as critical, the president directed the controller to organize an intensive effort to improve profit.

To implement the program, the head of one of the manufacturing departments was temporarily freed of his duties and assigned to coordinate the effort, reporting to the controller. Meeting monthly and consisting of the controller (chairman) and the vice presidents for manufacturing, engineering, and sales, a review committee was organized to review major proposals, authorize studies where required, and evaluate recommendations. Collectively, the members of the committee controlled close to 90 percent of the company's expenditures.

In addition, a working committee was set up, also meeting monthly; it consisted of the coordinator, the head of the industrial engineering department, the head of the systems department, the assistant to the president (responsible for organizational studies), and the director of budgeting. This committee's function was to obtain and develop proposals for profit improvement; to recommend specific studies to be undertaken, subject to authorization of the review committee; and to determine what personnel should be assigned to carry out these studies. In a number of instances, outside consultants were engaged to survey and study specific areas; they reported directly to the controller.

Unless strong direction is provided, it is likely that the profit improvement effort will produce too few proposals of substance or perhaps too many in one area and too few in another. It is an important part of the coordinator's job to initiate new proposals and to direct effort to those areas where there is the most need of or the greatest opportunity for improvement.

It seems clear that, in the absence of good proposals, initial emphasis in generating ideas be given to those product lines or areas of operation which do not measure up to management objectives in terms of profitability or return on investment. Once these have been studied, the next step is to search among the apparently profitable operations or product lines for "pockets" of unprofitability—that is, for individual items or classes of customers which are below par or for departments whose costs are not competitive with similar services available elsewhere within or outside the company.

The responsibility for developing this information falls in the controller's area, and it is beyond our scope to discuss methods of cost analysis and determination of product profitability. But we do wish to emphasize the need for these as a cornerstone of any profit improvement effort.

The most difficult areas to analyze, of course, are those of indirect and overhead expenses. In dealing with these, we must recognize two distinct approaches. The profit improvement program is primarily concerned with improvement of methods of operation; there is, however, the more basic question of whether a particular operation makes a contribution to the enterprise and should be continued. For example, a large manufacturing company was faced with the need for stringent economy. A major cost reduction was accomplished one morning when the president walked through the industrial engineering department and, after thinking upon the matter briefly, ordered the entire department of 200 employees disbanded. The decision was based on the premise that the work of studying operations, setting standards, and performing related functions was not essential to the enterprise at that particular time. Such decisions, however, are matters of organizational policy rather than methods improvement.

While some would declare this area beyond the bounds of the profit improvement program, the elimination or rearrangement of functions or projects undeniably offers great opportunities for profit improvement. The key lies, of course, in identifying what is necessary and what is not, and there is considerable room for individual judgment here. A prerequisite to the exercise of such judgment, however, is to relate the objectives of specific sections or projects of a department to the objectives of the company. The preparation of such objectives, and of the budgets which support these objectives, may lead to re-evaluation of the need for the function in question. The development of this information requires an individual of broad background and mature judgment and involves a more flexible approach than do methods improvement studies.

This approach has proved particularly useful in areas such as engineering or developmental research where work is normally controlled on a project basis. The need for expenditures in these areas can therefore be examined in increments—project by project.

Occasionally, a department or project is established to deal with a temporary situation, such as an expansion program or reorganization—or a profit improvement program—and continues its existence after the job is done by changing or broadening its objectives. Periodic updating and review of department and project objectives will serve to identify these. It is also unfortunately true that what is necessary depends on what one can afford. A company which has come upon bad times may find last year's necessity to be this year's extravagance, and the criteria for evaluation of functions may change from time to time. Because the economics are difficult to evaluate for indirect and staff functions, decisions in these areas tend to be reserved to top management levels.

Once management decides, for example, that it wants production standards, the cost and effectiveness of the methods whereby these standards are determined may be areas of concern for the profit improvement program. In such areas as engineering, accounting, research, quality control, or maintenance, the profit improvement program should be concentrated on the question of how or by what methods these projects are executed. It is generally possible, at least in principle, to compare the cost of one method with another. Such comparisons should, of course, consider the possibility of having the work done by outside sources.

As a rule it is not useful to bring the relatively ponderous mechanism of the profit improvement program into action unless the activity to be explored is one which involves several people over a reasonable period of time. The methods-improvement-program approach is best applied to operations which are repetitive, such as order handling and billing, quality testing and inspection, production scheduling, inventory control, and maintenance. The profit improvement program will generally focus on these activities. Some repetitive activities occur in the areas of selling and advertising. Despite their proximity to the customer, these should not necessarily be excluded from consideration. It is important, however, that the individuals assigned to study these functions be experienced and knowledgeable.

This question might now be asked: In any specific organization, how can we determine which area offers the greatest potential for improvement? In some industrial operations, materials costs are more closely controlled than payroll, possibly because it is easier to discontinue an order than to dismiss or even transfer an employee. We would not wish to de-emphasize materials costs by any means, however, particularly in the light of recent developments in value analysis and value engineering. From a practical point of view, it is quite safe to assume that where no previous studies have been made, there are bound to be opportunities. The best place to start would seem to be where expenditures are greatest and where management is most interested and sympathetic.

Studies are the key ingredient of the profit improvement program, since they serve both to generate ideas on improvement and to verify that the ideas are workable and economically preferable. Few managers, no matter how settled in their ways, can long resist a worthwhile change once it has been properly checked out through study and the result made known.

The term "study" as it is used here means the collection and presentation of factual information in sufficient detail and depth to permit a judgment. The facts must be structured to provide an argument in support of the proposed change and sufficiently complete to strongly suggest a conclusion for or against the change. When the facts are at hand or when no additional useful factual information can be obtained at reasonable cost, no study is required. Controversy must, in this case, be resolved by the line organization responsible, since it is in the best position to exercise judgment.

It is necessary to differentiate between two distinct study objectives and therefore between two kinds of study. The first is aimed at identifying opportunity for improvement, and it is best characterized as a *survey or review* of the operation under scrutiny. The purpose of the second kind of study is to confirm the desirability of making the change. The term *"feasibility study"* is sometimes used to describe this phase, although it is concerned as much with economics as with feasibility.

The factual information compiled for a *survey or review study* may include a description of how the operation is carried out; statistics on its performance in terms of throughput, output rates, organization, costs, delays encountered, and so forth; its relation to other areas of the company; and its problems. A survey may also be conducted of other similar operations within the company or on the outside to learn through comparison. All this information serves only to raise questions, not to provide answers on what can be done. The answers must come from the individual who makes the survey. To be effective, he must be familiar with the operation involved; he must know what constitutes good practice in this sort of work; and he must be trained to examine critically and to identify inefficiencies. He should, in short, be a trained engineer or systems specialist, depending on whether the operation studied is of a technical or clerical nature.

Mechanization and automation play increasingly important roles in cost reduction not only in production but also in office operations. For this reason, persons selected to perform survey studies must be familiar with appropriate devices and their relative merits in specific applications. The emergence of the industrial engineer in the role of specialist in production techniques and devices some 30 years ago has been paralleled in recent years by the advent of the systems specialist and the computer specialist in the area of clerical and data processing work. There is general recognition today that effective review and analysis of operating methods should be carried out by trained professional specialists.

The objective of the survey or review is limited to identifying methods changes which will probably lead to profit improvement. It is useful at this point to have this judgment reviewed by the management personnel of the affected department.

Next to management support, success or failure of a profit improvement program depends most critically on good *feasibility studies*. Failure, when it occurs, can usually be traced to too much reliance on persuasion and too little on factual information. The determination of what information is needed in a specific instance is not altogether a technical matter. It depends in part on an understanding of the individuals who must be convinced and on the nature of the resistance likely to be encountered. This does not, however, alter the basic requirement for factual information. Usually this includes a complete description of the new method or procedure proposed; a comparison of its operating cost with that of the present method and with the costs of other major alternatives; an evaluation of problems and costs of converting to the new procedure and of the effects on investment and capital budgets when applicable; and an assessment of the need for retraining or reorganizing personnel. In effect, the entire process of instituting the change must be thought through.

The scope, degree of detail, and format used in presentation are important and again are best determined by those professionally trained in carrying out such studies, although much of the data collection can often be done by others.

It is obvious—or should be—that the facts assembled must be accurate. Production rates, capacities, and technical problems should be checked by production or engineering personnel; forecasts, by sales or marketing; and costs, by accounting. The integrity of the profit improvement program, as evidenced by its factual reports and its recommendations, must be above suspicion or reproach. Reputation is as important to the internal profit improvement program as it is to the outside consultant who may be brought in to supplement the skill and experience of company personnel.

It should not be inferred that to determine the economic benefit of accepting a proposed change is a straightforward matter of getting facts or numbers and adding them up. There are many pitfalls.

Sometimes—perhaps usually—a change can be implemented by simple directive. In this case the only economic effect is the difference in operating cost between the old and new methods. To estimate this, however, is not as simple as it may seem, because of the indirect cost elements involved. Is the saving resulting from the elimination of a position measured in terms of direct payroll only, or does it include also indirect expense such as personnel benefits; and what portion of the overhead of the department can be considered as part of the savings? If not enough work is eliminated to free up a full-time position, can we count the elimination of a half-time job as a saving, and what value do we put on it? If the savings are in raw materials, how many units do the savings apply to—a year's supply or more? And how much is a year's supply?

We cannot answer these questions here in specific terms, but there are two basic conditions which the estimating procedure must meet. First, the rules for resolving these questions must be fixed beforehand on as realistic a basis as possible and must be understood by everyone involved. If they are not, continuous controversy will seriously detract from the profit improvement effort and render scorekeeping meaningless. Second, the method of estimating cost reduction must be not only defined and understood but also accepted by line management as a basis for the adjustment of budgets. Line management should participate in the estimating process and, once a change is adopted, must accept the responsibility of realizing the planned profit improvement. The establishment of firm ground rules in these areas is the controller's responsibility.

There is many an opportunity for slippage between the estimate of savings and the actual result; this makes it important to have effective control on the translation. This control is achieved through budget administration, and the approval of a profit improvement project is a signal for the budget director to adjust the budget at the proper time. To do this, the estimate must be effectively prepared, in a way which permits allocation of total estimated savings to individual accounts or budgets. The degree to which this can be accomplished depends on the sophistication of both the estimate and the budget system.

Estimating and scorekeeping in a profit improvement program are greatly facilitated through use of standard costs and variable budgets, which include:

- Documentation of standard operating procedures or process sheets, and determination of standard quantities of raw material, direct labor, and certain manufacturing expense elements per unit of product.
- Approval of standard procedures and quantities by manufacturing, engineering, quality control, safety, or other interested departments.
- Pricing of standard quantities and hours at standard unit purchase costs and standard labor rates developed by accounting.
- Predetermination of acceptable overhead expense at various operating or production levels and determination of what portion of overhead is to be considered fixed, what portion semivariable, what portion variable, and what basis (such as direct labor, for example) is to be used for budgeting the variable and semivariable portions.
- Establishment of the operating or production level of each product or department for the budget period, based on forecasts provided by sales or planning personnel.

Operating costs following adoption of a proposed change can be estimated by setting a new standard or budget and by using the same procedure as was employed in setting the initial standard or budget. The difference between the two—assuming neither the unit costs nor the forecasts have been altered—represents the best estimate of the result of the change. If forecasts do change, the variable budget makes it possible to determine the effect of the difference in volume on the budget, independently of the effect of change in method.

When each of the individual elements of the budget procedure (operating procedures, quantities, unit costs, bases for allocation, forecasts, and so forth) is reviewed and approved by the organizational unit responsible, the result represents the best estimate of all concerned as well as a realistic objective to be met by the department, regardless of any differences or variances between actual expenditures and budget which may subsequently develop. By adopting the new standard, the cost reduction is made part of a new budget and becomes an objective which the department must accomplish to avoid unfavorable variances.

Systems such as the one just described are still more the exception than the rule in industry. But one cannot ignore the fact that the results of a profit improvement program cannot be measured by "actual" accounting costs. Actual or historical costs are subject to so many distortions because of accounting allocations and variations in operating conditions that they usually fail to reveal the results of any but the most major changes in operation. The effect of methods changes on costs is most properly measured not by before-and-after differences in actual costs but by differences in budgeted costs. In the absence of suitable standards and variable budgets, estimates will serve, however, provided they meet the conditions established earlier.

Before-and-after differences in cost often tell only a part of the story. In order to put a change into effect, it may be necessary to provide new equipment or fixtures, to train operators, to accept a temporary loss of production, or to take other action leading to one-time costs or new investments. In some areas, such as production and inventory control, the proposed change may have as one of its objectives the reduction of investment in inventory. Before a change is made, these related economic effects must be evaluated.

Here again it is important that estimates be based on an established set of rules and, where possible, be related to the budget system. Expense items, if significant, would be reflected in the operating budget. Inventory reductions can be translated into reductions of purchases as well as into reductions of production labor and expense. Capital expenditures relate, of course, to the capital budget.

One of the functions of the coordinator is to maintain a log of all proposals submitted and to report periodically—usually monthly—on the status of each. This report would cover—

- A brief statement of each proposal and the date on which it was received.
- A list of the department heads to whom it has been submitted for initial review and a target date for their decision as to immediate implementation or further study.
- The name of the staff group to whom it has been assigned for further study and its estimate of the expected completion date of the study.
- A statement of the results of the study when completed, including the conclusion as to feasibility and an estimate of indicated savings or profit improvements.
- A record of dates of review by the review committee and its conclusions or recommendations.
- The final disposition of the proposal.

This report serves as a basis for expediting the processing of proposals and for follow-through on final recommendations. The control on putting changes into effect and realizing projected improvements lies, however, in the hands of the budget department, not the coordinator. The coordinator's function is to identify and explore opportunities and to secure agreement on implementation—the budget director's function is to translate these into budget adjustments based on the estimates provided.

The budget director should also keep a running log of budget revisions, identifying each as to whether it was generated through the profit improvement program and determining for each what portion of the budget reduction, on an annual basis, is the result of change of operating method and what portion is the result of change in price, pay rate, overhead rate, or volume. Based on this record, an annual report is prepared by the budget director, analyzing the total dollars of budget changes submitted and implemented during the year. This report identifies the effect of the profit improvement program on total company performance and also shows how much profit improvement was generated outside the program. The report also indicates the degree to which profit improvements from any source are offsetting adverse cost and price factors by product line or area of operation.

We noted earlier the desirability of conducting profit improvement on a continuing basis and noted the difficulties of maintaining sustained interest. Let us briefly consider what might be done to provide better motivation.

If a special effort is to be called for, there must be provision for special recognition. It is desirable that individuals be able to point to their own contributions and that the results be clearly visible for each individual change as well as in terms of their total impact on overall profitability or return on investment. If results are not carefully estimated in advance and evaluated in retrospect, effort may be wasted on meaningless or inconsequential changes; inability to demonstrate results eventually leads to loss of interest and perhaps to controversy. It is generally desirable, therefore, that a record of accomplished savings be prepared not only for the program as a whole but also for the affected department or area of responsibility. The interpretation of such individual scores is difficult, however, since the same intensity of effort may produce little improvement in one department and a great deal in another. For example, some production processes, which have been running for a long time and have already been studied thoroughly, are hard to improve; others, which are new and not as yet fully developed, may offer great opportunity for improvement. Thus there are no absolute criteria for comparing performance. Goals for each department can be set by management on a subjective basis, but there will always remain room for differences of opinion.

Because of this disparity between intensity of effort and result, it is good practice in organizing cost reduction programs to provide for some recognition of effort regardless of the results of that effort. This is generally accomplished by maintaining records of ideas submitted and study projects undertaken and by publicizing statistics on the number of submissions and completions of studies. Suggestions submitted must be screened for validity and substance before they are admitted. Aside from statistics, it is also useful to provide wide circulation for the ideas themselves, since many may be relevant in areas outside those for which they were originally intended.

After measurement and recording of effort applied and results achieved, the question still remains, "Who gets the credit?" Should it be the individual who originated the idea, the one who found a specific application for the idea, or the one who finally put it into practice? This question can be answered only by an arbitrary decision. In companies with formal scorekeeping procedures, credit is usually given to the originator of the idea, provided he was reasonably specific in describing it. This encourages employees who have ideas about their own jobs or departments to get them recorded before someone else beats them to it. Once an idea is on the record, other means can be brought into play to have it studied and, if it has merit, to put it to work.

In summary, the basic features in setting up a profit improvement program are—

1. Definition of the scope of the program, which is usually the identification and implementation of necessary and worthwhile changes in methods of operation and is generally limited to areas of internal operation where decisions are made largely on the basis of economics.

2. Recognition of three basic objectives: reduction of expense, reduction of unprofitable sales, and reduction of inventory and working capital investments.

3. Appointment of a coordinator or director (full or part time) to head the program, assisted by a management review committee.

4. Use of professional engineering and systems personnel to carry out studies both to identify opportunities and to verify desirability of proposed changes.

5. Establishment of a procedure for estimating savings based on fixed ground rules which are realistic, understood by everyone, and accepted as a basis for budget adjustment.

6. Use of budgetary procedures to monitor and control implementation of changes and also to provide information for keeping score on individual performance.

7. Use of a system of formal proposals, survey and study reports, and progress reports, with appropriate review and follow-up procedures.

8. Maintenance of high standards of accuracy and integrity in all facets of the program.

Case Study

The following case study illustrates how the concepts and principles discussed in this chapter were put to work in a live business situation. Although the company name is fictitious, the history of profit deterioration and subsequent reversal, through the application of sound management principles and techniques, is real. The case is based on a profit improvement program in a company quite similar to Get Well Quick, Inc.

Company Background

Get Well Quick, Inc. (GWQ) is a small consumer goods company that manufactures and distributes its own products directly to department, chain, and variety stores. GWQ has expanded rapidly since its inception, and over the past five years it has experienced a 10 to 15 percent annual growth in sales. However, during the past two years the company has incurred substantial net losses for the first time in its history (see Exhibit 116).

EXHIBIT 116 GET WELL QUICK, INC.
FIVE-YEAR INCOME STATEMENT IN THOUSANDS OF DOLLARS

	5 Years Ago	4 Years Ago	3 Years Ago	2 Years Ago	Last Year
Sales	$7,500	$8,600	$9,300	$11,500	$12,500
Cost of sales:					
Materials	2,400	2,750	2,970	4,050	4,370
Labor	1,200	1,360	1,580	2,410	2,620
Direct contribution	$3,900	$4,490	$4,750	$ 5,040	$ 5,510
Less:					
Variable burden	900	1,120	1,210	1,950	2,250
Fixed burden	600	600	560	1,150	1,150
Gross profit	$2,400	$2,770	$2,980	$ 1,940	$ 2,110
Selling expense	975	1,120	1,300	1,380	1,380
General and administrative expense	525	600	650	1,030	1,130
Net operating income (loss)	$ 900	$1,050	$1,030	($ 470)	($ 400)

The company's president, who had founded GWQ, was understandably concerned. To aggravate matters, word had reached his desk of a growing number of customer complaints about the company's inability to meet delivery dates, repeated backorders, and shortages in shipment. Several efforts on his part to get at the problems were frustrated by the immensity of the task and an inability to obtain the operating and financial data required for meaningful analysis.

Organization of the Effort

Consequently, and in view of the critical nature of the problem, the president decided to launch a formal profit improvement program. His first step in implementing the program was to establish a profit improvement committee composed of most of the members of the executive committee. The executive vice president presided over this group and was given the role of program coordinator. The committee's assignment was to establish the approach and direction which the profit improvement effort would take.

The initial problem facing the committee was to appoint a study team to perform the required fact-finding and analysis. The company had its own internal systems and procedures department, but the president decided to enlist the help of outside consultants. This strategy, he felt, would provide the critical objectivity that the program required as well as supplement the skills and competence of company personnel. When the study team was organized, the following tasks were identified as its initial responsibilities:

1. Conduct a complete review of the company's operations to identify opportunities for profit improvement.

2. Determine how and by whom action should be taken to increase the profit performance of these areas.
3. Establish priorities for further study in the areas requiring improvement.

About four weeks later, the study team reported its findings. As anticipated, many areas throughout the company apparently contributed to the poor overall performance. In an effort to organize the data and effectively communicate the findings, the study team grouped the results of its study into eight categories: (1) direct labor costs; (2) indirect factory labor; (3) production planning and inventory control; (4) warehousing and shipping; (5) clerical costs, plant; (6) clerical costs, headquarters; (7) cost information system; and (8) organization structure and management reports.

Results of the Study

The study team noted the following practices in this area:
1. Many work orders were delayed because materials availability was not determined when the orders were issued.
2. Production line staffing was tedious and slow.
3. Production lines contained bottlenecks, and the overall plant was poorly laid out.
4. Time reporting was subject to inaccuracies because a time clock was not used.

Apparently, the company's rapid growth had compromised the design of the plant and its operating procedures. The study team, however, was quick to see the profit leaks that were likely to result from these ineffective controls and practices.

Direct Labor Costs

In this area, the study team reported that no formal preventive maintenance program existed, and most work was done on an emergency basis. In addition, standards were not applied to the time required for machine repair, and each mechanic controlled his own supply of maintenance materials. These procedural inadequacies were compounded by the absence of any service or materials records. Practices in use at the time had prevented management from determining either the type or cost of maintenance work done in this department.

In the receiving area of the plant, the study team had found that materials were obtained from stores without a requisition and that the absence of locator files made it difficult to find items and led to an inefficient use of time.

Indirect Factory Labor

The method that was used to plan and develop production requirements was found to be wholly inadequate, the direct results being—
1. An excess inventory of certain finished goods and raw materials.
2. Poor customer service because a lack of materials and productive capacity resulted in the neglect of many orders.

Further, it was found that stock levels were not reviewed periodically and used

Production Planning and Inventory Control

as a guide for future production. Inventory records were cumbersome and not useful, since they focused on current and anticipated orders and failed to highlight those items on which action should have been taken.

Other Findings

The findings revealed opportunities for savings of approximately one-half to three-quarters of a million dollars. The principal findings that the study team uncovered in the remaining categories were as follows:
1. Warehousing and shipping.
    (*a.*) No control existed on backorders.
    (*b.*) Personnel were poorly utilized.
    (*c.*) Inventory was difficult to locate.
2. Clerical costs, plant.
    (*a.*) Supervision was inadequate and performance standards were not used.
    (*b.*) Overtime was not controlled.
    (*c.*) Most recordkeeping procedures contained duplications of data, were in excessive detail, and offered significant opportunities for streamlining.
3. Clerical costs, headquarters.
    (*a.*) Supervision of clerical employees was inadequate.
    (*b.*) There were excessive delays between shipping and invoicing.
    (*c.*) Customer credits were not analyzed to determine a pattern or to identify chronic complainers.
4. Cost information systems.
    (*a.*) Product cost information was not integrated into the accounting system and thus lacked reliability.
    (*b.*) Performance variances were not automatically developed and reported by the system.
    (*c.*) Associated overhead was not included in the cost of the product.
5. Organization structure and management reports.
    (*a.*) The assignment of responsibilities was not clear-cut.
    (*b.*) The importance of production planning and inventory control was not recognized by assigning someone at an appropriate level in the organization to exercise the required supervision.
    (*c.*) There was no system of planning and control that would provide meaningful reports as well as coordination and accountability for all functions.

Recommendations

As a result of these findings, the study team developed a list of recommendations to correct the inadequacies it had found. The following is a summary of the solutions presented:
1. Direct labor area.
    (*a.*) Adoption of production line balancing techniques to reduce bottlenecks.
    (*b.*) Revision of the plant's layout, methods, and work stations.
    (*c.*) Improvement of work scheduling.
    (*d.*) Improvement of personnel controls.

2. Indirect factory labor.
   (*a.*) Revision of work methods.
   (*b.*) Improvement of manpower scheduling and reporting of time.
3. Production planning and inventory control.
   (*a.*) Reduction in inventory levels.
   (*b.*) Revision of the production scheduling and control system.
   (*c.*) Elevation of the function of production planning and inventory control to a level reporting directly to the president.
4. Warehousing and shipping.
   (*a.*) Installation of a merchandise locator system.
   (*b.*) Increased utilization of available personnel.
   (*c.*) Batching of orders to reduce nonproductive walking time.
5. Clerical areas.
   (*a.*) Adoption of supervisory control techniques to increase productivity.
   (*b.*) Revision of procedures to simplify recordkeeping.
6. Cost information systems.
   (*a.*) Development of an integrated cost accounting system with revised standard costs for labor, materials, and associated overhead.
   (*b.*) Adoption of expense budgets for clerical and other overhead departments.
7. Organization and management reports.
   (*a.*) Development of charters of accountability defining functions, responsibilities, reporting relationships, and performance standards for all management personnel.
   (*b.*) Design and installation of a responsibility reporting system summarizing key dollar and statistical information for each area of accountability within the company.

The study team converted the company's income statements (Exhibit 116) from a dollar to a percentage basis (see Exhibit 117). This approach revealed a high proportion of total variable costs to sales. *Setting Priorities*

In addition, the previously discussed findings indicated that the major savings could be secured in the areas of direct labor, production planning and inventory control, and indirect factory labor and materials. In view of these facts, the study team recommended to the president that primary emphasis for the implementation of profit improvement recommendations be directed to these areas. Specifically, it felt that the following programs would provide the greatest payback for the company:

1. High priority programs.

(*a.*)	Direct labor cost reduction	$250,000
(*b.*)	Inventory cost reduction	150,000
(*c.*)	Indirect labor savings	60,000
(*d.*)	Clerical savings	40,000
(*e.*)	Reduction in warehouse cost	50,000
	Estimated dollar savings	$550,000

2. Longer-range programs.
   (*a.*) Analyze the product lines and purge them of unprofitable items.
   (*b.*) Reduce backorders and improve the control of product shipments.
   (*c.*) Shorten the time between order entry and shipment.
   (*d.*) Revise the organization structure.

EXHIBIT 117   GET WELL QUICK, INC.
FIVE-YEAR INCOME STATEMENT IN PERCENTAGES

	5 Years Ago	4 Years Ago	3 Years Ago	2 Years Ago	Last Year
Sales	100	100	100	100	100
Cost of Sales:					
Materials	32	32	32	35	35
Labor	16	16	17	21	21
Direct contribution	52	52	51	44	44
Less:					
Variable burden	12	13	13	17	18
Fixed burden	8	7	6	10	9
Gross profit	32	32	32	17	17
Selling expense	13	13	14	12	11
General and administrative expense	7	7	7	9	9
Net operating income (loss)	12	12	11	(4)	(3)
Components of variable cost:					
Materials	32	32	32	35	35
Labor	16	16	17	21	21
Variable burden	12	13	13	17	18
Total	60	61	62	73	74

Committee Review and Approval

After the findings and recommendations had been presented and the profit improvement committee and president had had an opportunity to carefully review all data, analyses, and conclusions, the president authorized the study team to begin with the implementation of the profit improvement program. This approval marked the end of the first phase of the program.

General Design

During the second phase, the study team embarked on the general design of the profit improvement program. This phase consisted of four tasks and covered all the areas of the company affected by the previous recommendations.

1. Definition of information and control requirements in terms of recommended reporting systems and procedures.

2. General description of the revised manufacturing and business systems.
3. Definition of supporting transaction system requirements in terms of source documents, control requirements, and processing alternatives.
4. Development of alternative methods of implementation and their estimated costs.

The material prepared as a result of the general design phase gave the president an opportunity to review and approve the proposed revisions. At this point, he was able to identify his particular preferences as they related to the new systems. Reports, procedures, and policies were then modified, as necessary, to meet these requirements. In addition, the president reviewed several alternatives for implementation and selected the one that he felt best met the needs of the company.

When all elements of the general design were completed and approved, the study team developed and presented a work program for the final detail design and implementation phase.

Detail Design and Implementation

The work program identified the specific tasks required to complete the design and fully implement the revised systems. In addition, the program was sequenced to reflect the originally approved schedule of priorities and contained time estimates for the completion of each major task. The individual or group responsible for each task was also identified.

In terms of total man-hours, the detail design and implementation phase represented the major segment of the profit improvement program. The detailed procedures, forms, and systems were designed, approved, and readied for installation during this stage. Periodic meetings between the study team, committee, and president permitted the group to solve specific design issues and to review progress to date. The time estimates and assigned responsibilities contained in the work program established a valuable method for project control and accountability. In addition, the work program provided the study team with an early warning device that quickly identified areas that were falling behind schedule.

The specific techniques and concepts utilized by the study team to correct system inadequacies were as varied as the problems that the team encountered. However, the success of the program was critically dependent upon the company's ability to substitute more effective and efficient business systems for those already in use. What follows briefly describes one of the approaches used by the GWQ study team in developing better systems and procedures.

A major area offering opportunities for improvement was that of developing companywide performance standards. The members of the study team felt that it was realistic to develop standards of performance for all levels of the organization so that management could objectively monitor personnel performance. They recognized, however, that the techniques that should be used vary with the classification of personnel. Consequently, all personnel in the company were classified into one of three categories:

1. Administrative. These individuals were typically managers and supervisors.
2. Program. This category included individuals who were responsible for activities such as research and development or systems and procedures.

3. Measurable. The individuals in this category were primarily responsible for routine and repetitive activities.

After completing the classification, the study team developed performance standards by undertaking a comprehensive work methods study of all areas where problems had previously been identified and where the majority of the employees were classified in the measurable category. The study team enlisted the assistance of those personnel performing the routine tasks, and together they designed and substituted improved methods and procedures that accomplished the same tasks more efficiently than the procedures in use at the time. The team then used historical performance data, stopwatch studies, and predetermined standard data to calculate standard completion times and output volumes for each task.

This approach, which encompassed many of the routine manufacturing, maintenance, and clerical tasks, actually improved the morale of the operating employees. The employees had had an opportunity to participate in the revision and upgrading of operating procedures, and now the revised methods and standards provided them with equal workloads and explicit procedures for executing their responsibilities, as well as a clearer understanding of the amount and quality of work that each of them was responsible for. In addition, the streamlined operations reduced total overtime hours worked, provided more accurate estimates of manpower requirements in view of pending workloads, and made workloads more uniform in spite of cyclical and backlogged situations. Periodic reports were also developed to establish the performance of individual employees. These reports, in addition to providing the basis for scheduling and controlling operations, were also valuable in reviewing personnel performance relative to the new standards and providing an objective evaluation to assist in the annual review of promotions and salary increases.

An important step in the profit improvement program was the follow-up review of results. As recommendations were implemented, the budget director would prepare a report containing the initial feedback of operating and financial results. The executive vice president supplemented the available data with a status report on the particular recommendations being reviewed. In the direct labor area, for example, the executive vice president indicated the following accomplishments:

1. Work assignments had been revised.
2. New work station layouts were being used.
3. Equipment had been rearranged.
4. Time reporting accuracy had been increased.

The budget director added that the new management reports revealed that production was up 25 percent, while labor costs actually decreased 10 percent. Similarly, each of the other areas was reviewed to establish the actual tasks accomplished and savings achieved. In this manner, the company was able to evaluate the profit improvement program itself, in terms of the degree to which it achieved its original objectives.

Not all systems were implemented within the first year of the program, and many of the effects of the installed revisions were not immediately felt. However, a dramatic reversal of the past two years' performance was achieved by GWQ in the following year (see Exhibit 118).

GET WELL QUICK, INC.   **EXHIBIT 118**
TWO-YEAR INCOME STATEMENT IN THOUSANDS OF DOLLARS

	Current Year		Last Year (See Exhibit 116)	
	Dollars	Percent	Dollars	Percent
Sales	$12,000	100	$12,500	100
Cost of sales (variances included):				
Materials	3,850	33	4,370	35
Labor	2,230	18	2,620	21
Direct contribution	$ 5,920	49	$ 5,510	44
Less:				
Variable burden	2,100	17	2,250	18
Fixed burden	1,120	9	1,150	9
Gross profit	$ 2,700	23	$ 2,110	17
Selling expense	1,060	9	1,380	11
General and administrative expense	1,040	9	1,130	9
Net operating income (loss)	$ 600	5	($ 400)	(3)

This case study is an example of how a company can improve its overall profit performance. The profit improvement program at GWQ secured its original objectives because the effort was effectively organized, endorsed by top management, and designed and implemented in a competent and thorough manner.

14

The Corporate Planning Model

THE PREPLANNING PHASE of the planning and budgeting cycle is described as a five-step process in Chapter 2. Included in this phase is an assessment of geographic and industry trends in consumer demand and an analysis of the company's past performance in relation to these trends. This planning activity includes a projection of industry demand and an assessment of what the company's share of the market will be, using historical performance and management's objectives as a base. This decision provides a basis for the company's sales objectives and leads to other considerations that must be resolved prior to the publication of management's final statement of objectives and policies. These considerations involve areas such as capital budget projections, new product introduction, and the extent to which expansion will be financed from internally generated funds, equity funds, or debt. Preplanning also deals with other questions of policy and company objectives, such as methods of distribution and development of sources of raw materials.

Resolution of each of these preplanning questions results in the formulation of management's policies and objectives supported by a long-range plan for implementation. The long-range plan—the key output of the preplanning activity—is based on a realistic analysis of the company's strengths, weaknesses, and position in the industry, and it sets forth the company's operating and financial goals for a meaningful planning period.

The development of the long-range plan is characterized by the evaluation of alternative courses of action on the basis of the return on investment, earnings per share, and other key financial ratios that can be related to management's objectives and policies. Realistic financial projection to assess alternatives requires the consideration of many factors and interrelationships, frequently in considerable detail. To be responsive to management's needs, the long-range planning capabilities should provide for rapid and systematic evaluations of alternative courses of action. To be meaningful, these evaluations should reflect the full effects of the company's financial and operating interrelationships and should provide profit and loss, balance sheet, and cash flow projections for decision making.

Unfortunately, many companies today do not possess this planning capability. To date most long-range planning has been performed using manual methods. This is time-consuming and expensive, and its slow pace and expense often force management to limit the number of alternatives evaluated as well as the scope and interrelationships to be considered. The difficulty in considering business questions in light of management's objectives lies in the need to insure that as many alternatives as possible are evaluated and that the full financial impact of each is adequately reacted to. Under manual approaches the decision maker is forced to use subjectivity, less than all the facts, and whatever business judgment he has developed from experience. In other words, once he has reached a tentative decision or at least restricted the number of alternatives, the facts he has managed to accumulate are then developed manually into financial projections to reflect the likely impact on the total corporation. It is not uncommon for management to make a decision and then measure the consequence. Typically, limitations in time and manpower preclude reworking many adjustments if the results appear to be unsatisfactory relative to management goals. Furthermore, there is an associated risk that some key elements of cost or revenue will be overlooked or "guesstimated" in redeveloping the projections.

These shortcomings are intensified by the increase in the size and complexity of business enterprises and by the rate at which individual companies are expanding and changing their practices. Growing companies with multiple product lines or businesses and complex internal organizations are becoming more common. Additionally, opportunities for expanding into new and often unrelated businesses through direct acquisition or merger with other companies also emphasize the need for effective long-range planning capabilities.

As a consequence of the limitations of manual methods and the increased complexities of business, many companies are moving toward the use of the computer to facilitate long-range planning.

The Corporate Model—What Is It?

Paralleling the movement toward computers in long-range planning is the emergence of the corporate planning model as a powerful planning technique. To understand about corporate planning models we must first understand the concept of models. In its most basic sense, a model is a meaningful abstraction of something real. For example, a road map is a graphic representation of a real network of roads and highways. Similarly, a corporate planning model represents the interrelated aspects of a total business enterprise symbolically by expressing them in logic consisting of a set of algebraic equations.

The key source for the interrelationships that describe a company's operating and financial functions is the budgeting system. This system contains the wage rates, product costs, production and inventory decision rules, relationships of indirect costs to sales—essentially, all the elements and interrelationships required to build the corporate planning model. The model should therefore portray the logical and mathematical relationships that reflect at a summary level the key operating and financial interrelationships as characterized in the budgeting system.

In addition, for effective financial planning, the structure of the planning model must be consistent with that of the budgeting system in terms of the operating and financial interrelationships and related accounting considerations. If the need for this consistency is not recognized, management runs the risk of failing to attain long-range profit objectives, since the vehicle for doing so is the budgeting system. Consistency in structure does not imply that the model must represent a mechanization of the total budgeting system as such. Rather, it must represent the enterprise at a summary level in order to facilitate use and rapid responsiveness to alternative assumptions. Consistency here does mean that the interrelationships and financial flow contained in the model agree with those contained in the budgeting system.

To be effective as a planning tool, the corporate planning model must calculate the financial effects of alternative courses of action and alternative policies as well as changing conditions. To attain the benefits of speed and to allow rapid assessment of many alternatives, the model must be operated by a computer. The corporate planning model provides output in terms of financial data, thereby enabling management to determine the profit and loss statement, balance sheet, cash requirement, and related financial impact of proposed courses of action. The model then projects these effects over a future period that corresponds to management's long-range planning period.

Schematically, the structure of a financial model (in Exhibit 119, for a retailing organization) can be viewed as having three basic elements. The first of these is made up of inputs to the model reflecting conditions that might be expected to change in the future. In retailing, these changing conditions relate to merchandising, operations, financial, and overall policy considerations. The format of these inputs—the way in which changes to basic factors can be initiated—can vary widely. In some cases such changes can be indicated as percentage growth rates. Under other circumstances, adjustments to basic historical expense ratios might be input.

The second element is a series of computer subroutines and data elements which make up the inner workings of the model itself. This aspect of the system contains an initial profile of the business, selected historical data that will be updated and built upon, and standard relationships that reflect the way in which certain costs are quantitatively related to certain levels of merchandising or operating activity. The function of the model is then to execute intermediate calculations—based on inputs of changing conditions to the basic profile—and generate the results in terms of net revenue, total merchandising costs, cash flows, and so forth. These intermediate calculations are necessary in order to generate the outputs of the system which are normally expressed in terms of projected profit and loss, balance sheet, and cash statements, as well as summarized key financial and statistical data.

The key to effective utilization of a corporate model is its ability to respond to management's what-if questions. In a sense, these questions are management's assessment of the possible future occurrences or conditions that will affect the outcome when any given alternative is pursued. There can be an infinite number of questions which management might need to evaluate in order to arrive at an appropriate decision consistent with long-range corporate goals. So a corporate financial model, appropriately designed and implemented for an individual company and its management, must facilitate inquiry and must rapidly respond with the financial impact associated with the what-if questions posed to it. The outputs of the model, when evaluated by management, provide the basis for recycling through this inquiry process until an appropriate alternative can be selected.

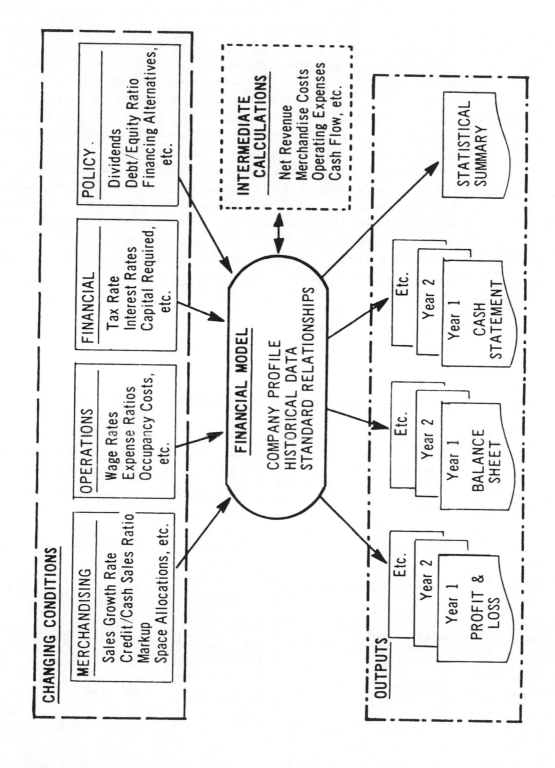

EXHIBIT 119   SCHEMATIC OF A CORPORATE PLANNING MODEL FOR A RETAIL SALES COMPANY

CHANGING CONDITIONS

MERCHANDISING
Sales Growth Rate
Credit/Cash Sales Ratio
Markup
Space Allocations, etc.

OPERATIONS
Wage Rates
Expense Ratios
Occupancy Costs,
etc.

FINANCIAL
Tax Rate
Interest Rates
Capital Required,
etc.

POLICY
Dividends
Debt/Equity Ratio
Financing Alternatives,
etc.

INTERMEDIATE CALCULATIONS
Net Revenue
Merchandise Costs
Operating Expenses
Cash Flow, etc.

FINANCIAL MODEL
COMPANY PROFILE
HISTORICAL DATA
STANDARD RELATIONSHIPS

STATISTICAL
SUMMARY

Etc.
Year 2
Year 1
CASH
STATEMENT

Etc.
Year 2
Year 1
BALANCE
SHEET

Etc.
Year 2
Year 1
PROFIT &
LOSS

OUTPUTS

As an illustration of alternative approaches to structuring the interrelationships of a company, consider the simple example in Exhibit 120. One approach to the design of the corporate model (shown on Alternative 1) might be to require the user to supply sales, cost of sales, and general and administrative expenses together with closing balance sheet figures as input data. The system would read the data, compute taxes and net income, do some summarization, and print the output reports. In essence, this concept requires the user to make a substantial number of the projections. Obviously, such a system is characterized by summarization capabilities and represents a very simple model. Although this would represent some advantages over manual methods, this approach has the disadvantage of putting too heavy a burden on the user to make computations external to the system, and it falls far short of fully utilizing the computer's abilities and capacity.

Another approach to the design (shown as Alternative 2 in Exhibit 120) would require the user to supply as input data the projection of sales. The corporate model would include relationships that calculate the cost of sales and general and administrative expenses on the basis of the projected sales level. The user requirement would be to input sales only, with all other calculations being made by the computer system. To extend the illustration, the corporate model could be designed to forecast future sales from historical sales data by application of a growth factor. As shown in Alternative 3, the purchases can then be used to calculate raw materials usage, which in turn is used to calculate cost of goods sold.

EXHIBIT 120   STRUCTURE OF A CORPORATE PLANNING MODEL

ALTERNATIVE 1

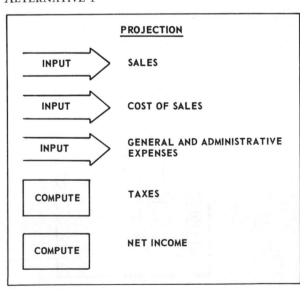

ALTERNATIVE 2

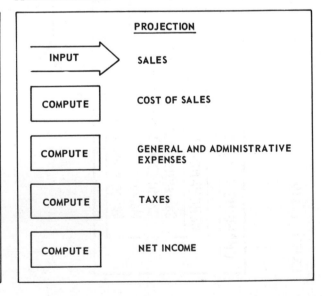

The motive behind these various steps in refinement is to improve the flexibility of the model by transferring the computational burden from the user to the system. As the example indicates, these refinements substitute relationships among basic underlying factors for figures which merely represent end-product results. The elaboration of the system, however, has advantages going far beyond those that relate to the production of figures, important as this result may be. The expansion of the system permits the user to investigate the financial effect of various changes in both the assumed conditions and the company's operations. For instance, the inclusion of sales prices, growth factors, and labor rates would permit investigation of the financial impact of variations in these elements. This elaboration and refinement of projection methods in the model should proceed until the desired level of what-if questions can be reflected.

ALTERNATIVE 3

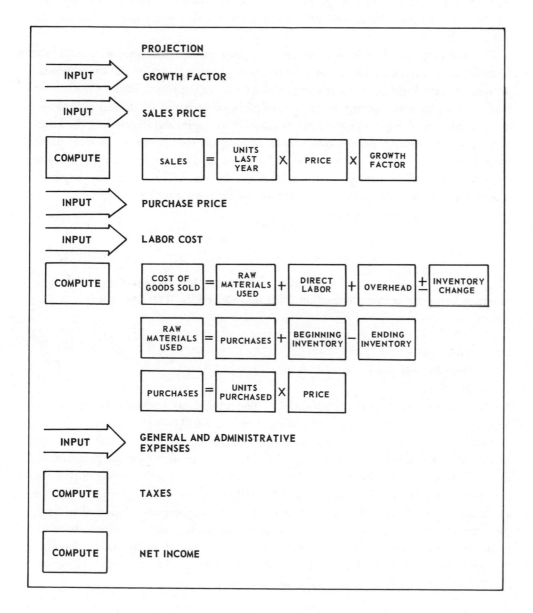

The corporate planning model can greatly expand the effectiveness of budgeting and planning, and distinct advantages and benefits can be derived from its use. First, it offers speed in the rapid evaluation of alternative courses of action. Second, it imposes a discipline on the user. The formal approach required by the use of a model can be expected to result in a higher-quality, less subjective level of planning. The development of a corporate model requires careful analysis of the important factors involved and an orderly procedure to make effective use of this tool. The corporate model reflects comprehensiveness, which is an additional benefit. The focus of the model is on an entire company, not just a division or a function. This encourages the comprehensive viewpoint in the analysis of problems and increases the likelihood of capturing the full financial impact of a proposed course of action. Another major benefit is the flexibility added to the planning cycle. Management can anticipate changes and revise its long-range plan as business conditions dictate. Finally, the corporate model provides an efficient basis for establishing operating guidelines and financial objectives.

The advantages and benefits that can be gained through the use of a corporate planning model must be viewed in relation to the key elements of the management process. As noted in Chapter 1, these key elements are expressed in the three major functions of planning, execution, and control. The objective of the model is to facilitate planning, specifically in evaluating alternative strategies and developing the long-range plan. Budgeting, on the other hand, focuses on the short-term annual plan; more important, it provides execution and control capabilities that are beyond the scope of the corporate model. It must therefore be emphasized that the corporate model is intended not to replace but rather to facilitate planning and budgeting.

A Case Study: Reliable Inc.

Reliable Inc. is engaged in the manufacture and sale of plastic products. The company competes in the toy market with its model kits. The four models it distributes are—

1. B-58.
2. Teddy Bear.
3. Stutz Bearcat Auto.
4. Ant Farm.

Reliable distributes its products nationwide. The annual sales volume has grown to $25 million in the current year, with profits exceeding $800,000 after taxes.

Reliable employs a planning and budgeting cycle similar to the one that is outlined in Exhibit 16. Additionally, this year Reliable plans to facilitate its preplanning through the use of a corporate planning model which has been developed during the past fiscal year. The structure of the model parallels that of the budgeting process on a summary level. Although Reliable does not have a computer installation of its own, the corporate model has been programed for a large-scale computer which the company can have access to through a time-sharing terminal. Reliable is a subscriber to a commercial time-sharing service which is used by accounting, manufacturing, and marketing for special studies and analysis.

Management is not satisfied with the present profit margins and believes they should be improved. The company's five-year record of return on investment and earnings per share has been—

	Return on Average Investment		Earnings per Share	
	%	% Increase (Decrease)	Amount	% Increase (Decrease)
Four years ago	11.9	–	$3.45	–
Three years ago	12.3	3	3.71	8
Two years ago	12.7	3	4.05	9
One year ago	12.2	(4)	4.15	2
Current year	11.3	(7)	4.10	(1)

Both these results and the company's recent growth rate are considered unsatisfactory. A careful study of the business and general industry trends and conditions has convinced management that Reliable should be able to earn $5 per share over the short term. This would be the result of a net income after taxes of $1 million for the coming year, which would represent a return on investment of approximately 13 percent. Both of these figures would represent a considerable improvement in Reliable's position, and, accordingly, the primary objective is to earn $1 million after taxes next year and to maintain a return on investment of at least 13 percent for the subsequent four years. Management will consider what plant expansion and capital investment are necessary to attain this objective.

To achieve higher earnings, a prime requirement will be an increase in gross profit. This can result from an increase in sales, a relative increase in the more profitable products, the introduction of a new product line (the addition of a new product called Wham is being considered), an increase in productivity and sales price, or a decrease in costs. Management intends to use the corporate model to evaluate alternative courses of action so as to establish guidelines and quantified objectives for the budget and to develop the long-range plan. Accordingly, the second objective is to achieve the proper level of sales at prices and costs that will produce the gross profit necessary to achieve earnings after taxes of $1 million for the next year and return on investment of at least 13 percent for the following years.

Labor negotiations for the coming year are another key concern of management. Currently the average hourly cost is $3 for molding, $2.75 for fabrication, and $2 for assembly. Management anticipates an increase for the coming calendar year of approximately 8 percent, and it wants to know how this increase will affect the profit picture. Furthermore, it may be in the company's interest to take a one-month strike at the beginning of the year and settle for a 2 percent smaller increase for the following 12 months. Accordingly, the corporate planning model will be used to evaluate alternative strategies for labor negotiations.

Reliable's corporate planning model is described in the schematic shown in Exhibit 121. The model operates on specific data inputs; it includes logical and mathematical relationships which project the operating and financial behavior of the company through a five-year period; and it provides balance sheet, cash flow, and profit and loss statements for management evaluation.

EXHIBIT 121 Reliable Inc. Corporate Planning Model

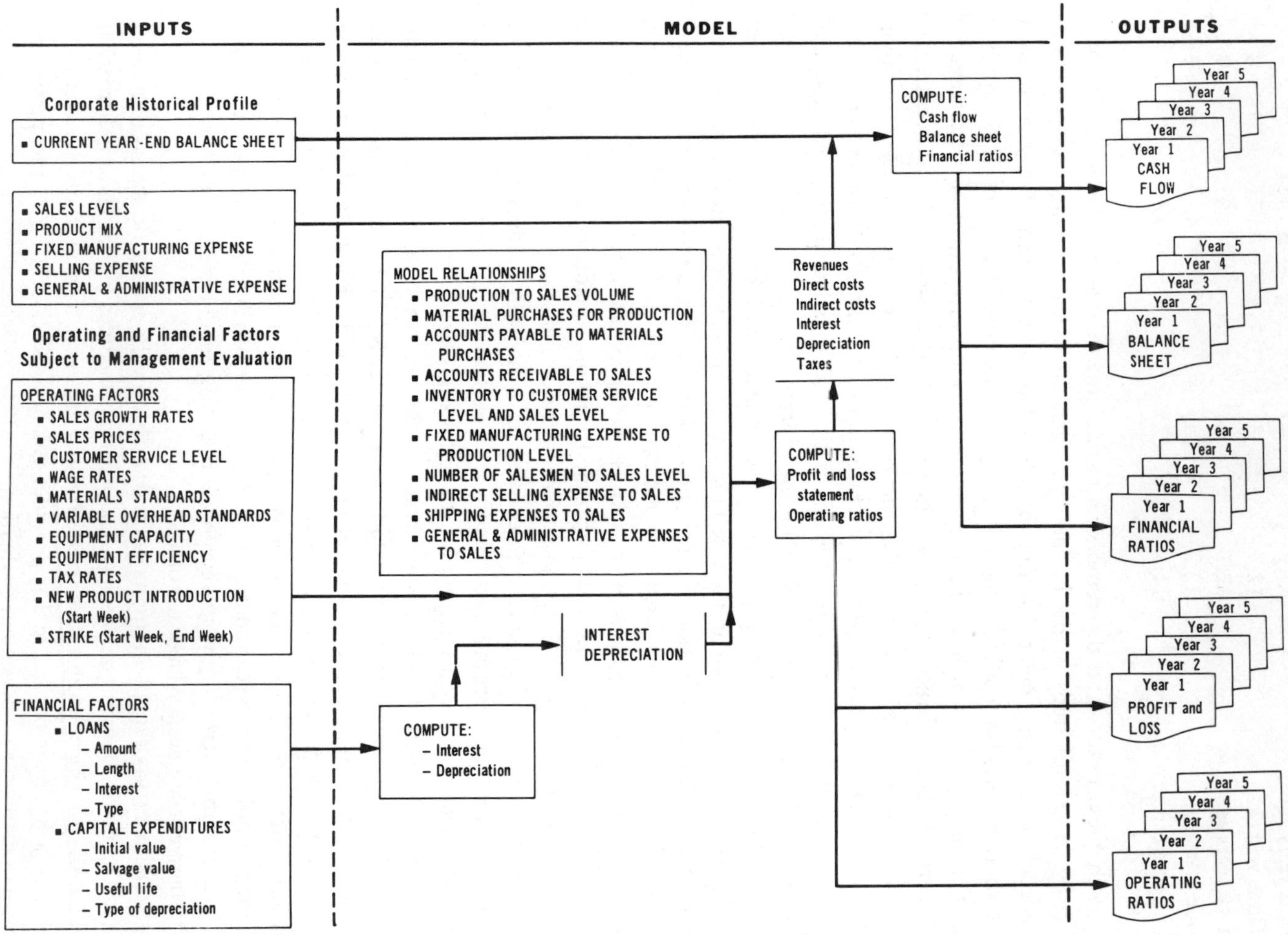

Data input requirements include—

1. A historical profile of the company in terms of the latest year-end balance sheet, sales level, product mix, and fixed manufacturing, selling, and general and administrative expenses. The historical profile provides a basis for projection of balance sheet line items, sales by product, and levels for the indicated expense items.

2. The operating and financial factors that are subject to management evaluation. The operating factors include such items as sales growth rates, prices, and wage and tax rates. The materials, price, cost, and labor standards included in this sector of the model were obtained from Reliable's budgeting system. Additional operating factors provide management with the capability to input the start week for a new product introduction and an anticipated start and end week to simulate the impact of a strike. The financial factors include existing loans and capital expenditures and also permit entry of proposed alternatives for financing and capital projects.

The relationships included in the model are a quantified and logical representation of Reliable's budgeting process. Reliable uses the concepts described in Chapters 2–6 dealing with the development of the sales, manufacturing and selling expense, and general and administrative budgets.

As an illustration consider how computations are performed by the model for the projection of sales, production, and inventory requirements. With the necessary inputs specified, the model proceeds to project the annual sales volume (units) by product for a five-year period by applying an annual growth rate to the latest year-end sales level. The growth rate represents management's objective based on an assessment of historical sales and profit performance and anticipated market growth and penetration. A key aspect in this consideration is that the model market is expected to expand by 5 to 6 percent per year over the next five years, primarily as a result of population growth and disposable income projections. The company products are expected to sell well, with performance generally better than the industry average.

Since the profitability of the Stutz Bearcat is marginal, management has decided to discontinue advertising and sales promotion on this product and consequently anticipates that sales will decrease at a rate of 3.3 percent per year. In contrast, the Teddy Bear has consistently exhibited an annual growth rate of 15 to 20 percent, with management anticipating a continuation of this trend. Accordingly, an annual growth rate of 17 percent has been specified for the Teddy Bear. The B-58 and Ant Farm, on the other hand, perform slightly better than the average for market growth, or about 7 percent per year. These anticipated growth rates are reflected in Exhibit 122, which shows the model's projection of annual sales broken down by quarter and valued at anticipated sales prices.

The model is now ready to calculate production requirements using a procedure similar in structure to the annual production budget development. At Reliable, the plant operates five days per week, three shifts per day, and is shut down for vacation during the last two weeks of the second quarter. Budgeted machine rates per thousand units for next year are as follows:

EXHIBIT 122   RELIABLE INC. CURRENT YEAR AND PROJECTED SALES BY PRODUCT AND QUARTER

(000 omitted)

Year	Quarter	Sales Stutz Bearcat Units	Dollars	Sales Teddy Bear Units	Dollars	Sales B-58 Units	Dollars	Sales Ant Farm Units	Dollars
Last year	1	776	$ 931	231	$ 691	486	$ 2,187	93	$ 326
actual	2	1,293	1,552	308	924	608	2,736	279	977
	3	1,293	1,552	615	1,845	608	2,736	233	816
	4	1,809	2,171	384	1,152	728	3,276	325	1,138
Total		5,171	$6,206	1,538	$ 4,612	2,430	$10,935	930	$3,257
Projected Year 1	1	750	$ 900	270	$ 810	520	$ 2,340	100	$ 350
	2	1,250	1,500	360	1,080	650	2,925	300	1,050
	3	1,250	1,500	720	2,160	650	2,925	250	875
	4	1,750	2,100	450	1,350	780	3,510	350	1,225
Total		5,000	$6,000	1,800	$ 5,400	2,600	$11,700	1,000	$3,500
Year 2	1	725	$ 870	316	$ 948	556	$ 2,502	108	$ 378
	2	1,209	1,451	421	1,263	696	3,132	323	1,131
	3	1,209	1,451	842	2,526	696	3,132	269	942
	4	1,693	2,032	527	1,581	834	3,753	375	1,313
Total		4,836	$5,804	2,106	$ 6,318	2,782	$12,519	1,075	$3,764
Year 3	1	702	$ 842	370	$ 1,110	595	$ 2,678	116	$ 406
	2	1,169	1,403	493	1,479	744	3,348	347	1,215
	3	1,169	1,403	986	2,958	744	3,348	289	1,012
	4	1,637	1,964	615	1,845	894	4,023	404	1,414
Total		4,677	$5,612	2,464	$ 7,392	2,977	$13,397	1,156	$4,047
Year 4	1	679	$ 815	432	$ 1,296	637	$ 2,867	124	$ 434
	2	1,131	1,357	577	1,731	796	3,582	373	1,306
	3	1,131	1,357	1,153	3,459	796	3,582	311	1,089
	4	1,583	1,900	721	2,163	956	4,302	434	1,519
Total		4,524	$5,429	2,883	$ 8,649	3,185	$14,333	1,242	$4,348
Year 5	1	656	$ 787	506	$ 1,518	682	$ 3,069	134	$ 469
	2	1,094	1,313	675	2,025	852	3,834	401	1,404
	3	1,094	1,313	1,349	4,047	852	3,834	334	1,169
	4	1,531	1,837	843	2,529	1,022	4,599	466	1,631
Total		4,375	$5,250	3,373	$10,119	3,408	$15,336	1,335	$4,673
Expected annual growth rate		3.3%		17.0%		7.0%		7.5%	
Expected selling price		$1.20		$3.00		$4.50		$3.50	

Products	Molding Machine Hours per Thousand Units
Stutz Bearcat	27.50
Teddy Bear	32.22
B-58	46.80
Ant Farm	37.50

The production requirements for assembly and fabrication of the products are based on molding operations, since molding is the production bottleneck in terms of availability of capacity and percentage of total process cycle.

The seasonal nature of Reliable's business makes it necessary to consider the cost of maintaining a stable workforce and carrying balanced inventories. Reliable has established a budgeting procedure to minimize the total cost of carrying inventory, employment change (hiring and firing), and third-shift operations. This procedure includes (1) setting the production rate at a level which will build up sufficient inventory to cover the two-week shutdown, and (2) after the shutdown, increasing the production rate to a level which will just cover demand during the remainder of the year. Accordingly, this procedure is the basis for projection of production and inventory requirements in the model.

As a first step, the projection of unit sales by quarter for the five-year period is converted to machine hours. This projection procedure, shown in Exhibit 123, is accomplished by applying the standard molding machine hours per thousand units to the projected product sales.

Next, safety stock requirements are established to compensate for variability in lead time and in the sales forecast itself. The inventory policy at Reliable requires a safety stock equal to the historical forecast error rate, plus two weeks' sales in machine hours at the current quarter's sales rate. Historical performance shows that sales for the first three quarters can be forecast with a 5 percent accuracy while the fourth quarter error rate has been averaging 10 percent. The computation of projected cumulative inventory requirements as shown in Exhibit 124 includes the safety stock as well as inventory to meet the projected sales level.

Finally, the model calculates the planned production schedule reflecting management's policy of maintaining a stable workforce and carrying balanced inventories. This includes planned second and fourth quarter ending inventories equivalent to safety stock requirements for those respective quarters and the calculation of half-year production requirements by week, net of the starting inventory position as shown in Exhibit 125.

Having calculated sales projections, weekly production requirements, and beginning and ending inventory balances (including safety stock), the model is now ready to calculate materials requirements, direct and indirect expenses, selling expenses, and so forth, using the appropriate relationships in conjunction with historical profile and operating and financial factor inputs. Upon completion of the computations, the model reports the company's financial and operating behavior, including cash flow, balance sheet, financial ratios, profit and loss, and key operating ratios through a five-year period.

EXHIBIT 123

RELIABLE INC. PROJECTION OF MOLDING MACHINE HOUR REQUIREMENTS*

Projected Year	Product	Projected Unit Sales				Standard Conversion Rate 1,000 Hrs/Units	Molding Machine Hour Requirements							
		1st Quarter	2nd Quarter	3rd Quarter	4th Quarter		1st Quarter		2nd Quarter		3rd Quarter		4th Quarter	
							Hours	% of Total	Hours	% of Total	Hours	% of Total	Hours	% of Total
Year 1	Stutz Bearcat	750	1,250	1,250	1,750	27.50	20,625	35.9	34,375	39.2	34,375	35.3	48,125	42.9
	Teddy Bear	270	360	720	450	32.22	8,700	15.2	11,600	13.3	23,200	23.8	14,500	12.9
	B-58	520	650	650	780	46.80	24,336	42.4	30,420	34.7	30,420	31.3	36,504	32.5
	Ant Farm	100	300	250	350	37.50	3,750	6.5	11,250	12.8	9,375	9.6	13,125	11.7
							57,411	100	87,645	100	97,370	100	112,254	100
Year 2	Stutz Bearcat	725	1,209	1,209	1,693	27.50	19,938	33.1	33,248	36.4	33,248	32.3	46,558	39.8
	Teddy Bear	316	421	842	527	32.22	10,182	16.9	13,565	14.8	27,129	26.3	16,980	14.6
	B-58	556	696	696	834	46.80	26,021	43.3	32,573	35.6	32,573	31.6	39,031	33.5
	Ant Farm	108	323	269	375	37.50	4,050	6.7	12,113	13.2	10,088	9.8	14,063	12.1
							60,191	100	91,499	100	103,038	100	116,632	100

* Years 3, 4, and 5 omitted.

EXHIBIT 124

RELIABLE INC. PROJECTION OF SAFETY STOCK AND CUMULATIVE INVENTORY REQUIREMENTS*

(Machine Hours)

Year	Quarter (13 Weeks)	Percent of Fore-cast Error	Product	Projected Sales	Safety Stock. Forecast Error	Safety Stock. Two Week Supply	Total Safety Stock	Cumulative Inventory Require-ments
1	1	5	Stutz Bearcat	20,625	1,031	3,176	4,207	
			Teddy Bear	8,700	435	1,340	1,775	
			B-58	24,336	1,217	3,747	4,964	
			Ant Farm	3,750	188	577	765	
				57,411			11,711	69,122
	2	5	Stutz Bearcat	34,375	1,719	5,294	7,013	
			Teddy Bear	11,600	580	1,786	2,366	
			B-58	30,420	1,521	4,685	6,206	
			Ant Farm	11,250	563	1,732	2,295	
				87,645			17,880	162,936
	3	5	Stutz Bearcat	34,375	1,719	5,294	7,013	
			Teddy Bear	23,200	1,160	3,572	4,732	
			B-58	30,420	1,521	4,684	6,205	
			Ant Farm	9,375	469	1,444	1,913	
				97,370			19,863	262,289
	4	10	Stutz Bearcat	48,125	4,813	7,411	12,224	
			Teddy Bear	14,500	1,450	2,233	3,683	
			B-58	36,504	3,650	5,621	9,271	
			Ant Farm	13,125	1,313	2,021	3,334	
				112,254			28,512	383,192
2	1	5	Stutz Bearcat	19,938	997	3,066	4,063	
			Teddy Bear	10,182	509	1,566	2,075	
			B-58	26,021	1,301	4,002	5,303	
			Ant Farm	4,050	2,025	6,229	8,254	
				60,191			19,695	434,566
	2	5	Stutz Bearcat	33,248	1,662	5,114	6,776	
			Teddy Bear	13,565	678	2,086	2,764	
			B-58	32,573	1,629	5,010	6,639	
			Ant Farm	12,113	606	1,863	2,469	
				91,499			18,648	525,018
	3	5	Stutz Bearcat	33,248	1,662	5,114	6,776	
			Teddy Bear	27,129	1,356	4,172	5,528	
			B-58	32,573	1,629	5,010	6,639	
			Ant Farm	10,088	504	1,552	2,056	
				103,038			20,999	630,407
	4	10	Stutz Bearcat	46,558	4,656	7,161	11,817	
			Teddy Bear	16,980	1,698	2,612	4,310	
			B-58	39,031	3,903	6,003	9,906	
			Ant Farm	14,063	1,406	2,163	3,569	
				116,632			29,602	755,642

Years 3, 4, and 5 omitted.

EXHIBIT 125   RELIABLE INC. PROJECTED PRODUCTION AND INVENTORY PLAN*

(Machine Hours)

Year	Quarter	Ending Inventory	Sales	Total	Beginning Inventory	Required Production	Effective Weeks	Weekly Production
1	1		57,411		13,190		13	
	2	17,880	87,645				11	
		17,880	145,056	162,936	13,190	149,746	24	6,239
	3		97,370		17,880		13	
	4	28,512	112,254				13	
		28,512	209,624	238,136	17,880	220,256	26	8,471
2	1		60,191		28,510		13	
	2	18,648	91,499				11	
		18,648	151,690	170,338	28,510	141,828	24	5,910
	3		103,038		18,648		13	
	4	29,602	116,632				13	
		29,602	219,670	249,272	18,648	230,624	26	8,870

* Years 3, 4, and 5 omitted.

An illustration of management's initial run of the model is shown in Exhibits 126 and 127, which contain reports of financial projections as obtained from the time-sharing terminal. This run includes the sales, inventory, and production requirements, together with other operating and financial factors that reflect current cost and operating efficiency. When management reviewed these pro forma statements and noted the net profit after taxes of $851,000 in the first year, it quickly realized that several alternative courses of action would have to be evaluated if it was to accomplish the objective of $1 million in net profit after taxes the following year. Furthermore, although the objective is realized in the third year, net profit after taxes takes a downturn in the fourth and fifth projected years. This is because the capacity limitation of the molding machines is exceeded, which in turn limits sales and shipments while fixed costs increase.

Before evaluating alternative courses of action to meet the stated objectives, Reliable must establish a strategy for labor negotiations and reflect the impact of anticipated wage increases in the corporate plan. The initial run of the model (Exhibits 126 and 127) includes the current hourly wage rates of $2, $2.75 and $3 per hour, as was previously indicated. Management has two negotiation alternatives to evaluate. The first would reflect contract settlement including a wage increase of 6 percent at the expense of a one-month strike. This run of the model required modifi-

RELIABLE INC. INITIAL RUN OF CORPORATE PLANNING MODEL **EXHIBIT 126**
PROFIT AND LOSS AND STATISTICAL DATA

($000 omitted)

PROFIT AND LOSS

LINE ITEMS	YR1	YR2	YR3	YR4	YR5
SLS STUTZ BC	6000.0	5803.1	5612.6	5170.8	4706.6
SLS TEDDY BR	5400.0	6318.0	7392.1	8238.4	9071.4
SLS B-58	11700.0	12519.0	13395.4	13653.0	13748.7
SLS ANT FARM	3500.0	3762.5	4044.7	4141.7	4190.2
SLS WHAM					
NET SALES	26600.0	28402.6	30444.7	31203.9	31716.9
TOTAL LABOR	4604.8	4895.9	5225.7	5333.7	5399.1
TOTAL MAT'L	6255.4	6622.1	7039.6	7158.0	7220.5
VAR MFG EXP	6151.0	6517.1	6933.3	7054.7	7120.4
TOT INV DECR	-102.2	-116.1	-131.9	-142.6	-152.3
FIX MFG EXP	2327.0	2600.0	2860.0	3150.0	3470.0
CST OF SALES	19236.0	20518.9	21926.8	22553.8	23057.8
GROSS PROFIT	7364.0	7883.6	8517.9	8650.2	8659.1
SALESMEN SAL	391.0	409.4	430.2	438.0	443.2
COMMISSIONS	528.4	564.2	604.8	619.9	630.0
OT DI SLS EX	374.5	390.9	409.5	416.4	421.1
SHIPPING EXP	296.4	306.9	318.8	323.2	326.2
ADVG & PROMN	1946.3	2100.0	2300.0	2550.0	2850.0
OT FX SLS EX	730.9	786.6	849.6	873.1	888.9
INTEREST-CM	107.0	107.0	107.0	107.0	107.0
DEPRECIAT-CM	706.0	706.0	706.0	706.0	706.0
G & A	579.4	645.6	720.7	748.7	767.5
OTHER INCOME	-59.0	.0	.0	.0	.0
OTHER EXPENS					
TOT IND COST	5600.9	6016.6	6446.6	6782.2	7139.9
NET BEF TAX	1763.1	1867.0	2071.3	1868.0	1519.1
PROV FOR TAX	911.3	933.5	1035.6	934.0	759.6
NET PROF A-T	851.9	933.5	1035.6	934.0	759.6

STATISTICAL DATA

LINE ITEMS	YR1	YR2	YR3	YR4	YR5
NPAT/COM SHR	4.3	4.7	5.2	4.7	3.8
RATIO GP/SLS	.28	.28	.28	.28	.27
RATIO IC/SLS	.21	.21	.21	.22	.23
RATIO OP/SLS	.07	.07	.07	.06	.05
U-SLS STUTZ	5000.0	4835.9	4677.1	4309.0	3922.2
U-SLS TEDDY	1800.0	2106.0	2464.0	2746.1	3023.8
U-SLS B-58	2600.0	2782.0	2976.7	3034.0	3055.3
U-SLS ANT FM	1000.0	1075.0	1155.6	1183.4	1197.2
U SLS WHAM					

EXHIBIT 127   RELIABLE INC. INITIAL RUN OF CORPORATE PLANNING MODEL CASH FLOW, BALANCE SHEET, AND FINANCIAL RATIOS

($000 omitted)

CASH FLOW

LINE ITEMS	YR1	YR2	YR3	YR4	YR5
1 SLS RECEIPTS	26388.	28163.	30173.	31103.	31649.
3 DIRECT EXP	19322.	20615.	21942.	22582.	23090.
4 INDIRECT EXP	4679.	5081.	5506.	5870.	6221.
5 INTEREST	107.	107.	107.	107.	107.
6 TAX	911.	934.	1036.	934.	760.
7 TOT DISBURSE	25019.	26736.	28591	29493.	30178.
8 OPER CASH	1369.	1427.	1583.	1610.	1471.
9 LOANS					
13 CAPITAL EXP					
14 DIVD COMMON	300.	300.	300.	300.	300.
18 NET CASH FLO	1069.	1127.	1283.	1310.	1171.
19 CASH BALANCE	2059.	3187.	4469.	5779.	6950.

BALANCE SHEET

LINE ITEMS	YR1	YR2	YR3	YR4	YR5
101 CASH BALANCE	2059.	3187.	4469.	5779.	6950.
102 ACCTS RCVBLE	1978.	2218.	2489.	2590.	2658.
103 INVENTORY	1129.	1273.	1336.	1388.	1439.
104 OTHER CURRNT	1000.	1000.	1000.	1000.	1000.
105 TOTAL CURRNT	6166.	7677.	9295.	10757.	12047.
106 PLANT&EQUIPT	11179.	11179.	11179.	11179.	11179.
107 ACCUM DEPREC	5217.	5923.	6629.	7335.	8041.
108 NT PLNT&EQPT	5962.	5256.	4550.	3844.	3138.
109 OTHR NON-CUR	1247.	1247.	1247.	1247.	1247.
110 TOTAL ASSETS	13375.	14180.	15092.	15848.	16432.
201 ACCTS PAYBLE	2372.	2543.	2720.	2842.	2966.
204 OTHER CURRNT	750.	750.	750.	750.	750.
205 TOTAL CURRNT	3122.	3293.	3470.	3592.	3716.
206 LNGTERM DEBT	2700.	2700.	2700.	2700.	2700.
209 COM OUTSTAND	2000.	2000.	2000.	2000.	2000.
211 RETAIND EARN	5553.	6187.	6922.	7556.	8016.
212 STOCKH EQUIT	7553.	8187.	8922.	9556.	10016.
213 TOTAL EQUITY	13375.	14180.	15092.	15848.	16432.

FINANCIAL RATIOS

LINE ITEMS	YR1	YR2	YR3	YR4	YR5
301 NP-AT/STH EQ	.11	.11	.12	.10	.08
302 LTDEBT/SH EQ	.36	.33	.30	.28	.27
303 QUICK RATIO	1.29	1.64	2.01	2.33	2.59

RELIABLE INC. USE OF CORPORATE MODEL TO EVALUATE LABOR
NEGOTIATION STRATEGY

EXHIBIT 128

($ 000 OMITTED)
6% WAGE INCREASE, 4 WEEK STRIKE
SELECTED LINE ITEMS
PROFIT AND LOSS AND STATISTICAL DATA

LINE ITEMS	YR1	YR2	YR3	YR4	YR5
TOTAL LABOR	4500.4	5189.6	5539.2	5653.7	5723.1
NET PROF A-T	476.8	787.5	879.9	775.1	598.7
NPAT/COM SHR	2.4	3.9	4.4	3.9	3.0
RATIO GP/SLS	.26	.27	.27	.27	.26
RATIO IC/SLS	.22	.21	.21	.22	.23
RATIO OP/SLS	.04	.06	.06	.05	.04

8% WAGE INCREASE, NO STRIKE
SELECTED LINE ITEMS
PROFIT AND LOSS AND STATISTICAL DATA

LINE ITEMS	YR1	YR2	YR3	YR4	YR5
TOTAL LABOR	4973.2	5287.5	5643.8	5760.4	5831.1
NET PROF A-T	674.9	738.9	827.9	722.1	545.1
NPAT/COM SHR	3.4	3.7	4.1	3.6	2.7
RATIO GP/SLS	.26	.26	.27	.26	.26
RATIO IC/SLS	.21	.21	.21	.22	.23
RATIO OP/SLS	.05	.05	.05	.05	.03

cation of the three hourly wage rates (increased by 6 percent) and an additional input indicating that a strike would occur during the first four weeks of the coming year. The second alternative represents early contract settlement, without a strike, but with an increase of 8 percent effective January 1 of the coming year. The results of the two runs are displayed in Exhibit 128.

On the basis of these projections it is desirable for Reliable to take an aggressive position toward early settlement and grant a wage increase of 8 percent for the coming year. Accordingly, subsequent runs of the model include labor rates of $2.16, $2.97, and $3.24 per hour for the assembly, fabrication, and molding positions.

Management next used the corporate planning model to evaluate two major alternatives that could have a pronounced impact on Reliable's future financial and operating performance. The first of these alternatives is the introduction of *Wham*, a new product with high profit potential that will require increased advertising and

*Wham Cost and
Sales Profile*

fixed manufacturing expense. Wham, if introduced, will have a factory price of $5.25 per unit and an estimated first-year sales volume of 500,000 units. The cost and sales profile for Wham has been submitted to the president of Reliable through the joint efforts of industrial engineering, marketing, and the controller's department. The breakdown looked like this:

Factory price		$5.25
Estimated product cost		
Material	.60	
Labor	.57	
Variable overhead	.83	
Total variable cost		2.00
Marginal profit		3.25
Fixed overhead		.60
Gross profit		2.60
Sales estimate:		
Initial year	500,000 units	
Growth rate	10% per year	

Advertising expenditures to support the sales forecast and growth rate are estimated at $1.3 million over a five-year period, with first-year advertising costs of $400,000. Wham is particularly attractive to management since it does not require molding (only fabrication and assembly), so production will not be limited by existing molding machine capacity.

With the cost and sales profile data, including advertising expenses, as input to the corporate planning model, a run projecting the impact of Wham was made. Key outputs from this run are displayed in Exhibit 129. Highly significant in this projection is the attainment of corporate objectives, in terms of both net profit after taxes and return on investment.

The second major alternative involves a proposed capital expenditure of $2 million in molding equipment improvements, which would result in a 20 percent reduction in the molding production cycle and an associated reduction in molding direct labor, also estimated at 20 percent. If this proposal were to be adopted, implementation of equipment improvements would be scheduled for completion at the end of the first quarter of the coming year.

To evaluate the projected impact of this proposed capital expenditure, the standard molding machine hours per thousand units and the standard man-hours per hundred units would be reduced by the indicated 20 percent. This change would take effect at the start of the second quarter of the coming year. These adjustments are as follows:

	Standard Molding Hours per Thousand Units		Standard Labor Hours per Hundred Units	
	Current	*Proposed*	*Current*	*Proposed*
Stutz Bearcat	27.5	22.0	3.025	2.420
Teddy Bear	32.2	25.8	3.545	2.836
B-58	46.8	37.4	5.149	4.119
Ant Farm	37.5	30.0	4.125	3.300

RELIABLE INC. USE OF CORPORATE MODEL TO EVALUATE THE INTRODUCTION
OF A NEW PRODUCT: WHAM

EXHIBIT 129

($000 omitted)

SELECTED LINE ITEMS
PROFIT AND LOSS AND STATISTICAL DATA

LINE ITEMS	YR1	YR2	YR3	YR4	YR5
SLS WHAM	2750.0	3025.0	3327.5	3660.3	4026.3
NET SALES	29350.0	31427.6	33772.2	34864.2	35743.2
NET PROF A-T	1034.0	1232.5	1450.9	1432.4	1351.4
NPAT/COM SHR	5.2	6.2	7.3	7.2	6.8
RATIO GP/SLS	.29	.29	.29	.29	.29
RATIO IC/SLS	.22	.21	.21	.21	.22
RATIO OP/SLS	.07	.08	.09	.08	.08
U-SLS WHAM	500.0	550.0	605.0	665.5	732.1

SELECTED LINE ITEMS
CASH FLOW AND FINANCIAL RATIOS

LINE ITEMS		YR1	YR2	YR3	YR4	YR5
18	NET CASH FLO	1139.	1360.	1630.	1766.	1716.
19	CASH BALANCE	1966.	3326.	4956.	6721.	8437.
301	NP-AT/STH EQ	.13	.14	.15	.13	.11
302	LTDEBT/SH EQ	.35	.31	.27	.25	.22
303	QUICK RATIO	1.27	1.68	2.13	2.55	2.91

Additionally, a $2 million capital expenditure with a useful life of 15 years, depreciated straight line and having a salvage value of $100,000, was specified as an input to the model. The results of this projection are displayed in Exhibit 130. This projection results in a net profit after taxes and a return on investment that meet management's objectives. Management also noted that the proposed capital expenditure would cause a negative net cash flow and a cash balance of only $272,000 at the end of the projected first year. In addition, since it is a policy at Reliable to maintain a quick ratio (cash plus accounts receivable divided by total current liabilities) of at least 1.0, management next used the model to evaluate financing alternatives. Exhibit 131 includes the projected financial effect of the proposed capital expenditure and a long-term loan for $1 million at an interest rate of 10 percent.

Having made these projections of alternative courses of action, management at Reliable decided on the introduction of Wham as a basis for attaining the stated objectives. Exhibits 132 and 133 contain the full schedule of pro forma statements that reflect management's labor negotiations strategy as well as the introduction of Wham. These outputs represent management's five-year plan as well as the guidelines for the next year's budgeting.

EXHIBIT 130 RELIABLE INC. USE OF CORPORATE MODEL TO EVALUATE IMPROVEMENT OF MOLDING EQUIPMENT—CAPITAL EXPENDITURE

(*$000 omitted*)

SELECTED LINE ITEMS
PROFIT AND LOSS AND STATISTICAL DATA

LINE ITEMS	YR1	YR2	YR3	YR4	YR5
NET SALES	26600.0	28402.6	30444.7	32758.1	35379.6
TOTAL LABOR	4783.4	5022.0	5364.3	5751.8	6190.5
VAR MFG EXP	5629.1	5788.7	6166.7	6595.5	7081.5
DEPRECIAT-CM	706.0	856.0	856.0	856.0	856.0
NET PROF A-T	1017.3	1158.6	1273.4	1392.9	1523.5
NPAT/COM SHR	5.1	5.8	6.4	7.0	7.6
RATIO GP/SLS	.29	.30	.30	.30	.30
RATIO IC/SLS	.21	.22	.22	.22	.22
RATIO OP/SLS	.08	.08	.08	.09	.09

SELECTED LINE ITEMS
CASH FLOW AND FINANCIAL RATIOS

LINE ITEMS	YR1	YR2	YR3	YR4	YR5
18 NET CASH FLO	-751.	1496.	1577.	1671.	1772.
19 CASH BALANCE	272.	1769.	3346.	5017.	6789.

LINE ITEMS	YR1	YR2	YR3	YR4	YR5
301 NP-AT/STH EQ	.13	.14	.13	.13	.13
302 LTDEBT/SH EQ	.35	.31	.28	.25	.23
303 QUICK RATIO	.72	1.22	1.69	2.14	2.55

RELIABLE INC. USE OF CORPORATE MODEL TO EVALUATE IMPROVEMENT OF MOLDING EQUIPMENT CAPITAL EXPENDITURE AND LOAN

EXHIBIT 131

($000 omitted)

SELECTED LINE ITEMS
PROFIT AND LOSS AND STATISTICAL DATA

LINE ITEMS	YR1	YR2	YR3	YR4	YR5
NET SALES	26600.0	28402.6	30444.7	32758.1	35379.6
TOTAL LABOR	4783.4	5022.0	5364.3	5751.8	6190.5
VAR MFG EXP	5629.1	5788.7	6166.7	6595.5	7081.5
INTEREST-CM	107.0	207.0	207.0	207.0	207.0
DEPRECIAT-CM	706.0	856.0	856.0	856.0	856.0
NET PROF A-T	1017.3	1108.6	1223.4	1342.9	1473.5
NPAT/COM SHR	5.1	5.5	6.1	6.7	7.4
RATIO GP/SLS	.29	.30	.30	.30	.30
RATIO IC/SLS	.21	.22	.22	.22	.22
RATIO OP/SLS	.08	.08	.08	.08	.08

SELECTED LINE ITEMS
CASH FLOW AND FINANCIAL RATIOS

LINE ITEMS	YR1	YR2	YR3	YR4	YR5
5 INTEREST	107.	207.	207.	207.	207.
18 NET CASH FLO	249.	1446.	1527.	1621.	1722.
19 CASH BALANCE	1272.	2719.	4246.	5867.	7589.
301 NP-AT/STH EQ	.13	.13	.13	.13	.13
302 LTDEBT/SH EQ	.48	.43	.39	.35	.32
303 QUICK RATIO	1.05	1.51	1.95	2.37	2.75

EXHIBIT 132 RELIABLE INC. FINAL RUN OF CORPORATE PLANNING MODEL PROFIT AND
LOSS STATISTICAL DATA

($000 omitted)

PROFIT AND LOSS

LINE ITEMS	YR1	YR2	YR3	YR4	YR5
SLS STUTZ BC	6000.0	5803.1	5612.6	5170.8	4706.6
SLS TEDDY BR	5400.0	6318.0	7392.1	8238.4	9071.4
SLS B-58	11700.0	12519.0	13395.4	13653.0	13748.7
SLS ANT FARM	3500.0	3762.5	4044.7	4141.7	4190.2
SLS WHAM	2750.0	3025.0	3327.5	3660.3	4026.3
NET SALES	29350.0	31427.6	33772.2	34864.2	35743.2
TOTAL LABOR	5260.8	5603.9	5991.7	6143.2	6252.1
TOTAL MAT'L	6558.2	6955.1	7405.9	7560.9	7663.8
VAR MFG EXP	6569.7	6977.8	7440.0	7612.1	7733.6
TOT INV DECR	-116.0	-131.5	-148.8	-161.2	-172.6
FIX MFG EXP	2627.0	2900.0	3160.0	3450.0	3770.0
CST OF SALES	20899.6	22305.3	23848.9	24605.0	25246.9
GROSS PROFIT	8450.4	9122.3	9923.3	10259.2	10496.4
SALESMEN SAL	419.1	440.2	464.2	475.3	484.3
COMMISSIONS	583.0	624.3	670.9	692.6	710.0
OT DI SLS EX	399.5	418.4	439.8	449.7	457.7
SHIPPING EXP	312.4	324.5	338.1	344.5	349.6
ADVG & PROMN	2346.0	2400.0	2500.0	2750.0	3050.0
OT FX SLS EX	815.8	880.0	952.4	986.2	1013.3
INTEREST-CM	107.0	107.0	107.0	107.0	107.0
DEPRECIAT-CM	706.0	706.0	706.0	706.0	706.0
G & A	680.5	756.9	843.1	883.3	915.6
OTHER INCOME	-59.0	.0	.0	.0	.0
OTHER EXPENS					
TOT IND COST	6310.3	6657.4	7021.5	7394.5	7793.5
NET BEF TAX	2140.1	2465.0	2901.9	2864.7	2702.9
PROV FOR TAX	1106.1	1232.5	1450.9	1432.4	1351.4
NET PROF A-T	1034.0	1232.5	1450.9	1432.4	1351.4

STATISTICAL DATA

LINE ITEMS	YR1	YR2	YR3	YR4	YR5
NPAT/COM SHR	5.2	6.2	7.3	7.2	6.8
RATIO GP/SLS	.29	.29	.29	.29	.29
RATIO IC/SLS	.22	.21	.21	.21	.22
RATIO OP/SLS	.07	.08	.09	.08	.08
U-SLS STUTZ	5000.0	4835.9	4677.1	4309.0	3922.2
U-SLS TEDDY	1800.0	2106.0	2464.0	2746.1	3023.8
U-SLS B-58	2600.0	2782.0	2976.7	3034.0	3055.3
U-SLS ANT FM	1000.0	1075.0	1155.6	1183.4	1197.2
U-SLS WHAM	500.0	550.0	605.0	665.5	732.1

RELIABLE INC. FINAL RUN OF CORPORATE PLANNING MODEL CASH FLOW, **EXHIBIT 133**
BALANCE SHEET, AND FINANCIAL RATIOS

($000 omitted)

CASH FLOW

LINE ITEMS	YR1	YR2	YR3	YR4	YR5
1 SLS RECEIPTS	28773.	31151.	33460.	34719.	35626.
3 DIRECT EXP	20942.	22410.	23872.	24643.	25289.
4 INDIRECT EXP	5179.	5742.	6101.	6471.	6862.
5 INTEREST	107.	107.	107.	107.	107.
6 TAX	1106.	1232.	1451.	1432.	1351.
7 TØT DISBURSE	27334.	29491.	31530.	32653.	33610.
8 ØPER CASH	1439.	1660.	1930.	2066.	2016.
9 LØANS					
13 CAPITAL EXP					
14 DIVD CØMMØN	300.	300.	300.	300.	300.
18 NET CASH FLØ	1139.	1360.	1630.	1766.	1716.
19 CASH BALANCE	1966.	3326.	4956.	6721.	8437.

BALANCE SHEET

LINE ITEMS	YR1	YR2	YR3	YR4	YR5
101 CASH BALANCE	1966.	3326.	4956.	6721.	8437.
102 ACCTS RCVBLE	2344.	2620.	2932.	3077.	3194.
103 INVENTØRY	1311.	1469.	1546.	1611.	1678.
104 ØTHER CURRNT	1000.	1000.	1000.	1000.	1000.
105 TØTAL CURRNT	6620.	8414.	10433.	12409.	14309.
106 PLANT&EQUIPT	11179.	11179.	11179.	11179.	11179.
107 ACCUM DEPREC	5217.	5923.	6629.	7335.	8041.
108 NT PLNT&EQPT	5962.	5256.	4550.	3844.	3138.
109 ØTHR NØN-CUR	1247.	1247.	1247.	1247.	1247.
110 TØTAL ASSETS	13829.	14917.	16230.	17500.	18694.
201 ACCTS PAYBLE	2644.	2799.	2961.	3099.	3241.
204 ØTHER CURRNT	750.	750.	750.	750.	750.
205 TØTAL CURRNT	3394.	3549.	3711.	3849.	3991.
206 LNGTERM DEBT	2700.	2700.	2700.	2700.	2700.
209 CØM ØUTSTAND	2000.	2000.	2000.	2000.	2000.
211 RETAIND EARN	5735.	6668.	7819.	8951.	10003.
212 STØCKH EQUIT	7735.	8668.	9819.	10951.	12003.
213 TØTAL EQUITY	13830.	14917.	16230.	17501.	18694.

FINANCIAL RATIOS

LINE ITEMS	YR1	YR2	YR3	YR4	YR5
301 NP-AT/STH EQ	.13	.14	.15	.13	.11
302 LTDEBT/SH EQ	.35	.31	.27	.25	.22
303 QUICK RATIØ	1.27	1.68	2.13	2.55	2.91

15

Budgeting and the Management Information System

Two IMPORTANT RECENT DEVELOPMENTS in industry provide the rationale for relating budgeting to the popular concept of a management information system.

1. Budgeting (or profit planning), as the system and process are described in this book, is the one basic system that integrates all the operational plans to express the financial results and economic performance of the business. This information must be central in any management information system because the total financial consequences, resulting from the sum of all operating plans, is the final measure of economic performance.

2. The notion of a management information system has increasingly struck the fancy of executive management, but the concept has been obscured by technical jargon and some confused promotional literature suggesting that a *computer* is a management information system.

Because the planning and control concepts which are here defined as budgeting are of central importance in the design and installation of a management information system, it is important to describe in a definitive way this core relationship and what in fact a management information system really is.

Defining the MIS

A management information system is a comprehensive system to provide information to all levels of management in a company so that the functions necessary to meet the objectives of the business can be effectively performed. Obviously, within this broad framework a number of component systems are needed to provide a wide range of information to many different people. Under this concept, however, these component systems are interrelated in a way similar to the way in which functional duties are interrelated in a management organization to achieve a coordinated business purpose. The interrelationships and the flow of information must be specified so that the flow is integrated to provide efficiency in the processing of data and to insure that different functions do not receive different information describing the same conditions or transactions.

The use of common data for multiple outputs and the integration of data flows have been made possible in large-scale enterprises largely because of modern computer processing and communications techniques. Nevertheless, the objective of a management information system—to provide the right information to the right executive for making the right decision—has always existed in business. Obviously, budgeting is only a part of the overall management information system. The importance of the budgeting system, or of a well-designed accounting system, is that it integrates key planning and control information from every other subsystem into a total plan expressed in financial terms. Only by reviewing the financial results indicated can top management have an ultimate test of the acceptability of action planned or taken by functional management. This is not to suggest that the budgeting system is the management information system. The development of a management information system in even a modest business is not a project that can be completed by a few technicians on a specific date. In fact, as we shall see, management information systems are constructed and installed on a modular basis, generally over an extended period of time. The important point is that the grand design or master plan for approaching the development of a management information system must be set forth in the early stages of the effort so that proper precautions are taken to define the proper system linkages as installation progresses.

Another point will be obvious as we proceed: A company that has developed a well-defined and viable budgeting system has a substantial advantage in the further development of its overall management information system. A major reason for this is that in developing the budgeting system, management will have had to focus on planning and control for each individual function of the business as well as for the business as a whole.

Essentially, a management information system is a marriage of a management system and information processing systems. By management system is meant the process by which management defines organizational accountabilities, establishes objectives, sets forth a plan of operation, and controls performance to insure that the objectives are met. Without a clear understanding of what the management system is, no sound management information system can be developed. Definition of the management system tells management what kinds of information it needs in order to plan and control—and how often the information is needed. The determination of how the data required to fill these needs will be processed, stored, and retrieved is the province of the information processing system, and we are then concerned with master file structure, data collection, computer capabilities, and so forth.

The Management System and the Information Processing System

Consider a basic information problem—in terms of both need and system—in a manufacturing company as illustrative of the implications of the need to convert a forecast of sales demand into materials and labor requirements and costs. From an information processing system viewpoint, this exercise might be described as processing a sales forecast of finished product items against an information file that "explodes" a bill of materials and operations sheets to ascertain the total requirements in terms of total materials and components and manufacturing hours by cost center. These materials requirements and operating hours are then matched against price and cost rate files, and the costs are accumulated into total cost of sales. This process could be described from an information processing standpoint in terms of inputs processed against master files to produce the required output (Exhibit 134).

From a business executive's point of view the use of this information system is meaningful only in the context of the management system. For example, consider that the preparation of the sales forecast, a responsibility of the marketing department, implies certain planning assumptions and is finally approved as a goal or standard of performance for sales management. In turn, the materials requirements in the bills of materials—used in processing the sales forecast—represent standard performance or predetermined plans established by engineering and approved by manufacturing management. Similarly, the manufacturing times predicted in the operations required by cost center represent standards or goals set by manufacturing management as good operating practice. To go a step further, the basic costs of the materials which will be used if this plan is approved represent commitments or objectives of procurement management that are based on certain planning assumptions. Viewed in this light, the systems notion of processing certain data through a computer carries with it important implications as to plans and standards approved by operational and functional management. Exhibit 135 illustrates this additional aspect. If the management system in the company is not such that the chief executive can rely on his functional officers to support the attainability of the goals or standards in the information being processed, the illustration discussed here would be nothing more than a systems or processing exercise.

EXHIBIT 134   SCHEMATIC OF PROCESSING SALES DEMAND TO DETERMINE REQUIREMENTS AND COST OF SALES

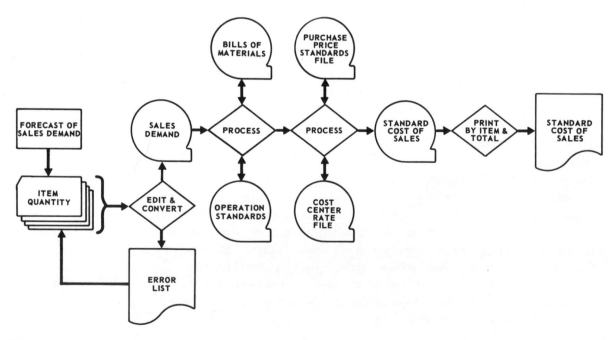

EXHIBIT 135

COMBINED MANAGEMENT SYSTEM AND INFORMATION PROCESSING SYSTEM

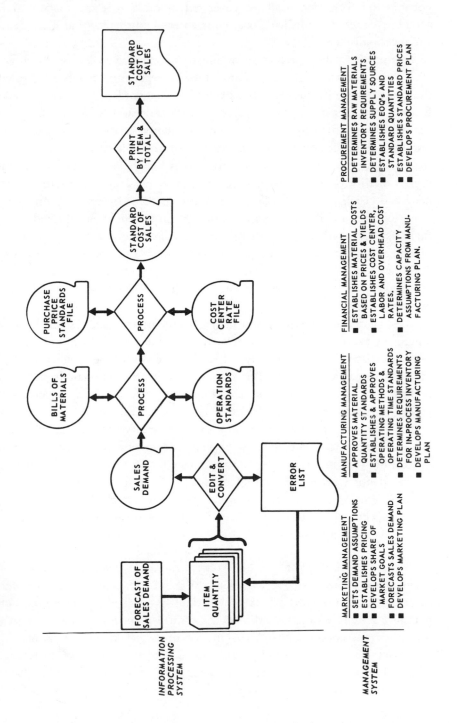

*Management
Information
Needs*

Before illustrating the approach to a management information system, let us summarize key ingredients in budgeting. Early in the book the budgeting system was described as one which contributes to the basic functions of planning, execution, and control of business operations. In describing the way in which budgeting should be carried out, emphasis was placed on (1) planning, which involved the setting of objectives, standards, and criteria for performance measurement, and (2) the reporting or information feedback generated monthly to show the extent to which actual revenues and costs had departed from the budget plan and the reasons for the variances indicated.

This process is best performed by functional executives. Reporting in accordance with the organization structure (responsibility reporting) has been stressed, as has the comparison of actual results with a plan, standards, or criteria, to sharpen the focus of management on the important information and reduce extraneous information which does not contribute to effective action or decisions. This illustrates an important point with respect to management information systems: that in many cases management does not need more information but in fact needs *less* information of higher quality or greater pertinence. Producing pertinent information related to a needed decision or action is best accomplished, then, by focusing on exceptions or opportunities; and the management information system should provide for management by exception to improve the effectiveness of executive control. As a result, executive management properly can view a management information system as an organized network of reports produced in recurring cycles, combined with specified retrieval capabilities, and organized to meet the accountability needs of various functional executives.

To suggest contrarywise that a management information system is like a library where any executive can browse endlessly for tidbits of interesting reading may imply systems artistry, but this certainly will do little to contribute to efficient management of a business enterprise. The library notion is not too different from the notion of budgeting as a continuing process of forecasting and reforecasting how a company will end the year on the basis of what has been happening lately.

Thus a management information system must serve the company's management system. Toward that end, it must provide information necessary for planning and controlling operations. It must do so in a way that furnishes the proper information in accordance with the division of organizational responsibilities and combines the subdivided information to report overall results to the chief executive and his staff. With respect to financial control, these purposes are essentially the same as the purpose of the budgeting system.

*Management
Information Sys-
tem Illustration*

In order to illustrate the MIS concept more concretely, a schematic of a management information system is shown in Exhibit 136. Notice that the schematic is constructed on three vertical levels. On the first level is the operational and profit planning system, on the second level the control reporting system, and on the third level the transaction systems. Across the top of the schematic are various representative functional areas in an industrial or manufacturing enterprise, including marketing, distribution, manufacturing, purchasing, and finance and control. This schematic highlights several important points.

MANAGEMENT INFORMATION SYSTEM SCHEMATIC (Part 1)

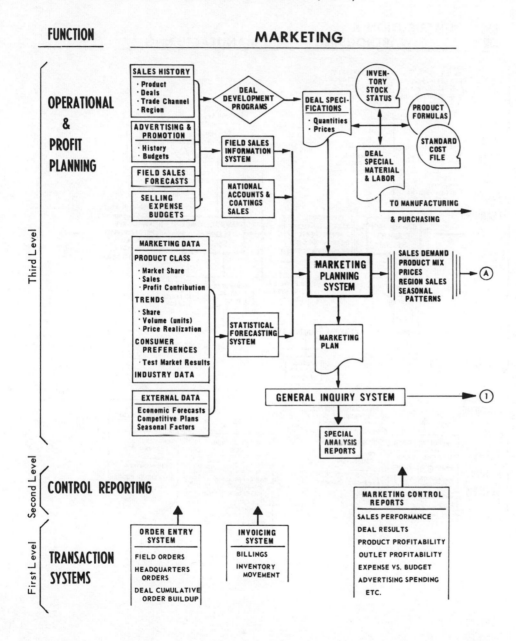

FUNCTION — MARKETING

EXHIBIT 136
(continued)

MANAGEMENT INFORMATION SYSTEM SCHEMATIC (Part 2)

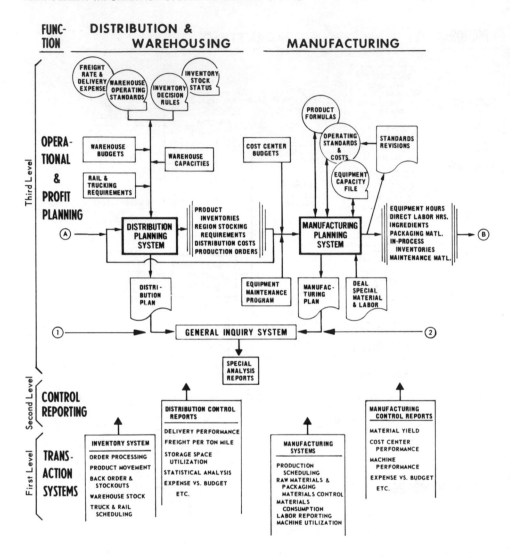

MANAGEMENT INFORMATION SYSTEM SCHEMATIC (Part 3)

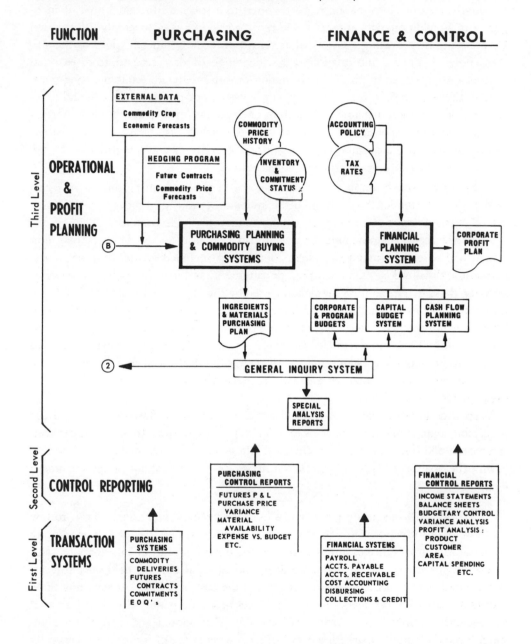

In the first place, the flow of transactions in a business provides basic raw material in the information system. Transactions are processed through subsystems which enter data, sort them, and compile them in a structured way into what systems people call data banks. The data are further summarized into control reporting systems which essentially organize information to be reported to a specific functional area of management. In addition, data are sorted and reorganized in a way to supply information for planning by providing a history of activity within the business. Added to this upward flow of internal information is a wide range of data secured from external sources and organized to provide information on sales demand, economic conditions, availability of materials, cost of money, and government policies. In the actual processing of information this flow of data from one systems level to another is important in achieving the proper degree of integration and efficiency in the use of data processing equipment. It is also important in assuring the accuracy and integrity of information to be used by various supervisors and executives.

In the illustrative example, let us consider the business planning process in terms of the way information flows through the system. Obviously, the example set forth is for a particular type of business and should be viewed in that context.

A glance across the schematic of the information flow in the business planning system will reveal the major subsystem components included in the illustration: the marketing, distribution, manufacturing, procurement, and financial planning systems. Between these major planning systems enclosed by three vertical lines on each side are information items flowing as output from one system and input to the next system. These are information interfaces, a necessary part of the management information system concept. The interfaces are important because, in practice, companies tend to develop these major subsystems and install them modularly; and to do so within the grand design or master plan of an MIS necessitates a clear understanding of what these interfaces should be.

Within each subsystem area, the schematic illustrates the flow of input and the processing against major master files in order to prepare output. In addition, between the second and third levels of the schematic is a general inquiry system which would permit the analysis of special information needs for the furnishing of specific stored data.

Marketing Subsystem

To see how business information is used for business planning, we can follow the flow of information through the various subsystems. In the area of marketing responsibility, for example, inputs deal with three basic classes of information: sales and selling expense history, marketing data, and external data. A field sales forecast is generated as part of the review of history and the cost of selling. At the same time, specific information on deals—including dealer promotions and allowances as well as consumer promotions—is made available for promotional and advertising planning. Inputs relating to marketing data include a wide range of information generally prepared outside the company—trade association forecasts, special statistical services, and so forth. Internal data of a marketing nature are also furnished with respect to brand profitability and market research and testing programs. Inputs involving external data relate to the state of the economy and the general competitive environment. Normally the sales history and field sales forecast are combined through a field sales information system and a promotion information system to establish the basis for the marketing plan. At the same time, environmental and marketing data are processed through a statistical forecasting system and the results are input to the marketing planning system. The master file also includes information relative to the finished stock positions of the company and the standard product cost file.

In accumulating this information, marketing management is focusing on the development of a marketing plan and will meld the forecast from the field sales organization and the statistical forecast into a marketing plan with the attendant planning for advertising, promotion, and selling expense required to execute the plan. As an illustration, note on the schematic the development of a deal program setting forth the specifications and requirements of promotional deals for the planning period and defining as output any special packaging material, size changes, or special labor necessary to complete the deals. This information then flows to manufacturing and purchasing for their planning. From the standpoint of the flow of information, the completion of a marketing plan will develop information that is necessary in other areas of the business—the flow into the distribution planning system of the sales demand properly time-phased; product mix; pricing strategies; sales broken down by territory, including regions and districts; and the impact of seasonality. Inputs such as these are vital to the proper planning of distribution and warehousing requirements.

Distribution Subsystem

The objective of the distribution planning subsystem in the management information system illustrated is to (1) determine a distribution and warehousing network plan that will satisfy the market demand in accordance with the marketing strategy and (2) print out information on requirements for manufacturing that can be melded into a manufacturing plan efficient and competitive enough to meet the required profit objective. It should be pointed out that because a given level of profitability is an overriding consideration, as management plans in each subsystem area there must be an intermediate management review and tentative approval of the strategy set forth.

From the standpoint of the management information system, the distribution planning process will require reference to master file data on freight rates and delivery expense, warehouse operating standards for manpower and costs, inventory stocking rules, and inventory stock status positions. In addition, the planning requires the development of warehouse budgets in the light of warehouse capacities and transportation requirements. The planning will produce a distribution plan and a flow of outputs relating to product inventory requirements by period, distribution of stock requirements by location, costs, and production orders necessary to meet these requirements.

Manufacturing Subsystem

In the manufacturing area, information categories resulting from the distribution planning system will be input for the development of a manufacturing plan which will express the production requirements in terms of equipment and direct labor hours, ingredients, packaging materials, and in-process stocking to manufacture in runs of efficient size. To develop these plans, manufacturing will need to use its

293

information system components with regard to product formulas or bills of materials, operational standards and standard costs, equipment capacity, and special deal pack requirements. While preparing the manufacturing plan, the information system will have to produce cost center budgets and equipment maintenance requirements.

Procurement Subsystem

Referring again to the schematic in Exhibit 136, the flow of information (insofar as it concerns ingredients) and packaging material requirements will go into the procurement subsystem. The planning process will require reference to both externally and internally generated information. Illustrations in the schematic include external data with respect to commodity markets and economic forecasts and in certain cases reference to the condition of commodity markets and future contracts for the possibilities of hedging programs. Internally, information will be required on commitments status, raw materials inventories, and commodity price history file. The procurement planning will then determine buying programs to meet the manufacturing plan, and those programs will become the procurement plan.

Finance and Control Subsystem

At this juncture, the functional plans in marketing, distribution, manufacturing, and procurement are brought together and consolidated on a business enterprise basis. This process establishes a budget in the format of a profit and loss statement. The schematic should have made it clear that the management information system has released cost standards and price information, equipment capacities, warehouse cost standards, and so forth to operating functions as the planning evolves. The functional plans incorporate much of the financial and accounting data, which will now be consolidated in the finance and control area. In this subsystem, however, the finance and control function has to apply accounting policies and generate a financial plan that distinguishes capital budget items, corporate program budgets, and the financial consequences of marketing and operational planning and tie them together into the corporate profit plan, taking into account tax rates and tax considerations. This is the integrative effect of the budgeting system.

The final review of the corporate profit plan by the chief executive officer and the corporate staff will be the ultimate test of the earnings acceptability of projected company operations. It may well be that additional revisions will be required, and a certain amount of recycling of plans or strategies may take place—again making reference to basic information files and new flows of input. In the process, each functional area of management will be revising certain standards, criteria, or objectives to take advantage of cost or profit improvements and to reflect more realistically the expected changes in wage rates, procurement prices, and capacity restrictions. An example of this can be seen in the manufacturing subsystems area of Exhibit 136, where standards revisions are input to update the operating standards and cost files as part of the development of the operational plan. These revisions could of course affect both basic standard data, such as methods changes, and cost standard data, such as revised direct labor wage rates.

The schematic discussed here is grossly oversimplified because of the limitations of space and should be construed as illustrative only. For example, not included are certain significant functions of any business such as the personnel function, which will also be developing manpower plans and referring to master file data with respect to company employees. This omission is simply in the interest of economy of space and should not be a significant bar to understanding the basic approach.

Having emphasized the MIS concept in the planning process, let us now turn our attention to the MIS structure with respect to control reporting and the requirement for retrieval of information in response to inquiry. As day-to-day operations are carried forward in any business, the information that comes into the company is processed in a series of systems that we can generally classify as transaction systems. Many of these systems are obvious and will be found in every business, such as the payroll system. Some are not so obvious and serve a special purpose for a particular company. All transaction systems are organized to do three things:

1. To process data for the preparation of basic business papers—invoices, payroll checks, order confirmations, shipping labels, and so forth—that produce an operating action or requirement or establish an accounting entry.
2. To develop a history of specific master file data, such as an earnings record card or a customer order master file, which is available for record purposes or for retrieval of specific data.
3. To produce organized information which can be fed to a higher-level control reporting system that will summarize the data and prepare meaningful management control reports.

It should therefore be obvious that, in the design of transactions systems, the systems analyst must consider the relationship of each transaction system to the overall management information system requirements. The flows of information into management control reports and the structuring of data files to make periodic inquiry most convenient are beyond the scope of this book, but an illustration of how the management information system produces a series of control reports is pertinent here. The management information system must produce control reports in such a way as to enable each responsibility area of management to compare the trend of actual results with the established plans so that the budgeting system can be effective and viable in assuring management that its overall objectives will be met.

By way of illustration, let us look at the field sales reporting system. The management information system may be designed to report weekly and monthly the order position and the invoices issued by sales district and by salesman. It may compare the actual and planned sales revenue for each district and salesman. It may combine in one report the district's selling expenses to show the ratio of sales revenue to selling expense. It can summarize the sales volume for the districts in each region and for the company as a whole. It may be programed to develop sales statistics by key or major accounts as a bellwether of trends on order and sales demand. It may break down sales by product classes and relate the actual mix of orders or shipments with the planned mix developed in the marketing plan. In addition, the sales reporting system may record a standard profit contribution on sales to show not only the sales trend, but the profitability of the mix and the pricing strategies. Sales by districts may be recast and reported by end use or customer classifications to show segmented market penetration.

In the area of special promotions and deals, the sales reporting system may show the cumulative order buildup in the early stages of a deal for comparison with a planned rate of sale and for immediate reaction as to reprograming manufacturing under the deal. In each of these cases the sales reporting should be summarized by responsibility according to the structure of the sales organization. Obviously these reports will be part of the marketing information system, but the information will also be available as part of the total management information system and ultimately will be summarized in the profit and loss statement each month for the company as a whole.

By careful design, inquiry needs can also be anticipated. In the sales reporting area it may be established that as the trends of order and sales activity are reported, sales managers will want to know the status of specific customer orders day by day. This then will require the ability of the management information system to secure selected listings of order status and projected shipment dates. Each of these features can be designed into a good MIS, but management must remember that the processing and computer programing are secondary to the basic problem of creating an effective reporting structure necessary to plan and control the operations of the business to meet a profit objective.

In sum, the purpose of budgeting in the overall management information system is not merely to prepare a budget which will project the financial results of a business one year hence. Its more fundamental purpose is to permit an integrated planning exercise which will develop the objectives, criteria, and standards of performance that are requisite to achieving the company's business purpose.

Standards, criteria, and objectives are particularly important in the working of the management information system. Without them, management would have no bench mark for evaluating individual performance or for projecting the consequences of revising plans or strategies. Without them it would be extremely difficult in a business of any size to develop an integrated plan which would insure that meeting certain sales goals would entail certain manufacturing requirements, manpower needs, procurement activities, and so on—and would achieve certain profit results. Without such standards, management would have difficulty in identifying the cost improvement or profit improvement potential in changing methods of doing business or in expanding capacities.

It is unlikely that any effective management information system can be developed without a good budgeting system because of the critical need for the objectives, standards, and criteria that have been discussed. In addition, the core relationship of the budgeting system is reflected in the fact that it is the only system that overlies the other subsystems in the planning and control process. To put it another way, in the development of, say, the marketing information system, the flow of information for planning marketing activities and for reporting marketing results is directly connected with the development of sales budgets and marketing expense budgets. The same is true in each other functional area of the business.

One aspect of a good management information system that has not yet been covered relates to the selection of key information for top management review that will provide an early warning or an indication that the business is headed for trouble. The accumulation of such selected data for high-level reporting, generally on a trend basis, is an important element of the management information system because it provides an extra dimension of top management control as a check on overall operational effectiveness. In the real world, of course, rarely does everything go as planned as the weeks go by, and without these key early warning indicators there may be a gap in the information flowing from functional or divisional management to senior officers. Therefore, it is generally wise to have certain key data identified with respect to the peculiar characteristics of key business problems and subjected to regular top management review. While considerable creativity must be brought to bear in developing this segment of information flow and reporting, one example will be helpful.

Key Early Warning Information

In the manufacture of injection molded plastic products on a custom order basis, it is the practice of management to book large orders for future delivery. Often competitive pressures are such that sales management will render quotations that are discounted so that the order can be secured. From a business point of view, booking orders is really booking equipment capacity on the injection molding equipment. In the case of one manufacturer, for example, conventional reporting indicated the order backlog and rate of incoming orders on a dollar basis. In addition, reporting was made of the percentage of quotations won or lost. Finally, the regular reporting to operational management included reports on equipment utilization and performance. In addition, however, a key early warning chart (Exhibit 137) was recommended to keep top management posted on the trend of the profit contribution of the order backlog and incoming orders, assuming manufacture at standard costs and standard running rates on equipment. This simple graphic picture of the spread of profit margin as related to the volume of the order backlog predicted for senior management the ultimate profit impact of the orders being accumulated and yet to be manufactured. This gave top management a basis for reviewing quotation pricing policy before the plants had been booked up for extended periods with low-margin business. Similar illustrations of key early warning information could be identified, of course, for any business. And the management information system can and should be designed to accommodate these needs for information.

Another technique, closely related to the budgetary planning and control system, can be valuable in the development or modification of management information systems. This technique is management by objectives. Clearly the budgeting system plays a critical role in integrating the establishment of objectives. Management by objectives attempts to relate corporate objectives to specific management positions and responsibilities. In the course of doing this, executives are typically asked during the planning process to identify and list key accountability areas and work objectives whose accomplishment will when taken together enable achievement of the corporation's objectives. This is a valuable planning tool—it helps to clarify organizational relationships and the key individual efforts required to achieve the business plan.

Accountability Charters

EXHIBIT 137   KEY EARLY WARNING CHART

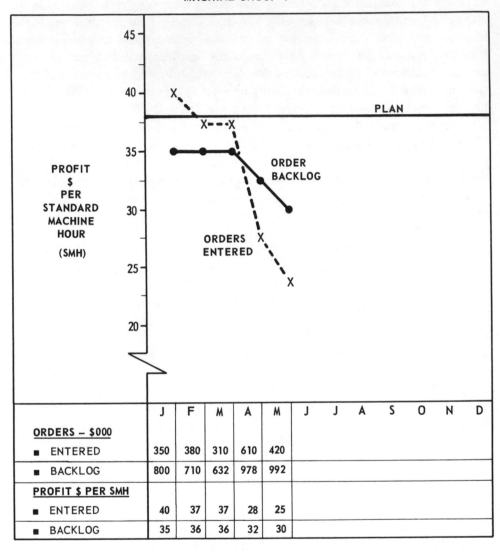

ORDER POSITION – PROFIT REALIZATION PER MACHINE HOUR
– MACHINE GROUP 1

	J	F	M	A	M	J	J	A	S	O	N	D
ORDERS – $000												
■ ENTERED	350	380	310	610	420							
■ BACKLOG	800	710	632	978	992							
PROFIT $ PER SMH												
■ ENTERED	40	37	37	28	25							
■ BACKLOG	35	36	36	32	30							

Summarizing these lists into individual "charters of accountability" for line and staff positions develops a valuable addition to conventional job descriptions. Exhibit 138 is an example of a charter of accountability for a manufacturing superintendent. Several features are obvious in the structure of the charter. For one thing, the position is referenced to an approved organization chart. Second, the reporting relation is defined in terms of accountability to a plant manager. Third, there is a basic statement of function which is output- or value-oriented. Fourth, the role of the job is identified in summary in terms of contribution to company goals. Finally, specific areas of accountability are identified in terms of standing requirements and in terms of special projects looking to some change in methods or some improvement in operations. In addition, as a rule information in the management by objectives system is entered on the form to define how performance will be measured.

This basis of performance measurement can greatly facilitate the identification of significant reports and information necessary not only to measure the accomplishment of objectives, but to assist the executive in managing toward that end. It will therefore help in the definition of information needs for the management information system. This approach helps to solve a major problem in management information systems design—the identification of the information needed to perform each management job.

Organizing to Improve the MIS

If this procedure is followed there is a real involvement of managers in the development of a management information system. This involvement is a must. It can be further organized—and should be—by the appointment of a multifunctional steering committee of top executives or their immediate subordinates to control the development of the management information system. The chairman of this steering committee should be a senior executive whose background and experience include exposure to several functional areas of the business and a keen appreciation of the interrelationships of functional planning to overall corporate profit planning. The particular post held by the executive is not as important as the respect in which he is held by others and the breadth of his vision and understanding of the total business. In a number of cases it has been found that the chairman was a man with a financial background, but this is not a necessary requirement. The chairman of the steering committee will be responsible to an executive review board, which should include the president or chief executive.

Working under steering committee direction, task forces can be formed to develop certain parts of the management information system, each headed by a project manager, and including technical specialists of the various disciplines necessary to do the job. Generally such task forces are organized to carry out general design or detailed computer design and programing. For example, one task force might be established to focus on the general design of a marketing information system. Another might be established to design a standard cost accounting system. A third might be established to review communications techniques and remote terminal operations. Certainly an important task force effort would relate to the development of budget procedures and the planning process. Exhibit 139 illustrates this ad hoc organization approach to the development of an MIS, with notation of the responsibilities of each group. This is the only effective way to develop or revise a management information system.

EXHIBIT 138   Charter of Accountability

XYZ COMPANY – PLANT X

1. **POSITION**:   SUPERINTENDENT – MACHINING GROUP (ORGANIZATION CHART 310 – 2).

2. **ACCOUNTABLE TO**:   PLANT MANAGER.

3. **BASIC FUNCTION**:   ACCOUNTABLE FOR THE EFFICIENT AND ECONOMICAL OPERATION OF MACHINE TOOLS WITH A PRODUCTIVE AND TRAINED LABOR FORCE SO AS TO PRODUCE THE GREATEST QUANTITY AND HIGHEST QUALITY PARTS AND COMPONENTS AT THE LOWEST COMPETITIVE COST FOR SALE, AS IS OR AFTER ASSEMBLY, TO OUR CUSTOMERS.

4. **ROLE OF THE JOB**:   THE SUPERINTENDENT – MACHINING GROUP CONTRIBUTES TO THE ACCOMPLISHMENT OF COMPANY GOALS BY:

     1. DIRECTING THE MANUFACTURE OF

AREAS OF ACCOUNTABILITY	BASIS OF PERFORMANCE MEASUREMENT

5. **STANDING REQUIREMENTS**:

   1. PRODUCING AT STANDARD OR PREDETERMINED COSTS.
     A. TOTAL OPERATING VARIANCE BY DEPARTMENT AND A SUMMARY OF OPERATING VARIANCES BY TYPE (DIRECT LABOR EFFICIENCY, INDIRECT LABOR PERFORMANCE VARIANCE, ETC.)

   2. STAFFING MANUFACTURING FUNCTIONS IN ACCORDANCE WITH PRODUCTION SCHEDULES.
     A. INDIRECT LABOR PERFORMED BY DIRECT LABOR PERSONNEL –– HOURS AND % OF THE TOTAL HOURS vs. PLAN BY DEPARTMENT AND CLASSIFICATION.
     B. INDIRECT LABOR EXPENSE vs. PLAN.
     C. PERSONNEL COUNTS vs. PLAN.

   3. MANUFACTURING TO SPECIFICATION.
     A. SCRAP AND REWORK COST DUE TO MANUFACTURING ERRORS vs. PLAN.
     B. MATERIAL USAGE VARIANCE.
     C. SUBSTITUTE MATERIAL VARIANCE.
     D. PRODUCT ENGINEERING EXPENSE ON REWORK DUE TO MANUFACTURING ERRORS vs. PLAN.

   4. MANUFACTURING TO PRODUCTION SCHEDULE.
     A. NUMBER OF SCHEDULE CHANGES AND REASONS.

EXHIBIT 138
(concluded)

AREAS OF ACCOUNTABILITY	BASIS OF PERFORMANCE MEASUREMENT
5. PLANNING AND CONTROLLING NON-DIRECT MANUFACTURING EXPENSE.	A. ACTUAL EXPENSES vs. PLAN.
6. USING PROPER RATED EMPLOY-EES FOR ALL WORK.	A. LABOR RATE VARIANCE.
7. OVERTIME PREMIUM DUE TO MANUFACTURING CAUSES.	A. ACTUAL PREMIUM vs. PLAN.
8. MACHINE REPAIR DUE TO MANUFACTURING MISUSE.	A. REPAIR COST vs. PLAN.
9. ENFORCING SAFETY STANDARDS AND CORRECTION OF SAFETY HAZARDS.	A. LOST TIME ACCIDENT SEVERITY RATE.
	B. LOST TIME ACCIDENT FREQUENCY RATE.
	C. SAFETY HAZARDS IDENTIFIED AND CORRECTIVE STATUS.
	D. SAFETY DISCIPLINARY ACTIONS TAKEN, CATEGORIZED BY TYPE.
10. ADHERENCE TO LABOR CONTRACT.	A. GRIEVANCES UPHELD/HOUR WORKED.
	B. GRIEVANCE COST vs. PLAN.
11. AFTER SHIPMENT COSTS CAUSED BY MANUFACTURING DEFICIENCIES.	A. CUMULATIVE NUMBER AND COST OF FIELD SERVICE PROBLEMS BY TYPE vs. PLAN.
12. COST IMPROVEMENT PLANNING AND RESULTS.	A. CUMULATIVE ANNUALIZED COST REDUCTIONS BY PROJECT AND IN TOTAL vs. TIME PHASED PLAN.

6. SPECIAL PROJECTS :

1. IMPROVE SAFETY RECORD FOR YEAR ENDED DECEMBER 31, 197X.	A. LOST TIME ACCIDENT SEVERITY RATE REDUCED BY 40 %.
	B. LOST TIME ACCIDENT FREQUENCY RATE REDUCED BY 50%.
	C. SPECIAL TRAINING DEVELOPED AND GIVEN TO ALL OPERATIONS.
2. REDUCE MATERIAL WASTE.	A. SCRAP METAL LOSS IN TONS REDUCED ON ANNUAL BASIS BY 10%.
	B. REDUCE REWORK COST BY 20%.
3. STUDY WAYS TO IMPROVE: a. BEARING LIFE b. TOOLING UTILIZATION	A. SPECIAL REPORTS TO BE DISTRIBUTED TO PLANT MANAGER BY 7/1/7X (a.) 9/15/7X (b.)

EXHIBIT 139   ORGANIZING AN MIS EFFORT

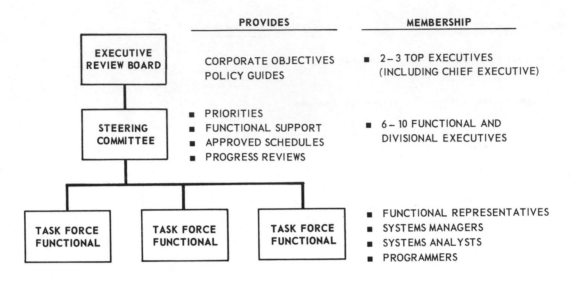

	PROVIDES	MEMBERSHIP

EXECUTIVE REVIEW BOARD

CORPORATE OBJECTIVES
POLICY GUIDES

- 2 – 3 TOP EXECUTIVES (INCLUDING CHIEF EXECUTIVE)

STEERING COMMITTEE

- PRIORITIES
- FUNCTIONAL SUPPORT
- APPROVED SCHEDULES
- PROGRESS REVIEWS

- 6 – 10 FUNCTIONAL AND DIVISIONAL EXECUTIVES

TASK FORCE FUNCTIONAL   **TASK FORCE FUNCTIONAL**   **TASK FORCE FUNCTIONAL**

- FUNCTIONAL REPRESENTATIVES
- SYSTEMS MANAGERS
- SYSTEMS ANALYSTS
- PROGRAMMERS

- CONDUCT INTERVIEWS
- DEVELOP REQUIREMENTS
- RECOMMEND SCHEDULES
- DESIGN, DOCUMENT & IMPLEMENT
- REPORT PROGRESS

This chapter has highlighted one concept of a management information system and why the budgeting system has a core relationship to it. It should be clear that planning and control are at the heart of management information needs and therefore of the management information system. More and more, in fact, budgeting systems are being included within the framework of developing management information systems.

Review of Budget Process

As with all systems, the management information system must have a certain amount of maintenance or updating, and it is logical for management to be alert to new techniques and information needs as a part of the annual budget process. As accountabilities change and as new needs for information are identified in the preparation of the profit plan, systems personnel should be consulted for assistance in improving the management information system.

A brief review of the sequence of events in a typical annual budgeting cycle of a manufacturing company should bring into focus the major points involved in the budgetary planning and control system. In this sequence, the first step usually involves the preparation of the sales budget, often called the marketing plan. (Work on this may start on September 1 for a calendar-year company.) At the same time, production management may well be engaged in an annual review of its operating standards with a view to incorporating improvements in operating methods and developing new product-cost standards.

With the help of the budget department, sales management sends instructions to the field for the preparation of a sales forecast. Certain guidelines are usually included with respect to general economic conditions and any known management policy changes. At about the same time, all managers are requested to pull together recommendations for capital improvements, in the form of requests for capital appropriations. Concurrently, sales management normally asks the market research or economics department to prepare a sales forecast, using pertinent statistical indicators and the best market and competitive information available.

By the end of September both sales forecasts are completed, and various levels of management review and adjust figures where appropriate. Based on the information available, sales management then completes the development of a marketing plan or sales budget; particular emphasis is given to such matters as market share, product line profitability, and the growth of the company's markets. Sales management attempts to improve the product mix so that greater emphasis is placed on the more profitable opportunities. Throughout this process many questions of policy are discussed in the budget committee (if one exists in the company) so that sound planning recommendations can be made to the president.

About mid-October the marketing plan is turned over to the budget director, and he applies product costs, taking into account any standards changes developed by production management. From this the budget director prepares a tentative or flash report for the president that indicates the profit impact of the marketing plan. Once the president and the budget committee (if one exists) give their tentative approval of the marketing plan, it is published and distributed to other departments. At this point, sales and production management work together to establish required finished-goods inventory levels to service the marketing plan. Financial management is also involved because of its concern with the financial cost of carrying inventory. Relying on the adopted inventory plan, production management develops budgets for materials, direct labor, and manufacturing expenses. Once again broad participation is sought by reviewing the requirements of each cost center right down to the foreman level. Frequently such budgeting is on a three-point basis, with foremen being asked to budget their manufacturing expenses not only at the control-volume level indicated by the marketing plan but also at a level below and a level above the control volume. This facilitates the establishment of variable budget rates. By the end of November the manufacturing budget is complete.

At the same time, other departments are engaged in preparing their budgets. In doing so, they classify jobs into the basic categories of administrative, measurable, and program work. For measurable activities, departments set activity levels in terms of expected volume and from this develop manning tables.

The area of program budgeting offers a particularly creative opportunity for management. All departments with program activities establish what might be viewed as an "idea budget" for the ensuing year. Each idea or program is set up as a separate budget authorization explaining the objective of the program, the commitment of manpower required, and the time it is expected to take to complete the work. In

303

addition, nonpersonnel costs, such as those for supplies and equipment, are added to the request for authorization.

By the end of November the budget director is an extremely busy man. His department has the job of consolidating all the plans of the operating departments into conventional financial statements. The marketing plan, production plan, and departmental expense budgets are summarized in the form of profit and loss statements. The projected profit is compared with the profit for the current year (actual figures to date plus an estimate for the remaining month or two), and significant differences are explained. This is a crucial juncture because it presents top management with the opportunity to see what relative improvements in operations can be expected. If each operating manager has done his job well, he has accounted for the major reasons why the planned budget differs from the actual experience of the current year. Then, for each department manager, the improvements from the prior period, as reflected in his planned operations, represent the objectives he expects to achieve.

*　　*　　*

It has been the intent of this book to provide an understanding of the overall budgetary planning and control system and of the related basic techniques and procedures. The concerned manager can relate this understanding of the budget objective to his own planning and control system in his own particular business environment. He should also make maximum use of the expertise of the budget director; he is a technical expert who can help with the procedural aspects of the budgeting operation. Nevertheless, the manager alone must carry the full burden of developing meaningful plans and executing them for results. When budgeting is done in this way, it need no longer be shunned as unnecessary work or as red tape imposed by the financial people; instead, it can actually be welcomed as a real help in the management function.

Index